THIRD EDITION

Critical Reasoning

Understanding and Criticizing
Arguments and Theories

Jerry Cederblom
University of Nebraska at Omaha

David W. Paulsen
The Evergreen State College

WADSWORTH PUBLISHING COMPANY
Belmont, California
A Division of Wadsworth, Inc.

Philosophy Editor: Kenneth King
Editorial Assistant: Karen Jones
Production: Greg Hubit Bookworks
Print Buyer: Martha Branch
Designer: Adriane Bosworth
Technical Illustrator:
Compositor: Kachina Typesetting, Inc.
Cover: Beginning by Kenneth Noland, courtesy of the Hirshhorn Museum
and Sculpture Garden, Smithsonian Institution.

Printed in the United States of America

2 3 4 5 6 7 8 9 10—95 94 93 92 91

Library of Congress Cataloging-in-Publication Data
Cederblom, J. B.
    Critical reasoning : understanding and criticizing arguments and
theories / Jerry Cederblom, David W. Paulsen. — 3rd ed.
        p. cm.
    Includes bibliographical references and index.
    ISBN 0-534-14688-0
    1. Reasoning. 2. Critical thinking. 3. Fallacies (Logic)
4. Induction (Logic) 5. Theory (Philosophy) I. Paulsen, David W.
II. Title.
BC177.C4   1991
160—dc20
                                                            90-46659
                                                              CIP

M326
22·00

ONE WEE
LO

THIRD EDITION

Critical Reasoning

002
Y 2005

Contents

CHAPTER FIVE

"That Depends on What You Mean by . . ."   96

CHAPTER SIX

Why Are Bad Arguments Sometimes Convincing?   133

Preface to the Third Edition

This text has evolved through succeeding editions alongside an educational movement. When the first edition was written, it was one of the very few texts designed to help students improve their ability to evaluate critically what they heard and read in a variety of everyday contexts. Most of the books in the field of logic did not address this need directly. But in the succeeding years the importance of developing and applying analytical and critical skills in everyday contexts became widely recognized. By the time the second edition was published, courses in informal logic and critical thinking had become common in colleges and universities across the United States and had been installed as a graduation requirement at some. As we began to prepare this third edition, it became apparent that the interest in critical reasoning is more than a short-term trend. Not only have course offerings and enrollments continued to increase in this area, but there is also a broadly based movement to infuse critical thinking instruction across the curriculum. Conferences related to critical thinking continue to draw large audiences, and publication of scholarly literature in this area has shown strong development.

In this context, teachers and students are well served by the availability of a variety of texts displaying different approaches to many topics. In this edition, we have sought to maintain features that have appealed to a broad range of users of previous editions: readability, diversity of examples and exercises, and clear presentation of step-by-step procedures for reconstruction and criticism. In addition, ours remains one of the few texts that provide techniques for understanding and criticizing theories as well as arguments. In response to a variety of helpful suggestions, we have added new features to the third edition.

New Features in the Third Edition

- A new introductory chapter—"Deciding What to Believe"—that thoroughly describes what critical reasoning is and that develops the case in favor of the practice of critical reasoning.
- Expanded informal characterization of the validity of arguments in Chapter 4, using physical models to convey the notion of logical necessity.
- A more detailed formal treatment of validity in the appendix. This allows instructors more flexibility in choosing whether and how deeply to pursue formal logic in connection with critical reasoning.
- Concise definitions of each fallacy we discuss in Chapter 6.
- A useful glossary of important concepts at the end of the text.
- An expanded selection of answers to exercises, including exercises requiring longer answers.

Suggestions for Using the Text

The main body of the text is divided into two parts. Chapters 2 through 8 concentrate on deductive arguments; Chapters 9 and 10 concentrate on induction and empirical theories. Within the section on arguments, Chapters 2 and 3 concentrate on analysis and reconstruction of simple passages, Chapters 4 and 5 introduce techniques of criticism, Chapter 6 discusses fallacies, and Chapters 7 and 8 apply techniques to more complicated passages. Even though the early chapters may seem relatively easy, it is important for the reader to master this material, because the more complex exercises in Chapter 7 and especially Chapter 8 are very difficult unless the step-by-step procedures of identifying premises and conclusions, adding missing premises and conclusions, determining validity, criticizing premises, assessing underlying conceptual theories, and paraphrasing passages have been carefully studied. Even if the steps of analysis and criticism have been learned individually, this learning will be wasted unless it can be brought together in a more systematic manner to understand and criticize real-life arguments, such as those in Exercise 8.

A main concern in selecting a text and planning a course in critical thinking is how much attention to devote to more formal aspects of logic. In this edition, we have sought to give users a maximum of flexibility in this regard. Chapter 4 contains an introduction to the concept of validity by means of analogy with physical necessity as well as some informal techniques involving counterexamples and parity of reasoning that can be used to demonstrate invalidity. The appendix provides an introduction to symbolism, definition of truth functional connectives, and the use of truth tables and Venn diagrams, as well as comments about natural deduction. The appendix can be omitted, used in part (for example, as an introduction to symbolic notation), taught as a free-standing chapter (with assigned exercises), or treated as an introduction and supplement to a more elaborate discussion of symbolic logic.

Instructors might consider varying passages to be analyzed and criticized by asking students to select articles from newspapers or magazines. We have found it useful to have students keep a journal of such articles, as well as a transcription of interesting arguments or theories they have heard in conversation, encountered in lectures, or seen on television. As a final exercise, students can then be asked to apply the techniques discussed in the text to some of the items in their journals. These and other ways of extending the text are considered in greater detail in the *Critical Reasoning Instructor's Manual*.

Acknowledgments

Special thanks are due to Wadsworth's philosophy editor, Kenneth King, and the Wadsworth staff for organizing reviewers' comments on the first two editions and providing encouragement in shaping the third. The first two editions went through numerous revisions, and the authors were helped by constructive comments from many people. The current edition has benefitted greatly from a variety of supportive, but sometimes critical comments by colleagues who have read and used the text. Of particular help were William Blizek and Cassia Spohn of the University of Nebraska at Omaha, as well as Al Leisenring, Kirk Thompson, Gonzalo Munevar, and Camille Coffey of The Evergreen State College. We would also like to thank reviewers of the third edition for their many helpful suggestions. They were Bradley Dowden, California State University, Sacramento; Michael McMahan, College of the Canyons; Deborah Mayo, Virginia Polytechnic and State University; Lauren Miller, Longview Community College; Michael Pritchard, Western Michigan University; and Everett Traverso, Santa Rosa Junior College. We appreciate as well the editorial assistance of Greg Hubit.

Jerry Cederblom
David W. Paulsen

CHAPTER ONE

Deciding What to Believe

When you read a book or a newspaper or listen to someone speak, or even when you are thinking by yourself, you face a decision about what to believe. Should you accept a newspaper columnist's argument in favor of undermining drug cartels by legalizing drugs? Should you be persuaded by your professor's reasoning that plea bargaining in the criminal courts should be eliminated? Should you be led by your own considerations to the conclusion that women should not be entirely free to choose whether to have an abortion? Critical reasoning—the subject of this book—is a collection of procedures that will help you make decisions concerning what to believe. More specifically, exercise of critical reasoning can help you understand what is at issue and guide you in judging whether the reasons supporting a point of view are strong enough that you should accept it.

This is not to say that critical reasoning *alone* can tell you what to believe. Critical reasoning is not a magical technique guaranteed to tell you whether to accept a particular belief in isolation. It does not operate in a vacuum. In order to decide whether drugs should be legalized, for example, you would need supporting information. You would probably want to know the extent of drug use under present laws, the nature of illegal drug trafficking and the harm it produces, the probable effects of different plans for legalization (Would drug use increase? By whom? How much?), and so on. But in evaluating what appears to be "information" on these subjects and in judging whether this information justifies taking a particular position on the issue, critical reasoning should play a crucial role.

The techniques of critical reasoning that we describe in this book assume that you already have many beliefs and that you use these beliefs to decide whether to accept new arguments presented to you. For example, suppose someone claims that drug use wouldn't increase significantly if drugs were legalized. You will be inclined to accept or reject this, depending on your beliefs about people—how tempted they are to use drugs, whether it is the threat of punishment that now keeps them from using drugs, and whether they would become more inclined to use drugs if the threat of legal punishment were lifted. If you believe that the threat of legal punishment has very little to do with whether people use drugs, this would support the claim that legalization wouldn't result in higher drug use.

Of course, you can always pursue the question further, asking whether a supporting belief is itself well supported. Why do you believe that threat of punishment isn't what keeps people from using drugs? You could try to find out whether there is support for this belief, perhaps by looking at research done on why some people use drugs while others don't. Moreover, it is crucial for critical reasoners to be willing to give up some previously held beliefs if they appear to be inconsistent with claims that have better support.

The techniques of critical reasoning that we present here are not techniques for generating beliefs or cleverly presenting arguments. They are not techniques that tell you how to move from premises you now accept to conclusions you haven't yet considered. They are techniques for *evaluating* some beliefs in the light of others. By contrast, the detective in fiction is often depicted as "deducing" unexpected conclusions from a set of clues. Critical reasoning does not operate in this way. It is a procedure for judging beliefs, not for generating them.

We can describe our approach to critical reasoning more clearly by contrasting it with two other kinds of activity: (1) passive reading or listening (as in the case of students who expect a lecturer to fill them with information) and (2) mere disagreement (as in the case of a combative person who is not willing to listen to reason).

Critical Reasoning Versus Passive Reading or Listening

Sometimes, when we listen to a lecture or read a book or an essay, we take each statement as information to be remembered. Suppose you are listening to a professor lecturing on the criminal courts. If your main purpose is to prepare yourself for a multiple choice test, you might simply try to remember as many of her statements as you can: "Most criminal cases don't go to trial. About 90 percent of defendants plead guilty. Most legal scholars account for this high rate of guilty pleas as being the result of plea bargaining. If this is so, then eliminating plea bargaining would swamp the courts with cases." If you are taking notes, your mind will be active to the extent that you select some statements as worth writing down, and you probably group statements together under topical headings. But you are passive in the sense that you don't evaluate which of the professor's statements to accept and which to doubt or reject.

By contrast, critical reasoning demands a more fully active approach. First, in order to evaluate what you hear, you listen for structure: Are some statements presented as conclusions (e.g., that eliminating plea bargaining would swamp the courts) and others as supporting reasons (e.g., that plea bargaining results in guilty pleas)? Are some presented as explanations? What are they intended to explain? (Is the availability of plea bargaining intended to explain the high rate of guilty pleas?) Next, you evaluate: Has this conclusion been adequately supported? Do you have reason to doubt the supporting statements? Does the conclusion follow from them? Is this explanation an adequate one? These are some of the questions this book will address.

Critical Reasoning Versus Mere Disagreement

In contrast to passive reading and listening, mere disagreement is critical as well as active, but it nevertheless lacks some essential features of critical reasoning. As we conceive mere disagreement, the listener/reader is poised to reject that with which she disagrees. She approaches what she hears or reads with her own established beliefs well in mind. She considers each statement presented to her and accepts, rejects, or holds it as uncertain, depending on how it squares with her prior set of beliefs. So as she reads from the editorial on legalizing drugs, "Many of the deaths associated with drug trafficking are the result of disputes between rival drug gangs," she thinks, OK, I agree with that. She reads further that, if drugs were legalized, the commerce of drugs could be regulated by law. She thinks, Well, I guess so. She proceeds through the editorial to the conclusion of the article, which suggests the limited legalization of drugs, and she makes the judgment, No, that's too radical, I've always been against drugs.

This process is active in that, as each statement is considered, a judgment is made. And the process is critical insofar as the judgments are evaluative (some statements are accepted, some are rejected). But critical reasoning differs from mere disagreement in certain crucial ways.

Mere disagreement is applied to separate, individual statements, and they are judged solely against the background of the reader's own beliefs. Critical reasoning, by contrast, requires reading the whole editorial for argumentative structure, looking at some statements as justifications for believing others. Rather than judging the main thesis of the article in isolation and evaluating it on the basis of her prior beliefs alone, critical reasoning requires that the reader be open to having her mind changed. Even if she would have disagreed with the editor's thesis initially, she might be persuaded by the content of the editorial to believe it.

Critical reasoning, then, involves looking at reasons on which a point of view is based and judging whether these reasons are strong enough to justify accepting this point of view.

The Attitude of the Critical Reasoner

This activity of critical reasoning typically carries with it an attitude quite different from that of the person engaged in mere disagreement. When we engage in mere disagreement, we seek to maintain the same beliefs we held prior to considering a new position. When we engage in critical reasoning, we cultivate an attitude of relative detachment. Of course, we can't give up our whole set of beliefs at once because we use these beliefs to judge whether to accept the argument being presented to us. But if an arguer points out that reasons we ourselves would accept really support his conclusion and would compel us to give up some conflicting view we used to hold, then we see this as a gain, not a loss.

If we have been against abortion and someone points to beliefs we ourselves hold that would rationally compel us to the view that the fetus should not be considered a person, then as critical reasoners we would embrace this view even though it threatens our antiabortion position. And the same can be said if we are in favor of allowing abortion and we are given good reasons for taking the fetus to be a person. The object is not to "save face" by attempting to justify past beliefs, but to embrace whatever is most reasonable now. We are committed to being consistent and to following reason wherever it leads.

An issue like abortion typically reduces potential reasoners to mere disagreers. Because the issue is heartfelt and because those on both sides tend to see their opponents as villains, it is difficult to accept a point that might give support to the opposing view, even if you have good reason to accept it. The object becomes the "winning" of the argument—by making the opposition look and sound bad—rather than the winning of new understanding by careful consideration of points made.

Self-Identity: Two Options

These two attitudes—the mere disagreer's attitude of wanting to sustain past beliefs and the critical reasoner's attitude of wanting to judge what *should* be believed—correspond to two ways of viewing ourselves. I might associate what I truly am with my present set of beliefs. Then, if I find that I was mistaken about something, I must admit that until now my self has been defective—a difficult thing to do. In this situation, it is important for me to *already* be right—not to have to change my beliefs or learn from someone else. Maintaining this attitude will hold me at the level of mere disagreement.

On the other hand, I might identify myself more closely with the belief-forming process itself. Rather than characterizing myself in static terms, by the set of beliefs that I try to maintain, I can think of myself dynamically as actively engaged in replacing less adequate beliefs with more adequate ones. I can characterize myself as the kind of person who takes pride in carrying out this activity well. Critical reasoners are like athletes engaged in the activity of their sport. Mere disagreers are more like bodybuilders, taking pride in the static features of their bodies, not in how their bodies perform.

Benefits of Critical Reasoning

What is to be gained from approaching disputes as opportunities to improve your set of beliefs rather than as contests? Many people enjoy winning arguments, and they would be disappointed to learn that studying critical reasoning won't prepare them to win more arguments. Neverthe-less, there are several points to consider in favor of critical reasoning.

First, not all disputes in which you engage are with other people. Perhaps the most important dialogues that occur in your mental develop-ment are with yourself. If you have acquired the habit of arguing with others only for the purpose of winning, then you have not prepared yourself adequately to reason well in these dialogues with yourself. There are sidetracks along which an individual can be drawn, just as a pair of people can be drawn away from reason and into competition and attempts to dominate. In a conversation with yourself, unless habits of reasoning have been well established, it is easy to choose the position that is the most comfortable or the most self-serving, rather than the one that is the most reasonable.

Second, from a broader perspective, the practice of critical reasoning can promote substantial social values. Perhaps foremost among them is the defense it can provide against our vulnerability as citizens in a society increasingly ruled by experts. Even though we might not be experts ourselves, we can mitigate our status as amateurs by honing our reasoning skills.

Moreover, our guiding assumption in promoting critical reasoning is that our beliefs form the basis for our actions, and, the better justified our beliefs, the more appropriate to the world our actions will tend to be.

Still, considerations such as these might be insufficient to motivate you to begin what you anticipate as being the long and not particularly enjoy-able task of developing your critical reasoning skills—especially if you picture critical reasoning as having shortcomings and disadvantages of its own. Let's look at this side of the case.

Some Common Misconceptions about Critical Reasoning

Perhaps the most common misconception people have about critical rea-soning is that they picture it as locking us into very structured patterns of thought. They associate it with "being logical," which calls up a picture of moving from proposition A to proposition B to proposition C in a boring mechanical way. This regimented, "linear" way of thinking is sometimes contrasted with a spontaneous, creative, free and easy manner of thought that sounds much more appealing.

This picture of critical reasoning and its effects on the mind is a mistaken one. In the first place, in order to criticize a position someone has offered, you may sometimes need to put statements into a pattern. But learning to do this will not suddenly make the thoughts that come into your head fit into patterns. You may *get* your ideas any way you want; critical reasoning won't have any effect on this. Your thoughts might float through your head in any order, mixed with the wildest fantasies and daydreams—critical reasoning has nothing to say about this. But if, on some later occasion, you wish to evaluate a certain thought that occurred to you, you might *then* need to fit it and certain other thoughts into a pattern. Critical reasoning doesn't tell you to spend a large portion of your mental life doing this, but if and when you want to evaluate a statement you have considered or someone else has offered, *at that time* you will need to consider whether there are other statements that adequately support the one in question. This involves looking at the pattern of the statements.

The notion that a person thinks either logically or nonlogically all the time, and that learning to reason will transform you from doing the latter to doing the former, is preposterous. If thinking nonlogically means think-ing spontaneously, freely, in no imposed order, then everyone thinks nonlogically a good deal of the time, and no one would want to stop doing so. But on some occasions, everyone needs to determine whether a certain belief is well supported and worth holding. On these occasions, there is really no choice about whether to do this logically or nonlogically. Critical reasoning, in other words, is something we all do some of the time. The question is whether to learn to do it better.

Another common misconception about critical reasoning is that it supposes there is a right and wrong point of view. Some people are more attracted to the notion that each person has his or her own way of looking at things and one way is no better than another. Actually, engaging in critical reasoning doesn't force you to assume that there is always one right position on an issue. It could be that more than one position can be held equally reasonably. We do not assume that the truth can always be known, or even that it can ever be known with certainty. But to engage in critical reasoning is to assume that sometimes one point of view can be seen to be more reasonable than another. We also assume that it is sometimes more reasonable to doubt a certain position than to believe it.

Perhaps the notion that one person's opinion is always as good as another's seems the more humane and tolerant attitude. A more thorough assessment of this relativism will be given in the final chapter of this book. For now it is worth noting that this attitude has a profound and dangerous consequence. If one holds that there is no way of determining what is reasonable to believe—that one opinion is as good as another—then, when it comes to deciding what belief to *act* upon, what procedure is available for making this decision? If it is assumed that no opinion can be shown to be more reasonable than another, it is a short step to the view that the only final appeal in settling differences is an appeal to force.

A Preview of the Text

Thus far we have claimed critical reasoning to be a process that emphasizes a rational basis for belief and provides a procedure for resolving disagreements by means of further inquiry. And we have contrasted critical reasoning to a *mere* disagreement or quarrel in this respect. We now indicate briefly some of the ways in which critical reasoning can accomplish its ends. This overview also introduces the materials contained in Chapter 2 through Chapter 11.

We can illustrate the main techniques of critical reasoning by applying them to the following lecture fragment on the subject of plea bargaining. Suppose you have taken notes on this lecture, and you now want to critically evaluate what has been said. How do you put this content into a structure that prepares it for fruitful evaluation? What should you accept of what has been said? What should you call into question? Why? These are the kinds of questions we hope to prepare you to answer for yourself in the chapters that follow.

Plea bargaining (agreeing to plead guilty in exchange for a reduced sentence) generates problems. Innocent defendants who can't afford bail may plead guilty just to avoid jail time waiting for trial. The process makes no presumption of innocence. Guilt is not determined in an adversarial process, it is negotiated. It makes work easier for prosecutors, defense attorneys, and judges, but it sacrifices the interests of society.

Given these problems, some have suggested that plea bargaining be eliminated. But this might create an even worse problem. Ninety percent of defendants plead guilty, and most of those do plea-bargain. Suppose plea bargaining were eliminated and the percentage of guilty pleas dropped to 80 percent. This would double the number of criminal trials, placing a staggering burden on the criminal justice system.

The experience of Alaska, however, calls this fear into question. Alaska has virtually done away with plea bargaining. There was some increase in the number of trials, but not as much as expected. In the year before elimination of plea bargaining, there were seventy-two felony trials in Fairbanks. In the year after, there were ninety. This is only a 25 percent increase.

Why was the increase so small? The explanation of why defendants plead guilty could be because most of them are factually guilty, and they don't have a viable legal argument for their defense (i.e., they are legally guilty as well); so they believe it is unlikely that they would win in a trial. If this is the case, then, as Alaska's experience indicates, while it may be difficult to eliminate plea bargaining, it is not impossible.

An important part of critical reasoning is identifying, understanding, and evaluating *arguments,* and these topics are the primary focus of this book. By viewing a collection of statements as an argument, we are seeing it as a *conclusion* based on *reasons* (premises). What arguments can we find in the lecture fragment on plea bargaining?

If we survey the passage, we can see that the first paragraph contains reasons in favor of the conclusion that plea bargaining should be eliminated. The second paragraph presents reasons supporting the opposite conclusion—that plea bargaining should not be eliminated. The third and fourth paragraphs cast doubt on the second argument—they suggest that the reasons given for keeping plea bargaining may be weak. The last statement of the passage (". . . while it may be difficult to eliminate plea bargaining, it is not impossible") indicates that the lecturer is supporting the first argument and rejecting the second.

In applying critical reasoning to this passage, you will want to decide for yourself whether to accept the first argument and reject the second. To do this, you will first need to restate each argument clearly, listing all the premises and the conclusion for each. Often, this requires rewriting parts of the passage in a more clear, direct manner. For example, the first premise of the first argument might be stated, "Plea bargaining may cause innocent defendants to plead guilty." You will want to include in your reconstruction of the argument any premises that are implied but not stated. We discuss how to identify premises and conclusions in Chapters 2 and 3, and we discuss in Chapter 7 how to rewrite arguments in a complete form, based on their fragmentary presentation in prose passages.

After you reconstruct the arguments in the passage, you will want to evaluate them. This is a two-step procedure of asking (1) whether the conclusion follows from the premises and (2) whether the premises themselves should be believed. These basic steps of argument evaluation are discussed in Chapter 4 and elaborated in Chapters 5, 6, and 8.

The first eight chapters focus on what is called a *deductive* argument. Chapter 9 turns to an argument (usually called *inductive*) that has a different relationship between its premises and its conclusion. This discussion involves us in an analysis of how generalizations can be based on particular observations. This in turn leads us to a discussion of causal generalization and prediction.

Paragraphs 3 and 4 of the lecture fragment can be seen as generalizing from particular data. The particular case of Fairbanks, Alaska, in which felony trials increased only 25 percent, is used to suggest that it may not be impossible to eliminate plea bargaining generally (i.e., in other states as well). Chapter 9 will give you a procedure for judging whether generalizations such as this one are warranted.

Chapter 10 extends the discussion of critical inquiry to the topic of theories. Theories are often set forth either as premises of arguments or as explanations of why certain patterns occur in the observable world. Evaluating theories sometimes requires specialized knowledge, but we present some general procedures that are helpful in understanding many theories and provide a direction for evaluating them.

The lecture fragment can be interpreted as presenting two theories, both intended to explain why most defendants plead guilty. The first theory (suggested in paragraph 2) supports the argument that plea bargaining should not be eliminated. According to this theory, most defendants plead guilty simply because they are offered a lesser sentence under plea bargaining than they would stand to get if they went to trial. The second theory is presented in paragraph 4. In essence, this theory claims that defendants plead guilty because they *are* guilty. The techniques described in Chapter 10 will help you reconstruct these theories more precisely and understand how to evaluate them. This reconstruction in turn will help you choose between the two opposing arguments presented in the lecture.

Sometimes we feel unqualified to judge what we hear and read because we lack expertise. In the case of plea bargaining, for example, we might feel tempted to leave the matter to specialists in the field of criminal justice and simply adopt the views of those specialists. However, taking this approach raises difficulties of its own. How do we know who to count as an expert in a particular field? What do we do if the experts disagree? How do we avoid being controlled by experts? The difficulties we face in making decisions based on theories and arguments proposed by experts and specialists is the subject of Chapter 11.

Through its treatment of all of these topics, a strong underlying purpose of this book is to provide procedures for determining what is reasonable to believe. When presented with an argument or theory, one might take this as an occasion for a contest, an occasion for defending prior beliefs and defeating anything that contradicts them, or as an opportunity to determine whether past beliefs are inadequate and should be modified. Our basis for urging the latter course is the proposition that there is more to be gained by building a more reasonable set of beliefs than by winning contests when disagreements occur.

Exercise 1.1   **Taking Notice of Disagreements and Reasoning**

---

1. Write a short account of a dispute that you overheard or in which you participated recently. State whether you think anyone's point of view was changed as a result of reasons presented by the opposition. If not, why not? To what extent did the exchange consist of mere disagreement, and to what extent reasoned criticism?

2. As a starting point in developing your reasoning skills, it will be useful for you to produce a short piece of writing. This exercise will be used later to help you improve your writing. In a paragraph or two, express a position on one of the following issues and support it:

   a. censorship
   b. capital punishment
   c. abortion
   d. use of alcohol or other drugs
   e. marriage
   f. U.S. foreign policy

3. Consider the situations of a courtroom trial and a formal debate. Contrast the procedures followed in these situations (as you understand them) to the procedures of reasoned criticism that have been outlined in this chapter.

4. In an important sense, critical reasoning is intimately involved with critical reading and listening. The first step in carrying out this task is putting someone else's ideas in your own words. We will be discussing how to do this in detail throughout the text, but as a start, for each passage, (a) write what you take to be the author's main point, and (b) list any claims the author makes that support this point. Set aside for the moment your own position on the issues raised, and try to capture the author's position as best you can. It is often useful to simplify a passage, using your own words.

   a. America has got to slash unmercifully its budget deficit. In the last decade, America has become the world's greatest debtor nation. We can only hope to reverse this sorrowful state of affairs if we seriously engage in reducing the budget deficit.
   b. People are dying all over the United States as victims of the drug war. These victims often have their lives destroyed, if not by the

drugs themselves, then by a disease like AIDS that often comes with drug taking. But of course, drug takers are not the only victims. The drug trade brings with it the violence we see in cities all over the United States. Gangs supported by drug money bring terror to the streets. But our political system is also a victim. The truly incredible amount of money available to drug kingpins inevitably leads to corruption among the police and in the government. The fabric of the country is in danger. The war on drugs is one of the greatest problems the country will face over the next decade.

c. I've got a tough decision. I'm thinking about what area to major in. I've taken a course in philosophy and found it very interesting, but I don't see how it can fit into my career plans. After all, what really counts in college is getting the training you need for a good job. Philosophy is irrelevant to the job market. Perhaps I should take some business courses instead. Well, maybe I'll take a course in Business Ethics sometime.

d. The abortion issue seems to be in the news practically every week. There are rallies and political speeches. Various candidates are jockeying for political advantage by embracing one side or the other on this controversial issue. Abortion raises some fundamental issues that bring into conflict our very conception of humanity and our ideals of liberty. In spite of the importance of the topic, abortion should not be made the central issue in political campaigns. Candidates for public office differ in a variety of ways, some of which are more important to the fate of the country than to abortion policy. If we do not adequately deal with the deficit and the drug problem, both our ideals of humanity and our liberty will be threatened. There should be no "litmus test," no single criterion, in judging people for public life in our complex and increasingly vulnerable world.

5. Review your notes from a lecture that you heard recently. Briefly state the most important points in your own words.

CHAPTER TWO

The Anatomy of Arguments: Identifying Premises and Conclusions

When someone gives reasons to support a point of view, that person is usually offering an *argument*. You encounter arguments in your reading and in your conversations with others, and you commonly offer arguments to support your own beliefs. When you are presented with an argument, you can take the opportunity to decide whether the reasons given are good enough to warrant incorporating the point of view that is being advanced into your own set of beliefs. To make this decision, you need to clearly understand the argument and then evaluate it. This and the following chapters present a step-by-step procedure for understanding and evaluating arguments.

The parts of an argument are called the *premises* and the *conclusion*. In order to understand arguments fully, you need to first learn to identify these parts. Ultimately, understanding them will help you to distinguish good arguments from bad. As in medicine, you must learn the anatomy of an animal before you can systematically diagnose its ills and improve its health.

The Key to Identification: Seeing What Is Supported by What

We shall begin our investigation of premises and conclusions by looking at short, simple passages that contain arguments. These first examples might seem contrived, but they have been stylized in order to make it easier for you to see the structure of arguments. Once the preliminaries have been thoroughly developed, we shall return to more natural cases, such as argumentative passages found in magazines, newspapers, and books.

Suppose someone who is talking politics says:

Example 2.1   *If the president were really doing his job, the budget deficit would be reduced. But the budget deficit hasn't been reduced. So the president is not really doing his job.*

The first two statements support the third. They provide reasons why the listener should believe that the president is not really doing his job. We call statements offered to support a position the *premises* (each one individually is a premise). The *conclusion* is the statement that the premises are supposed to support. Together the premises and the conclusion make up the argument. In this argument we are asked to move from the claims made in the two premises to the claim made in the conclusion, which depends on them in such a way that, if both of the premises are true, the conclusion must also be true.

Consider a second example. Suppose someone who doesn't know much about biology argues as follows:

Example 2.2   *Whales are not mammals, since no fish are mammals and whales are fish.*

In this argument the premises and the conclusion are not separate sentences, but we can nevertheless distinguish what is supported from what is offered as support. The first statement, *whales are not mammals,* is supposed to be supported by the two statements that follow: *no fish are mammals* and *whales are fish*. The latter two statements are the premises, and the first statement, *whales are not mammals,* is the conclusion. This conclusion happens to be false, but it is nevertheless the conclusion of the argument.

Two cautions are in order: (1) Some people misconstrue the conclusion as a mere summary of the premises. A conclusion in our sense does not, however, simply restate the sentences in a passage. (2) Others tend to think of the conclusion as the most important point in the passage. Often it is, but it need not be. The conclusion can be singled out because it stands in a special relationship to the other statements; that is, it is supposed to be supported by the other statements. In order to find the conclusion in a passage, we must see which statement is supposed to be supported by the others.*

Clues to Identifying Argument Parts: Indicator Words

Sometimes the person offering an argument provides clues that identify the premises and conclusion. Imagine a pessimistic lecturer trying to convince his audience that we are going to face a time of economic woes.

Example 2.3   *Either we actually reduce the budget deficit or we will face severe economic problems within a decade. But we won't actually reduce the budget deficit. We can conclude that we will face severe economic problems within a decade.*

In this case the speaker tells us which statement is the conclusion of the argument by using the phrase "We can conclude that. . . ." We call expressions that explicitly mark a conclusion *conclusion indicators*. Numerous expressions can play this role, including the following:

CONCLUSION INDICATORS

    so

    thus

    therefore

    hence

    we can conclude that

    consequently

There are also expressions that help identify premises. Among the most common of these are:

---

*In later chapters, when we deal with more complicated passages, we shall find that some arguments can be interpreted as having more than one conclusion.

PREMISE INDICATORS*

since

for

because

for the reason that

The statement that immediately follows a conclusion indicator is the conclusion; that following a premise indicator is a premise. This latter will seem natural when you consider that premises are reasons given in support of the conclusion, and all the premise indicators mean roughly "for the *reason* that."

Additional indicators typically come between premises and conclusions:

PREMISE AND CONCLUSION INDICATORS

(premise)	. . . shows that . . .	(conclusion)
"	. . . indicates that . . .	"
"	. . . proves that . . .	"
"	. . . entails that . . .	"
"	. . . implies that . . .	"
"	. . . establishes that . . .	"
"	. . . allows us to infer that . . .	"
"	. . . gives us reasons for believing that . . .	"

Or, alternatively, between conclusions and premises:

CONCLUSION AND PREMISE INDICATORS

(conclusion)	. . . is shown by . . .	(premise)
"	. . . is indicated by . . .	"
"	. . . is proven by . . .	"
"	. . . is entailed by . . .	"
"	. . . is implied by . . .	"
"	. . . is established by . . .	"

---

*These words are not *always* used as premise indicators. For example, *since* can also be used to indicate order in time as in the statement, "Since Joe went to medical school, he has established a practice in the field of AIDS treatment."

Exercise 2.1   Techniques for Marking the Parts of Arguments

The distinction between the premises and conclusion in an argument can be formally marked in several ways. We can graphically set them apart by putting the argument into standard form. To do this, we list the premises, numbering each separate statement. Then we draw a line to separate premises from the conclusion. The conclusion is below the line. Traditionally, conclusions have been marked by a sign consisting of three dots. The argument in Example 2.3 would be written in standard form as:

Sample A

(1) *Either we actually reduce the budget deficit or we will face severe economic problems within a decade.*

(2) *We won't actually reduce the budget deficit.*

∴   *We will face severe economic problems within a decade.*

Note that we leave out premise and conclusion indicators, as well as words that connect the premises such as *and** or *but*. These words become unnecessary because our manner of displaying the argument already indicates which statements are premises, how many there are, and what is asserted as the conclusion.

For simple arguments written out in detail, a second, abbreviated version of the process of putting an argument in standard form involves circling the parts of a passage that contain premises and conclusion and marking the premises with the symbols "Pr1," "Pr2," and so on, and the conclusion with "C."

Sample B

(1) Since (whales and dolphins are mammals) *Pr1* and (mammals need to breathe air,) *Pr2* (whales and dolphins need to breathe air.) *C*

Notice that premises and conclusion must be complete statements. In Sample C below, the fragment "If the president were really doing his job" alone can't serve as a premise because it is not a complete statement.

Sample C

(If the president were really doing his job, the budget deficit would be eliminated.) *Pr1* But (the budget deficit hasn't been reduced.) *Pr2* So (the president is not really doing his job.) *C*

---

*If the word *and* occurs *within* a premise, rather than *between* premises, it should not be omitted.

Try these techniques on the following exercises. Put exercises 1 and 2 into standard form; for exercises 3–16, circle and label the premises and conclusions.

1. You shouldn't lie to friends. Carla is your friend. Therefore, you shouldn't lie to Carla.

2. If you want to catch Bruce's attention, then you should make sure that your teeth are white. You want to catch Bruce's attention. So you should make sure your teeth are white.

3. Abortion raises serious moral questions because abortion involves the taking of a human life, and anything that involves the taking of a human life raises serious moral questions.

4. If a person's desk is organized, her mind is organized. Sue's desk is organized. We can conclude that Sue's mind is organized.

5. All living things need some external source of energy. The sun is the only external source of energy for living things on earth. Thus, all living things on earth need the sun.

6. It is wrong for society to kill a murderer. This follows for the reason that if a murderer is wrong in killing his victim, then society is also wrong in killing the murderer. And a murderer *is* wrong in killing his victim.

7. All pornography should be banned. This allows us to infer that *National Geographic* magazine should be banned, because anything that contains pictures of naked people is pornographic, and *National Geographic* contains pictures of naked people.

8. Any area of study that contributes to the field of medicine should be well supported. Therefore, biology should be well supported, since it contributes to the field of medicine.

9. Only adult citizens can vote and Peter is not a citizen, so Peter can't vote.

10. An activity pays if the people who engage in it come out ahead economically more often than not. The people who engage in many crimes come out ahead economically more often than not. It follows that many crimes pay.

11. The Pentagon must be in Washington, D.C., because it is either in Washington, D.C., or in Baltimore, Maryland. But my brother, who works at the Pentagon, says he has never been in Baltimore.

12. Capital punishment is not justified for the reason that, with capital punishment, an innocent person might be executed, and no practice that might kill innocent people is justified.

13. That there won't be a quiz on Monday is implied by the fact that we had a quiz on Friday, and we never have quizzes in two class meetings in a row.

It might seem more difficult to identify premises and conclusions in passages with long, complex sentences. Actually, the task remains fairly simple if you can locate the indicator words that divide an argument into its parts, as in the following exercises.

14. There are only four possible solutions to the long-range problem of energy for the industrialized world: We develop a program of greater energy conservation, we develop a new technology based on nuclear fusion and solar energy, we permit the establishment of a plutonium economy, or we experience economic collapse. But we will not embark on a program of greater energy conservation, or develop a new technology based on nuclear fusion and solar energy, or permit the establishment of a plutonium economy. As a result, we will experience economic collapse.

15. The United States has nothing to lose by cutting back on planned military expenditures. This is because the United States already has enough military resources to protect the country from any likely military action against it. And if the United States already has enough military resources to protect the country from any likely military action against it, the United States has no need to increase military expenditures or even to keep them at current levels. If the United States has no need to increase military expenditures or even to keep them at current levels, then the United States has nothing to lose by cutting back on planned military expenditures.

16. If Americans continue to reject candidates for public office who propose significant tax increases, then the needed improvements to our infrastructure, including our educational system, will be impossible. If the needed improvements to our infrastructure will be impossible, then we will be unable to retain our economic competitiveness with Europe and Japan. Consequently we will be unable to retain our economic competitiveness with Europe and Japan, because Americans will continue to reject candidates for public office that propose significant tax increases.

What to Do When There Are No Indicator Words: The Principle of Charitable Interpretation

Indicator words explicitly mark the intended role of statements in an argument. But authors often omit indicator words on the assumption that it is obvious which of their statements are offered as support and which statement is being supported. When there are no indicator words, and it is questionable what an argument's premises or conclusion are, you should employ what might be called the *Principle of Charitable Interpretation: When more than one interpretation of an argument is possible, the argument should be interpreted so that the premises provide the strongest support for the conclusion.** This principle is in keeping with the rationale for critical reasoning that was offered in Chapter 1. The object is not to make your opponent's argument look as weak as possible but to determine what is most reasonable to believe. It is to this end that arguments under consideration should be given the strongest possible interpretation.

The procedure this principle suggests for identifying the premises and conclusion involves trying each statement of an argument in the role of conclusion, with the remaining statements acting as premises. Whichever statement is best supported by the others should be taken to be the conclusion. Note the following argument:

Example 2.4   *You should have come to the party. You promised Alice you would come. If you promise to do something, you should do it.*

It can be seen fairly readily that the first statement is better supported by the remainder of the argument than either of the other two. If we put the argument into standard form, alternating each statement in the role of conclusion, we can see more easily that this reading is the best. Although this lengthy process is seldom necessary in actually interpreting an argument, it might be helpful in this case to go through it to show how the plausibility of the different alternatives varies.

---

*As will be explained in Chapters 3 and 7, this principle must be amended to take account of the intent of the arguer and information that is provided by the context of the argument.

Putting the argument into standard form with the first sentence as the conclusion gives us:

Reading 1   *(1) If you promise to do something, you should do it.*

(2) You promised Alice you would come.

∴   You should have come to the party.

This interpretation of the passage is best because if the premises are true, the conclusion must also be true. And, as shall be explained in succeeding chapters, this is precisely the relationship of support between premises and conclusion that is one requirement for a good argument. By considering what each statement means, you can see that the premises adequately support the conclusion. The first premise states that if you satisfy a certain condition (making a promise), then you have an obligation (keeping the promise). The second premise adds that you did satisfy the condition of promising something (that is, to come to the party). But if these premises are true, then the conclusion, *you should have come to the party,* must be true.

In contrast, the supposed premises in the other readings do not adequately support their supposed conclusions. The premises could very well be true without the conclusion being true.

Reading 2   *(1) You should have come to the party.*

(2) You promised Alice you would come.

∴   If you promise to do something, you should do it.

It could very well be true that you should have come to the party, and that you promised Alice, but these facts do nothing to support the more general conclusion that if you promise to do something, you should do it.

Reading 3   *(1) You should have come to the party.*

(2) If you promise to do something, you should do it.

∴   You promised Alice you would come.

The claims that you should have come, and that if you promise something, you should do it, do not support the claim that you promised Alice you would come. It could be that you should have come (perhaps you would have had the chance to meet some interesting people), and that you should keep your promises; but it could at the same time be false that you promised Alice you would come.

Again, in actual practice, the context in which you find a passage limits the number of possible interpretations that can reasonably be made. This point will be discussed in some detail in Chapter 7. The formulation of the Principle of Charitable Interpretation, which has been stated here, should be taken as preliminary and subject to this later qualification.

Exercise 2.2   **Using the Principle of Charitable Interpretation to Pick Out Premises and Conclusions without Explicit Indicator Words**

Identify the premises and the conclusion in each of the following arguments. Interpret each argument so that the premises give the best support for the conclusion. As we have indicated, arguments do not ordinarily occur in such simplified form, with every statement in a passage serving as either a premise or a conclusion. We are presenting these stylized passages in order to sharpen your skills at identifying argument parts.

1. If you take too much pride in your physical beauty, you will come to dread growing older. You take too much pride in your physical beauty. You will come to dread growing older.

2. Either today's students will be given computer education very soon, or tomorrow's adults will enter the world of work with outmoded skills. Today's students will not be given computer education very soon. Tomorrow's adults will enter the world of work with outmoded skills.

3. If you respected my opinion you would seek my advice. You don't seek my advice. You don't respect my opinion.

4. Richard will end up hating himself. Anyone who is steeped in vice will end up hating himself. Richard is steeped in vice.

5. If Rob breaks up with Edna, then he will be free to date Karen. If he will be free to date Karen, then Arnold will be out of luck. If Rob breaks up with Edna, then Arnold will be out of luck.

6. Interest in women as sex objects will be on the rise again. If feminism is losing ground, then interest in women as sex objects will be on the rise again. Feminism is losing ground.

7. Every person has the capacity to kill. But anyone who has the capacity to kill should avoid keeping loaded guns around the house. Every person should avoid keeping loaded guns around the house.

8. If Edward made a deposit, then he got the money from his wife. If he got the money from his wife, then she is the thief. Edward made a deposit. His wife is the thief.

9. Either the United States will tackle the real social ills that beset its cities or it will lose the "war on drugs." The United States will not tackle the real social ills that beset its cities. The United States will lose the "war on drugs."

10. Body is not the only important characteristic in a white wine. If body were the only important characteristic, then California Chardonnay would always be preferable to a Sauvignon Blanc. But it is not the case that it is always preferable.

Patterns of Argument

The Principle of Charitable Interpretation asks us to interpret an argument so that the statements we take as premises best support the statement we take as the conclusion.* We have assumed that you are already able to see, in the simplest cases, which statement is best supported by the remaining statements. But in order to become clearer about this relationship of support, consider two ways of interpreting the following argument.

Argument   *If my car is out of fuel, it won't start. My car won't start. My car is out of fuel.*

Interpretation 1   *(1) If my car is out of fuel, it won't start.*

(2) My car is out of fuel.

∴   *My car won't start.*

Interpretation 2   *(1) If my car is out of fuel, it won't start.*

(2) My car won't start.

∴   *My car is out of fuel.*

---

*Again, when you apply this principle, you are limited by what can plausibly be interpreted as the intent of the passage.

In interpretation 2, the conclusion does not follow from the premises. There are other reasons a car might not start than that it is out of fuel; perhaps the ignition system has failed. Even if the first premise is true and the car does not start, it doesn't follow that it is without fuel. Now contrast this to interpretation 1. If it is true that the absence of fuel prevents starting, then it is unavoidable that if you are out of fuel, the car will not start. We can't find a situation for interpretation 1 (like the ignition problem for interpretation 2) that would make the premises true but the conclusion false.

You could try to reason through to the best interpretation in this way each time you encounter a passage without indicator words and are unsure of what to pick as premises and what as the conclusion. But it is helpful to note that the two interpretations that were just considered are instances of argument patterns that you will encounter again and again; every time you see an instance of the pattern in interpretation 1, the conclusion does follow from the premises, whereas for the pattern in interpretation 2, the conclusion doesn't follow.

The pattern in interpretation 1 might be represented as:

(1) If A, then B.

(2) A.   *MODUS PONENS*
_____   *AFFIRMING THE ANTECEDENT*

∴ *B.*

This pattern is so common that it has been given a name: *modus ponens*. The faulty pattern in interpretation 2 might be represented as:

(1) If A, then B.

(2) B.   *AFFIRMING THE CONSEQUENT*
_____   *(Faulty)*

∴ *A.*

Even though this is a faulty pattern, it is so commonly used that it also has acquired a name. It is known as the *fallacy of affirming the consequent* (because the second premise *affirms* the "then . . ." part, i.e., the *consequent* of the first premise).

The point of the foregoing discussion is that if a passage could be fit into either of the two patterns, the Principle of Charitable Interpretation would dictate fitting it into the *modus ponens* pattern, because with this interpretation the premises provide the best support for the conclusion.

A related but different pair of interpretations can be given for the argument: If you respected my opinion, you would seek my advice. You don't seek my advice. You don't respect my opinion. Here are two ways of identifying the premises and conclusion.

Interpretation 1

(1) If you respected my opinion, you would seek my advice.

(2) You don't seek my advice.

∴ *You don't respect my opinion.*

Interpretation 2

(1) If you respected my opinion, you would seek my advice.

(2) You don't respect my opinion.

∴ *You won't seek my advice.*

In interpretation 1, the conclusion does follow from the premises. The first premise states that if you respected my opinion, then you would seek my advice. But the second premise states that you don't seek my advice. Now in order to make both these premises true, we are compelled to say that you don't respect my opinion. If we tried to claim both that the first premise is true and that you do respect my opinion, then we would be forced to say that you would seek my advice. But this would make the second premise false. In other words, the only possible way to make both premises true is to make the conclusion true also. This pattern of argument is called *modus tollens* and is represented as:

(1) If A, then B.

(2) Not B.   *MODUS TOLLENS* or

---   *DENYING THE CONSEQUENT*

∴ *Not A.*

In interpretation 2, the conclusion *doesn't follow from the premises.* It could well be that if you did respect my opinion, you would seek my advice—suppose you need information badly and will go to any source you consider reliable. It could also be that you don't respect my opinion—maybe you have heard that I have been mistaken more times than not. But it doesn't follow that you won't seek my advice. You might do so just to flatter me and keep me as a friend. That is, there might be more than one reason for a given consequent. It is perfectly possible for the premises of this argument to be true without the conclusion being true.

Arguments of this pattern are often persuasive, even though they shouldn't be. The pattern, called *denying the antecedent*, looks like this:

(1) If A, then B.

(2) Not A.   DENYING THE ANTECEDENT
                              (Faulty)

∴ *Not B.*

Although there are countless argument patterns besides *modus ponens* and *modus tollens* whose premises guarantee the truth of their conclusions, there are a few that occur so frequently that they are worth learning at the outset. By becoming familiar with these patterns, you will get a feel for the kind of relationship between premises and conclusions you are looking for when you attempt to apply the Principle of Charitable Interpretation. Chapter 4 and the appendix discuss argument patterns in greater detail, explaining some of the ways to determine whether an argument pattern is a good one.

The chart below and on the following page displays seven common argument patterns, including *modus ponens* and *modus tollens*. Any argument that fits one of these patterns will satisfy the criterion that if the premises are true, the conclusion must be true. Therefore, any plausible reading of a passage that fits one of these patterns would be supported by the Principle of Charitable Interpretation.

Some Common Successful Argument Patterns

Statement-Based Patterns*	Example
i. *(1) If A, then B.*	*(1) If I lie, then I'll be sorry.*
(2) A.	*(2) I'll lie.*
∴ *B.*	∴ *I'll be sorry.*
ii. *(1) Either A or B.*	*(1) Either I should jog or I should diet.*
(2) Not A.	*(2) I should not jog.*
∴ *B.*	∴ *I should diet.*

---

*The capital letters A, B, and C in patterns i–v stand for whole *statements*; we call this type of argument pattern "statement-based." In patterns vi and vii, the terms P_1, P_2, and P_3 stand for parts of statements, such as "good teacher," which refer to classes of objects. The lowercase letter m in pattern vi stands for a name or description of a particular person or thing. These names or descriptions can be seen as subjects that fit with a *predicate* such as "is a good teacher" to form a whole statement "Jones is a good teacher." We will call the argument patterns vi and vii "predicate-based."

iii. *(1) If A, then B.*

    (2) Not B.

———————————————————

∴   *Not A.*

(1) If wishes are horses, then beggars can ride.

(2) Beggars cannot ride.

———————————————————

∴   *Wishes are not horses.*

iv. *(1) If A then B.*

    (2) If B, then C.

———————————————————

∴   *If A, then C.*

(1) If I pay now, then I'll save.

(2) If I'll save, then I'll have money later.

———————————————————

∴   *If I pay now, I'll have money later.*

v. *(1) A.*

  (2) If A, then B.

  (3) If B, then C.

———————————————————

∴   *C.*

(1) The whole group is coming.

(2) If the whole group is coming, then we'll need more refreshments.

(3) If we'll need more refreshments, then we'll have to go to the store again.

———————————————————

∴   *We'll have to go to the store again.*

Predicate-Based Patterns

vi. *(1) All P_1's are P_2's.*

    (2) m is a P_1.

———————————————————

∴   *m is a P_2.*

Example

(1) All good teachers are sensitive to the needs of students.

(2) Jones is a good teacher.

———————————————————

∴   *Jones is sensitive to the needs of students.*

vii. *(1) All P_1's are P_2's.*

    (2) All P_2's are P_3's.

———————————————————

∴   *All P_1's are P_3's.*

(1) All good teachers treat students with respect.

(2) All who treat students with respect listen to what students say.

———————————————————

∴   *All good teachers listen to what students say.*

Exercise 2.3   **Using Argument Patterns to Pick Out Premises and Conclusions in Arguments without Explicit Indicator Words**

Each of the exercises in this section fits one of the patterns identified on the preceding page or a combination of them. Several tips will help you apply these patterns in written passages. First, the order of the premises makes no difference:

(1) If B, then C.

(2) A.

(3) If A, then B.

∴   *C.*

exhibits the same pattern for our purposes as

(1) A.

(2) If A, then B.

(3) If B, then C.

∴   *C.*

Second, in an either-or type sentence, order does not make any difference (though it does in an if-then type sentence):

(1) Either B or A.

(2) Not A.

∴   *B.*

exhibits the same pattern as

(1) Either A or B.

(2) Not A.

∴   *B.*

Third, arguments can fit these patterns even if some key words are missing. For example, if-then sentences often occur without the "then," as in: "If you lend me ten dollars, I'll love you forever." They may even have the "if" part at the end of the sentence, as in: "I'll bring the money, honey, if you'll bring the beer." Either-or type sentences may occur without the "either" stated: "I'll have coffee or tea." And the word *all* may be replaced by other expressions such as "every" or "any," as in: "Every person needs a friend."

In the process of identifying premises and conclusion, other features of a passage may provide further clues. First, since the conclusion is often the main point in an argumentative passage, look carefully at those readings that treat the beginning or the final sentences as the conclusion. Second, the conclusion of an argument is seldom longer and more complex than the premises. For example, we should be suspicious of a reading in which the conclusion is an if-then sentence, but the premises are not.

As we have indicated, arguments do not ordinarily occur in such simplified form. We are presenting these "unnatural" passages in order to sharpen your skill at identifying premises, conclusions, and argument patterns.

1. Go back to Exercise 2.2 and use the argument patterns to identify premises and conclusions. Note any arguments you interpreted incorrectly before you learned the argument patterns.

2. Identify the premises and conclusion, as well as the argument pattern, for each of the following exercises:

   a. John is bound to sharpen his argumentative skills. He is studying critical reasoning, and anyone who studies critical reasoning is bound to sharpen his argumentative skills.
   b. If we expect interest rates to go down, then the government will have to balance the budget. But the government won't balance the budget. Interest rates won't go down.
   c. If Mary finds sensitive men appealing, then she will be attracted to Roger. If she will be attracted to Roger, then she will end up being frustrated. Mary does find sensitive men appealing. She will end up being frustrated.
   d. Anyone who deceives other people is guilty of a form of coercion. Anyone who deceives others is manipulating their choices. Anyone who manipulates the choices of others is guilty of a form of coercion.
   e. If Paul can find the strength to resist Sheila's advances, then he will be able to salvage some measure of self-respect. He will find this strength. He will salvage some self-respect.

f. Alvin has not fulfilled the graduation requirements. If he has fulfilled the graduation requirements, then he is eligible for graduation. Alvin is not eligible for graduation.

g. Students will not become more interested in learning for its own sake. Universities will become more vocationally oriented. Either students will become more interested in learning for its own sake or universities will become more vocationally oriented.

h. If a human person is created at the moment of conception, then abortion always kills a human person. If abortion always kills a human person, then it is never justified. If a human person is created at the moment of conception, then abortion is never justified.

i. John will eventually become conservative. Everyone who goes to medical school will eventually become conservative. John will go to medical school.

j. Casual sex is justifiable in some cases. If some people can't find a partner who is willing to enter a serious relationship, casual sex is their only alternative to abstinence. Some people can't find a partner who is willing to enter a serious relationship. If casual sex is the only alternative to abstinence for some people, then casual sex is justifiable in some cases.

3. The following arguments don't exactly fit any of the seven patterns listed on the chart in this chapter. Try to determine their patterns. Identify the premises and conclusion and formulate the (new) patterns.

a. All liberals support spending for social programs. Our senator doesn't support such spending. Our senator is not a liberal.

b. We shouldn't abolish capital punishment. If we do, prisons will become more crowded. If prisons become more crowded, then we will have to build more prisons. We don't want to build more prisons.

c. Some judges have been subjected to corrupting influences. Anyone who has practiced law has been subjected to corrupting influences. Some judges have practiced law.

d. Either we should get married or we should break up completely. But if we get married I'll have to stop seeing Carl. I couldn't handle that. We should break up.

Applications to Writing

In this and many of the succeeding chapters we discuss how to put critical techniques into practice. It is difficult to discuss a particular aspect of criticism without presupposing a broader range of critical skills. The situation is similar to that of learning a sport like tennis. The tennis instructor must start with some particular aspect of the swing, leaving the others in rough form. Then the remaining aspects of the swing are developed one by one and fitted into the whole. Similarly, many of our exercises and examples presuppose some understanding of a range of skills that may not have been explicitly discussed in the text at that stage. We hope that you will be able to sharpen the particular skill that is the subject matter of each chapter, while at the same time seeing how this skill fits into the broader context of critical reasoning. We begin by discussing how identifying premises and conclusions can be helpful in presenting arguments in written essays. This is just a short first step.

When you present an argument in writing, it is important to convey to the reader what position you are supporting and what reasons you are offering in support. This might seem so obvious as to not be worth mentioning, but an essay that is hastily written or not well thought out often presents a series of loosely related statements with no hint of what is to be taken as premises or as the conclusion. The reader is left in the position of considering each assertion, agreeing with some, disagreeing with others, but being led nowhere. This sort of reading experience is neither enjoyable nor edifying. Consider this example:

Example 2.5   *In the United States there is supposedly freedom of expression, and yet there are laws against obscenity. No one can say what obscenity really is. And is obscene material really harmful? Psychologists are not at all certain that it is. Some forms of censorship are probably necessary. But we shouldn't keep saying we have a free country when we really don't.*

As a first step in editing such a passage, it is useful to mark the main points or conclusions it contains. Some of the statements can be taken to support the view that the United States is not truly free. Other statements seem to support the position that there should not be laws against obscenity. But neither of these points is used to support the other, and it is questionable whether they belong in the same paragraph. If the writer of this passage had considered which statement she intended as her conclusion, she would have focused the paragraph on one or the other of these points. Editing and rewriting might then have produced either of the following:

Rewrite 1   *We should admit that freedom of expression is not truly realized in the United States, since any censoring of materials constitutes a definite limitation of this freedom.*

Rewrite 2   *If a law is so vague that it is difficult to know what counts as a violation of it, and if there is really no harm that this law prevents, then the law should be abolished. Laws that prohibit obscenity have both of these defects. The conclusion to which we are driven is obvious.*

When you rewrite a loosely organized passage, do not be afraid to delete substantial portions in order to give the passage focus. If the deleted points are worth making, they can be made in another part of your essay.

We are not claiming that a polished paragraph of prose consists of nothing but premises and a conclusion. Indeed, neither Rewrite 1 nor 2 would qualify as a polished paragraph—they are both far too spare. What should be added to fill them out are not the extraneous points from Example 2.5. Rather, each would benefit from an introductory sentence and from examples illustrating the points made by the premises, as well as explanations of important concepts that might not be clear to the reader.

The move from Example 2.5 to Rewrite 1 or Rewrite 2 might be seen as an intermediate step between an initial draft and a more polished piece of writing. An initial, exploratory draft is often done best in a spontaneous, unstructured way in order to get some ideas on paper. The advice we are giving here and in later chapters concerning writing deals primarily with editing and rewriting such a first draft, attending particularly to structure and logical flow. Additional steps of editing will be touched on only occasionally.

Exercise 2.4   Making Premises and Conclusions Clear in Your Writing

1. Edit the following passages, making the premises and conclusion clear. Don't be afraid to eliminate some sentences or to change the wording of the remaining sentences. There is no single "correct" way of rewriting any of these, but some ways of rewriting will be better than others. One point that is helpful to keep in mind is that an argument should proceed from premises the reader is already inclined to believe to a conclusion she is less inclined to believe. Using a premise that is at least as doubtful as the conclusion it supports is not effective. And it is not interesting to be led to a conclusion that was obvious from the beginning.

For *one* of the following exercises, write a complete, polished paragraph. It should contain not only premises and a conclusion but also an introductory sentence, examples to reinforce points made, and explanations of important concepts.

a. Regardless of whether your religious beliefs are true or false, you need *some* beliefs to hang onto. The universe couldn't have just started itself—it had to come from something. If we didn't have a God to believe in, our lives would have no meaning and we would have no hope. How can people rationally deny the existence of God?

b. People who favor capital punishment are mainly just looking for a way to satisfy their blood lust and get revenge. Capital punishment doesn't accomplish any constructive purpose, and it probably just makes society more violent to see killing condoned by the state. It is appalling that so many Americans favor this practice.

c. If the United States won't provide clear constitutional guarantees assuring completely equal rights for women, then it had better not allow women to face any possibility of combat. When you bring women into the armed forces you have all kinds of problems with harassment and sexist abuse that women receive in training and on duty. Women should have equal rights, but some propositions can be pushed too far.

d. The decline in the number of lasting marriages poses a serious threat for the stability of American society. More and more children have to cope with the separation of their parents. Divorce reinforces the attitude that it is legitimate to break a commitment any time it becomes burdensome. Couples should consider these facts before they get married. If they aren't willing to enter the relationship seriously, it might be better for them to just live together.

e. The United States needs to formulate a coherent policy to improve its international economic competitiveness. We are simply sitting back and letting Japan, Germany, and many other parts of the world outstrip us economically. If we do so, we may well become a backward nation supplying raw materials and food to the rest of the world during the twenty-first century. We have already seen a rearrangement in basic industry. High-paying jobs in basic industries have been eliminated in favor of much lower-paying work in the service economy. This makes it difficult for single mothers to support a family. It has also helped accelerate the movement of population out of the older industrial centers of the East and

Midwest into the West. But such transformation requires large amounts of investment in basic public utilities such as streets, sewers, and water services. Water is especially important in California.

2. Reread the passage you wrote for problem 2 of Exercise 1.1 in Chapter 1. Rewrite it as you have the passages in problem 1 of this exercise (unless you think no such improvement needs to be made).

CHAPTER THREE

Understanding Arguments through Reconstruction

Many of the arguments considered in Chapter 2 sound contrived because we don't ordinarily hear or read arguments spelled out in such painful detail. If you were discussing sex discrimination with a friend, for example, he might argue:

Example 3.1   *I don't care what you say; if it's wrong to discriminate against a woman on the basis of her sex, then it is equally wrong to discriminate against a man on the basis of his.*

In this example, there is no explicit conclusion, and a necessary premise is missing. In everyday discourse, arguments are often presented with implicit (that is, unstated) premises, and even implicit conclusions. In this chapter, we explain how the argument fragments that we commonly hear and read can be reconstructed so their entire content, including implicit premises or conclusion, is explicitly displayed. In many situations this is unnecessary. However, when you encounter complicated passages or seek to criticize an argument, it is often helpful to create such reconstructions. After you work some reconstruction exercises, you should find it easier to see what has been left implicit in fragmentary arguments, like the one stated in Example 3.1, even when you do not actually restate or rewrite the argument in reconstructed form.

Understanding Arguments by Identifying Implicit Conclusions

The least complicated case of reconstruction is one in which premises are supplied with the audience left to "draw its own conclusion." In such circumstances the person offering an argument expects the context to make clear the conclusion. Suppose we hear a disc jockey giving this radio spot:

Example 3.2   *The smoother the sound, the better the station. The music is smoother at WIMP radio.*

The obvious conclusion is that station WIMP is better. In many cases like this, where only the conclusion is missing, the argument is relatively easy to reconstruct—the stated premises seem to point directly to the implicit conclusion.

Unfortunately, it isn't always so simple. Sometimes you might be in doubt about whether the conclusion of an argument is actually missing. In such a circumstance the technique of considering alternative readings, which was discussed in Chapter 2, might help. Consider the following example:

Example 3.3   *If most Americans recognize the need to eliminate the budget deficit, then Congress will be able to take strong action. But everyone who watches the news recognizes the need to eliminate the budget deficit. And most Americans watch the news.*

Clearly, this passage has to do with elimination of the federal budget deficit in the United States. But what is the conclusion? To see whether it is one of the statements in the passage, we can try treating each one in turn as the conclusion.

Reading 1   (1) *If most Americans recognize the need to eliminate the budget deficit, then Congress will be able to take strong action.*

(2) *Everyone who watches the news recognizes the need to eliminate the budget deficit.*

∴   *Most Americans watch the news.*

Reading 2   *(1) If most Americans recognize the need to eliminate the budget deficit, then Congress will be able to take strong action.*

(2) Most Americans watch the news.

∴   *Everyone who watches the news recognizes the need to eliminate the budget deficit.*

Reading 3   *(1) Everyone who watches the news recognizes the need to eliminate the budget deficit.*

(2) Most Americans watch the news.

∴   *If most Americans recognize the need to eliminate the budget deficit, then Congress will be able to take strong action.*

Think about the meaning of the premises and conclusion in each case. Does the conclusion *follow from the premises?* In Reading 1, for instance, the premises offer no reason for believing that "most Americans watch the news." Although this statement might follow from the premises in some *other* argument, the premises supplied here are irrelevant. In each of the other readings, the premises also fail to give reasons that adequately support the conclusion. Such a mechanical process of developing alternative readings for an argument might seem overly cumbersome, but working through it a few times will help you begin to get the feel for argument structure and to sharpen your sense of whether a conclusion has been explicitly stated or left implicit.

Because in this case we have found that the conclusion is not explicitly stated, our next step is to formulate the implicit conclusion. To discover the hidden conclusion that the premises support, you will often find it useful to list the premises.

Reading 4   *(1) If most Americans recognize the need to eliminate the budget deficit, then Congress will be able to take strong action.*

(2) Everyone who watches the news recognizes the need to eliminate the budget deficit.

(3) Most Americans watch the news.

∴   *???*

Think about what statement these premises jointly support and how they are linked. The second and third premises together support the statement that most Americans recognize the need to eliminate the budget deficit. This taken with the first premise supports the conclusion of the entire argument: "Congress will be able to take strong action."

Reading 4 illustrates two important features of a good reconstruction for arguments with missing elements. First, it strives, other things being equal, to interpret the argument in such a way that *the conclusion does indeed follow from the premises.** In this reading the conclusion follows from the premises, whereas in each of the other three readings, the supposed conclusion does not follow from the premises. Further, it is difficult to find acceptable implicit premises that could be used to support these "conclusions." Second, the argument *makes use of as much of the passage as possible:* Notice the way in which Reading 4 uses all three premises to support the conclusion and compare this reading with the following example, which makes some of the premises contained in the passage unnecessary:

Reading 5   (1) *If most Americans recognize the need to eliminate the budget deficit, then Congress will be able to take strong action.*

(implicit)   (2) *If Congress takes strong action, then the power of the presidency will be enhanced.*

(implicit)   ∴ *If most Americans recognize the need to eliminate the budget deficit, then the power of the presidency will be enhanced.*

Reading 5 does not use all the available material in the passage. It picks out one element as a premise, disregards the rest, and reaches a conclusion that is not even hinted at in the passage. Of course, in order to do so, an implicit premise also needs to be added.

Understanding Arguments by Identifying Implicit Premises

More common than the argument with an implicit conclusion is the argument that presents a conclusion and some of the premises needed to support it but leaves out one or more statements necessary to guarantee the

---

*Other things are *not* equal if the passage actually suggests a reading in which the conclusion does not follow.

truth of the conclusion. These missing premises are sometimes referred to as *presuppositions* of the argument. Consider this example:

Example 3.4   *America will succeed in solving the crisis of international economic competitiveness because whenever America has truly devoted itself to solving a crisis, it has succeeded.*

The indicator word *because* flags the second statement in this sentence as a premise and the first as the conclusion. In standard form we have:

Example 3.5   *(1) Whenever America has truly devoted itself to solving a crisis, it has succeeded.*

∴   *America will succeed in solving the crisis of international economic competitiveness.*

What is missing in this argument is the presupposition that links the stated premise to the conclusion. As the argument is now written, it is assumed that American industry has truly devoted itself to solving the crisis of international economic competitiveness, a presupposition that might well be doubted. This presupposition is made explicit in the following version of the argument, which is easier to understand and to critize.

Example 3.6   *(1) Whenever America has truly devoted itself to solving a crisis, then it has succeeded.*

(implicit)   *(2) America has truly devoted itself to solving the crisis of international economic competitiveness.*

∴   *America will succeed in solving the crisis of international economic competitiveness.*

Sometimes the missing premise is a presupposition about the definition of some term in the argument. For example:

Example 3.7   *Abortion involves intentionally taking the life of an innocent human being, so abortion is murder.*

What is missing here is a statement that characterizes *intentionally taking the life of an innocent human being as murder.* Once this definitional assumption is made explicit, it is even more apparent that the conclusion follows from the premises.

The implicit premise in itself is not very controversial although the argument might provoke debate.* Indeed, if you have a choice in adding implicit elements to an argument reconstruction, *the more plausible, less questionable statements should be selected.* In the argument in Example 3.7, for instance, the conclusion would still follow if we added a premise that the taking of a human life constituted murder, irrespective of whether it was done intentionally or involved an innocent being. But in the context of the passage, which includes the words "intentionally" and "innocent," such a reading would not be charitable.

Although the Principle of Charitable Interpretation enjoins us to add the most reasonable implicit premises or conclusions that can be plausibly attributed to the author, given what is stated in the passage, it need not be one that *we* believe is true. In fact, one of the advantages of reconstructing an argument is that we sometimes expose a hidden premise that is controversial, as in Example 3.8:

Example 3.8   *Stealing is wrong. Using a friend's car without asking is taking property without permission. So using a friend's car without asking is wrong.*

The implicit premise needed to reconstruct this passage can be stated: *Taking property without permission is stealing.* This premise is, at best, doubtful. Special circumstances, such as an emergency or the absence of any intention to keep the car, suggest that sometimes taking property without asking permission is not an act of stealing.

Example 3.9   *(1) Stealing is wrong.*

(2) Using a friend's car without asking is taking property without permission.

(implicit)   *(3) Taking property without permission is stealing.*

∴   *Using a friend's car without asking is wrong.*

Adding Both Conclusion and Premises

There are also cases in which both the conclusion and some of the premises are missing. In such cases the best way to begin is to supply what appears

---

*The explicit premise would probably be the focus of concern because it is true only if we consider the fetus to be a full-fledged human being. If not (as some maintain), then it is false to say that abortion involves taking the life of an innocent *human being*.

to be the intended conclusion and then to consider the premises needed as plausible assumptions to support it. In making this reconstruction, it is helpful to pay close attention to the context, as you can see in the following example:

Example 3.10   *The voices of despair have misled us. If Americans will mobilize the forces that have made them great, then they will ultimately weather the crisis of international economic competitiveness and develop effective new products to meet the challenge.*

The editorial comment that the voices of despair have misled us indicates that the author would assert a conclusion that is not one of despair. The second clause of the next sentence offers hope—namely, "they will ultimately weather the crisis of international economic competitiveness"— suggesting that this is the author's intended conclusion. This first step in reconstruction yields:

Example 3.11   *(1) If Americans will mobilize the forces that have made them great, then they will ultimately weather the crisis of international economic competitiveness and develop effective new products to meet the challenge.*

(implicit)   ∴   *Americans will ultimately weather the crisis of international economic competitiveness and develop effective new products to meet the challenge.*

What is missing from this formulation is the hidden assumption that Americans will indeed mobilize the forces that have made them great. The Principle of Charitable Interpretation directs us to understand the argument in this more fully developed way.

Example 3.12   *(1) If Americans will mobilize the forces that have made them great, then they will ultimately weather the crisis of international economic competitiveness and develop effective new products to meet the challenge.*

(implicit)   *(2) Americans will mobilize the forces that have made them great.*

(implicit)   ∴   *Americans will ultimately weather the crisis of international economic competitiveness and develop effective new products to meet the challenge.*

The implicit premise, premise 2, is the most controversial part of the argument. Only when it is made explicit can we criticize the contention effectively.

Guidelines and Warnings in Adding Implicit Premises and Conclusions

Our discussion of the Principle of Charitable Interpretation suggests several guidelines in reconstructing arguments with missing elements. The following general rules apply when there is no *explicit* evidence to the contrary.

GUIDELINES FOR RECONSTRUCTION

Other things being equal, the reconstructed argument should:

1. Contain a conclusion that follows from the premises.
2. Use as much of the passage as possible, that is,
   a. use *all* explicit premises
   b. include premises compatible with other elements of the passage.
3. Avoid obviously false or highly questionable premises.
4. Bring out underlying presuppositions in a way that promotes critical discussion.

As we have indicated, these criteria for evaluating alternative reconstructions cannot be followed blindly. For some arguments or argument fragments, there is no way, faithful to the text, that allows us to reconstruct them so that the conclusion follows from the premises. Suppose we confronted the following:

Example 3.13   *It is true that, if America fails to become more economically competitive internationally, then it will become a relatively backward nation supplying raw materials and food to more successful nations. But America needn't worry because it is not failing in this regard.*

This passage is one with a missing conclusion. The context of the passage, particularly the phrase "America needn't worry," suggests that the author wishes to maintain that America needn't worry about becoming a relatively backward nation. This contention can be captured in the conclusion: *America will not become a relatively backward nation supplying raw materials and food to more successful nations.* In standard form, the argument looks like this:

Example 3.14   *(1) If America fails to become economically competitive internationally, then it will become a relatively backward nation supplying raw materials and food to more successful nations.*

(implicit)   *(2) America is not failing to become economically competitive internationally.*

(implicit)   ∴ *America will not become a relatively backward nation supplying raw materials and food to more successful nations.*

Unfortunately, in this argument the conclusion does not follow from the premises. It is an instance of the argument form:

Example 3.15   *(1) If A, then B.*

(2) Not A.

∴ *Not B.*

As indicated in Chapter 2 in our discussion of some common, inadequate argument patterns, this argument is faulty (even though it resembles *modus ponens*). One way of thinking about this matter is to realize that America might not fail, that is, it might succeed in becoming economically competitive, but still not avoid becoming a relatively backward nation. The most successful countries might move farther and faster in developing and distributing new technological advances. The point to note about this example is that, even with a charitable interpretation, the conclusion does not follow from the premises.

Although these guidelines need to be applied cautiously, they nonetheless help distinguish better from worse reconstructions. Look at the following passage and the attempted reconstructions:

Example 3.16   *America cannot overcome the drug crisis. Most of the drug supply cannot be stopped before it comes to market (even with a massive "war on drugs"); taxpayers are unwilling to provide money to tackle the underlying social and economic conditions that are the root cause of the demand for drugs.*

Reconstruction 1
(implicit)   *(1) If America is to overcome the drug crisis, then most of the supply must be stopped before it comes to market.*

(2) Most of the drug supply cannot be stopped before it comes to market (even with a massive "war on drugs").

∴ *America cannot solve the drug crisis.*

The conclusion of this reconstruction follows from the premises, and the implicit premise has some plausibility. The major problem is that it doesn't use all of the relevant statements. In particular, it makes no mention of the need to fund efforts to tackle the underlying social and economic causes of drug use. For this reason, a better reconstruction would include this information in a premise and add an implicit premise that includes comments limiting both supply and demand.

Reconstruction 2

(1) Most of the drug supply cannot be stopped before it comes to market (even with a massive war on drugs").

(2) Taxpayers are unwilling to provide money to tackle the underlying social and economic conditions that are the root cause of the demand for drugs.

(3) America can overcome the drug crisis only if most of the drug supply can be stopped before it comes to market and the taxpayers are willing to provide money to tackle the underlying social and economic conditions that are the root cause of the demand for drugs.

∴ *America cannot overcome the drug crisis.*

Finally, notice that there is an overly easy way of adding a premise to complete any argument. It should be used only as a last resort. Let's use the following example of a partially reconstructed argument:

Example 3.17

(1) No one who wants power can be trusted.

(2) Edward is on the corporate "fast track."

∴ *Edward can't be trusted.*

It is always possible to write an if-then premise that connects the premises already stated with the conclusion. Using this procedure, we can complete Example 3.17 in this manner:

Easy way of completing Example 3.17

(1) No one who wants power can be trusted.

(2) Edward is on the corporate "fast track."

(implicit)   (3) If no one who wants power can be trusted and Edward is on the corporate "fast track," then Edward can't be trusted.

∴ *Edward can't be trusted.*

Using the easy way, we have made premises 1 and 2 into the "if" part of our added premise, and the conclusion into the "then" part. However, there is an alternative way of completing Example 3.17 that adheres more closely to the guidelines.

Preferred way of completing Example 3.17 (implicit)

(1) No one who wants power can be trusted.

(2) Edward is on the corporate "fast track."

(3) All people on the corporate "fast track" want power.

∴ *Edward can't be trusted.*

This latter formulation is better because it states more specifically what is presupposed in argument 3.17. If you were to criticize the argument, the preferred reconstruction would direct you to scrutinize the claim that all people on the corporate "fast track" want power. With the easy if-then reconstruction, you can see only that the argument presupposes some connection between the stated premises and the conclusion, but it is not clear what this connection is. The if-then premise, premise 3, simply restates argument 3.17 in a single sentence. You can just as easily question whether the conclusion of 3.17 follows from the premises, as you can whether the if-then implicit premise is true. For this reason the "easy" reconstruction violates Reconstruction Guideline 4 from the list on page 42 because it does *not* bring out underlying presuppositions in a way that promotes critical discussion.

Picking out an interesting, not overly easy, implicit premise was relatively straightforward for the partially reconstructed argument in Example 3.17. But deciding what implicit premise to add in reconstruction in less stylized contexts can be a greater problem. If Example 3.17 were an argument embedded in a passage that focused on Edward's education in a very competitive business school, we might have added this to premise 2, and modified the implicit premise:

(3) All people on the corporate "fast track" want power.

to take this into account:

(3′) All people on the corporate "fast track" who were educated in competitive business schools want power.

Alternatively, if the argument were embedded in a context that discussed the cutthroat corporate climate in which Edward worked, then another version of the implicit premise would be appropriate:

> *(3″) All people on the "fast track" in a cutthroat corporate climate want power.*

Notice that implicit premise 3 makes the boldest claim. It applies to "all people on the corporate 'fast track.' " The other two, 3′ and 3″, make less bold statements about all people on the fast track who had a certain kind of education or worked in a certain kind of climate. These qualifications might make one version of a prospective implicit premise more defensible than another. If, however, the passage gives no hint about such a more qualified version, then you are not required by the guidelines to supply it. At a certain point, the burden of clearly stating the argument falls on its author.

There is no simple formula for selecting which version of an implicit premise to include. Sometimes elements of the passage will suggest which version is more appropriate. Other times you will need to rely on the Principle of Charitable Interpretation and pick the version that seems most acceptable from among those that can be plausibly attributed to the author.

Exercise 3.1   **Recognizing Argument Patterns and Adding Implicit Premises, Conclusions, or Both**

This exercise should help prepare you to identify premises and conclusions that are left unstated. When it is not immediately obvious what premise or conclusion has been left unstated, identifying the pattern of the argument can be very helpful.

Suppose you are trying to identify the missing premise in this argument:

> *(1) If Dan lied, then he kept the money for himself.*
>
> *(2) [.]*
> _____
>
> ∴   *Dan didn't lie.*

To identify the pattern of an argument, look for words or word pairs like "if . . . then," "either . . . or," "not"; and look for statements or parts of statements that are repeated in the argument. If we substitute "A" for *Dan lied* and "B" for *he* [Dan] *kept the money for himself,* we can represent the argument with the following "partial" pattern.

(1) If A, then B.

(2) [.]

∴ *Not A.*

Now compare this partial pattern to the list of complete patterns in Chapter 2. Our partial pattern is a fragment of the following complete pattern:

(1) If A, then B.

(2) Not B.

∴ *Not A.*

The implicit premise, then, is: *Not B.* To put this into an English sentence, you have to find what B stands for in premise 1, and then deny that sentence. In this case, premise 2 is: *Dan did not keep the money for himself.* And the complete argument is:

(1) If Dan lied, then he kept the money for himself.

(2) [Dan did not keep the money for himself.]

∴ *Dan did not lie.*

To review, the steps we went through are:

(i)   Look for words or word pairs like "if . . . then," "either . . . or," "not," "all," or "every"; look for statements or parts of statements that are repeated.

(ii) Write out the partial pattern for the portion of the argument that is stated.

(iii) Determine what the complete pattern is.

(iv) From the part of the pattern that is missing, determine what statements are missing. (For example, where *Not B* was missing, we looked to see what statement B stood for in premise 1, and negated that statement.)

1. Go through steps i–iv for the following problems. We havehelped you by filling in key words in some of the missing premises and conclusions.

Write patterns here.

a. *(1) If the Nerdic computer runs Wordswift software, then it can meet my computing needs.*

   (2) [.]

   ∴ *The Nerdic computer can meet my computing needs.*

b. *(1) Either [   ] or I should buy the Hacker 386 computer.*

   (2) I shouldn't buy the Nerdic computer.

   ∴ *I should buy the Hacker 386 computer.*

c. *(1) If the Hacker 386 computer does not run Wordswift software, then I can't do word processing on it.*

   (2) If [,] then [.]

   ∴ *If the Hacker 386 computer does not run Wordswift software, then it doesn't meet my needs.*

d. *(1) If David can afford a new computer, then [,]*

   (2) David can't afford to pay his debts.

   ∴ *David can't afford a new computer.*

Write patterns here.

e. *(1) Either [   ]*
   or [.]
   (2) I shouldn't buy a Hacker 386 computer.

∴ *I should buy a Nerdic computer.*

f. *(1) If the Nerdic computer has only 256K*
   memory,
   then [.]
   (2) If it can't run Wordswift, then I
   shouldn't buy it.
   (3) [.]

∴ *I shouldn't buy it.*

g.* *(1) All Hacker 386s are products guaranteed*
   three years.
   (2) All [   ] are [.]

∴ *All Hacker 386s are products that give you*
   a lot of protection against faulty workman-
   ship.

h.* *(1) Any addition to my computer system is*
   an extravagance.
   (2) [   ] is [.]

∴ *A new Laserspeed printer is an extrava-*
   gance.

---

*Fill the slots in these examples with words that apply to classes of objects (for example, "Hacker 386s") or that designate a particular object belonging to a class (for example, "my Hacker 386s"). Do not insert a complete sentence into the slots for these examples.

The following exhibit more complicated patterns, not listed in Chapter 2. Can you figure out the patterns they exhibit?

Write patterns here.

    i. *(1) If the Nerdic computer can run Word-swift and it is cheaper than the Hacker 386 then I should buy it.*

        (2) [.]

        (3) [.]

        ∴ *I should buy the Nerdic computer.*

    j. *(1) Either I'll spend my bonus on a new computer or I'll replace my bald tires (but not both).*

        (2) If I do not replace my bald tires, then I risk a serious accident.

        (3) [.]

        ∴ *I won't spend my bonus on a new computer.*

    k. *(1) Either I should buy more books or more computer games.*

        (2) If this money was given to me for my education, then I should not buy more computer games.

        (3) [.]

        ∴ *I should buy more books.*

2. Put the following arguments into standard form. Add implicit premises, conclusion, or both. Leave out any editorial comments. For problems a–k, indicate the argument pattern, using letters to represent repeated elements.

a. You promised to be here at 8:00. If you promised to be here at 8:00, then you should have arrived at 8:00.

b. I should either study more or prepare to accept failure. I should study more.

c. If you tell lies frequently, then you must remember not only what you have done but also what you said you have done. Therefore if you tell lies frequently, your memory becomes burdened.

d. Harold should be sensitive to other people because any teacher should be sensitive to other people.

e. The American universities are eroding their public support. Any social institution that spends beyond the willingness of the public to pay is eroding its public support.

f. If being affectionate were the only important virtue, then Maurice would be a saint. So being affectionate is obviously not the only important virtue.

g. We will face substantial energy shortages by the year 2000 because there are not enough nuclear power stations under construction. (*Note:* Sometimes there is no alternative to adding the easy linking premise: "If *premise 1,* then *conclusion.*")

h. Many college faculty members are reaching retirement age. But if that is so, then many new, younger faculty members will be hired. It follows that, before long, college faculties will become more energetic.

i. Every successful politician has to compromise his principles occasionally. Everyone who has to compromise his principles occasionally loses integrity.

j. The number of unmarried adults in the United States is continuing to increase. If there is an increase in people unsupported by the bonds inherent in the nuclear family, there will be an increase in alcoholism and suicide. So there will be an increase in alcoholism and suicide.

k. The Third World countries have a chance to solve their mounting economic problems if banks and governments in the industrialized countries continue to be willing to forgive some massive debts accumulated in the seventies and early eighties. If taxpayers take seriously the need for such foreign assistance, then the governments and banks will be willing to forgive some of the Third World debt. The fear of instability in the Third World and new prospects for democratic government have convinced taxpayers to take seriously the need for debt relief. The conclusion is clear.

Passages l–r do not fit into the common patterns of argument we have considered previously.

l. The burglar was under five feet tall, so Albert was not the burglar.
m. The higher the interest rates, the better the bank. The interest rates at CASH National Bank are the highest in town.
n. Apparently, you don't smoke opium, since everyone who smokes opium is happy.
o. Either I should spend my tax refund on paying off my debts or I should buy books for this term. But if I don't buy books, I'll risk failing my courses. So I shouldn't spend the refund on paying off my debts.
p. I will be moving up in the world. Bruce has a new job in Minneapolis. If so, he'll be moving and that will create an opening for either Armand or me.
q. Every human action is determined by laws of nature. But for a person to deserve praise or blame, it is necessary for the person to have been able to act differently than she in fact did act. So no person deserves praise or blame.
r. The industrialized nations will resolve the environmental crises that are looming for the near future if these nations mobilize all the technological resources at their disposal. If political incentives are sufficiently high, then the mobilization of resources will occur. Public awareness about oil spills, depletion of the ozone layer, and

the "greenhouse effect" is growing rapidly. If so, political incentives are sufficiently high. The conclusion is clear.

In the following passages much of what is stated is either not part of the argument, or must be restated to make the structure of the argument clear. There may be more than one acceptable reconstruction.

s. The facts speak for themselves. The existence of adult bookstores and the lawlessness they engender cannot be hidden from children. We must protect our children. We are forced to the conclusion that we must prevent the existence of adult bookstores and the lawlessness they engender.

t. As we all know, American taxpayers are reluctant to face tax increases. But with mounting budget deficits, deterioration of our transportation system, and crises in education, the taxpayers are finally becoming convinced the era of the free lunch is over. They realize that either they start paying now or they will bequeath to their children an impossible burden. They are not willing to do that.

u. It isn't a bad environment that causes people to become criminal. For every criminal who comes from a bad environment, there are thousands who hold jobs.

v. We have before us the question of rights for homosexuals—a question which I hope disturbs you as much as it does me. My friends, I am as much concerned about other human beings as anyone. But I am opposed to these so-called rights. The reason is that if the United States passed rights for homosexuals, then the United States would support what is unnatural. But the United States should never support what is unnatural.

3. Use the Guidelines for Reconstruction to determine which, if any, of the reconstructions provided are adequate for the passages given. Indicate why you reject the reconstructions you do. If you find all of them faulty, supply one yourself.

a. *Passage*

Either we should cut spending drastically or we should raise taxes to eliminate the budget deficit. We shouldn't let our transportation, health care, and education systems deteriorate even further; the conclusion is clear.

Reconstructions

   i. *(1) Either we should cut spending drastically or we should raise taxes to eliminate the budget deficit.*

      (2) We shouldn't let our transportation, health care, and education systems deteriorate even further.

   ∴ *We should cut spending drastically to eliminate the budget deficit.*

   ii. *(1) Either we should cut spending drastically or we should raise taxes to eliminate the budget deficit.*

      (2) If we cut spending drastically, our transportation, health care, and education systems will deteriorate even further.

      (3) We shouldn't let our transportation, health care, and education systems deteriorate even further.

   ∴ *We should raise taxes to eliminate the budget deficit.*

   iii. *(1) We should prevent the deterioration of social and economic systems in the United States.*

      (2) We shouldn't let our transportation, health care, and education systems deteriorate even further.

   ∴ *We shouldn't cut spending drastically in order to eliminate the budget deficit.*

   b. *Passage*

I don't care what you say: if it's wrong to discriminate against a woman on the basis of her sex, then it is equally wrong to discriminate against a man on the basis of his. Permitting combat roles in the military for men only is unjust.

Reconstructions

   i. *(1) If sex discrimination is wrong, then combat roles for men only is unjust.*

      (2) Combat roles for men only is unjust.

   ∴ *Sex discrimination is wrong.*

ii. *(1) If it is wrong to discriminate against a woman on the basis of her sex, then it is equally wrong to discriminate against a man on the basis of his.*

(2) Combat roles for men only discriminates against a man on the basis of his sex.

∴ *Combat roles for men only is unjust.*

iii. *(1) If sex discrimination against women is wrong, then it is unjust to discriminate against a man on the basis of his sex.*

(2) Sex discrimination against women is wrong.

∴ *Combat roles for men only is unjust.*

c. *Passage*
Since Mervin has devoted himself to making it to the top by the time he is 35, you shouldn't cross him without taking special care.

Reconstructions

i. *(1) If Mervin has devoted himself to making it to the top by the time he is 35, you shouldn't cross him without taking special care.*

(2) Mervin has devoted himself to making it to the top by the time he is 35.

∴ *You shouldn't cross Mervin without taking special care.*

ii. *(1) If Mervin has devoted himself to making it to the top by the time he is 35, no one should cross him without taking special care.*

(2) Mervin has devoted himself to making it to the top by the time he is 35.

∴ *You shouldn't cross Mervin without taking special care.*

iii. *(1) Nobody should cross anybody who wants to make it to the top by age 35 without taking special care.*

(2) Mervin wants to make it to the top by age 35.

∴ *You shouldn't cross Mervin without taking special care.*

d. *Passage*

Reliance on abortion as a means of birth control will cheapen American social commitment to protecting life. It should be banned except in the case in which the mother's life is in danger.

Reconstructions

i. *(1) If reliance on abortion as a means of birth control will cheapen American social commitment to protecting life, then it should be banned except in the case in which the mother's life is in danger.*

   (2) Reliance on abortion as a means of birth control will cheapen American social commitment to protecting life.

∴ *Abortion should be banned except in the case in which the mother's life is in danger.*

ii. *(1) Anything that cheapens American social commitment to protecting life should be banned.*

   (2) Abortion as a means of birth control cheapens American social commitment to protecting life.

∴ *Abortion should be banned.*

iii. *(1) Anything that cheapens American social commitment to protecting life should be banned.*

   (2) Except in the case in which the mother's life is in danger, abortion cheapens American social commitment to protecting life.

∴ *Abortion should be banned except in the case in which the mother's life is in danger.*

Using Techniques of Reconstruction in Writing

Some of the same considerations that are relevant to understanding somebody else's argument also apply to presenting one yourself. After developing some ideas in a preliminary draft, you will be able to decide whether you want to present an argument in your essay, and if so, what that argument will be. Argumentative prose, even more than other kinds of writing, requires you to have a clear idea of what you want to say before you develop a final draft of your essay. Some skilled authors do not need to spend much time thinking out the structure of their argument. But for students who find writing difficult it is a good idea, after writing a preliminary draft but before writing a final draft, to write out or sketch in standard form any arguments they are advancing. As students become more proficient they will no longer need to work out the argument in detail, although even skilled writers find it helpful to do so when they weave complex arguments.

Shaping Lean Prose   The techniques and exercises found in this section are designed to help develop your ability to move from an argument in standard form back to a prose passage. In essence, you will be reversing the process of adding implicit premises and conclusion. Once you have clearly formulated an argument, including all premises needed to support the conclusion, you are free to attend to matters of style, in particular to economy, emphasis, and clarity of presentation. Four steps are useful in making this move from the more formal statement of argument in standard form to an actual passage.

1. Find and eliminate any premises that are obvious and uncontroversial.

2. Avoid unnecessary repetition of sentences or parts of sentences.

3. Place the parts of the argument you wish to emphasize at the beginning or (secondarily) at the end of the passage.

4. Use illustrations or examples if the argument contains concepts that are abstract or unfamiliar to your audience.

The first suggestion helps you focus the reader's attention on the more interesting parts of your argument—although, if your argument is weak, this move will only highlight its difficulties. The technique is sometimes misused in debate to cover up weaknesses in argument; that is, premises that cannot be adequately defended are left out in the hope that listeners will fail to see that the argument depends on these hidden assumptions. When used properly, however, such elimination can streamline your prose by preventing you from belaboring the obvious. Correlatively, you should also recognize the need to provide additional support for premises most vulnerable to disagreement. As an example, suppose you have created the following argument:

Example 3.18   *(1) Overconsumption of salt is hazardous to our health.*

(2) We ought to avoid what is hazardous to our health.

∴   *We ought to avoid overconsumption of salt.*

The second premise is unlikely to provoke much debate (though many people have difficulty living up to it). With this in mind, we can reformulate the argument and provide additional information.

Example 3.19   *Doctors have recently come to understand the influence of salt in the development of heart conditions. They have warned us that eating too much salt is hazardous to our health. Consequently, we ought to avoid such overconsumption.*

The second suggestion helps us shorten the prose presentation of our argument by eliminating redundant material. The most obvious application is to eliminate some of the repetitions created by if-then sentences, especially in cases in which the consequent of one sentence is the antecedent of the next. Often the repeated sentence can be replaced by saying, "If so, then . . ." or "If that is the case, then. . . ." An argument can also be shortened by dropping some of the connective words such as the *either* in either-or sentences or the *then* in if-then sentences. Finally, sentences such as "I like Alice and I like Mike" can be trimmed into "I like Alice and Mike."

Numerous other devices to shorten and provide a more effective presentation of an argument can be employed as long as the basic meaning and connections in the passage remain clear. The amount of simplification that is appropriate depends in part on the stylistic level you seek in your writing. A more formal style will contain more connective words than a conversational style.

The third and fourth suggestions do not shorten your presentation of an argument, but they do make you more effective in conveying what you intend. People attend more strongly to the first and last sentences of a short passage than to the intervening sentences. In recognition of this fact (and perhaps as its cause), writers customarily fill these slots with the sentences they wish to emphasize. Sometimes the focus is on the conclusion; at other times the most controversial premise is placed at the beginning where it serves to concentrate attention on what is most significant in the argument.

Adding Illustrations   We can make our argument more accessible to readers by providing some concrete illustrations for concepts that are abstract or that might be misconstrued. These examples do not support our premises directly, but they make it easier to understand our argument.

We can try our tactics on this sample:

Example 3.20

(1) Americans are overly concerned with the pleasures of the moment.

(2) If Americans are overly concerned with the pleasures of the moment, then they are unlikely to sacrifice private gain for public projects.

(3) If Americans are unlikely to sacrifice private gain for public projects, then America will fail to solve the social and economic problems it will face in the future.

∴ *America will fail to solve the social and economic problems it will face in the future.*

By removing the repetition of elements in the if-then sentences and focusing on the conclusion, we can obtain a paragraph that reflects this argument.

Example 3.21

The prospects for America look bleak. It will fail to solve the social and economic problems it is bound to face in the future because Americans are unwilling to make sacrifices for the sake of the country. This is just another manifestation of a growing phenomenon: devotion to immediate pleasures at the expense of public concerns.

A second version can be created that focuses on the first premise and illustrates the phrase *concerned with the pleasures of the moment* with concrete examples.

Example 3.22

Devotion to immediate pleasures will have dire consequences for America. The country will not mount an adequate attack on the multitude of social problems it faces because it is unable to make the sacrifices their solution requires. Effective social action will have widespread public support only if Americans are prepared to look beyond their own personal lives and feel themselves fully a part of the larger community. The allure of drug-induced experiences and the self-indulgence of fancy automobiles make such a social vision impossible.

Exercise 3.2   Moving from Arguments in Standard Form to Prose Passages

1. Transform each of the following arguments in standard form into a short prose passage that adequately reflects the basic thrust of the argument without use of extraneous material.

   a.   *(1) Bruce does not need and cannot use the Hacker 386 computer.*

        (2) People shouldn't buy what they don't need and can't use.

   ∴   *Bruce shouldn't buy the Hacker 386 computer.*

   b.   *(1) If capital punishment is justified through its deterrent effect, then the killing of an innocent person as a scapegoat is sometimes justified.*

        (2) The killing of an innocent person as a scapegoat is never justified.

   ∴   *Capital punishment is not justified through its deterrent effect.*

   c.   *(1) If a drunken driver kills a person, then he has unintentionally taken the life of a person in circumstances he could reasonably foresee.*

        (2) If a person unintentionally takes the life of another in circumstances he could reasonably foresee, then he has committed either second degree murder or is guilty of criminal negligence.

   ∴   *If a drunken driver kills a person, then he has committed either second degree murder or is guilty of criminal negligence.*

   d.   *(1) If Darwin's theory of evolution is correct, then every animal is adapted to its particular biological niche.*

        (2) If every animal is adapted to its particular biological niche, then large-scale environmental change will radically affect most animals.

   ∴   *If Darwin's theory of evolution is correct, then large-scale environmental change will radically affect most animals.*

e. *(1) If Americans overconsume now, then they borrow against the future.*

(2) If Americans borrow against the future, then they leave their children in an untenable position.

(3) If Americans leave their children in an untenable position, then they have failed their children.

∴ *If Americans overconsume now, then they have failed their children.*

2. *Writing Essays with Complex Arguments*

The writing exercises so far have been concerned with shaping relatively short passages. But it is sometimes helpful for the beginning writer to use an argument in standard form to structure a more complex essay. We are *not* offering a model that is to be blindly applied to all the argumentative essays you write, but it might be useful for you as a first step in developing your own writing style. More sophisticated essays may emphasize certain elements more than others or leave some of them out altogether.

Suppose an essay aims at establishing a certain conclusion by appeal to premises A, B, and C, and that each of these premises in turn can be supported by further argument. The whole essay can be cast into the following form.*

a. Introduction.

b. First Section. Indicate reasoning for premise A.

c. Second Section. Indicate reasoning for premise B.

d. Third Section. Indicate reasoning for premise C.

e. Fourth Section. Present Main Argument.

(1) Premise A.

(2) Premise B.

(3) Premise C.

∴ *Conclusion.*

---

*We are assuming here that none of the premises is obvious or uncontroversial. If one or more premises *is* obvious or uncontroversial, it need not be given a paragraph of support. It may be worthwhile, however, to mention such premises in the summary of the main argument, to make the structure of the argument clear.

In such an essay, the introduction should be a preview, setting out the author's intentions and setting the stage for subsequent sections. In a long essay, a concluding section that reviews the essay might be added. Of course, such a full-blown argument might not leap out at you when you begin preliminary or "free" writing, in which case you might impose the structure suggested here when you edit.

Use the following arguments to structure an essay of a page or more in which you provide some support for each of the premises (unless a premise is too obvious or uncontroversial to merit a paragraph of discussion). The support need *not* be a full-blown argument, but merely some reason for believing that the premise in question is true. The final paragraph should tie the premises together by presenting the main argument.

a. *(1) Anything that cheapens American social commitment to protecting life should be banned.*

(2) Except in the case in which the mother's life is in danger, abortion cheapens American social commitment to protecting life.

∴ *Abortion should be banned.*

b. *(1) Cigarette smoking in public places forces the nonsmoker to risk her health against her will.*

(2) Nobody should be forced to risk her health against her will unless there is an overwhelming benefit.

(3) Allowing cigarette smoking in public places provides no overwhelming benefit.

∴ *Cigarette smoking in public places should not be allowed.*

c. *(1) Capital punishment is acceptable social policy only if it either deters capital crimes or is justifiable retribution.*

(2) Capital punishment does not deter capital crimes.

(3) Capital punishment is not justifiable retribution.

∴ *Capital punishment is not acceptable social policy.*

d. *(1) If all abortion should be prohibited, then a mother can be forced by law to give up her life for the sake of her unborn child.*

(2) If a mother can be forced by law to give up her life for the sake of her unborn child, then the state is justified in taking a life without due process of law.

(3) The state is not justified in taking a life without due process of law.

∴ *Not all abortion should be prohibited.*

e. *(1) Research on weather modification is likely to produce a new technology, which, if abused, would have a substantial destructive potential.*

(2) Research on a new technology, which, if abused, would have a substantial destructive potential, would be a danger to mankind.

(3) We ought to avoid whatever would be a danger to mankind.

∴ *We ought to avoid research on weather modification.*

f. Create an argument, put it in standard form, and use it as the basis for writing an essay.

CHAPTER FOUR

Evaluating Arguments: Some Basic Questions

What makes an argument a successful one? Think about the different kinds of qualities that might be desirable in an argument. Our concern in this chapter, as elsewhere in the text, is with features of arguments that are central to their role in providing adequate reasons for belief. We will evaluate the success of an argument primarily in terms of (1) how its parts "fit together" and (2) whether the premises of the argument are well founded. Success on dimension 1 is called *validity* by logicians, and we can call success on dimension 2 *truth of premises.**

In addition, an argument can be assessed in terms of (3) how well it is suited to convince a particular audience. We will designate success on this dimension *legitimate persuasiveness*. Arguments cast in language readily understood by the audience, expressed in a way that makes the audience sympathetic enough to overcome bias against them, and based on premises that the audience believes have greater promise of being persuasive than those that aren't.** We include the qualification "legitimate" because

---

*Strictly speaking, we are primarily concerned in this chapter with *deductive* arguments. These are arguments that are interpreted as having parts that fit together so tightly that it is impossible for all the premises to be true and the conclusion to be false. We discuss the distinction between deductive and other, nondeductive, arguments in Chapter 9.

**This is especially the case if an argument is successful on the first two dimensions as well—that is, if it is sound.

sometimes persuasiveness is used for questionable purposes. If your purpose is to have the audience believe your conclusion regardless of its truth, you would want the argument to use tricks and gimmicks—to sway the audience by appeal to emotion, to distract attention from an argument's weak points, and so forth. Such an argument might be persuasive but could mislead the audience toward unreasonable beliefs. Arguments like this are the tools of some advertisers and politicians. From the standpoint of the critical reasoner seeking justified belief, they are bad arguments—even fallacies—not good arguments. We explore them in Chapter 6. Overall, however, we are most interested in arguments that are persuasive without being misleading, that is, those that are legitimately persuasive.

When an argument is successful on dimensions 1 and 2, that is, when it is *valid* and has *true premises,* we call it *sound.* In addition, when it is also *legitimately persuasive,* we will call it *successful.** These relationships are displayed in Table 4.1.

A sound argument has the potential to persuade reasonably, but soundness is not dependent on the particular audience to which the argument is addressed—soundness is a characteristic of the argument itself. You might think of it as based on criteria you would apply if you were to consider an argument privately, as both the presenter and the audience, and your interest were in evaluating the reasons (premises) on which you based

Table 4.1

Criteria	Terms Used for Success in Satisfying Criteria		
1. Structural fit	Validity	Soundness	Successfulness
2. Foundation	Truth of premises		
3. Convincing an audience	(Legitimate) Persuasiveness		

*Our concern in this text is primarily with issues of *soundness* for deductive arguments, though in the process of critical assessment of arguments it is also relevant whether the argument is or is likely to be *legitimately persuasive* and hence whether it is or is likely to be *successful.* But deductive arguments can be further judged by additional criteria. For example, the conclusion might be one that the audience had previously doubted. A sound argument that persuaded this audience to change its beliefs would be both interesting and productive—it would provide a kind of progress in the audience's thinking, surely another virtue for an argument.

your beliefs (your conclusions). As you considered each argument, your attention then would be on two questions:

1. Does the truth of the conclusion follow from the truth of the premises?

2. Should the premises be accepted?

These questions are the focus of this chapter.

When we say that truth of the conclusion does not follow from truth of the premises, we are saying that something is wrong with the form, or pattern, of the argument. On the other hand, when we say that the premises are not acceptable, it is the content, not the pattern, of the argument that we are criticizing.

Think of an argument as like a building, with the premises being the foundation, the conclusion being the superstructure that sits on this foundation, and the form, or pattern, of the argument being the blueprint or design of the building. The design could be a perfectly good one, but if the foundation is made of weak material the superstructure will fall. On the other hand, the foundation could be perfectly strong but the design could be faulty, so that the superstructure doesn't sit on the foundation correctly. The superstructure could still fall because of this poor design. Similarly, an argument could fit a correct pattern, but if the premises are false, the conclusion could still be false. And an argument could have true premises but an incorrect pattern, in which case the conclusion could be false.

Here is an example of each kind of faulty argument we have just described. Example 4.1 is like a building with a good design but a faulty foundation (a false premise). Example 4.2 is like a building with a strong foundation (true premises) but a bad design.

Example 4.1
(Correct pattern,
false premise) *(1) If AIDS is harmless, then we need not take precautions against it.*

(2) AIDS is harmless.

(False conclusion) ∴ *We need not take precautions against AIDS.*

Example 4.2
(True premises,
incorrect pattern) *(1) Any disease that threatens many lives is worth our concern.*

(2) Mumps is worth our concern.

(False conclusion) ∴ *Mumps is a disease that threatens many lives.*

Again, an argument's conclusion follows from its premises because of the form, or pattern, of argument. This property of having a correct pattern, so that the conclusion does follow, is called *validity*. The first question we now must address is the question of when an argument is valid.

The Validity Question: When Does the Conclusion Follow from the Premises?

An important first step in evaluating a deductive argument is considering whether it is valid. In Chapter 2 we presented a chart of seven argument patterns. A portion of this chart is repeated below. We claimed that, for any argument that fits one of these patterns, its conclusion follows from its premises.

"Picturing" Argument Structure   Valid arguments have a structure in which the premises are linked in such a way that they assure the truth of the conclusion when all the premises are true; invalid arguments

---

Some Common Successful Argument Patterns

i. *(1) If A, then B.*

    (2) A.

    ∴   *B.*

ii. *(1) Either A or B.*

    (2) Not A.

    ∴   *B.*

iii. *(1) If A, then B.*

    (2) Not B.

    ∴   *Not A.*

iv. *(1) If A, then B.*

    (2) If B, then C.

    ∴   *If A, then C.*

v. *(1) A.*

    (2) If A, then B.

    (3) If B, then C.

    ∴   *C.*

vi. *(1) All P_1's are P_2's.*

    (2) m is a P_1.

    ∴   *m is a P_2.*

vii. *(1) All P_1's are P_2's.*

    (2) All P_2's are P_3's.

    ∴   *All P_1's are P_3's.*

allow the possibility that the conclusion is false even when all the premises are true. This relationship can be "pictured" in a variety of ways, depending on the pattern of argument. Suppose we have a *modus ponens,* or "chain" type, argument (pattern i on the chart) that has the form:

PATTERN

SAMPLE

Example 4.3

(1) *If A, then B.*

(2) *A.*

∴   *B.*

(1) *If Maria is a student, then she is eligible to use the college pool.*

(2) *Maria is a student.*

∴   *Maria is eligible to use the college pool.*

We can represent the if-then statement as the physical relationship between two blocks or dominos placed close enough to each other so that, if the first were to be pushed to the right, then the second would fall to the right.

If A, then B.

The bare assertion of the statement A (premise 2) can be represented as actually pushing block A to the right, so that, according to this scheme, the argument can be pictured liked this:

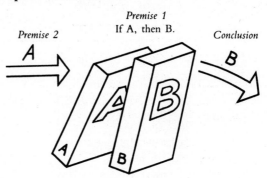

Premise 2   Premise 1   Conclusion
              If A, then B.

In this picture, it is physically impossible for the situation representing the premises to occur without the conclusion occurring as well.

A similar model can be applied to *modus tolens,* or the reverse "chain" argument (pattern iii).

	PATTERN	SAMPLE
Example 4.4	(1) If A, then B.	(1) If Jian Loc is a registered student, then he paid his fees.
	(2) Not B.	
	————————————	(2) Jian Loc did not pay his fees.
	∴ Not A.	————————————————
		∴ Jian Loc is not a registered student.

As in the first case, we can represent the if-then sentence as a configuration of blocks. We can represent the negative sentence as pushing a block to the *left* (not to the right). So the argument can be pictured as follows:

Again, given the placement of the blocks and a push of block B to the left, we are assured that block A will also fall to the left.

Contrast these two *valid* argument patterns with two similar but *invalid* versions. First, consider

Example 4.5   (1) If I'm in Aspen, then I'm in Colorado.

(2) I'm not in Aspen.

————————————————————

∴ I'm not in Colorado.

which has the form

(Invalid) (1) If A, then B.

(2) Not A.

————————————————————

∴ Not B.

We would picture the argument in Example 4.5 as

Premise 1
If A, then B.

Premise 2   *Conclusion*
                          ?

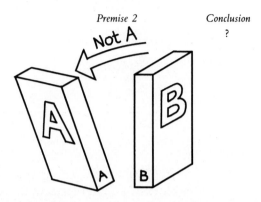

In this case, block A could fall to the left without block B falling. Such a circumstance would count as a *counterexample*. In this "physical" configuration, the falling of A to the left does not assure the falling of B to the left.

Similarly, consider the *invalid* pattern

Example 4.6

(Invalid)   *(1) If A, then B.*

(2) B.

∴   *A.*

Here again, the situation depicted in the premises will not result in block A falling to the right.

Premise 1
If A, then B.

Conclusion   *Premise 2*
      ?

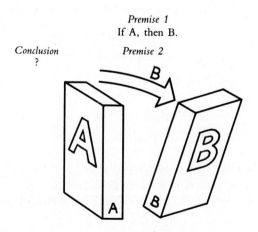

This technique of visualizing structure can help us to see the force of other patterns from our list "Some Common Successful Argument Patterns." Consider pattern v.

Example 4.7

(1) A.

(2) If A, then B.

(3) If B, then C.

∴   *C.*

To depict this argument, set block A "close enough" to B, and block B "close enough" to C. Clearly, given this structural relationship, A's falling to the right would result in C's falling to the right.

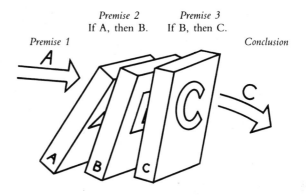

Accordingly, we can also picture pattern iv:

Example 4.8

(1) If A, then B.

(2) If B, then C.

∴   *If A, then C.*

We can see that if A is placed close enough to B that A's falling right will cause B to fall right, and B is placed close enough to C that B's falling right would cause C to fall right. This assures us that, if we were to push A to the right, C would fall to the right.

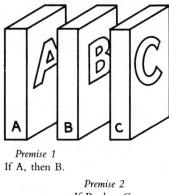

Premise 1
If A, then B.

Premise 2
If B, then C.

Conclusion
If A, then C.

These pictures represent only a kind of idealized physical necessity, not the *logical* necessity that is spelled out by the logician and presented in the appendix of this text. Nevertheless, pictures like these may help to fix in your mind that certain structures or structural relationships determine consequences with *necessity*. In other words, it is *impossible* for these structures to exist without these consequences following. This is precisely what is involved in answering the *validity* question. We ask whether the argument is of such a structure that the truth of the premises assures the truth of the conclusion.

We can use a different type of model to picture pattern ii:

Example 4.9   *(1) Either A or B.*

(2) Not A.

∴   *B.*

Imagine a game show with the big prize behind at least one of two curtains. We say at least one because on this game show some contestants are lucky enough to have the prize behind both. We picture premise 1 as the situation in which the prize is behind one curtain or the other (or both). Premise 2 is represented by the situation in which the prize is not behind curtain A. (An unlucky contestant might have chosen A, but found that the prize wasn't there.) If the game is structured as described, then we can be assured that the prize is behind the second curtain.

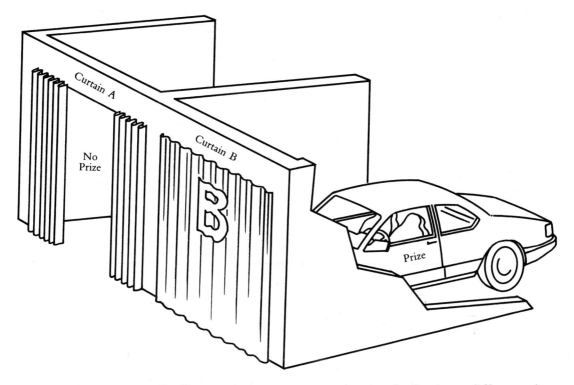

Finally, we can represent patterns vi and vii using a different scheme that emphasizes the image of containment.

Consider pattern vi:

Example 4.10

(1) *All* P_1*'s are* P_2*'s.*

(2) m *is a* P_1.

∴   m *is a* P_2.

Premise 1 can be pictured as two nested containers—container P_1 within container P_2. Premise 2 places an item, *m,* inside container P_1. It can readily be seen that *m* must also be inside P_2.

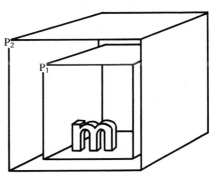

Contrast this to the situation for the *invalid* argument:

Example 4.11   *(1) All P_1's are P_2's.*

(2) m is a P_2.

∴   m *is a P_1.*

Knowing that *m* is in the P_2 container doesn't tell us whether it is in P_1, as illustrated:

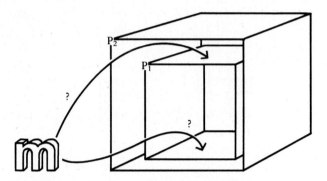

Again, we can use the containment model for the *valid* pattern vii:

Example 4.12   *(1) All P_1's are P_2's.*

(2) All P_2's are P_3's.

∴   *All P_1's are P_3's.*

We nest container P_1 within container P_2 within container P_3. Clearly, P_1 is within P_3.

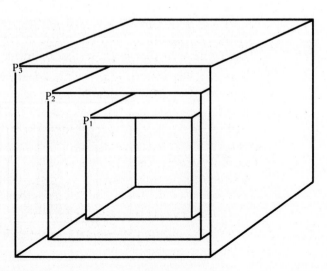

A more systematic version of this way of thinking about arguments has been developed by logicians. This is treated in expanded form in the appendix. All three methods of depicting arguments were introduced to make more meaningful the idea that a structural necessity can exist. Valid arguments exhibit such a structural necessity; invalid arguments don't.

How should you use this concept of validity in evaluating arguments that you hear and read? Most arguments in actual discourse aren't stated in enough explicit detail to judge whether they are valid or not without some further work. As we saw in Chapter 3, premises are typically left unstated or only vaguely suggested. Or a premise might be clearly stated but a conclusion left implicit. Our Principle of Charitable Interpretation would tell you to reconstruct such arguments so that they *are valid* unless you find some reason to assume that the author of the argument indeed embraced an invalid argument form. The concept of validity is especially important for us because it is useful for reconstructing arguments in this way.

It is actually a rare case in which someone will fully state an argument in all its detail. But when this does occur, it is such a grave error of reasoning that you want to be sure that you are able to detect it. If an argument is invalid, then it doesn't matter whether the premises are true or not, they simply don't support the conclusion.

But even when we reconstruct an argument fragment in a way that makes it valid, we are performing an important preliminary to the next step of evaluating: determining whether the premises are acceptable. By adding premises to make an argument valid, we are stating all of the premises that need to be evaluated before we can decide whether to accept an argument.

Showing Invalidity   Our brief look at ways of picturing arguments has *clarified the concept* of logical necessity for an argument (the impossibility of the premises all being true and the conclusion being false). In some cases of everyday argumentation, we can supplement our list of common argument patterns, by this picturing of arguments in order to help answer questions about validity and aid in charitable reconstruction. We can further interpret it as part of a more broadly based attempt to find a *counterexample* to the claim that an argument is valid. Such a counterexample is an instance in which the premises are true but the conclusion is false. We found just such counterexamples when we used the idealized "physical" analogies to depict invalid argument structure.

There are other ways to present counterexamples that demonstrate how all the premises could be true and the conclusion, false. Suppose, for instance, it were argued:

Example 4.13   *(1) If police departments improve their effectiveness, crime rates go down.*

(2) Crime rates have gone down.

∴   *Police departments have improved their effectiveness.*

We could point out *how,* in the particular case, both premises might be true, but the conclusion, false. The police department in this example might not have improved its effectiveness at all. Perhaps improving police effectiveness *would* make crime go down, even though police effectiveness has not improved. And perhaps crime *has* gone down, but for some other reason—perhaps a drop in the number of young people.

This method—discussing in the particular case how the premises can be true and the conclusion, false—is one common way of showing invalidity. Another way is to produce an argument that has the same pattern as the one in question, but in which it is *obvious* that the premises are true and the conclusion, false. The argument just stated in Example 4.13 has the following pattern:

(1) If A, then B.

(2) B.

∴   *A.*

The following argument fits the same pattern:

Example 4.14   *(1) If I'm the president, then I'm a citizen.*

(2) I'm a citizen.

∴   *I'm the president.*

If an argument is valid, then all arguments of the same form or pattern must also be valid. Since Example 4.14 obviously *can have true premises and a false conclusion, it provides a counterexample* that undermines the argument pattern (affirming the consequent) and thereby shows that the original argument in Example 4.13 is *invalid.*

Exercise 4.1   **Showing Invalidity**

Determine whether the following arguments are valid, using one of the techniques discussed so far in the text. They include (1) appeal to the list

"Some Common Successful Argument Patterns," (2) construction of a physical analogy (e.g., falling blocks or containers), (3) explanation of a counterexample showing how all the premises could be true and the conclusion, false, and (4) presentation of a counterexample exhibiting the same pattern but with obviously true premises and a false conclusion.

1. *(1) Either Coolidge was elected U.S. president in 1924 or Harding was.*

   (2) Harding was not elected U.S. president in 1924.

   ∴ *Coolidge was elected U.S. president in 1924.*

2. *(1) All dogs are mammals.*

   (2) All mammals are animals.

   (3) Zeke is a dog.

   ∴ *Zeke is an animal.*

3. *(1) All cats are animals.*

   (2) All dogs are animals.

   ∴ *All mammals are animals.*

4. *(1) If the price of stocks goes up, the price of bonds will go down.*

   (2) If the price of bonds goes down, the price of gold will drop.

   (3) The price of stocks won't go up.

   ∴ *The price of gold won't drop.*

5. *(1) Either the drug crisis will continue or the government will devote more resources to solve the underlying social problems.*

   (2) The drug crisis will continue.

   ∴ *The government will not devote more resources to solve the underlying social problems.*

6. *(1) If Congress puts significant new money into social programs, then the budget deficit will get worse.*

   (2) If the budget deficit gets worse, then interest rates will rise.

   (3) If interest rates rise, then home ownership will become increasingly difficult.

   (4) If home ownership becomes increasingly difficult, then great political pressure will have to be borne by Congress.

   (5) Great political pressure will not be borne by Congress.

   ∴   *Congress will not put significant new money into social programs.*

When Are the Premises True or Acceptable?

An argument can be valid, that is, have the right kind of structural "fit," even though some or all of the premises are false.

Example 4.15

(1) If an effective cure for AIDS is available, the government should provide it to all who need it but can't afford it.

(2) An effective cure for AIDS is available.

∴   *The government should provide it to all who need it but can't afford it.*

Unfortunately, though this argument is valid, the second premise is false. (At least, we take it to be false at the time of the writing of this book.) The conclusion of the argument follows from the premises, but because the second premise is false, the argument is not sound; it doesn't justify our belief in the conclusion.

In general, validity of a deductive argument is relatively easy to establish. Logicians have developed techniques that can tell us whether an argument is correctly structured even when we are dealing with more complex arguments than those illustrated in our list of patterns. Establishing the truth of premises is a more complex matter. There is no general method of doing this.

Most of the arguments we encounter in our everyday lives have premises whose truth or falsity cannot be determined with certainty.

Consider our judgment that the argument about an AIDS cure (Example 4.15) is *unsound* because the premise *An effective cure for AIDS is available* is *false*. We are not as certain about this judgment of falsity as we would be if an argument contained statements from arithmetic. We can only give reasons why it is highly unlikely that an AIDS cure is available. For example, we can point out that this would be such important news that we surely would have heard about it, and that it would be difficult to suppress news of the discovery of an AIDS cure.

We use reasons such as these to justify our *judgment* that the premise *A cure for AIDS is available* is false even though we are not absolutely certain that it is false. And we use comparable reasons for making judgments that some premises of arguments are true. Sometimes we are relatively certain about premises because of clear, direct observations we have made (for example, that a friend has acted aggressively) or because we have evidence from many independent sources (for example, that the U.S. balance of trade is unfavorable). But at other times, we must decide whether to accept the premises of an argument when we are not all that certain of their truth or falsity.

Most of the examples and exercises in the remainder of the book are not ones in which you will be led to a clear, definite decision: "This argument is sound." You will sometimes be able to determine absolutely that an argument is *unsound* because it is *invalid*. But typically, you will be reconstructing the arguments you read in a way that makes them valid. Then the question remains of whether you should accept the premises as true. Answering this will be an exercise in using the background information and beliefs you already possess to give reasons for or against accepting premises.

Tips on Casting Doubt on Premises   Since any kind of statement can serve as a premise in an argument, the question of how to cast doubt on premises is obviously too broad to be dealt with here in detail. How can you cast doubt on any statement? We have to assume that this is the sort of thing you already know how to do. But we can provide a few tips concerning the kinds of premises that can be criticized most easily and fruitfully.

If a premise is a general one—*All killing is wrong; No sea animals are mammals*—try to think of a counterexample (self-defense; whales or seals). As will be pointed out in Chapter 5, many definition-like statements make a universal claim that can be criticized most effectively with a counterexample.

An if-then premise claims a connection between two things. If the premise is of this type, try to think of ways that the first thing could occur without the second occurring. For example, consider the premise *If birth-rates continue to increase, the world will become overcrowded.* What if death rates increase more rapidly than birthrates? What if people start colonizing the planets?

Every premise has further implications—statements that *would* be true if the premise in question were true. Try to think of such implications. For example, someone might use as a premise the claim that punishment does not deter crime. This implies that if there were no punishment, there would still be no more crime than there is now. Do you believe this? Would you personally still refrain from stealing, for example, to the same extent that you do now, even if you knew you wouldn't be punished? Would you still pay your income tax?

Sometimes scientific theories are used as premises. In Chapter 10, we discuss in some detail how these can be criticized. But for now, don't fall into the mistake of assuming that just because something is called a theory, it is automatically doubtful. Some theories are deserving of belief and some are not.

When you are criticizing an argument, avoid wasting your time quibbling over matters that require research and documentation to verify and of which you are uncertain. That is, avoid such matters unless you are willing and able to actually do the research and documentation in question. Avoid, for instance, making unsubstantiated claims about such things as divorce rates, employment rates, relative strengths of armed forces, oil profits, and so on. Direct your first attention (after determining the validity of an argument) to premises that can be discussed on the basis of generally shared background information.

Exercise 4.2   Casting Doubt on Premises

Each of the following statements might occur as a premise in an argument. (Indeed, some of them are used as premises in the arguments in Exercise 4.5 at the end of this chapter.) For each statement, think about what you might say to persuade someone that the claim being made is not true (or at least that it is doubtful). If you need more information about a topic, do a little research, either by consulting a library or by talking with someone you consider knowledgeable about the subject. Then put your ideas into writing, formulating a short paragraph casting doubt on each statement. Keep in mind the tips for casting doubt on universal claims and on if-then claims. If you find yourself initially inclined to agree with a statement, try to imagine what an intelligent critic on the other side of the issue might say to cast doubt on it.

1. Any practice that is harmful should be illegal.

2. If the average couple has more than two children, then the population will rise drastically.

3. The fetus is a part of a pregnant woman's body.

4. If the tenure system in colleges and universities were abolished, then academic freedom would not be protected.

5. If drugs such as cocaine were made legal in the United States, then countries like Colombia and Mexico would benefit.

6. People shouldn't make promises unless they are certain they can keep them.

7. If capital punishment is abolished, then the homicide rate will continue to increase.

8. If abortion continues to be legal, then respect for life will decline.

9. Any activity that makes people aggressive should be discouraged.

10. If Japan is becoming more technologically advanced than the United States, then the United States should adopt the educational methods of Japan.

Sample Appraisals: Examples of Techniques of Criticism

As we have learned in our discussion of *validity* and *soundness* in the previous sections, an argument can be criticized by showing that it is not valid or by casting doubt on whether the premises should be accepted. Suppose we were to criticize each of the following arguments:

Example 4.16

(1) John withheld information.

(2) Withholding information is lying.

(3) Anyone who has lied has done something wrong.

∴ *John has done something wrong.*

Example 4.17

(1) It is wrong for any person to kill another person.

(2) If the state executes a murderer, the state is killing a person.

∴ *It is wrong for the state to execute a murderer.*

The initial question is whether an argument is valid. Consider the argument in Example 4.16. If withholding information is lying and John has withheld information, then John has lied. And it follows from this and the third premise—anyone who has lied has done something wrong—that John has done something wrong. So the argument is valid. To admit this is not to admit that the premises are true; but if they are true, then the conclusion must be true as well.

But in the second argument (Example 4.17), there is no such relation between premises and conclusion. Even if it is wrong for any person to kill another person, and granting that the state, by executing a murderer, is killing a person, it doesn't follow that it is wrong for the state to execute a murderer because the state is not a person. There may be special considerations that justify killing by the state. So the second argument can be criticized as invalid.

The second kind of criticism (casting doubt on premises) can be raised against either argument. But before we discuss specific criticisms of premises, we should make some general points about the relation between the two kinds of criticisms. First, as we can see in Example 4.16, if an argument is valid, then the only means of criticism left is an attack on the premises. If you decide that there are adequate grounds for believing the premises, then you should be compelled by these reasons to believe the conclusion. If it is impossible for the premises to be true and the conclusion false, and you believe the premises, then it is irrational not to believe the conclusion. Second, if an argument is invalid, then it is not necessary to criticize the premises. You can point out that it does not matter whether the premises are true or not—even if they are true, the conclusion still does not follow.

There is a fairly obvious move, however, that might be made in defense of an argument that has been called invalid: this is to claim that there are implicit premises that, if added, will make the argument valid. In the case of Example 4.17,

(1) It is wrong for any person to kill another person.

(2) If the state executes a murderer, the state is killing a person.

∴   *It is wrong for the state to execute a murderer.*

it might be claimed that the argument should be expanded by the addition of an implicit premise.

> *(1) It is wrong for any person to kill another person.*
>
> *(2) If the state executes a murderer, the state is killing a person.*
>
> *(implicit)* *(3) Everything that is wrong for a person to do is wrong for the state to do.*
>
> ---
>
> ∴   *It is wrong for the state to execute a murderer.*

Your criticism will be more effective if you show that you are aware that an argument can be made valid by adding premises. (This point was made in Chapter 3.) Often the premise or premises left unstated are precisely the ones that, if made explicit, can be seen to be doubtful. A good procedure, then, is to point out first that the argument, as stated, is invalid. Second, you can raise the possibility of adding premises yourself. You might formulate the premise or premises that would make the argument valid, then discuss whether these premises are deserving of belief. In our expanded version of Example 4.17, the added premise says that everything that is wrong for a person to do is wrong for the state to do. In order to cast doubt on this premise, you can point out that if it were true, then not only would the state be wrong in executing murderers, the state would also be wrong in imprisoning *any* offenders, levying taxes, or generally carrying out any of the functions of government that are beyond the just power of any individual citizen.

We can now return to criticizing the premises in Example 4.16. They were:

1. John has withheld information.
2. Withholding information is lying.
3. Anyone who has lied has done something wrong.

Premise 3 can be criticized by giving counterexamples to this generalization. It is doubtful that someone who has lied to prevent great harm to another has done something wrong.

Premise 2 turns on a definitional or conceptual relationship between withholding information and lying. We discuss the criticism of claims such as these at some length in Chapter 5. The arguer in this case is guilty of stipulating a meaning of "lying" that is not ordinarily assumed by people who use this word, then proceeding in the argument with this misleading definition.

Premise 1 is the kind of claim that might be criticized on the basis of direct observation or reports of direct observation. Suppose John has been accused of selling his house without telling the buyer that the basement walls leak. Maybe you or someone else actually heard John say that the basement walls leak. Or, in the absence of such direct evidence, the premise could be supported by a further argument that we would then have to evaluate. For example, the buyer of the house could argue that all the junk John piled up against the water-stained wall was a deliberate attempt to hide its condition.

Even if there is direct observational evidence, this doesn't settle the matter with absolute certainty. We sometimes make mistakes about what we see and hear. And studies of "eyewitness testimony" in connection with criminal justice research has clearly indicated that our memory for what we have supposedly seen can be notoriously inaccurate.

Although philosophers and other students of reasoning have been trying at least from the time of Descartes (d. 1648) to establish unassailable foundations for all our reasoning, such efforts have fallen short of establishing general methods for establishing the truth or falsity of premises in deductive arguments. Nevertheless we are sometimes in a position to claim that an argument is *sound*. On some occasions the premises we use in an argument (or at least in further arguments on which an original argument is based) are not in doubt. In such circumstances we can hold the premises to be true or at least justified. If so, we are then in a position to maintain that a *valid* argument containing only these premises is *sound*.

In subsequent chapters we will discuss at greater length some of the techniques for establishing truth of premises. The latter part of Chapter 5 deals with *conceptual* or *definitional* support for premises that relies on clarification of meaning in the evaluation of arguments. Chapters 7 and 8 deal with techniques for understanding more complex passages that contain a series of linked arguments such that one is *further argument* for another. Finally, Chapters 9 and 10 examine more complex justifications that can be given for premises through appeal to techniques of empirical generalization and scientific theorizing, which go well beyond simple appeals to observation and memory, such as those we have just discussed. The discussion in these sections should be seen as directly relevant to the question of truth of premises in a deductive argument and thereby to the evaluative question of whether an argument is *sound*.

The Rationale for Using These Critical Techniques

How can we justify the use of the techniques of criticism we have recommended? Perhaps this can best be done by explaining what is *not* a fruitful way of criticizing an argument, and then by showing in contrast the effectiveness of the strategies we have recommended. *Perhaps the most common and least fruitful way of criticizing an argument is simply to deny the conclusion.* When one person states a position and the other just denies it or states an opposing position, there is really no place to go from there. The same result is produced by merely denying the conclusion of your opponent's argument.

The point of interpreting your opponent's position as an *argument* is that then you can make progress toward determining whether one of you should change your position. You can ask whether the reasons (premises) given for the conclusion are ones that you have grounds for believing, or grounds for doubting. And you can ask if the conclusion follows from these reasons (premises).

Let us illustrate this point. Suppose someone has claimed that killing is wrong and capital punishment is killing, so capital punishment is wrong. The least fruitful way of replying would be: "No, capital punishment is not wrong." To stubbornly adhere to this, without regard for the argument that has been presented, is to miss the point of argument and criticism. You have been given reasons for believing that capital punishment is wrong. If you agree with the statements given as reasons, and if the conclusion follows from these reasons, then you should change your mind and agree to the conclusion. If you can show your opponent that he should *not* believe the statements he has given as reasons, or that his conclusion does *not* follow, then he should give up this argument as a basis for believing his conclusion. You could then press him or her: "Was this the only reason you had for believing this? Let's look at any other arguments you might have made. Let's look at some arguments against believing that capital punishment is wrong. Perhaps we can find an argument on one side or the other that we find conclusive."

Admittedly, there are cases in which it would be appropriate to deny the conclusion of someone's argument. Suppose that someone is presenting an argument that it will not rain today because of the combination of barometric pressure, temperature, and humidity. Just as he is finishing his argument you look out the window and see the rain coming down. Of course, it is perfectly appropriate to say, "I don't know where your argument went wrong, but we can see that your conclusion is false."

Still, this is an exceptional case. Usually, we make an argument when our conclusion is one that someone might doubt and we do not have a direct means of determining if it is true. That is why we must look for premises to support our conclusion. And in this standard sort of case, it is not appropriate simply to deny the conclusion.

The same considerations apply when you are defending your own position. It is not enough merely to assert unsupported statements. You should build your argument on the firm foundation of true premises interconnected in a valid argument form.

Exercise 4.3   **Distinguishing the Validity of an Argument from the Truth of Its Premises**

---

1. State for each argument (1) whether or not the conclusion follows and (2) whether or not the premises are true.

   a. *(1) If Jones is in Washington, D.C., then he is in the state of Maryland.*

   (2) Jones is in Washington, D.C.

   ∴ *Jones is in the state of Maryland.*

   b. *(1) Either Harding was elected U.S. president in 1924 or Coolidge was.*

   (2) Harding was not elected U.S. president in 1924.

   ∴ *Coolidge was elected U.S. president in 1924.*

   c. *(1) Everything is either immoral, illegal, or fattening.*

   (2) Alice's brownies are not immoral.

   (3) Alice's brownies are not illegal.

   ∴ *Alice's brownies are fattening.*

2. Write in standard form an example (of your own creation) of each of the following:
   a. An argument that is valid but obviously unsound.
   b. An argument that is obviously sound, given common knowledge.
   c. An argument that is invalid and has at least one false premise.
   d. An argument that is invalid but has true premises and a true conclusion.

3. One aspect of the terminology we have introduced may be confusing. In ordinary speech, we occasionally refer to individual statements as "valid," as in "He made a valid point." In these cases, *valid* means "acceptable" or "true." As we are using the term, however, it is only *arguments* that are valid or invalid. Validity does not apply to individual statements. Likewise, only arguments are sound or unsound. On the

other hand, only individual *statements* are true or false. It is inappropriate to call an argument true or false.

i) Which of the following statements make sensible use of the terms?
   a. The argument you just gave is true.
   b. Your premises are unsound.
   c. Your conclusion is false.
   d. Your statement is true.
   e. Your statement is invalid.
   f. You are arguing from true premises to an invalid conclusion.

ii) Which of these statements are consistent; that is, for which of them can the two parts both be true together?
   a. Your argument is sound, but not valid.
   b. Your argument is valid, but your conclusion is false.
   c. Your argument is valid, but not sound.
   d. Your argument is sound, but your conclusion is false.

Arguments That Create Special Problems

The procedure we have recommended for understanding and criticizing arguments is fairly simple: Boil a passage down to its stated premises and conclusion (rephrasing if necessary); add any unstated premises or conclusion; and determine whether the conclusion follows from the premises and whether you can cast doubt on the premises.* Now we raise the question, Can this procedure be applied to all arguments, or are there categories of arguments that must be handled in different ways? Arguments concerning values have been treated as particularly troublesome.

Arguments Concerning Values Arguments concerning values can be handled adequately by the procedures already described. In fact, many of the arguments already used as examples concern values. One common pattern of argument that uses premises concerning values is exhibited by:

---

*A more elaborate procedure, which can be applied to arguments occurring in the context of longer prose passages, will be presented in Chapter 8.

Example 4.18

(1) *If the United States continues to use energy at a prodigious rate, then the country will collapse.*

(2) *The country shouldn't collapse.*

∴ *The United States shouldn't continue to use energy at a prodigious rate.**

There is a widespread belief that arguments concerning values must always be inconclusive—that all value judgments are subjective, and therefore arguments based on value judgments cannot be settled. We believe this position is mistaken. First, as Example 4.18 shows, we do accept some arguments that include value terms as valid.** Nevertheless, we may question whether the premises are true. We can ask, in particular, whether the second premise, which contains the value term, is true. Some people hold that conflicts about such value judgments can never be resolved.

---

*This argument closely resembles those of the valid *modus tollens* form

(1) *If A, then B.*

(2) *Not B.*

∴ *Not A.*

The examples concerning value are similar except that a value term such as *should* or *ought* occurs in the second premise and the conclusion.

**Contrast the valid argument in Example 4.18 with an invalid argument involving value statements such as:

(1) *If we force people to eat less salt, then they will be healthier.*

(2) *People ought to be healthier.*

∴ *We ought to force people to eat less salt.*

This argument is like those that exhibit the invalid form

(1) *If A, then B.*

(2) *B.*

∴ *A.*

which assume there is only one way of achieving the state described in B, but there may be others. For example, educating people to eat less salt may be better than forcing them to do so.

Many things are commonly included under the term *value judgment*—assessments of the aesthetic value of objects (paintings, films, novels, and so on), assessments of objects or experiences as being worthwhile in themselves or for some purpose, and (as in the example) assessments as to whether actions or policies are right or just. Whether these judgments can be made objectively is a difficult philosophical question we will not pretend to settle here. However, a few points can be made that are relevant to the criticism of arguments from each category.

Arguments Concerning Aesthetic Value   In discussing arguments concerning aesthetic value, our purpose is *not* to give a procedure for determining whether a work of art is beautiful, or aesthetically good. Rather, we wish to counteract the view that all arguments concerning aesthetic value can be dismissed because all questions of aesthetic value are in some sense subjective, that is, questions of taste.

If this subjectivist argument amounts to the claim that people differ in what they like, and therefore, no one can be convinced that someone else's judgment is correct, then the argument's conclusion doesn't follow from its premise. It is obvious that people differ in what they like, but equally obvious is that they are sometimes convinced that their initial judgment about a work of art was mistaken. A good critic can point out qualities in a work that might have been missed at first glance. Works that did not seem to hang together can be made sense of; flaws that were overlooked can be brought to light. In cases such as these, critical arguments might well convince you that your assessment of a work was mistaken.

Sometimes the impulse to dismiss all arguments concerning aesthetic value seems based on a skepticism concerning whether qualities can be identified that would make something aesthetically good or bad for all observers. If, for example, it were argued that a certain song is aesthetically bad because it is overly sentimental, we might reply that some people like sentimental music, so it doesn't follow objectively or universally that the song is bad—just that it is bad to people who don't like sentimental music.

This line of attack, however, is inconclusive. In the first place, the person who is attempting to establish that an object is aesthetically good or bad need not equate this goodness or badness with being liked or disliked. Most of us would readily admit that there are works of art we like a great deal even though they are not very good. So the reply that some people like sentimental music doesn't defeat the claim that a certain song is aesthetically bad because it is overly sentimental. Furthermore, our critic might claim that to call something aesthetically good goes beyond the personal report of liking or disliking. Judgments of aesthetic value might be claimed to be predictions of whether observers with a cultivated taste will appreciate a work in the long run.

To carry this discussion further would involve us in some fine points of aesthetic theory. But it should be fairly clear that arguments concerning aesthetic value cannot be summarily dismissed simply on the basis that different people like different works of art.

Even Matters of Taste Can Be Argued   There is one major category for which the subjectivist's claim seems well founded—classic cases of "taste." This is a category in which objects or states of affairs are assessed in terms of the experiences they produce. The best meal I can imagine is poached oysters. You can't stand seafood. These are matters of taste, pure and simple.

If this is what is meant by the subjectivity of value judgments, then the claim must be granted. But two cautions are in order. First, just because poached oysters make a good meal for me but a bad one for you, it does not follow that each person is the only one who knows what is good for him. We all often make mistakes in predicting what objects will be a source of experience that is good in itself. You might *think* that a certain house, car, suit of clothing, or meal will bring enjoyment (or its opposite), but find out that you are wrong. And someone might have presented an argument to you stating reasons why you would not find these things to be good. If you had dismissed this argument on the grounds that all value judgments are subjective, you would have been mistaken.

The second caution is this: Just because the question of which objects produce good experiences is in some sense subjective, it does not follow that questions of which acts are right are also subjective.

Assessments of Actions and Policies as Right or Just   An important distinction is made in ethical theory between *the good* and *the right*. Whereas objects, states of affairs, or experiences might be good or bad, it is actions that are right or wrong. While the same object might be good for me but bad for you, this does not hold for actions. From a moral point of view, if an act is right to perform, it must be right for anyone in a similar kind of situation to perform. According to some theories, what is right depends at least in part on the good or bad that it produces. The same act might have good consequences for one person and bad consequences for another person. But according to any defensible moral theory, a correct judgment that an act is right would not be based on the subjective standpoint of the person who benefits from it. If an act is right, it would be judged right from an impersonal point of view, taking into account both those who are benefited and those who are harmed by the act. So arguments concerning what is right cannot all be dismissed with the claim that "what is right for you is different from what is right for me, and no one can tell what is really right."

This same point can be made concerning arguments about justice. The concept of justice is close to the concept of moral rightness, except that the concept of justice is more typically applied to actions or policies that distribute a benefit or burden among a group of people. As with moral rightness, no defensible theory of justice allows that the same act or policy is just to the person who benefits but unjust to the person who suffers. If an act or policy is just or unjust, it is so from an impersonal or universal perspective.

To summarize, some arguments concerning values or concerning rightness or justice are reasonable, defensible arguments, and some arguments are not and should be criticized. It is a mistake, however, to give no consideration to any of these arguments just because they concern values or rightness or justice.

In some cases, a premise of an argument concerning values or rightness or justice will be a definition or theory of "good" or "right" or "just." Some help in criticizing premises such as these will be provided by Chapter 5, which discusses definitions and conceptual theories.

Exercise 4.4   **Arguments Concerning Values**

---

1. Develop an argument that contains a judgment of value as a conclusion. It may be:
    a. A judgment of aesthetic value, such as "Picasso's *Guernica* is a fine painting"; "*Midnight Cowboy* is a great film"; "Modern art is all trash."
    b. A judgment of taste, such as "Try it, you'll like it"; or "The blue suit with the green stripe is just the thing for you."
    c. A judgment of right or just action or policy, such as "The United States should never be the aggressor in a nuclear war"; "Alice shouldn't just walk out on Alvin"; or "It isn't just for the United States to use one-third of the world's energy production each year."

2. Suppose someone dismisses your entire argument simply on the grounds that it involves a question of value and claims that value questions cannot be decided. Drawing from the discussion in the text, how would you respond? We don't expect you to accept unquestioningly the view about values that we have presented, but you

should take it into account. Write a short passage in which you state both your response to someone's dismissal of your argument and your general view about whether matters of value can be argued.

Writing Critical Comments

The techniques of criticism discussed in this chapter may be used to structure critical comments. You should always consider whether an argument is valid and its premises true. The four-step process suggested below will help you draft a critical remark or expand on critical statements you have already written. Of course, as in any piece of writing, you must keep in mind the expectations of your audience. Critical comments will take different forms, depending on whether, for example, you are responding to a passage in a critical reasoning course, writing a short answer on an examination, or creating a paragraph that will be placed in a longer essay.

1. Present the elements of the argument that are relevant to your criticism, but not in painful detail. Include any important, implicit premises.

2. Indicate whether the conclusion follows. (If it does not, add remarks to help the reader see its inadequacies.)

3. If the premises are questionable, say what you can to cast doubt on them.

4. Consider whether a modest reformulation will produce an improved argument. (Employ the Principle of Charitable Interpretation in a liberal manner.)

A passage constructed in accordance with these four suggestions may well be edited later in the process of producing a polished criticism. Let's apply these suggestions to an argument cited in a news item.

News Item   *Senator Malcom Bismark emerged from the State Economic Development Committee meeting with the gloomy prediction that we will not be able to overcome the crisis of lagging industry. He said, "If Washington would support the states in encouraging new industry, we could survive this crisis. But as recent budget cuts indicate, the federal government is unwilling to support the states in this endeavor."*

A reconstruction of the argument, setting out the basic elements of the passage, helps us to see that the conclusion doesn't follow.

(1) If the federal government supports the states in encouraging new industry, then we can overcome the crisis of lagging industry.

(2) The federal government won't provide this support.

∴   *We will not be able to overcome the crisis of lagging industry.*

Since the conclusion does not follow, we need not consider whether the premises are true. However, there is another interpretation of the first premise that makes the argument valid; unfortunately this restated premise is questionable.

Reformulated Argument

(1) We can overcome the crisis of lagging industry only if the federal government supports the states in encouraging new industry.

(2) The federal government will not support the states in encouraging new industry.

∴   *We will not be able to overcome the crisis of lagging industry.*

These observations about the argument in the news item can be formed into a critical comment.

> *Senator Bismark, in a recent news item, suggests that Americans will not be able to overcome the crisis of lagging industry. He argues that if the federal government would support the states in encouraging new industry, we would be able to overcome this crisis. But he claims that Washington won't lend this support. As he states his argument, Bismark's conclusion doesn't follow from his premises. Federal support may be one way to overcome the crisis, but there may also be other ways.*
>
> *Perhaps the senator meant to say that we will overcome the crisis of lagging industry* only if *the federal government supports the states. His conclusion would then follow, but it is questionable whether this new premise is true. It is at least possible that the incentives of private investment, together with support from the states themselves, will suffice to revitalize American industry.*

Exercise 4.5   Criticizing Arguments

Write a paragraph or two criticizing each of the following arguments. Use the four suggestions offered in the text. (1) Set out the argument. (You might find it useful to sketch a version of the argument in standard form on a scratch paper to help you determine its structure and whether it has any missing premises.) (2) Indicate whether the conclusion follows. (3) See if you can cast doubt on any of the premises. (When you do this, don't just make a general statement aimed at discrediting several premises at once; instead, tackle the premises specifically, one at a time, clearly saying which premise you are attacking.) Finally, (4) consider relevant reformulations and whether they can be criticized.

1. Football should be discouraged, for the reason that football makes people aggressive, and any activity that makes people aggressive should be discouraged.

2. The United States is *not* really democratic, since if it were democratic, each person's opinion would have a significant effect on government.

3. If the government's antidrug policies are effective, then drug use will begin to decline. Drug use *is* beginning to decline. So the government's antidrug policies are effective.

4. If you should not be blamed for what your ancestors did, then neither can you take pride in their deeds. It would follow that you are not entitled to take pride in what your ancestors accomplished.

5. If the average couple has more than two children, the population will rise drastically. But we should prevent the population from rising drastically. So we should prevent any couple from having more than two children.

6. If the universe was created, then there was a time at which it did not exist. If there was a time at which it did not exist, then there was a time at which nothing was converted into something. But this is impossible. So the universe was not created.

7. We shouldn't allow doctors to determine the gender of a fetus whenever parents request it. This is so because if we allow such testing, then some parents will abort a fetus simply because of its gender.

8. People have the right to do whatever they want to with their own bodies. Therefore, a pregnant woman has the right to have the fetus aborted if she wants to.

9. All tax increases are unjustified at this time. But since user fees to get into national parks are not taxes, increasing them is justified.

10. No one should get married. This is so because getting married involves promising to live with a person for the rest of one's life. But no one can safely predict that she will remain compatible with some other person for the rest of her life. So no one should get married.

11. People should pay taxes to support only parts of government they use. It stands to reason that people without children shouldn't be required to pay for schools.

CHAPTER FIVE

"That Depends on What You Mean by . . ."

In Chapter 4, we distinguished two tasks that must be carried out in the evaluation of arguments: (1) determining whether the conclusion follows from the premises and (2) determining whether the premises should be accepted. Until now, we have assumed that the words that make up our arguments are reasonably clear in their meaning. This assumption simplifies the tasks we just mentioned. As we will see in this chapter, when we look at arguments whose words and phrases are unclear in their meaning, it becomes more difficult to judge whether a conclusion follows and whether to accept premises.

Often, the question of how to judge an argument seems to depend on the meaning of a word or phrase.

Example 5.1   *John is emotionally disturbed, and emotionally disturbed people shouldn't be allowed to own guns. So John shouldn't be allowed to own guns.*

Example 5.2   *Frank is not a war veteran since he fought only in Vietnam, and the conflict in Vietnam was not a war.*

Example 5.3   Flesh *magazine contains pictures of people in sexually explicit poses. Since such pictures contribute to lewd desires, it follows that* Flesh *magazine is pornographic.*

You can almost hear the quick replies: "That depends on what you mean by 'emotionally disturbed,' " "That depends on what you mean by 'war,' " "That depends on what you mean by 'pornographic.' " But if the discussion proceeds at all, it is likely to get confused. Suppose the arguer in Example 5.1 indicates what *she* meant by "emotionally disturbed," and according to her definition, John *is* emotionally disturbed. Does this save her argument? Or suppose the arguer in Example 5.2 supports his premise that "Vietnam was not a war," by insisting that a conflict is not a war unless one country officially declares war on another. Should we then accept the conclusion? Suppose the listener in Example 5.3 disagrees with the arguer's assumptions about the meaning of the word *pornographic*. Is there a way to proceed?

If there is a disagreement about meaning in any of these cases, someone will probably claim, "Now we're just arguing semantics, so there's no use in continuing." What do people mean by "just arguing semantics?" Are they making a worthwhile point? Is it true that there is no use in continuing? Can the issue of meaning be decided? How? By using a dictionary?

In an attempt to sort out and answer these questions, we note that situations in which problems with meaning arise are not all of the same kind. We distinguish three different situations in which considerations of meaning might affect our appraisal of an argument.

First, there might be a shift in meaning from one premise to the next, so that the argument's pattern is made invalid. Depending on the circumstances, this might be true of Example 5.1. The meaning of "emotionally disturbed" might shift from one premise to the next.

Second, the premises of an argument might support the conclusion only if an expression is given a special meaning. Unless this is pointed out, the argument's conclusion can be misleading. This criticism could be made about Example 5.2. The conclusion "Frank is not a war veteran," could be misleading.

Third, an argument might contain a premise that rests on a claim about the meaning of an expression. In order to evaluate the argument, we will need to decide whether to accept this claim about meaning. Example 5.3 could be interpreted as having the implicit premise, "Material that arouses lewd desires is pornographic." And this claim could be thought to express something about the *meaning* of "pornographic." How do we tell whether a claim like this should be accepted? In the remainder of this chapter we shall explore each of these problems in turn.

Unclear Expressions in the Premises: Looking for Shifts in Meaning

When an expression that is unclear in its meaning is used in more than one premise, its meaning might shift from one premise to the next. If this happens, the usual result is that the conclusion does not follow from the premises. This kind of mistake is called *equivocation*.

Let's return to Example 5.1, focusing on the expression "emotionally disturbed," which occurs in both premises.

(1) John is emotionally disturbed.

(2) Emotionally disturbed people shouldn't be allowed to own guns.

∴   *John shouldn't be allowed to own guns.*

It might be thought that the arguer can protect the argument from criticism by saying what she means by "emotionally disturbed." Or, if the arguer is not present, perhaps we could help the argument by suggesting a definition that makes at least one of the premises true. Suppose the arguer is present and she says, "I mean by 'emotionally disturbed,' anyone who would score outside the normal range of the Minnesota Multiphasic Personality Inventory (MMPI) test, and John would score outside the normal range of the relevant scales."

This definition saves the truth of the first premise, but it raises doubts about the second. As long as we vaguely suppose the expression "emotionally disturbed" to apply to people with certain severe disturbances such as paranoid delusions, it is easy to accept the claim that they shouldn't be allowed to own guns. But if we accept the stipulation that *emotionally disturbed* means "anyone who would score outside the normal range in the MMPI," then the second premise becomes doubtful. This is particularly apparent when we realize that the MMPI has a scale according to which homosexuality is "outside the normal range." It is implausible to maintain that sexual preference alone is relevant to whether people should own guns. The problem is not that the second premise remains vague, but that it is probably false if *emotionally disturbed* is stipulated to mean "anyone who would score outside the normal range on the MMPI."

The lesson from this example is important, and it can be applied in many instances of criticism. When an expression is used in more than one premise, it must have the same meaning in all premises (unless the structure of the argument does not depend on these terms having the same meaning).* When the meaning shifts in structurally relevant ways, the pattern of the argument is destroyed, and the conclusion does not follow from the premises. If "emotionally disturbed" kept the same meaning throughout the argument, the argument would have the following pattern, in which the conclusion follows:

John is a P_1.

All P_1's are P_2's.

∴ John is a P_2.

But if "emotionally disturbed" shifts its meaning, then the pattern becomes the following, in which the conclusion does not follow:

John is a P_1.

All P_3's are P_2's.

∴ John is a P_2.

As a second example of equivocation, consider the following reconstruction of an argument from the final exercise set of Chapter 4. We'll focus on the expression, "significant effect."

Example 5.4

(1) *If the United States were democratic, each citizen's opinion would have a significant effect on government.*

(2) *Each citizen's opinion does not have a significant effect on government.*

∴ *The United States is not really democratic.*

"Significant effect" could mean many things, but let's try to interpret it in a way that makes both the premises of this argument plausible. In premise 2, having a "significant effect" might be taken to mean having the government do what each person wants it to do. It is certainly true that each person's opinion doesn't have this kind of effect. But if we interpret "significant effect" in this same way in premise 1, then that premise

---

*We have to add this qualification to handle special cases such as those involving two distinct meanings for a single word. Take, for example, the argument: "Don't build your bank near the bank of the river, it floods over its banks regularly, and your bank would be open to substantial damage." This argument is *not* faulty even though there is a (harmless) shift between the two meanings of "bank."

becomes completely implausible. If we refused to call the United States a democracy unless each person in it could have the government do what he wanted, then we are requiring something that is impossible.

On the other hand, we could make premise 1 plausible by interpreting "significant effect" in a more modest way, requiring only that citizens be allowed to vote and have their vote counted. But then premise 2 becomes false.

The question is whether there is some interpretation of "significant effect" that makes both these premises true, and this is beginning to appear doubtful. Unless there is such an interpretation, Example 5.4 is an equivocation.

The way in which we dealt with Examples 5.2 and 5.4 suggests a three-step procedure for judging whether an argument is guilty of an equivocation:

1. Locate any unclear expressions that occur in more than one premise.

2. Determine what the expression must mean to make one of the premises true.

3. Determine whether the other premise(s) can be made true without changing the meaning of the unclear expression.

The Possibility of Misleading Definition

A slightly different problem can arise when an unclear expression occurs both in a premise and in the conclusion, and a different critical approach is required. The way in which the expression is used in the premise can give it a special meaning. If we interpret the expression as having its ordinary meaning in the conclusion, then the conclusion is misleading. Suppose it is argued that:

Example 5.5

(1) *The average height of women in the United States is five feet five inches.*

(2) *Any woman over the average height for women in the United States is tall.*

(3) *June is five feet five and one-half inches tall.*

∴   *June is tall.*

This problem is not one of equivocation. The meaning of "tall" need not shift in order to make both premise 2 and the conclusion true. The problem is that the definition of "tall" that would make premise 2 true is not a definition that would ordinarily be assumed if we heard someone referred to as "tall." So if the arguer proceeded, on the basis of this argument, to go around preparing people to meet a tall woman when they meet June, these people would be misled.

A fruitful way of criticizing this kind of argument is to point out to the person presenting it that he should simply substitute his stipulated definition for the unclear term in the conclusion. We could say, "If all you mean by 'tall' is 'above the average height for women in the United States,' then why not simply say June is slightly above average height."

The same critical approach could be used with Example 5.2:

(1) Frank fought only in Vietnam.

(2) The conflict in Vietnam was not a war.

∴ *Frank is not a war veteran.*

In order to keep the meaning of "war" from shifting, we must take it to mean "declared war." But it would be misleading to formulate this argument and at other times, without explaining the stipulation, to claim that Frank is not a war veteran. If the arguer were required, however, to substitute his stipulated definition and say, "Frank didn't serve in a declared war," then his claim would lose its misleading effect.

Kinds of Unclarity: Vagueness and Ambiguity

So far in this chapter, we have referred broadly to "unclear meaning." Two kinds of unclarity are commonly distinguished: vagueness and ambiguity.

Vagueness "Emotionally disturbed," as it is used in Example 5.1 concerning who should own guns, is a typical vague expression. Where do you draw the line between people who are emotionally disturbed and people who are not? "Tall," as it is used in Example 5.5 concerning the height of women in the United States, is another vague expression. There is no definite boundary between people who are tall and those who are not. There is a range of height, and we would not hesitate to call people at the high end of the range tall, but it is somewhat arbitrary where to draw the line between those who are tall and those who aren't. *When there is no definite boundary (as in these cases) between the objects an expression applies to and those to which it does not, the expression is vague.*

It is no particular fault of an argument that it uses vague language. Most of the expressions we use could be called vague to some degree. As we can see from the examples in this chapter, a problem can arise when an argument uses the same vague expression in more than one premise. Then the question is whether it is used *consistently*. That is, does the vague expression apply to one portion of a range of objects in one premise, but to another portion of the range in the other premise?

In Example 5.4, concerning whether the United States is a democracy, the expression "significant effect" is vague. We can imagine a range of effects that citizens could have on government, from the most slight (voting for a losing proposition) to more significant (deciding what is to be law). The problem with argument 5.4 is that, in order to be plausible, one premise must be taken to use "significant effect" in a way that refers to less weighty effects within this range, while the other premise refers to more weighty effects. There is no answer to—and in this case no point to answering—the question, What does "significant effect" really mean? The question is whether "significant effect" can mean the *same* thing throughout the argument.

If a vague expression is used in a premise and a conclusion, it might be used consistently but still be misleading. As we saw in Example 5.2 concerning whether Frank is a war veteran, "war" is vague enough that it could be used to refer only to declared wars. But it is misleading not to stipulate this when asserting the conclusion.

Ambiguity   A second kind of lack of clarity is *ambiguity. An ambiguous expression has more than one meaning.* "Dream," for example, can mean either something that is hoped for or a sequence of images occurring during sleep. An expression can be ambiguous without being vague—both meanings of dream are fairly precise. Or an ambiguous expression can be vague also. A person might be called "educated," for example, if he has had a good deal of formal schooling or if he has acquired considerable knowledge through his own study. But in addition to having these two fairly distinct meanings, which make the word ambiguous, it is also vague because neither meaning has a definite boundary. How much schooling (or individual study) does it take before one can be properly called "educated"?

We can contrast this kind of unclarity of meaning and the kind of "shift" in meaning that can result, to the kind of unclarity and the kind of shift that can result from vagueness. A vague expression like "tall" is unclear because of the haziness of the boundary between things that are tall and those that are not. By "shifting in meaning," we meant that a vague term like *tall* can make a shift from premise to premise in the range of objects to which it refers. In the case of ambiguity, it might be unclear which of two distinct meanings an expression like *dream* should be given in a particular premise, and an expression might shift from one distinct meaning to another within an argument.

Ambiguity is less likely than vagueness to lead to difficulties in an argument. If an expression has wildly different meanings, then using it as though the meanings were the same would be too obvious to fool most listeners. Problems can arise, however, if the meanings are closely related. For example, there is a family of expressions that are used both in legal contexts and in moral contexts—*responsible, right, entitled,* and so on. It is easy to slip from one context to the other, giving these expressions a slightly different meaning, as in the following argument.

Example 5.6   *If you bought the car from me, then I'm entitled to the money. And if I'm entitled to the money, then it isn't wrong for me to ask for it now.*

The speaker in this argument may well be shifting from a legal to a moral context in his use of the word *entitled.* The first statement has to do with a legal right to payment. But the person he is addressing might be complaining about the ethical propriety of being asked for the money in special circumstance—being in dire need, for example, or having just been insulted by the person who is owed the money. If the first premise is only true if "entitled" is used in a legal sense, but the second premise requires that "entitled" be used in a moral sense, then it wouldn't follow that it's not wrong for me to ask for the money now. This is an example of an ambiguous expression leading to equivocation in an argument.

Interpreting and Evaluating: A Dialogue-Process

It can be seen from the discussion of these examples that when an argument contains unclear terms, the task of evaluating it and of determining what the unclear terms mean are not separate. This point can be brought more clearly into focus through a discussion of an argument that you already attempted to criticize in Exercise 4.5. It might have been reconstructed in the following way:

Example 5.7   (1) *Getting married involves promising to live with a person for the rest of one's life.*

(2) *No one can safely predict compatibility with another person for life.*

(3) *If two people aren't compatible, then they can't live together.*

(4) *No one should make a promise unless she or he can safely predict that she or he can keep it.*

∴   *No one should get married.*

As we shall see, an adequate evaluation of this argument and an interpretation of its unclear terms are two parts of a dialogue-process in which each part affects the other. We call this a *dialogue-process* because it simulates a dialogue that might actually occur if the author of the argument were present. We imagine the critic asking the arguer what he means by certain expressions, and the arguer responding in turn by clarifying his meaning. The critic then assesses the implications of this interpretation for the argument as a whole.

It is possible simply to dismiss some of the premises in the argument given in Example 5.7 (and in many others) by interpreting vague or ambiguous expressions in ways that make the premises false. But by seeking interpretations (within reason) that will make the premises true, we can try to discover whether the argument advanced is making a point worth our consideration. This approach, which might be seen as an extension of the Principle of Charitable Interpretation, supports our objective of using critical reasoning to determine what is reasonable to believe rather than to humiliate opponents in argument.

Since a written text provides no opportunity for a real dialogue, the reader must play the arguer's role as well as his or her own in interpreting and evaluating this document. The first premise of our argument states that *Getting married involves promising to live with a person for the rest of one's life.* But the term *marriage* is broad (that is, vague) enough to cover common-law marriages and the recent phenomenon of self-styled marriage contracts that include no such promise. These cases suggest that the premise is false.

This criticism has a point; the first premise is at best misleading as stated. But it is both interesting and worthwhile to give the arguer the benefit of the doubt by interpreting *getting married* in a sense that restricts the term to cases involving the traditional vow "until death do us part" or some equivalent. This interpretation now makes the first premise true since traditional marriages *do* seem to involve a promise, that is, a marriage vow.

The second premise may also be subjected to the dialogue-process. It states that *No one can safely predict compatibility with another person for life.* The expression "safely predict" is vague here. Would a prediction with 90 percent certainty be a safe prediction? 80 percent? 51 percent? Again, we can pick a meaning that will make premise 2 false since we can predict compatibility if we set the level of safe prediction low enough. But let us see where a more generous interpretation might lead us.

We can pick a level of certainty high enough to make the second premise true—one such that no one will be able to safely predict compatibility for life. But notice that the same expression, "safely predict," is used again in premise 4. We must interpret it in the same way there.

Now a problem emerges. The high standards of predictability that were necessary to make premise 2 true, make it less likely that *No one should make a promise unless she or he can safely predict that she or he can keep it.* We might be justified, for instance, in promising to return a book even though we know that a variety of factors, such as a house fire, might make the promise impossible to keep. To demand nearly absolute certainty of being able to keep a promise would rule out all but a few promises. Such a stipulation, if actually carried out in practice, would virtually eliminate the very useful custom of making promises.

We are now left with the question of whether there is a range of "safe prediction" that is low enough to make this premise about promises true, but high enough that it is also true that no one can safely predict compatibility with another person for life. It is doubtful whether there is such a range.

There is a problem of interpretation regarding premise 3 as well. It maintains: *If two people aren't compatible, then they can't live together.* We have the same dilemma with *compatible* that we had with *safely predict.* For premise 3 to be true, we would have to call people "compatible" unless they had extremely serious conflicts. After all, many people continue to live together in spite of minor incompatibility. But by interpreting the notion of "compatible" in a liberal way, we make premise 2 less plausible—many people might be able to safely predict that they won't have serious conflicts (especially if they share a great many values and have known each other for some time). Therefore, an interpretation that makes premise 3 more plausible makes premise 2 less plausible.

What is the outcome of our dialogue-process? Even being generous with the meanings of unclear terms, the argument in question is probably not sound—some premises are implausible. But reaching this conclusion through a dialogue-process that makes every effort to find truth in the argument's premises is more important than jumping at easy ways to dismiss the argument. As an added benefit, the dialogue-process has raised interesting questions about the nature of commitment in marriage. In actual practice, you need not act out a dialogue in order to interpret an argument. But you should try to provide sympathetic, even generous, interpretation of crucial expressions.

The discussion of this example should have made clear how interpreting the words used in an argument, and evaluating the argument itself, are interrelated. We can often choose one of several meanings for an expression, and the choice we make can affect the truth or falsity of premises. But we must make our choices consistent in order to preserve the validity of an argument.

Exercise 5.1   **Criticizing Arguments That Contain Unclear Words or Expressions**

---

1. Discuss the ways in which vague or ambiguous expressions might be clarified in the following statements. Suggest how assigning different interpretations affects their truth or falsity.

   a. Man is born free.

   b. Exceptional children should be given special attention by the public education system.

   c. Suicide, whether direct or indirect, should be strongly condemned.

   d. The average American family has 3.2 members.

   e. The war on poverty was no war.

   f. Marriage is a bond of trust between equals, but the partners in a marriage are rarely equal.

   g. The accused argued that he should not be required to pay the parking ticket because the sign said, "Fine for Parking" (from Mike Mailway, *Seattle Post-Intelligencer*).

   h. The public school system can never treat students equally; they come to the schools unequal in talent, experience, and family background.

   i. America did not become a democracy until the 1960s. Women could not vote until the Nineteenth Amendment was ratified in 1920, and it was only in 1965 that a Voting Rights Act was passed that did away with property qualifications and literacy tests, and paved the way for the genuine participation of all people, regardless of race, creed, or national origin.

2. Write a brief critical assessment of the following arguments, focusing particularly on possible shifts in meaning of vague or ambiguous terms. Try to create a dialogue—suggesting possible meanings of

unclear terms, evaluating the argument in the light of these stipulations of meaning, and suggesting alternative interpretations that might get around any objections. Refer to the discussion of Example 5.7 for a model of this kind of dialogue.

a. The United States is a democracy. This follows from the fact that the United States is ruled by the people and *democracy* means "government ruled by the people."

b. If the average couple has more than two children, the population will rise drastically. But we should prevent the population from rising drastically. So we should prevent the average couple from having more than two children. *(Note that this argument has been altered from the version presented in Chapter 4 so that it is now valid.)*

c. Space cannot be expanding unless it is finite. But space is not finite. Hence, space cannot be expanding.

d. Equal rights for women should not be constitutionally guaranteed. This follows from the fact that men and women are different physiologically and emotionally. But if this is so, then men and women are not equal. And if men and women are not equal, then they should not be called "equal" by the law.

e. Nobody should undertake college education without at least some idea of what she wants to do and where she wants to go in her life. But our world is full of change. We can't predict which fields will provide job openings in the future. If we can't confidently predict future employment, then we can't form a reasonable idea of what to do with our lives. So nobody should go to college.

f. A game is time-bound . . . it has no contact with any reality outside itself, and its performance is its own end. Further it is sustained by the consciousness of being a pleasurable, even mirthful, relaxation from the strains of ordinary life. None of this is applicable to science. Science is not only perpetually seeking contact with reality by its usefulness, i.e., in the sense that it is applied, it is perpetually trying to establish a universally valid pattern of reality, i.e., as pure science.*

(HINT: Assume that the conclusion being argued is that science is not a game.)

g. "Man is born free," said Rousseau, "and is everywhere in chains," but no one is less free than a newborn child, nor will he become free as he grows older. His only hope is that he will come under the

---

*John Huizinga, *Homo Ludens: A Study of the Play Element in Culture* (Boston: Beacon Press, 1955), p. 203.

control of a natural and social environment in which he will make the most of his genetic endowment and in doing so most successfully pursue happiness.*

(HINT: Assume that Skinner is arguing in support of the conclusion that happiness does not involve freedom from control.)

Argument and Definition

At the beginning of this chapter we pointed out that when an argument has been presented and the meanings of terms are challenged, the discussion is likely to get frustrating and confused. Some people become impatient with further discussion because they believe there is an easy resolution: a trip to the dictionary. Other people see the debate over meaning as pointless ("mere semantics") because they believe that definitions are arbitrary—anyone can use a word to mean most anything he or she wants. We believe both of these points of view are mistaken.

Consider first the view that substantial problems of meaning can all be solved by consulting a dictionary. This presumption is faulty in two ways. First, dictionary entries often do little more than provide synonyms whose meaning is closely allied to the term being defined. As such, they fail to clarify meaning as is illustrated in the following series of dictionary entries:

recondite—incomprehensible to one of ordinary understanding or knowledge

incomprehensible—impossible to comprehend; unintelligible

unintelligible—not intelligible; obscure

obscure—not readily understood or not clearly expressed; abstruse

abstruse—difficult to comprehend; recondite

Second, dictionaries give precise definitions for only a limited range of

---

*B. F. Skinner, *About Behaviorism* (New York: Knopf, 1974), p. 201.

scientific or technical terms. They can define precisely, for instance, specially coined terms from physics, such as:

> pion—a short-lived meson that is primarily responsible for the nuclear
> force that exists as a positive or negative particle with mass 273.2
> times the electron mass or a neutral particle with mass 264.2 times the
> electron mass

But dictionaries give only incomplete analyses of more familiar terms:

> marriage—the institution whereby men and women are joined in a
> special kind of social and legal dependence for the purpose of found-
> ing and maintaining a family

Even if we overlook the vagueness of certain terms ("social and legal dependence," "family"), this dictionary entry faces difficulty. It is inadequate because people can be married without intending to found or maintain a family (that is, without intending to have children). It is not even clear that marriage must customarily be associated with intending to have children. In order to fix the dictionary entry to avoid this problem, we would need to investigate more closely the connection between the concept of marriage and related concepts such as that of a family or social and legal dependence. The latter part of this chapter examines techniques that can be used to improve our understanding of crucial concepts used in arguments. The dictionary, however, as we have seen, provides little help in resolving uncertainty about concepts.

A second perspective is taken by those who believe that discussion about meaning and definition should be dismissed because they are merely a matter of semantics. Such skeptics assume that we are free to attach whatever meaning we like to the words and statements we use, and for this reason believe that inquiry into meaning (and definition) must be fruitless.

An unlikely, but well-known, supporter of this perspective is Humpty Dumpty, as recorded in his discussion of the matter with Alice in Lewis Carroll's classic *Through the Looking Glass.** They have just finished a conversation about birthdays and *un*-birthdays (we have 364 days for *un*-birthday presents).

> *"And only one for birthday presents, you know. Here's glory for you!"*
>
> *"I don't know what you mean by 'glory,' "* Alice said.

---

*Lewis Carroll, *The Annotated Alice* (New York: Clarkson N. Patter Inc., 1960), pp. 268–269.

Humpty Dumpty smiled contemptuously. "Of course you don't—till I tell you. I meant 'there's a nice knock-down argument, for you!' "

"But 'glory' doesn't mean 'a nice knock-down argument,' " Alice objected.

"When I use a word," Humpty Dumpty said, in rather a scornful tone, "it means just what I choose it to mean—neither more nor less."

"The question is," said Alice, "whether you can make words mean so many different things."

"The question is," said Humpty Dumpty, "which is to be master—that is all."

This snippet illustrates an extreme version of the thesis that the meaning of words reflects the momentary intentions of speakers. Alice raises the telling question whether we *can* mean what we choose at the moment. A certain stability is necessary for communication to be possible at all. Communication is possible only if people can share meanings for the words they use and hence share concepts. If people use words as they please, with no regard for the meaning recognized by others, then they limit the amount of communication possible. Some people might be momentarily amused by a strange, unorthodox use of expressions, but they would quickly tire of the game. If you give words meaning according to a personal code, you make it virtually impossible for others to understand you. But even more generally, if the "words" (that is, sounds) a person uses are completely arbitrary and unsystematic, she won't even be able to begin to communicate. She won't be speaking a language but merely babbling sounds.

Of course, sometimes it is useful to specify or choose a meaning. Such specifying is commonly done within a field through its technical vocabulary; we do it as well when we stipulate a meaning for a vague expression or select among the meanings of an ambiguous expression. Such choices need not be arbitrary. But extensive use of technical expressions, especially those that have non-technical meanings as well, can make communication difficult. Learning to use words in a technical manner is like learning to use another language.

This emphasis on stability is not meant to suggest that meanings are unchanging over time, or from person to person, or group to group—people can miscommunicate. The process of examining the meaning of crucial concepts in an argument is designed to limit faulty communication. The process presupposes a certain amount of agreement between the person producing an argument and those to whom the argument is directed. If there is no such agreement on the application of a concept to even a single case (either real or imagined), then we should conclude that the people involved have different concepts—even though they might employ the same words to express them. This is what most people are prepared to do with Humpty Dumpty. His concept of "glory" is certainly not theirs (however much they might relish a "nice knock-down argument").

Evaluating Definition-like Premises

At the beginning of this chapter we pointed to three kinds of situations in which considerations of meaning can affect our appraisal of an argument. The first two we discussed involved unclear expressions that are used more than once in an argument, raising the possibility of equivocation, or misleading definition. The comments just made concerning argument and definition are intended to clear the way for a discussion of the third kind of situation. That is, a premise of an argument might make or imply a claim about the meaning of an expression. When this occurs, we must consider whether this claim about meaning is acceptable as a part of our appraisal of the argument. We have just made a case that this can not be done by simply consulting a dictionary, but neither are meanings so arbitrary that words can mean whatever we want them to. So how do we decide whether to accept a claim concerning meaning?

Let's consider again the argument we posed at the beginning of the chapter, in which the acceptability of some premises seems to depend on the meaning or definition of concepts.

Example 5.3

(repeated) Flesh *magazine contains pictures of people in sexually explicit poses. Since such pictures contribute to lewd desires,* Flesh *is pornographic.*

or in standard form:

(1) Flesh *magazine contains pictures of people in sexually explicit poses.*

(2) Pictures of people in sexually explicit poses arouse lewd desires.

(implicit) *(3) Any material that arouses lewd desires is pornographic.*

∴   Flesh *magazine is pornographic.*

Imagine how we might explore the truth of these premises. We could test premise 1 by looking at a copy of the magazine (or perhaps several issues) to see whether they contain pictures of people in sexually explicit poses. Premise 2 is more difficult to assess. Presumably it depends at least on some sort of psychological investigation. Such a claim might well rest on the observations and theories of psychologists concerning the causes of "lewd desires." Thus premises 1 and 2 can both be easily interpreted as needing justification that appeals to features of the world and, either directly or indirectly, to observation of it. The term *empirical* is often used to mark this dependence. Premise 3, on the other hand, is more a matter of definition. Appeal here is to the meaning of the concept of pornography. Further, part of the process of assessing the truth of not only premise 3, but premise 2 as well, depends on making clear the meaning of "lewd desires."

In deciding whether to accept the premise, "Any material that arouses lewd desires is pornographic," we could simply test it like any other universal generalization—we could try to find a counterexample to it. We could, for example, point out that for some people who are readily inclined to lewd desires, almost anything remotely related to sex could arouse such desires—pictures of fully clothed but physically attractive people, for example. For someone not disposed to lewd desires, material that many would call "pornographic" might only arouse disgust.

In many situations in which a definition-like premise is to be evaluated, this sort of testing by counterexample will probably suffice. But our discussion of the inadequacy of dictionary definitions raises a deeper question than how to determine whether a particular claim about meaning is acceptable. We might wonder how a particular claim could be supported—what kind of theory would provide a basis for a claim about the meaning of "pornographic," or of "lewd desire," or of any other concept. In order to address this deeper question, we present the following analysis of conceptual theories.

Conceptual Theories

Conceptual theories are seldom stated fully and explicitly in ordinary argumentative passages or discourse, although they are common in such disciplines as philosophy, logic, and mathematics, where conceptual clarity is essential. In those disciplines, a conceptual theory will be offered where there is conceptual uncertainty. A philosopher wonders which laws are just and which objects should be considered works of art. A logician wonders which arguments should be considered acceptable. A mathematician wonders how to give an account of a crucial concept such as "number."

We are also called upon to make conceptual distinctions in ordinary, less formal contexts as well. The local community wants to encourage recycling, cut down on the amount of material sent to the local landfill, and generate usable compost. It announces that "lawn and garden wastes" can be brought to a specified site. What are lawn and garden wastes? If someone brings a broken water heater, that is clearly outside the boundaries of the concept. Leaves, grass clippings, and old tomato plants are clearly within it. What about pesticide containers and old fertilizer bags? What about large tree limbs or stumps? Even though the pesticide containers and fertilizer bags are wastes attendant to the lawn and garden, they pose a danger to those who would use the compost and would for this reason be inappropriate. The limbs and stumps, though recyclable in the long run, take such a long time that, without special processing, they too would be inappropriate. The town could more fully articulate the requirements for using the recycling facility. They might add that the site is for "recyclable vegetable matter from lawns and gardens." This might help, at least if the citizens were clear about what counted as recyclable vegetable matter. They might even specify it in more specific ways—for example, require that it be less than one inch in diameter and three feet in length.

This example suggests some important features of conceptual reasoning that apply not only in the more abstract speculation of philosophers, logicians, and mathematicians, but in more everyday contexts. First, we had some clear cases in mind: water heaters were out (though they might be recyclable in a different project); leaves and grass clippings were in. Furthermore, we might raise issues that would help decide less clear-cut cases—for instance, trees and stumps. In trying to clarify the concept, we face the danger that our attempt might not be illuminating, if for instance, the public doesn't already have an idea of what "recyclable vegetable matter" might be. Finally, we might want to make somewhat arbitrary decisions on borders for ease of use. If a one-inch-diameter branch is acceptable because it would decay in a reasonable amount of time, a one-and-one-eighth-inch branch would not take much longer. The exact point at which one draws the boundary might not be critical, though having a boundary might be necessary for actually using the concept as a tool for admitting waste into the public compost pile. If the context changed, for example, if the city bought a wood chipper, then the boundary for acceptable wastes might be altered significantly.

We borrow the model of conceptual theory* from the disciplines of philosophy, logic, and mathematics in order to set out a systematic way of reconstructing definition-like claims found in arguments, even everyday arguments, and as a way of seeing what these claims look like when fully articulated. This way of reconstructing these claims also helps promote critical assessment. In later sections we suggest several techniques for criticizing conceptual theories and tie these criticisms into the larger task of reconstructing and criticizing whole arguments.

A Model for Conceptual Theories

Ideally, a conceptual theory designates precisely the conditions under which a certain concept applies to an object. Some conceptual theories (not necessarily adequate ones) might be:

Example 5.8   *A film is* <u>pornographic</u> *if and only if it explicitly depicts the sex act.*

Example 5.9   *A law is* <u>just</u> *if and only if it is passed democratically.*

Example 5.10   *An object is* <u>a work of art</u> *if and only if:*
(1) It is manmade.
(2) It resembles an object in nature.
(3) It is beautiful.

Example 5.11   *An argument is* <u>valid</u> *if and only if the conclusion follows from the premises.*

Often it is not an isolated concept that is unclear, but rather a group of related concepts. In such a case, a conceptual theory tries both to state the way in which the concepts are related and to designate which objects are to be included under each of the concepts. For example, an ethical theory might try to explain what acts are right, what things are good, and the relation between right and good, in the following way:

---

*We use the uncommon expression "conceptual theory" (rather than the term "definition") for the full account of the meaning of a concept, in order to distinguish it from a simple dictionary definition.

Example 5.12   *An act is* <u>right</u> *if and only if it produces more good than any alternative.*

Something is <u>good</u> *if and only if:*

(1) It is happiness;

OR *(2) It produces happiness.*

Each of these theories is stated in a standard form that is useful for clearly expressing conceptual theories. The part of the statement that comes before "if and only if" indicates what is being explained: the use of a certain concept in a certain context. The word or phrase designating the concept is underlined in these examples. This first part of the statement, before "if and only if," also indicates the context. In Example 5.8, the conditions under which the concept of *pornography* applies to any film are being explained. In Example 5.9, the concept of *justice* is being explained in the context of law. The theory explains the conditions under which a law is just. In Example 5.10, the context is not limited. What is being explained (not necessarily adequately) are the conditions under which the concept of *being an artwork* can apply to any object whatsoever.

The middle phrase in each stated theory—"if and only if"—indicates that what follows is a set of *requirements,* or *conditions to be met;* these select precisely those objects to which the concept applies. The part of the statement following "if and only if" is the list of requirements or conditions. The theory in Example 5.10 claims that the conditions an object must meet in order to be a work of art are:

1. It is manmade.

2. It resembles an object in nature.

3. It is beautiful.

It is claimed that, taken by itself, each condition is a necessary one, in the sense that an object *must* meet this condition in order to be a work of art. There may be other conditions as well, but nothing can be a work of art without satisfying this one. For instance, the theory in Example 5.10 claims that it is necessary for an object to be manmade in order to be a work of art. But each condition by itself is not enough to make the object a work of art. All the conditions must be met in order for an object to qualify fully as art. In this sense, while each condition is necessary, the entire list of conditions is said to be sufficient to ensure that an object is a work of art.

The preceding discussion might be misleading in that it represents conceptual theories as being rather simple, brief formulations standing by themselves; nothing has been said about the context in which a conceptual theory is developed. Typically, a conceptual theory is not offered in isolation from a discussion of (1) why it was chosen, (2) what alternatives were considered and why they were rejected, (3) how the analysis in question is related to a broader area of inquiry, and (4) further conclusions or implications that can be drawn from it. Example 5.12, for instance, is a simplification of an ethical theory that has been the focus of attention in hundreds of books and essays. In these writings, a rationale for choosing this theory over others is carefully discussed. Possible objections to the account are raised, and the reasons for overriding the objections are presented. The analysis or theory of valid arguments introduced in Chapters 2, 3, and 4 and the appendix has been developed through an on-going program in the field of symbolic logic.

Much of the development of a conceptual theory takes place in the context of the dialogue-process discussed in this chapter. In such a dialogue an inadequate account is rejected and a stronger one is constructed to meet objections. You will better understand this process after we explain how a conceptual theory is criticized.

Reconstructing Fragmentary Theories

In an ideal case (in a careful philosophical essay, for example), a conceptual theory will be presented completely and precisely. If it is not presented in the form we have discussed, it is at least apparent how the theory will fit into this form. In less formal discourse, however, theories are sometimes presented in a fragmentary, loosely expressed manner. It is often helpful to reconstruct such a theory in order to organize the task of criticism. To do this, we determine how the writer's or speaker's statements can be fit into the form we have discussed, while both preserving the meaning and making the theory as defensible as possible.

Suppose someone has written:

Example 5.13   *When can we consider two people to be married? This is a particularly difficult question in this age which has seen the rise of self-styled marriage contracts and even homosexual marriage. I would venture to say that marriage requires cohabitation. But it also requires having the intention of sharing love—by which, to be explicit, I mean sexual love.*

As with reconstructing an argument, a good portion of the task is eliminating remarks that are incidental. The first part of the passage conveys the difficulty of saying what marriage is, but it does not state a theory. From the second half of the passage we can elicit the following theory:

Reconstruction   *Two people are* <u>married</u> *if and only if:*

(1) They live together.

(2) They have the intention of sharing sexual love.

Consider a second example that is more fragmentary and therefore requires more extensive reconstruction.

Example 5.14   *Some people claim that the institution of marriage has not declined. But this is due to a misunderstanding of the true nature of marriage: it is a lifelong commitment, ...*

Again, we must eliminate remarks that are not a part of the theory. The first statement in this example has no part in the conceptual theory being reconstructed, although it presents the position the author is criticizing. On the basis of the second statement, however, we could take the writer to be asserting:

Reconstruction 1   *Two people are* <u>married</u> *if and only if they have made a lifelong commitment.*

But we should presume that the writer is more reasonable than this. First, the writer probably has in mind not just any commitment, but the specific commitment to live together. Second, the writer probably sees this as only one condition necessary for marriage. For example, he would probably not believe that two brothers were married just because they had made a lifelong commitment to live together. Often, fragmentary theories present only the most important or controversial conditions. In this case, since the writer has not spelled out the remaining necessary conditions, we should attribute to him only the incomplete theory:

Reconstruction 2   *Two people are* <u>married</u> *if and only if:*

(1) They have made a lifelong commitment to live with each other;

AND (2) other (unspecified) conditions.

We can also use a somewhat similar pattern of reconstruction when we interpret a passage as setting out one of several possible conditions sufficient for us to apply a concept.

Example 5.15   *All people born within the boundaries of the United States are U.S. citizens.*

This can be reconstructed by adding "OR other (unspecified) conditions."

Reconstruction   *A person is a* <u>U.S. citizen</u> *if and only if:*

(1) He or she is born within the boundaries of the United States;

OR (2) other (unspecified) conditions (e.g., he or she is born abroad of parents who are U.S. citizens).

You may find it easier to see the kinds of glaring weaknesses that should be avoided in reconstructing fragmentary theories after we examine the kinds of criticisms that can be made against conceptual theories. We turn to this topic in the next section.

Exercise 5.2   Reconstructing Conceptual Theories

Reconstruct the conceptual theory presented in each of the following passages and present it in the form illustrated in the text. In each case, begin by asking what concept is being discussed in the passage. The words designating this concept should be underlined. Second, look for the condition(s) that explains the concept. The condition(s) should be listed after the phrase *if and only if.* Try to make your statement of conditions as brief as possible. This may require substantial summarizing and rephrasing of some passages. Eliminate any irrelevant material and be as charitable as possible.

1. It is easy to see that squares are precisely those figures with four sides of equal length.

2. Much of the trash hung in art galleries these days is not really art, for to be art something must represent an object found in the real world.

3. It cannot be argued whether this law is just. It is obvious that it is just, since it was passed democratically.

4. Many questions of ethics could be resolved if people would be mindful that an act is right if it produces happiness and wrong if it produces unhappiness.

5. Traffic gridlock is a total standstill of traffic for at least 15 minutes extending eight blocks or more in any direction.*

---

*Adapted from *Science 84*, October 1984, p. 84.

6. A work of art can be characterized by noting two features. First, works of art are the product of man's activity, i.e., they are artifacts. But unlike most tools, which are also artifacts, a work of art is an artifact upon which some society or sub-group of a society has conferred the status of candidate for appreciation.*

7. There are certain indicators of humanhood, included among them are an IQ of at least 20 and probably 40, self-awareness, self-control, a sense of time, and the capability of relating to others.**

8. What is a work of art, granted that there is something in art proper (not only in art falsely so called) to which that name is applied, and that, since art is not craft, this thing is not an artifact? It is something made by the artist, but not made by transforming a given raw material, nor by carrying out a preconceived plan, nor by way of realizing the means to a preconceived end. What is this kind of making? . . . If the making of a tune is an instance of imaginative creating, a tune is an imaginary thing. And the same applies to a poem or a painting or any other work of art . . . the music, the work of art, is not the collection of noises, it is the tune in the composer's head. The noises made by the performers, and heard by the audience, are not the music at all; they are only means by which the audience, if they are listening intelligently (not otherwise), can reconstruct for themselves the imaginary tune that existed in the composer's head.[†]

9. Art is a human activity consisting in this, that one man consciously by means of certain external signs, hands on to others feelings he has lived through, and that other people are infected by these feelings and also experience them. Art . . . is a means of union among men, joining them together in the same feelings, and indispensable for the life and progress toward well-being of individuals and of humanity.[‡]

10. The "positive" sense of the word "liberty" derives from the wish on the part of the individual to be his own master. I wish my life and decisions to depend on myself, not on external forces of whatever

---

*Adapted from George Dickie, "Defining Art," *American Philosophical Quarterly* 6 (1969):253–255.
**Adapted from Joseph Flecher, "Indicators of Humanhood: A Tentative Profile of Man," in the Hasting Center Report 2.5 (November 1972).
[†]R. G. Collingwood, *The Principles of Art* (Oxford: Oxford University Press, 1958), pp. 125 and 139. Reprinted with permission.
[‡]Leo Tolstoy, from "What Is Art" in *Aesthetics: A Critical Anthology*, ed. George Dickie and Richard Sclafani (New York: St. Martin's Press, 1977), p. 66.

kind. I wish to be the instrument of my own, not of other men's acts of will. I wish to be a subject, not an object; to be moved by reasons, by conscious purposes which are my own, not by causes which affect me, as it were, from outside. I wish to be somebody, not nobody; a doer—deciding, not being decided for, self-directed and not acted upon by external nature or by other men as if I were a thing, or an animal, or a slave incapable of playing a human role, that is, of conceiving goals and politics of my own and realizing them.*

The Criticism of Conceptual Theories

The two most effective ways of criticizing a conceptual theory are:

1. Presenting a counterexample.

2. Pointing out that the theory uses concepts that are as difficult to understand as the concept being explained (that is, the theory *does not elucidate*—does not make things clear).

The application of these techniques can be illustrated by considering some examples. Suppose someone offers the following theory to explain what things qualify as works of art.

Example 5.16   *An object is a* <u>work of art</u> *if and only if:*

(1) It is made by an artist.

(2) It expresses the emotions of the artist.

Criticism 1: Presenting a Counterexample   The first kind of criticism—presenting a counterexample—can be done in either of two ways. First, an object that clearly *is* a work of art but does not satisfy the two conditions stated can be described. Or second, an object can be described that clearly is *not* a work of art, but *does* satisfy the two conditions. The theory asserts that these two groups of objects are equivalent; either kind of counterexample just described shows that they are not.

---

*Isaiah Berlin, "Two Concepts of Liberty" in *Four Essays on Liberty* (Oxford: Oxford University Press, 1958), p. 16. Reprinted with permission.

Something that is a work of art but that does not satisfy both conditions is a painting with a purely geometrical design, expressing no emotion whatsoever. This would fail to satisfy the second condition. Something that would not count as a work of art but *would* satisfy the two conditions would be a note written by an artist, demonstrating (inartistically) by use of intemperate language that he is angry.

Although we have provided two counterexamples, even one clear case is enough to show that a conceptual theory is inadequate. No matter how many instances are covered by it, a full-fledged conceptual theory does not merely describe the characteristics of *some* of the objects that fall under a concept. Such a theory would not be particularly interesting. A conceptual theory ideally states that a concept applies to *all and only* those objects having certain specified characteristics.*

Criticism 2: Showing That a Theory Fails to Elucidate The second kind of criticism points out that the theory uses concepts that are as difficult to understand as the concept being explained (that is, the theory fails to elucidate). As in the case of criticizing an argument for lack of clarity, this criticism should not be overused. It is always possible to quibble about terms and to claim that a certain term has not been defined. What is more interesting to point out is that if a person did not already understand the concept being explained, he would not understand the explanation being offered. For instance, in the theory presented as Example 5.16, the term *artist* is used in the explanation of what a work of art is. In order to apply the theory to determine what things to count as works of art, we need to know what an artist is. But if we really did not know what things to count as works of art, we most likely would not know which people to count as artists either, so the theory is not very helpful.**

For this kind of criticism to be justified, it is not necessary for a theory to use a concept as closely related to the one being explained as "artist" is to "art." For example, if someone were to explain the concept of "morally

---

*There is a related criticism that notes the "inapplicability" of a concept in a particular domain. We could, for instance, have an interest in studying political behavior of legislators who are resistant to change and offer the following "stipulative" definition: *A legislator is refractory if and only if he or she refuses to admit any grounds for changing policy.* The problem here is not so much that we have a counterexample, but that given this stipulation it is unlikely that any actual legislator is *refractory*. The concept is inapplicable to the "real" world of actual legislators.
**A particularly vivid example of this failing arises if someone characterizes a work of art as the product of an artist and goes on to characterize an artist as a person who produces a work of art. Such a process is clearly circular and does not help to explain what a work of art is. For this reason these so-called "circular definitions" should be avoided.

right action" simply as "an action that has good consequences," it would be appropriate to point out that "good" is a concept that is not clearer than "right"; so if the theory is going to explain "right" in terms of "good," the theory should also explain what things are good.

Exercise 5.3   **Criticism of Conceptual Theories**

---

1. Criticize each of the following conceptual theories by finding a counterexample (actual or imagined). Counterexamples may be generated in two ways:
   (i) By describing an uncontroversial example to which the concept applies but that does *not* satisfy at least one condition.
   (ii) By describing an example that satisfies *all* the conditions, but to which the concept does *not* apply.

Sample
An action is *morally right* if and only if it is legal.

Counterexample

(i) Jaywalking in order to give first aid	is morally right	but	is *not* legal.
(ii) Insulting a depressed friend in order to make him even sadder	is *not* morally right	but	is legal.

   a. A figure is a *square* if and only if it has four equal sides.
   b. A law is *just* if and only if it is passed by majority vote.
   c. A group is a *society* if and only if it is composed of members who live close to each other.
   d. A film is *pornographic* if and only if it explicitly depicts the sex act.
   e. A person is a *compulsive programmer* if and only if nothing for that person is worthwhile except time spent with the computer.
   f. An argument is *valid* if and only if it has true premises.
   g. A person is *intelligent* if and only if the person scores above 130 on the Stanford–Binet IQ test.
   h. An object is a *work of art* if and only if:
      (1) it is manmade;
      (2) it resembles an object in nature;
      (3) it is beautiful.
   i. A belief is *true* if and only if:
      (1) it is accepted by most people;
      (2) it is supported by some evidence.

    j. A society is *democratic* if and only if:
       (1) it has a constitution;
       (2) it has a court system;
       (3) it has elected officials.
    k. A person is *courageous* if and only if:
       (1) the person has been in a position of danger;
       (2) acted with disregard for personal safety;
       (3) did so for some noble purpose.

2. For each of the following determine whether the conceptual theory should be criticized for failing to elucidate. If it should, indicate which term or terms lack clarity.

    a. An argument is *valid* if and only if it follows from the premises.
    b. An action is *morally right* if and only if it is the sort of action a morally upright man in possession of all the facts would choose.
    c. Something is *good* if and only if:
       (1) it is happiness itself;
       (2) it produces happiness.
    d. Someone is *lascivious* if and only if he is wanton.
    e. A policy is *just* if and only if it provides for a fair distribution of benefits and liabilities.
    f. An object is *beautiful* if and only if it is aesthetically successful. An object is *aesthetically successful* if and only if it springs from creative imagination.
    g. A line is an *arc* if and only if it is part of a circle. An object is a *circle* if and only if it is a locus of points in a plane equidistant from a given point.
    h. A group of organisms is a *society* if and only if its members can communicate about their wants and expectations.
    i. An organism *communicates* with another if and only if its behavior results in the transmission of information from this other organism.
    j. An object is a *work of art* if and only if:
       (1) it is an artifact;
       (2) some society or subgroup of a society has conferred the status of candidate for appreciation on it.*
    k. An object is *appreciated* if and only if, in experiencing it, someone finds it worthy or valuable.
    l. A book is *pornographic* if and only if:
       (1) it offends standards of decency;
       (2) it has no redeeming social value.

---

*Adapted from George Dickie, "Defining Art," *American Philosophical Quarterly* 6 (1969):253–255.

Conceptual Clarification and Argument

The soundness of an argument can depend on an assertion about meaning. Consider this argument about the showing of a film.

Example 5.17   *The film "Last Tango in Paris" shouldn't be shown at the university because it is pornographic. It is quite explicit in its portrayal of the sex act.*

This argument can be restated as follows:

Example 5.18   *(1) "Last Tango in Paris" contains explicit portrayals of the sex act.*

(implicit)   *(2) Any film that contains explicit portrayals of the sex act is pornographic.*

(implicit)   *(3) Pornographic films shouldn't be shown at the university.*

∴   *"Last Tango in Paris" shouldn't be shown at the university.*

Controversy over this argument is most likely to arise concerning premise 2. Since the argument is valid, the argument's soundness hinges primarily on this premise. The conceptual theory implicit in the premise can be reconstructed in this way:

Example 5.19   *A film is pornographic if and only if:*

(1) It contains explicit portrayals of the sex act;

OR   *(2) other unspecified conditions.*

First, we might criticize this theory by pointing out that it contains the expression "explicit portrayals of the sex act." Although this expression might not need further elucidation in many contexts, its application is questionable in the case of "Last Tango in Paris." That film contains, for example, little nudity but highly suggestive bodily movement. The question of whether such portrayals of the sex act are "explicit" might be as difficult to answer as the question of whether the film was pornographic. So this theory fails to elucidate.

Second, we could hold that condition 1 is not a sufficient condition for being a pornographic film. We could cite counterexamples, such as medical films or films having substantial redeeming social and cultural value.

To the extent that we could maintain these criticisms of the conceptual analysis, we have provided grounds for rejecting the premise contained in the passage cited. If this premise is questionable, the soundness of the argument that contains it is also questionable.

Conceptual theories can be related to arguments in another way. Given a conceptual analysis, we can ask about its *implications*.* Its implications are those *conclusions* that can be drawn from it indirectly, with the addition of some set of obvious premises. Suppose we have the conceptual theory:

Example 5.20

A group is a society if and only if:

It is composed of members who live close to each other.

One implication of this analysis is that the American Chemical Society is not a society. This is shown by the argument:

Example 5.21

(1) A group is a society if and only if it is composed of members who live close to each other.

(2) American Chemical Society members do not live close to each other.

∴ *The American Chemical Society is not a society.*

A second, obvious implication would be that the increased mobility of people in a society would result in the group becoming smaller. Here again if we wished to spell this out in detail we could construct an argument in standard form that would have as a conclusion: If a society increases its mobility, then it will become smaller.

We could generate indefinitely many such arguments using the conceptual analysis as a premise. These would be the implications of the conceptual theory in a technical sense, but the term "implication" is often limited to just those conclusions that can be drawn with the help of obvious or relatively uncontroversial supplemental assumptions.

Exercise 5.4

Reconstructing and Criticizing Conceptual Theories and Arguments Based on Them

1. This exercise will give you the opportunity to apply all the techniques of reconstruction and criticism you have learned in this chapter. For each of the following passages, write a paragraph or two in which you first present a reconstruction of the conceptual theory then apply *all*

---

*We introduced the term "implication" in Chapter 4. Our discussion here explains it more fully.

criticisms that are appropriate. Several passages were presented earlier for reconstruction only.

a. Listen then, Thrasymachus began. What I say is that "just" or "right" means nothing but what is to the interest of the stronger party. Well, where is your applause? . . .*

b. Once conceived, the being was recognized as a man because he had man's potential. The criterion for humanity, then, was simple and all embracing: If you are conceived by human parents, you are human.**

c. Any adequate account of morality must concern itself with both what is right and what is good. They are related in this way; a morally right action produces more good than any available alternative. But this leaves open the question of just what counts as a good. Ultimately the goodness of something must be measured in terms of the pleasure it produces in normal individuals.

d. A work of art can be characterized by noting two features. First, works of art are the product of man's activity, i.e., they are artifacts. But unlike most tools, which are also artifacts, a work of art is an artifact upon which some society or sub-group of a society has conferred the status of candidate for appreciation.†

e. There are certain indicators of a humanhood, including among them are an IQ of at least 20 and probably 40, self-awareness, self-control, a sense of time, and the capability of relating to others.‡

f. What is a work of art, granted that there is something in art proper (not only in art falsely so called) to which that name is applied, and that, since art is not craft, this thing is not an artifact? It is something made by the artist, but not made by transforming a given raw material, nor by carrying out a preconceived plan, nor by way of realizing the means to a preconceived end. What is this kind of making . . . If the making of a tune is an instance of imaginative creating, a tune is an imaginary thing. And the same applies to a poem or a painting or any other work of art . . . the music, the

---

*Plato, *The Republic,* 1338, trans. Francis Cornford, Oxford University Press, Oxford, 1945.

**John Noonan, "An Almost Absolute Value in History" in John Noonan, ed., *The Morality of Abortion,* Harvard University Press, Cambridge, 1970, p. 51.

†Adapted from George Dickie, "Defining Art," *American Philosophical Quarterly* 6 (1969):253–255.

‡Adapted from Joseph Flecher, "Indicators of Humanhood: A Tentative Profile of Man," in the Hasting Center Report 2.5 (November 1972).

work of art, is not the collection of noises, it is the tune in the composer's head. The noises made by the performers, and heard by the audience, are not the music at all; they are only means by which the audience, if they are listening intelligently (not otherwise) can reconstruct for themselves the imaginary tune that existed in the composer's head.*

g. Art is a human activity consisting in this, that one man consciously by means of certain external signs, hands on to others feelings he has lived through, and that other people are infected by these feelings and also experience them. Art . . . is a means of union among men, joining them together in the same feelings, and indispensable for the life and progress toward well-being of individuals and of humanity.**

h. The "positive" sense of the word "liberty" derives from the wish on the part of the individual to be his own master. I wish my life and decisions to depend on myself, not on external forces of whatever kind. I wish to be the instrument of my own, not of other men's acts of will. I wish to be a subject, not an object, to be moved by reasons, by conscious purposes which are my own, not by causes which affect me, as it were, from outside. I wish to be somebody, not nobody; a doer—deciding, not being decided for, self-directed and not acted upon by external nature or by other men as if I were a thing, or an animal, or a slave incapable of playing a human role, that is, of conceiving goals and policies of my own and realizing them.†

i. [The original position] is understood as a purely hypothetical situation characterized so as to lead to a certain conception of justice. Among the essentials of this situation is that no one knows his place in society, his class position or social status, nor does anyone know his fortune in the distribution of natural assets and abilities, his intelligence, strength, and the like. I shall even assume that the parties do not know their conception of the good or their special psychological propensities. The principles of justice are chosen behind a veil of ignorance. . . . I shall maintain . . . that the persons in the initial situation would choose two rather different principles;

*R. G. Collingwood, *The Principles of Art* (Oxford: Oxford University Press, 1958), pp. 125 and 139. Reprinted with permission.
**Leo Tolstoy, from "What Is Art" in *Aesthetics: A Critical Anthology*, ed. George Dickie and Richard Sclafani (New York: St. Martin's Press, 1977), p. 66.
†Isaiah Berlin, "Two Concepts of Liberty," in *Four Essays on Liberty* (Oxford: Oxford University Press, 1958), p. 131. Reprinted with permission.

the first requires equality in the assignment of basic rights and duties, while the second holds that social and economic inequalities, for example inequalities of wealth and authority, are just only if they result in compensating benefits for everyone, and in particular for the least advantaged members of society . . .

The first statement of the two principles reads as follows.

First: each person is to have an equal right to the most extensive basic liberty compatible with a similar liberty for others.

Second: social and economic inequalities are to be arranged so that they are both (a) reasonably expected to be to everyone's advantage, and (b) attached to positions and offices open to all.*

2. The following passages contain arguments that depend on definitions or conceptual analyses. (1) State the underlying conceptual theory upon which the argument depends. (2) Reconstruct the argument. (3) Criticize the argument by criticizing the underlying conceptual analysis.

   a. The Museum of Modern Art in New York City shouldn't show any of the French Impressionists. Its mandate is to collect and exhibit the best of modern art, but the French Impressionists painted during the nineteenth century.

   b. People shouldn't be given capital punishment for treason. The state is justified in taking a life only as a penalty for murder. Since treason involves no killing, a traitor doesn't deserve the death penalty.

   c. Since a valid argument is a good argument, all valid arguments must have a true conclusion.

   d. Public sale of pornography violates the civil rights of women. Pornography involves the sexually explicit exploitation of women whether graphically or in words. As such, it promotes the sexualized subordination of women.

   e. The hope of computer scientists to create Artificial Intelligence is misguided. Computers must be programmed. If they're programmed, they can't be creative. If they're not creative, then they can't be intelligent. Perhaps *artificial* intelligence is the correct term. Computer intelligence must remain artificial not genuine.

3. Trace some of the implications of the conceptual theories implicit in the following passages and reconstruct the argument leading to the implications you cite.

---

*John Rawls, *A Theory of Justice* (Cambridge, Mass.: Harvard University Press, 1971), pp. 12, 14, 60.

a. Being a work of art is not some objective characteristic of a thing like its color or shape, nor is it merely a matter of individual taste. Rather, an object becomes a work of art by being put in contention as a candidate for appreciation by people who constitute the art world—those whose life and social relations are dedicated to creating, identifying, assessing, and evaluating objects as works of art.

b. Four ingredients are essential for a revolution. There must be a vision easily grasped by the majority. The vision must be credible. There must be widespread faith and conviction that the vision can be achieved. The new order promised by the vision must be perceived as better than the current order. I believe all these ingredients are present in the changes occurring now during this time we sometimes call "The Computer Revolution." . . .

Revolutionary Ingredients

The four basic ingredients of revolution are present. First, the basic vision—machines behaving intelligently—is easily grasped by the majority. Who can fail to understand the concept of a personal doctor machine? A personal lawyer machine? A personal banker machine? An assembly line robot?

Second, the basic vision is credible. Fifteen years ago, hand calculators were curious toys; now they fit in watches. A $200 box transforms an ordinary TV set into a deep-space battleground. Desk top computers come with advanced interactive graphics. Some of these machines have synthetic voice output, which is a fancy way of saying they talk. Racks offering software cartridges replace record and book displays in many stores. No toys, these cartridges—some contain complete operating systems.

Third, there is faith and conviction that the vision will be achieved. In less than fifteen years, we have seen computers leap from the dark wings into center-stage prominence. Yesterday's room-filling computers have been compressed into the stems of pens; yesterday's multiman-year operating systems are duplicated like phonograph records. How big a leap of faith is required by the ordinary person to go from a $250 chess-champion machine to a personal doctor machine? Or from a block-stacking robot arm to one that builds cars? Not much. Many people believe that intelligently behaving machines are already here.

Fourth, the new order is generally perceived as an improvement over the present. Who would believe that a personal doctor machine that seldom errs and costs, say $2000, is a step backwards in a time of sharply rising medical costs? Or would not help a poor country desperately in need of doctors? Who would believe that a personal lawyer machine that costs little more than a library of popular how-to law books would be a waste of time? You can be sure that there are today shrewd investors backing projects to develop such machines and bring them to market in the next decade. These investors are betting that many consumers will find such machines valuable.

Another way of looking at this: Both hardware and software are now being mass-produced cheaply. Current machines and programs are of such sophistication that the average person believes the generation of intelligent machines is inevitable; it's just a matter of time.*

c. Since I use the term *authority,* in this book and elsewhere, in a wider sense than is common, I will say once more what I mean by it. A person accepts authority whenever he takes decision premises from others as inputs to his own decisions. Rewards and punishments provide the most obvious motives for accepting authority—especially, in organizations, the economic rewards associated with employment. But these are not the only motivating forces. Provided that a person is basically motivated to work toward the goals of an organization, much of the authority he accepts derives from the "logic of the situation." Decision premises are likely to be accepted if there is reason to believe that they are appropriate to the task and the situation. Expert advice is authoritative if it reflects the requirements of the situation. And a communication is frequently accepted as authoritative because it comes from an organizational source that is in a position to be "expert" for that kind of communication.

Closely related to the expertness of a source of decision premises is its legitimacy. The division of labor in an organization establishes expectations that certain kinds of decision premises will emanate from certain departments in the organization. A regulation about personnel practices has prima facie legitimacy if it comes from the personnel department.

Under some circumstances people chafe at accepting authority; under other circumstances they do not feel it as being in the least demeaning. In particular, authority is accepted more readily if it appears consistent with the logic of the situation than if it appears arbitrary or capricious. The experience of freedom and responsibil-

---

*Peter J. Denning, "Editorial: Childhood's End." *Communications of the ACM,* vol. 26 #9 (1983): pp. 617–618. Copyright 1983, Association for Computing Machinery, Inc. Reprinted with permission.

ity does not require complete independence from outside influence. Rather, it requires that the outside constraints and demands be understandable and reasonable. One does not feel unfree handling a sailboat, even though most of one's responses are governed by the moment-to-moment demands of wind and wave.

As the sailboat example illustrates, the physical environment is often as important a source of decision premises as are other human beings. One way to control a driver's behavior is to pass and enforce a speed law; another is to attach a governor to his motor or reduce its horsepower. Human reactions to authority are not particularly different as the authority resides in a human or in a physical source. Human beings react negatively to human authority that they view as inimical or frustrating to their goals; they also react negatively to rain at a picnic.*

d. THE EOLITHIC ALTERNATIVE

The alternative ways of focusing an evaluation listed above are relatively straightforward in conceptualization. . . . Alternative conceptualizations are important and powerful because they direct our attention toward some things and away from other things, just as goals do. New conceptualizations can be helpful in opening our minds to potentially new ways of perceiving and experiencing the world. The eolithic alternative, *partly through the very strangeness of the term,* is meant to serve this thought-provoking, awareness-enhancing function. The notion of eolithism is meant to alert us to the limitations of goals-based evaluation designs, while making us aware of, not simply an alternative technique, but a totally different way of proceeding and perceiving.

The eolithic alternative was introduced into evaluation by David Hawkins. In a highly provocative paper, Hawkins draws on the work of American engineer/novelist Hans Otto Storm to differentiate the principle of eolithism from the principle of design. The principle of design is fundamental to logical, rational, goals-based planning, and evaluation: One must know where one is going, have ways of measuring progress toward the specified goal(s), and select those means most likely to result efficiently in successful goal attainment. An evaluation design specifies a specific purpose and focus for the evaluation, methods to be used to

---

*Herbert A. Simon, *The New Science of Management Decision,* Revised Edition, © 1977, pp. 120–121. Reprinted by permission of Prentice-Hall, Inc., Englewood Cliffs, N.J.

achieve desired evaluation outcomes, measurements to be made, and analytical procedures to be followed. Proposals are usually rated, and funded, on the basis of clarity, specificity, efficiency, and rigor of design. The principle of design is logical and deductive in that one begins with goals (a purpose and desired outcomes) and then decides how best to attain those goals, given resources known in advance (at the design stage) to be available.

The principle of eolithism, on the other hand, directs the investigator to consider how ends can flow from means. One begins by seeing what exists in the natural setting and then attains whatever outcomes one can with the resources at hand. Storm adopted the term "eolithism" for this approach in order to focus our attention on the eoliths that are available all around us, but that are often overlooked in our preoccupation with attainment of preordinate goals and our commitment to follow paradigmatically validated designs. An eolith is "literally a piece of junk remaining from the stone age, often enough rescued from some ancient burial heap. . . . Stones, picked up and used by man, and even fashioned a little for his use". . . . The important point here is that eoliths are discovered in modern times already adapted to and suggestive of some ancient end. More generally, and metaphorically, the principle of eolithism calls to mind a child (or stone-age human) happening upon some object of interest and pondering, "Now what could this be used for?"

There are two ways in which the principle of eolithism is important to creative evaluation, and therefore, important to include in the repertoire of creative evaluators. The principle is important first as a conceptual distinction for understanding how certain programs function. Evaluations of programs operating according to an eolithic principle may be best served by evaluation approaches other than the traditional, goals-based model of evaluation—at least in terms of the standards of utility, feasibility, and propriety. Second, the principle of eolithism is important as an alternative approach to evaluation, regardless of whether the program being evaluated is eolithic in orientation.*

---

*Michael Patton, *Practical Evaluation* (Beverly Hills, Calif.: Sage, 1982), pp. 112–113. Reprinted by permission.

CHAPTER SIX

Why Are Bad Arguments Sometimes Convincing?

A *fallacy* is a kind of argument or appeal that tends to persuade us even though it is faulty. At the beginning of Chapter 4, we indicated that being persuasive can be a virtue in a successful argument, but that it is also a quality that can be used for bad purposes if the argument that is persuasive is not a sound one. Some bad arguments employ tricks and gimmicks that can persuade not only the listeners but also the person presenting the argument. In this chapter, we identify some of the most common kinds of arguments that use trickery to persuade us, and we try to understand why these tricks often work. This approach is intended to serve two purposes. First, you can be on the alert against either committing these kinds of fallacies yourself or against accepting them when they are presented by others. Second, you can learn to explain to someone who commits a fallacy why he might have thought he was offering a good argument when he was not. It is for this latter purpose that we place considerable emphasis on why the fallacies tend to persuade us.

A difficulty in presenting a discussion of fallacies should be understood before we begin. As we introduce each kind of fallacy, we need to state an example that shows clearly the flaw in this kind of argument. But if the flaw is made obvious, you may doubt that this kind of argument will ever fool you. So our clear, illustrative examples may make you feel it unnecessary to take the study of fallacies seriously. It is important, however, to overcome this temptation. Although the flaws will be obvious in many of the examples we present, there is a trick or ploy involved in each kind of fallacy that *can* be effective. It is as though, by seeing a sleight-of-hand artist work slowly, watching him from the most revealing angle, you will be learning how he fools people. Such knowledge doesn't guarantee that you wouldn't be fooled by similar tricks if you were in the audience. But you would have an advantage in knowing what to look for.

Another reason for approaching this subject carefully is that some fallacies depend heavily on emotional context. In making a fallacious appeal to pity, for example, the arguer conveys that it will hurt her feelings if you don't believe what she is claiming. In reading such an example from a textbook it is unlikely that you will be swayed, and you might doubt that such an obvious ploy could work on you in real life. But, given a context of strong emotions, even the best thinkers might be convinced by fallacies such as appeal to pity. And unfortunately, the more important the issue, the more likely it is that strong emotions will come into play and that fallacies will be effective.

What Is a Fallacy?

Not all invalid or unsound arguments are fallacies. Some writers do not distinguish between unsound and fallacious arguments. However, lumping these categories together ignores the aspect of trickery or deceit that is present in fallacies but not in all unsound reasoning. If someone were so misguided in his reasoning as to tell you that you should buy either a car or a motorcycle, therefore you should buy both—his argument would be obviously unsound; but since nothing in this kind of argument tempts us to be persuaded, it is not a fallacy. If, on the other hand, we are told that the streets in our town should not be repaved because the city councilman who proposed the repaving has a financial interest in the cement industry, we are not listening to sound reasoning, but there *is* a tendency for arguments like this to persuade us. Hence it is a fallacy. Although there is an element of trickery in fallacies, not everyone who offers a fallacious argument intends to trick or deceive; the arguer may be deceived by his own reasoning.

There is another reason for not equating fallacies and unsound arguments: some arguments are fallacious even though they are sound. Suppose someone argues:

Example 6.1   *Whatever is less dense than water will float, because such objects won't sink in water.*

Here the premise is just the conclusion stated in different words. The conclusion obviously follows from the premise (since it says the same thing), and the premise happens to be true; so the argument is sound. But it still commits the fallacy we call "begging the question"; although we might be persuaded by it, the premise does not really give a *reason* for believing the conclusion—it just restates it.

Fallacies, then, are arguments that tend to persuade but should not persuade. Of course, we shall not call a bad argument a fallacy just because it happens to persuade some unwary person. There must be a common tendency for an argument of a certain kind to persuade people, even though they should not be persuaded, before we call the argument a fallacy.

Categorizing the Fallacies According to Their Sources of Persuasiveness

We can avoid and explain fallacies more easily if we divide them into categories according to the kinds of tricks they use. There are two primary ways in which an argument can trick you. First, an argument can trick you by something similar to sleight of hand as used by a magician or illusionist. Second, an argument can trick you by confusing emotion with reason, or more precisely, by providing a motive for belief in place of support for belief. In addition, some particularly dangerous fallacies use both these tricks at once. We shall deal first with *sleight-of-hand* fallacies, explaining this source of persuasiveness and the forms it can take and describing seven fallacies we place in this category. Next we deal with *motive-in-place-of-support* fallacies and with the fallacies that draw from both sleight of hand *and* motive in place of support as sources of persuasiveness.

Two Kinds of Sleight of Hand

A sleight-of-hand artist uses two kinds of tricks to persuade you that you saw something that really didn't happen. One distracts you so you don't see the false move. The other substitutes counterfeit objects—props or dummies—for the things they resemble. Sleight-of-hand fallacies use these same two tricks. The first kind of argument fools you by distracting your attention from the weak point of the argument. The second kind of argument appears to be sound because it is similar in form to an argument that *is* sound.

Accordingly, *distraction* and *counterfeit* are the two kinds of sleight-of-hand fallacies. We discuss three common fallacies under the first category, and four under the second category.

Sleight of Hand: Distraction

1. False dilemma

2. Slippery slope

3. Straw man

False Dilemma   The technique of distraction is easiest to spot in the case of false dilemma. Here is an example of this fallacy:

Example 6.2   *Either we pass a constitutional amendment requiring a balanced budget, or we let deficits ruin us.*

The implicit premise, obviously, is that we should not let deficits ruin us, and the conclusion is that we should pass a constitutional amendment requiring a balanced budget. This type of argument is typical of a false dilemma. *The arguer claims that there are two alternatives and that one is unacceptable, so we should choose the other. But in fact, there are more alternatives than the two stated.* We are distracted by how horrible, or preposterous, one of the alternatives is, and we tend not to ask whether these are the *only* two alternatives. In Example 6.2 there are other alternatives. We could scale down our deficits year by year. We could continue to run deficits each year, but deficits of more manageable size, representing a smaller percentage of federal revenues. It *may* be that an amendment should be passed requiring a balanced budget. But if this is true, it is not because the *only* alternative is letting deficits ruin us.

It is interesting that the false dilemma argument is *valid*. Its form is:

Either A or B.

Not A.

∴   *B.*

But if it is really a *false* dilemma argument, then it is unsound because the premise *Either A or B* is not true. In fact, there are other alternatives. Examples 6.3, 6.4, and 6.5 are also examples of false dilemma. Notice that one premise and the conclusion are often left implicit. Sometimes a false dilemma is stated in the form: If we don't choose alternatve A, then we will be left with the (undesirable) outcome of alternative B.

Example 6.3   *If we don't give people the death penalty, they will get off with a few years in prison and then parole. So we should not abolish the death penalty.*

Example 6.4   *Either we allow abortion or we force children to be raised by parents who don't want them.*

And, of course, there was the motto from the era of war protesters and their opponents:

Example 6.5   *America: Love it or leave it.*

Notice how easy it is to be distracted from the issue of whether these are the only alternatives.

Slippery Slope   *Slippery slope* is similar to false dilemma. *The slippery slope fallacy occurs when we object to something on the grounds that if it is done, something else will happen or is likely to happen as a result, and then something else, and then something else, right down the "slippery slope" to a situation that is clearly undesirable.* For example:

Example 6.6   *Now they just want to register handguns. Next it will be all guns, and then they'll want to take our guns away. We'll be set up for a police state.*

As with false dilemma, our attention is distracted by the thought of how horrible the situation is that threatens us (according to the argument). We do not attend to the question of whether all the steps down the slippery slope are really connected. If it is doubtful that all the steps are connected, as in Example 6.6, then an argument of this sort is fallacious.

Another example of the slippery slope fallacy is:

Example 6.7   *We must keep the classics of European thought at the core of our college curriculum. If we move our curriculum in a multicultural direction, quality will be sacrificed in the name of diversity. Pretty soon we'll be treating pop music and pulp fiction as serious art.*

In Example 6.7 the conclusion of the argument is made explicit in the first sentence. When it is not, as in Example 6.6, the implicit conclusion is usually that the first step on the slope should not be taken.

Straw Man   The *straw man* fallacy is more complicated than false dilemma or slippery slope, but it also relies on the sleight-of-hand technique of distraction. *Straw man consists of making your own position appear strong by making the opposing position appear weaker than it actually is.* An example is:

Example 6.8   *Now is no time to reduce defense spending. Senator Toski claims we should spend less, but he apparently thinks the potential instability in Eastern Europe poses no threat to our interests.*

Your attention is drawn to how weak the senator's argument is for reduced defense spending, and there is a strong tendency to move directly to the conclusion that we should not reduce such spending. We do not stop to think that some opposing arguments are much tougher to knock down. If you are really trying to test a position that you hold, you should build the *strongest* case you can in opposition to it, not the weakest.

Here is another example of the straw man fallacy:

Example 6.9   *We desperately need a nationalized health care program. Those who oppose it think that the private sector will take care of the needs of the poor. But this has not been the case in the past and will not be in the future.*

The fact that *this* particular argument against nationalized health care can be easily refuted is irrelevant to whether we should in fact have such a program.

Keep in mind that the person who commits this fallacy cites *someone else's* argument. She points out the weakness in this argument, and uses the weakness as a reason for holding an opposing view. Do not confuse this with false dilemma, in which it is claimed that there are only two alternatives and one of them is unacceptable, so we must choose the other. In the case of the straw man fallacy, it is someone else's argument that is claimed to be unacceptable. The flaw here is that stronger arguments than the one cited support the same view. The flaw in false dilemma is that there are other alternatives than the two cited.

To keep the two fallacies distinct in your mind, contrast these examples:

Example 6.10   **False dilemma:** *Either we ban all guns or we let crime run amok.* (Arguer claims there are only two alternatives; one is unacceptable.)

Example 6.11   **Straw man:** *We should ban all guns. Those who oppose a ban on guns don't think very many crimes involve guns, but statistics prove otherwise.* (Arguer makes his position look strong by citing an opposing argument that is obviously weak.)

Exercise 6.1   **Identifying Fallacies: False Dilemma, Slippery Slope, Straw Man**

---

1. We have discussed three of the seven sleight-of-hand fallacies. You can solidify what you have learned by identifying the fallacies in the following passages and by writing a brief description of why each fallacy might be persuasive. There may be more than one fallacy in some passages.
   a. Sample:
      You're either part of the solution or part of the problem.
      Passage A—false dilemma—could be persuasive because the thought that you might be part of the problem distracts you from considering that there are more alternatives than these two. A third alternative is that you are *both* part of the solution and part of the problem.
   b. I'm in favor of legalized gambling. There are those who oppose it, but they apparently think that anything that's fun is sinful.
   c. If you're not going to save a *lot* of money on fuel, then you might as well not waste the effort. Putting weather stripping around your doors doesn't save you that much.
   d. The main argument for drug legalization seems to be a hedonistic one—that we're all entitled to pursue any pleasure we want, regardless of the consequences. But surely any pleasure drugs bring is far outweighed by the harm they cause. I oppose legalization.
   e. In the early stages the compulsive gambler doesn't behave differently from the casual gambler. He plays a little poker on Friday night; he bets on the Sunday football games. Slowly, he begins to bet more. Winning becomes the high point of his week. A loss means several days of depression. Finally, he runs out of his own money and is forced to get it any way he can. He begs, borrows, and ultimately steals. Beware! That first flip of the coin can spell disaster.
   f. Those who support the practice of prayer in the classroom must believe that there is no constitutional provision for separation of church and state. But such a separation is clearly provided for. Prayer in the classroom cannot be tolerated.
   g. I urge you to vote against the bill requiring a deposit on all bottles. There are many kinds of litter besides bottles. We should require a

deposit on everything that might be thrown on the roadside or on nothing.

h. I think it would be a mistake to return to the welfare programs of the sixties and seventies. If we give people something, they come to expect it. And this attitude will spread to the point that everyone thinks society will support them. Pretty soon we'll be left with an ineffective socialism. There are many people who disagree with me about this—who support welfare. But they seem to think that it is beneath the dignity of people on welfare to do the same kinds of menial jobs that many of us had to do.

2. Creating examples of fallacies: Write one example (of your own creation) of each of the following fallacies: false dilemma, slippery slope, straw man.

Sleight of Hand: Counterfeit

1. Affirming the consequent

2. Denying the antecedent

3. Equivocation

4. Begging the question

The second kind of trick the sleight-of-hand artist uses is to substitute props and dummies for the objects they resemble. The counterfeit fallacies can trick you in the same way—they can seem like good arguments because they resemble good arguments. The first two fallacies we discuss are sometimes categorized as formal fallacies, because they can be recognized by their form or pattern. It is more helpful, however, to use categories that remind you of the ways in which fallacies can persuade you.

Affirming the Consequent and Denying the Antecedent   *Affirming the consequent* and *denying the antecedent* resemble two of the most common valid argument patterns—*modus ponens* (or *affirming the antecedent*) and *modus tollens* (or *denying the consequent*). We introduced both the valid and fallacious forms in Chapter 2 and mentioned them again in Chapter 4. We can display these patterns as follows. (Remember, in an if-then sentence, the "if" part is the antecedent and the "then" part is the consequent.)

VALID

Modus Ponens (Affirming the Antecedent)

(1) If A, then B.

(2) A.

∴ B.

Example 6.12

(1) If I'm in Reno, then I'm in Nevada.

(2) I'm in Reno. (This premise affirms the antecedent.)

∴ I'm in Nevada.

VALID

Modus Tollens (Denying the Consequent)

(1) If A, then B.

(2) Not B.

∴ Not A.

Example 6.14

(1) If I'm in Reno, then I'm in Nevada.

(2) I'm not in Nevada. (This premise denies the consequent.)

∴ I'm not in Reno.

FALLACIOUS

Affirming the Consequent

(1) If A, then B.

(2) B.

∴ A.

Example 6.13

(1) If I'm in Reno, then I'm in Nevada.

(2) I'm in Nevada. (This premise affirms the consequent.)

∴ I'm in Reno.

FALLACIOUS

Denying the Antecedent

(1) If A, then B.

(2) Not A.

∴ Not B.

Example 6.15

(1) If I'm in Reno, then I'm in Nevada.

(2) I'm not in Reno. (This premise denies the antecedent.)

∴ I'm not in Nevada.

In these initial examples of the fallacies, the conclusion obviously does not follow from the premises. It is apparent that I could be in Nevada without being in Reno, and I could be outside of Reno but still be in Nevada. But in other arguments of the same patterns it is easy to get confused. Consider these examples:

AFFIRMING THE CONSEQUENT

Example 6.16   *If the president does a good job, the economy remains stable. The economy has remained stable. So the president has done a good job.*

DENYING THE ANTECEDENT

Example 6.17   *If he denies that he knows her, then he's been cheating on me. He admitted that he knows her. So he hasn't been cheating on me.*

These *are* fallacies. The president could have done a poor job, even though the economy remained stable. Maybe the economy remained stable *in spite of* mistakes the president made. And the man in Example 6.17 could be cheating on his woman friend even though he didn't get caught. But the reasoning is good enough that it will often get by. Why is this? We have suggested that these fallacies resemble valid arguments. But which valid arguments? Surely we don't transpose the second premise and the conclusion of Example 6.16, changing it into the following *modus ponens* argument:

Example 6.18   *If the president does a good job, the economy remains stable. The president has done a good job. So the economy has remained stable.*

We are more likely to confuse the first premise of Example 6.16, *If the president does a good job, the economy remains stable*, with *If the economy remains stable, the president has done a good job*. This would make 6.16 a valid argument. Perhaps we tend to confuse *If A, then B*, with *If B, then A*, because if B follows from A, it is fairly common for A to follow from B also. (If there's smoke, there's fire; if there's fire, there's smoke. If someone flips the switch, the lights come on; if the lights are on, someone flipped the switch.)

Thus, we might be fooled by Example 6.17 because we might confuse *If he denies that he knows her, then he's been cheating on me*, with *If he's been cheating on me, then he will deny that he knows her*. This confusion *does* seem likely. And this change in the first premise would make 6.17 a valid argument.

In general, then, the fallacies of affirming the consequent and denying the antecedent can be persuasive because we tend to confuse *If A, then B* with *If B, then A*; and once we make this change, these fallacious forms become valid. When you identify these fallacies in Exercise 6.2, see if this account is not a plausible one.

Equivocation   We discussed *equivocation* at some length in Chapter 5. We review it here with a focus on why this fallacy can be persuasive. When a word or expression occurs in more than one premise of an argument, it must have the same meaning in each occurrence. If it shifts meaning from one premise to the next, it is guilty of *equivocation*.

Example 6.19

You are perfectly willing to believe in miracles like a man landing on the moon. If this is so, you shouldn't be so skeptical of the miracles described in the Bible.

In the first occurrence, "miracle" means something that is amazing, that you wouldn't have thought could be done. But in the second occurrence, "miracle" means something that defies the laws of nature. The fact that the first kind of miracle occurred doesn't make it more likely that the second kind occurred.

Example 6.20 might commit the fallacy of equivocation if it shifts the meaning of the term *small*.

Example 6.20

In these times of scarce resources, people who drive small cars are to be commended. McGruder drives a small car. So McGruder is to be commended.

A sense of "small car" that would make the first premise true would be "light car with a small engine." Perhaps McGruder's car has a small wheelbase, but is a gas-guzzler.

Here is a more subtle example:

Example 6.21

The law says that insane people should not be punished. Anyone who murders must be insane. So murderers should be treated in mental wards, not punished.

The sense of "insane" that makes the first premise true concerns a person being unable to act intentionally or not knowing right from wrong. The sense of "insane" that might make the second premise true concerns a person being abnormally cruel (which could still allow that the person knows that cruelty is wrong). But if the same definition of "insane" is used in both premises, then one of them becomes false.

Why can arguments such as these be persuasive? Like the other counterfeit fallacies, they closely resemble good arguments. Typically, an argument that commits the fallacy of equivocation would be valid if it were not for the shift in meaning. (In 6.21, for example, it would follow that murderers should not be punished.) Furthermore, all the premises can be made true by the shift in meaning (and sometimes the shift in meaning is barely noticeable). So if you lose track of the fact that the meaning has shifted, an argument that commits this fallacy seems sound.

Begging the Question   An argument that *begs the question* is fallacious even though it might be sound (see also page 134). For example:

Example 6.22   *Whatever is less dense than water will float, because such objects won't sink in water.*

Here the premise happens to be true, and the conclusion follows from the premise; but the reason the conclusion follows is because it just restates the premise in different words.*

The fallacy is fairly obvious in an argument as short as the one in Example 6.22, but in a longer, more complicated argument, you might not see that the conclusion is just a restatement of one of the premises. Consider, for example, the following exchange:

Example 6.23   **Realtor:** *If you're choosing between the house our competitors have listed and this one, you ought to buy this one. You'd make more money on it.*

Customer: *Why would I make more money on it?*

Realtor: *Well, you said you planned to sell in five years. You have to consider real appreciation, not just how many dollars you pay and how much you sell for. That means figuring in the rate of inflation. I would estimate that at the rate houses like this appreciate, taking account of fees, taxes, and so on, in five years you'd come out with a greater net profit on this house than on the other one.*

All the realtor has really said is that you'd make more money on this one because you'd make more money on this one.

In any valid argument, fallacious or not, the conclusion is, in a sense, "contained in" the premises. Taken together, the premises guarantee the truth of the conclusion. But remember that the object of presenting an argument is to make the conclusion more reasonable to believe. To accomplish this, you must use premises which, individually, will be taken to be more certain than the conclusion. *If a premise is either a restatement of the conclusion or a statement that will be equally doubtful on grounds similar to those which make the conclusion doubtful, then the argument doesn't make any progress toward supporting the conclusion, and is guilty of begging the question.*

The following example begs the question even though the conclusion does not simply restate a premise:

---

*The name "begging the question" indicates that an argument is *missing* (begging) the question at issue by simply assuming what it is trying to prove.

Example 6.24   *The Bible says God exists, and everything the Bible says is true since God wrote it. Therefore God exists.*

Anyone who doubted the conclusion—God exists—would have the same reason for doubting the premise that God wrote the Bible.

Review

A fallacy is a kind of argument that tends to persuade, even though it is a bad argument. So far, we have explained two ways in which a fallacy can be persuasive: by *distraction* (taking your attention away from the weak point of the argument); and by *counterfeit* (resembling a good argument). We described seven of the most common fallacies that use these tricks. They are listed below. As you read through the list, try to state a general definition of each kind of fallacy. If you have difficulty, refer back to the appropriate section.

SLEIGHT OF HAND: DISTRACTION

1. *false dilemma* Either we pass a constitutional amendment requiring a balanced budget or we let deficits ruin us.

2. *slippery slope* Now it's register handguns. Next it will be all guns. Then they'll ban guns, and we'll be set up for a police state.

3. *straw man* Senator Toski claims we should spend less on defense. He must think the instability in Eastern Europe poses no threat to our interests.

SLEIGHT OF HAND: COUNTERFEIT

1. *affirming the consequent* If the economy is healthy, unemployment is down. Unemployment *is* down. So the economy is healthy.

2. *denying the antecedent* If she loves you, she'll marry you. She doesn't love you. So she won't marry you.

3. *equivocation* Insane people shouldn't be punished. Someone who commits murder must be insane. So murderers should not be punished.

4. *begging the question* The Bible says God exists. Everything in the Bible is true, since God wrote it. So God does exist.

Exercise 6.2   More Sleight-of-Hand Fallacies

1. The following are all fallacies from the sleight of hand: counter-feit category (which includes affirming the consequent, denying the antecedent, equivocation, and begging the question). Identify the fallacy in each selection and discuss briefly why it might be persuasive.

   a. If everybody benefited from the present education system, then there would be no reason to change it drastically. But not everybody is helped by current teaching methods. So we should radically overhaul the way in which kids are educated.

   b. Callous though it sounds, I do not believe we have an obligation to redistribute wealth to the less fortunate. The reason that I believe this is that what a person earns is rightfully hers. No one else has a claim to it.

   c. They say that nice guys finish last. So let's finish last to show that we're nice guys.

   (HINT: Write the first premise as an if-then statement.)

   d. It won't be dangerous to ride with Gary, because he hasn't been drinking. If he had been drinking, it would be dangerous.

   e. The senator's denial that he was influenced by lobbyists is hardly credible, since it is obvious that he was not telling the truth.

   f. If Alvin really loved Alice, then he would have given up his evil ways. He does seem to have reformed—he's even quit hanging out in pool halls and doing drugs. He must really love Alice.

   g. I believe that reality is made up of more than material objects—there is also spirit. The spiritual aspect of reality is demonstrated by man's interest in such things as art and religion, as well as material well-being.

   h. Placing a lid on federal spending is not a wise policy. If the lid bill had achieved its purposes in California, it would be reasonable to pass such a bill at the federal level also. But the California bill didn't achieve its purposes.

   i. The welfare state rests on the ideal that man is unselfish. But it is futile to attempt to run a society on any other principle than that of individuals seeking their own interests, since all humans are essentially selfish. Even actions that seem charitable actually have some selfish end, such as gaining respect of others, or soothing a guilty conscience.

2. Creating examples of fallacies: Write one example (of your own creation) of each of the following fallacies: affirming the consequent, denying the antecedent, equivocation, begging the question.

3. Identifying fallacies—comprehensive review: The following is a collection of fallacies from both sleight-of-hand categories (distraction and counterfeit). It may include instances of false dilemma, slippery slope, straw man, affirming the consequent, denying the antecedent, equivocation, and begging the question. Identify the fallacy in each selection and discuss briefly why it might be persuasive.

a.

FUNKY WINKERBEAN   **Tom Batiuk**

PHILOSOPHY I-(Prerequisite-five hours of sitting around doing nothing)

Philosophy I is where you learn how the great thinkers of the past view man's existence, such as Descartes who said,"I think, therefore I am."

It turns out he was right because he stopped thinking a while back, and now he no longer is!

© 1980 Field Enterprises, Inc. Courtesy of Field Newspaper Syndicate.

b. If you can't lick them, join them.
c. According to my theory, men who had doting mothers will seek women who are hard, independent, and not overly affectionate. This is a reaction to having been smothered by their mother's affection. Now if my theory is correct. Ed would be attracted to someone like Carla. Ed *is* attracted to Carla. So I would say that my theory is correct.
d. Show me a good loser and I'll show you a loser.
e. If a society encourages freedom of thought and expression, then creativity will flourish. New theories will replace old ones; traditions will be challenged; inventiveness will reign. The eighteenth century was perhaps the period of American history when creativity flourished most, showing the degree to which free thought was encouraged during that period.
f. Most students go to college to improve their job prospects. But the fact is that many areas of study—particularly the liberal arts—don't strike students as preparing them for a vocation. They fail to see that living a life enriched by ideas *is* a kind of vocation. So when they quit college to get a job they are making a big mistake.

g. If I continue to live in the dorm, the noise will make me nervous and irritable. I'll worry all the time about not getting my studying done. I'm honestly afraid that I'd have to start seeing a psychiatrist about these problems. I'd have to borrow the money for the psychiatrist from my parents. And if I flunk out of school I wouldn't be able to get a good job to pay them back. The alternative is to move into a nice apartment complex near campus. It's pretty expensive, but actually it might save money in the long run.

h. So the thing to do when working on a motorcycle, as in any other task, is to cultivate the peace of mind which does not separate one's self from one's surroundings. When that is done successfully, then everything else follows naturally. Peace of mind produces right values, right values produce right thoughts. Right thoughts produce right actions and right actions produce work which will be a material reflection for others to see of the serenity at the center of it all.*

(HINT: This might be interpreted as committing one of the fallacies "in reverse.")

Note: What seems to be a fallacy may not be one. Some additional arguments that may or may not commit fallacies are presented at the end of the chapter.

Emotion and Reason in Argument

In the first part of this chapter, we discussed fallacies that can be persuasive because of the sleight-of-hand tricks they play. In this part, we discuss a source of persuasiveness that is quite different: confusing emotion with reason. We identify three prominent fallacies that draw their persuasiveness from this source. Then, to complete our discussion of fallacies, we identify two fallacies that rely on a combination of sleight of hand and

---

*Robert M. Pirsig, *Zen and the Art of Motorcycle Maintenance: An Inquiry into Values* (New York: Bantam Books, 1974), p. 290.

emotion in order to persuade and that can be extremely effective as a result.

Before examining the illegitimate use of emotion in argument, note that there are many cases in which it is quite appropriate for an argument to appeal to emotion. We may become clearer about what is involved in fallacious appeals to emotion if we contrast these cases to legitimate ones.

Suppose a friend tries to convince you to wear a helmet when you ride your motorcycle. He describes some severe head injuries received by other riders who didn't wear helmets. He reminds you how miserable your friends and parents would be if you suffered such an injury. And he points out that if you wear a helmet you are much less likely to be seriously injured. Your friend has certainly appealed to emotion in his argument, but was his appeal illegitimate? It would hardly seem so. When you are considering an action that will affect you or other people for good or for ill, one kind of consideration that is relevant is just *how* well or *how* badly you or others will be affected. If certain consequences of your actions have only limited probability of occurring, or will occur far into the future, or will be removed from your sight, then you tend to ignore them. You need to be reminded graphically of them—have them brought before your consciousness as though they were immediate.

Consider a different example. Suppose that you are deciding whether to give political support to a government policy that may make war more probable. If a friend reminds you of the horrors of modern warfare, all its innocent victims, the chances of escalation leading to nuclear war, the devastation that such a war would wreak upon the planet—all of this appeals to emotions, but is certainly legitimate.

The *amount of weight* that should be given to such an appeal, however, is open to question. The possible bad consequences could be pictured so graphically that you would lose sight of any potential benefits of the policy in question—benefits that should be weighed against possible risks. Suppose the policy involves making a strong response to a foreign power that has acted aggressively. Perhaps the reaction in question is not so strong as to *significantly* raise the probability of war. Perhaps a weaker reaction would have some chance of leading to war also, because it would encourage future aggression. All these considerations must be weighed; they must not be lost sight of. An appeal that arouses emotion, even if it is relevant to the issue, runs the risk of leaving a one-sided impression because of the way such an appeal can command your attention. The point remains, nevertheless, that an emotional appeal can be a legitimate kind of appeal, as we have seen from our two examples.

When Is an Emotional
Appeal Illegitimate?

Let's contrast the cases we have just described to one in which the appeal to emotion is illegitimate. Suppose that you are deciding which of two candidates is better qualified for office. You discuss the choice with your parents and they get upset about the candidate you are favoring. They support the other candidate and claim that you are being disloyal. You decide their candidate isn't so bad after all.

If the question to be decided is which candidate is better qualified, then the appeal to loyalty is an illegitimate appeal to emotion.* There is a difference between this example and the earlier examples in this chapter. In the earlier examples, the question was whether a certain act should be done: Should you wear a helmet? Should you support a certain foreign policy? These actions might have certain consequences—injury, death—and considering these consequences arouses emotions. But these consequences *must* be considered in order to determine whether the actions in question should be taken. In the candidate example, however, the question of whether your choice will upset your parents is *not* relevant to whether your candidate is better qualified. The fact that your parents want you to be loyal might give you a *motive* for believing that their candidate is better. But this consideration does not provide support, in the sense of evidence, for the belief that their candidate is better qualified. Does the candidate in question have good judgment? Would his programs succeed? Is he honest? These are the relevant kinds of considerations that would determine his qualifications.

We must be careful here to make a certain distinction. If you are considering whether to state your political preference in front of your parents, or even whether to act on the basis of your preference when you go to vote, then the question of loyalty *might* be considered relevant. This question of how to act is a question of ethics. Should you let family loyalty override your own political principles? You may feel that one of these factors clearly outweighs the other. For example, you may feel that it is much more important to maintain your own integrity by voting according to your conscience than to remain loyal to your family. But although this factor of loyalty might be outweighed when it comes to voting, it is totally

---

*We are not, at this point, identifying the particular fallacy being committed here. We are still in the process of characterizing a general category of fallacies. Depending on how your parents stated their argument, they could be committing any one or more of the fallacies to be discussed later: *appeal to force, appeal to pity, or prejudicial language.*

irrelevant when it comes to deciding which candidate is better qualified. When you are deciding how to act, all motives are in a sense relevant. But when you are deciding what to believe, motives are not relevant. The fact that it would be more comfortable for you to believe that your parents' candidate is better qualified gives you a *motive* for holding that belief, but it does *not* provide evidence that the belief is true.

In keeping with this distinction, we shall adopt the name "motive in place of support" for the category of fallacies that makes an illegitimate appeal to emotion. Three fallacies within this category deserve discussion. Two of them are commonly recognized and have acquired names: "appeal to force" and "appeal to pity." The other, although it is commonly used, is not as commonly identified and is referred to by different names at different times. We call it "prejudicial language."

Motive in Place of Support

1. Appeal to force

2. Appeal to pity

3. Prejudicial language

Appeal to Force and Appeal to Pity   *Appeal to force* and *appeal to pity* can best be explained together because they have an important similarity. *When a person gets you to agree to something because he will be hurt if you don't agree, this is an appeal to pity. If someone gets you to agree because he will hurt you if you don't agree, this is an appeal to force.** In both cases, the factor that makes the argument persuasive is motive in place of support. That is, both appeal to force and appeal to pity make it undesirable not to believe that the conclusion is true even though they do not give support (in the sense of evidence) for believing that the conclusion is true. This seems fairly clear in the following examples.

APPEAL TO FORCE

Example 6.25   *So you're an environmentalist. I'd think twice about that if I were you. There are a lot of us miners in this town who aren't too partial toward environmentalists.*

---

*Notice that although this fallacy is called *appeal to force,* the harm threatened need not be physical harm.

Example 6.26   **Diplomat A:** *We think the interference of your country in our internal affairs is unjustified.*

Diplomat B: *That is a very unwise opinion to hold when we are considering a trade embargo against you.*

APPEAL TO PITY

Example 6.27   *I am qualified for the job. I have a little experience in the area, and I've been out of work for two months so I really need the money.*

Example 6.28   *Your mother and I devoted years of our lives raising you to believe in the Christian religion. Don't you know how it hurts us for you to abandon those beliefs now?*

In each of these examples, it is not that a certain belief is made desirable, but rather that it would be harmful (either to yourself or others) to *not* hold a certain belief—that environmentalism is a bad policy, that a political action was justified, and so on.

It might seem unlikely that you would be fooled into *believing* these things; rather, you might just *say* you believed them in order to avoid certain undesirable consequences. If this were the case, you really couldn't be accused of committing a fallacy—you might be doing a very reasonable thing. The problem is, we often end up convincing ourselves that we really do believe the position we publicly state. Perhaps we convince ourselves because we don't like to admit that we didn't stand up for the truth. Let's look at two other examples in a little more detail.

APPEAL TO PITY

Example 6.29   *A friend asks you to write a letter of recommendation for him, for a job he is not really qualified for. You write the letter saying he is qualified, because you know it will hurt his feelings if you don't. (And you end up convincing yourself that he really was qualified.)*

APPEAL TO FORCE

Example 6.30   *You are asked to evaluate the performance of your supervisor at work. She has done a very poor job, but you give her a high evaluation because she has made it clear that she can make it tough on you if you don't. (You end up saying to yourself, "I didn't really lie. The supervisor did a pretty good job.")*

Two issues must be kept separate in situations like these. One is whether you should state something in order to avoid harm to others or to yourself, even though the statement is probably not true. This is a moral question, not a question of logic, and the answer will vary depending on the circumstances. The second issue is whether you should believe such a statement if you do make it. This *is* a matter of logic, and the answer is no. To do so would be to commit a fallacy. It is important to see that these two issues are often confused. The desirability of a conclusion and the evidence for it (the motive and the support) seem to operate as competing forces; either one can be strong enough to produce belief, even though they are totally different. If you think about the plausibility of Examples 6.29 and 6.30, about the discomfort people feel in acknowledging that they have lied, and about the uncanny ability of people to tailor their beliefs to make themselves comfortable, then you will probably agree that appeals to force and to pity *can* be persuasive.

One point of clarification: We have spoken loosely of a fallacy being "committed," without specifying whether it is the person offering the fallacious argument or the person accepting it who is committing the fallacy. It seems reasonable to say that *both* parties are committing the fallacy. However, as stated before, if a person makes a statement in order to avoid harm to himself or others but does not believe it, then he is not committing a fallacy of appeal to force or pity. His *argument* is nevertheless fallacious, and might mislead whoever hears it.

Prejudicial Language   An argument can also provide a motive for belief without providing support for belief by using *prejudicial language*. Consider these examples:

Example 6.31   *I hope you aren't going to say that you support the backward philosophy of emphasizing basic skills in primary and secondary education. I tend to take the progressive view that there are many things at least as important for students to learn as reading, writing, and arithmetic.*

Example 6.32   *He outgrew the naive view of man as a mechanistic, robotlike creature, and came to the more sophisticated view of man as autonomous and possessing a free will.*

Identifying a position using such words as "backward" or "naive" provides a motive for rejecting the position, and using such words as "progressive" and "sophisticated" provides a motive for adopting a position, all without giving any evidence either for or against the position.

There is an element of trickery or distraction here, since in each example two issues are falsely presented as one: (1) Do you support teaching basic skills? (2) Is such a philosophy backward? and (1) Did he give up a mechanistic view of man? (2) Is such a view naive? But the main persuasive factor is motive in place of support. You would often not separate the two issues and argue each one through, because the prejudicial language causes you to either endorse or reject the position in question before any discussion can get started.

Exercise 6.3

Identifying Fallacies: Appeal to Force, Appeal to Pity, and Prejudicial Language

---

Identify instances of the fallacies of appeal to force, appeal to pity, and prejudicial language that occur in the following passages:

1. How can you call my serve "out" when it's that close and I'm behind five games to one?

2. Politicians should keep in mind, when they are deciding whether abortion is right or wrong, that we pro-lifers have big families who grow up to be part of the voting public. Pro-abortionists tend to have no families at all.

3. You've been contradicting everything I say. The point I'm making is an obvious one. Nationalized health care will ruin the quality of medical practice.

4. Congressman Adamson has been critical of every policy this administration has proposed. Perhaps we should instruct him in the errors of his ideology by suggesting to him that we can arrange an audit of his income tax.

5. I've poured my soul into the task of writing this novel. I've worked on it late at night after spending the day on my regular job. I've endured rejections, gone through revisions, and at last it's published. What do you think about it?

6. You say it's government spending that has caused high federal deficits? Sounds like you're falling for what the compassionless penny-pinchers are preaching.

7. Do I need to remind you how difficult it might be if you decide that you won't go out with me? After all, I help make personnel decisions around here.

8. More tax "incentives" for the ultrarich? When are you going to grow out of that outdated, Reaganite, "trickle-down" mentality?

Double Trouble

1. Appeal to authority

2. Attacking the person

These two fallacies—and particularly *attacking the person*—are probably the most common and the most persuasive fallacies. They draw from *both* the sources of persuasiveness we have discussed, and for this reason we are calling them "double trouble."

Appeal to Authority and Attacking the Person We often doubt a statement because there is something wrong with the person who makes it, or give additional credit to a statement because a famous or highly admirable person makes it. Sometimes it is legitimate to do this, but more often, these moves constitute a fallacy.

APPEAL TO AUTHORITY

Example 6.33   *A majority of doctors think that the morals of our young people have declined.*

Example 6.34   *Meryl Streep doesn't approve of using pesticides on crops. It's probably a bad idea.*

ATTACKING THE PERSON

Example 6.35   *Our former mayor favored legalizing prostitution. But he was the most corrupt mayor we ever had. There's no way we should legalize it.*

Example 6.36   *Most of the men who say war is wrong are cowards.*

Although doctors may be much admired and knowledgeable in the field of medicine, there is no reason to believe they are experts in the field of morals. A similar criticism can be made of the argument concerning the use of pesticides on crops. The question of whether prostitution should be legalized is independent of the question of the character of its supporters;

and the question of whether war is wrong is independent of the question of
the courage of its opponents. But, since these criticisms seem fairly easy to
make, the same question should be asked of these fallacies as was asked of
the previous fallacies: Why do they tend to persuade? The answer is they
rely on both motive in place of support and sleight of hand, but in rather
subtle ways.

How Both These Fallacies Use Motive in Place of Support

If you like a person, this is a motive for agreeing with him. You
treat agreeing with someone as a way of honoring him. Similarly, if you
don't like a person, this is a motive for disagreeing with him. For example,
liking an actress such as Meryl Streep might make you inclined to agree
with her position on the use of pesticides. And the idea that someone is a
coward might make you less inclined to honor him by agreeing with his
view on war.

But there is a further dimension to be explored here. Recall our
discussion in Chapter 1 of the double arena in which argument takes place.
An exchange of views is unfortunately often seen as a sort of contest, as
well as an occasion to determine what is reasonable to believe. It is in part a
victory to discredit the other person's point of view and a defeat to be
discredited. In this arena, discrediting your opponent is on a continuum
with insulting and physically attacking. A *person* is being engaged in a
contest, not just a point of view. Looked at in this way, the fallacy of
attacking the person gains effectiveness because it identifies a person as a
common enemy—someone it would be satisfying to defeat—and it associates a certain point of view with this enemy. This approach helps create a
motive for the person hearing the argument to attack the enemy's point of
view as a way of doing battle with him. And by contrast, associating a
point of view with someone who is generally admired makes one less
inclined to attack the view because to do so would be to take this person on
as an opponent.

How Appeal to Authority Uses Sleight of Hand

It is often
legitimate to defend a statement by appeal to authority. Because of this,
even when an appeal to authority is fallacious, it draws some persuasiveness from its similarity to the legitimate cases.

It is certainly not a fallacy to say you should take a particular medicine
because a doctor prescribed it. Since we don't have time to become experts
in every field, it often makes sense to trust someone (within limits) who
has proof of expertise in a certain field. Unfortunately, a "halo" effect
seems to apply to statements that lie outside an expert's area of knowledge.

This is particularly the case if some relationship is believed to exist between the area in which the person *is* an expert, and the area in which he or she is offering an opinion. As a result, we have examples such as:

Example 6.37   *Astronaut Willard has been to outer space, and he believes there is a God.*

Example 6.38   *Judge Walker believes that most murderers are really mentally ill.*

Sponsors apparently believe that viewers will even be taken in when an actor who plays a doctor on a television show endorses a certain medicine.

In between the cases in which appeal to authority is clearly legitimate and cases in which it is clearly fallacious, there are a disturbingly large number of cases that are difficult to decide. If someone has the title "physicist" and supports nuclear power, how much more weight should his opinion carry than the opinion of an ordinary citizen who has done some reading on the subject? If someone teaches economics, what additional weight should be given to her views on how to combat inflation? We examine this troublesome issue in Chapter 11.

How Attacking the Person Uses Sleight of Hand   It is also legitimate in some cases to criticize a statement by attacking the person who makes it. This similarity to legitimate arguments lends persuasiveness to *attacking the person,* even when such an attack is fallacious. To see why attacking the person is sometimes legitimate, let's consider the example of a witness in a court of law. Suppose that Thompson says he saw Smith take a woman's purse. If we have no reason to believe that Thompson wants to deceive us, then we will take his statement as evidence (at least partial evidence) that Smith did take the purse. But if we hear testimony that Thompson hates Smith or has often lied before, then these attacks on the person will justifiably discredit his testimony by showing an ulterior motive.

It is legitimate to attack Thompson's statement by attacking his credibility because our initial faith in his statement was based on the fact that Thompson had been in a position to see what went on, had presented his statement, and had had no apparent reason to lie. But in other cases it is *not* legitimate to attack the person making a claim. Suppose someone is offering an argument—premises in support of a conclusion. In such cases it is legitimate to attack either his premises or the validity of his argument, but attacking the person making the argument is irrelevant.* Still, because

---

*If he is simply expecting you to take his word that his premises are true, an attack on the person might still be relevant. But if he is drawing from information that is generally accessible to anyone, an attack on the person is not legitimate.

attacking the person is relevant in the courtroom testimony kind of case, it can *seem* relevant in this latter case also.

Perhaps we can clarify the distinction between a legitimate attack on a person and an illegitimate one by applying it to more examples. Contrast the attack made by the supervisor against the foreman with that made by the father against the daughter in these examples:

Example 6.39

Foreman: *Charles shouldn't get the promotion. I worked with him two years ago and he never did his share.*

Supervisor: *I doubt that you can judge him impartially. You've been hostile toward him ever since that young woman chose to marry him instead of you.*

Example 6.40

Daughter: *I don't believe that God exists. If there were such a being, then it would not allow all the suffering we see in the world.*

Father: *You've just turned against religion because you think it isn't fashionable. None of those so-called intellectuals you hang out with believe in it.*

In Example 6.39, the supervisor's attack on the foreman *is* relevant. The foreman expects his testimony about Charles's work record to be taken as evidence by itself that Charles doesn't deserve the promotion. But the credibility of this testimony *is* damaged by the information about the foreman's attitude toward Charles. Example 6.40 is different in that the daughter is not simply expecting her father to believe her testimony against God's existence. She is giving a reason, the strength of which can be judged independently of an assessment of the daughter's character or circumstances. Her father's attack upon her is irrelevant.

It is not always easy to judge how much weight to give to an attack on a person's credibility. Even with the example of the foreman, although it is *relevant* to point out his hostility toward Charles, does it follow that his testimony should be discounted completely? A judgment must be made of how biased the foreman is and how able and inclined he is to overcome bias in making claims about other people. These judgments, although they lack precision, are not impossible to make. Often, corroboration from other sources helps determine a person's credibility.

In analyzing legitimate and fallacious cases of attacking the person, we have sought to do two things. First, we have tried to show that there are legitimate cases; this fact accounts, in part, for why fallacious cases tend to be convincing. (This is the sleight-of-hand source of persuasiveness.) Second, we have sought to show how you can distinguish, if you are careful, between the legitimate and fallacious cases of attacking the person.

Variations of the Fallacy of Attacking the Person

Certain common variations of this fallacy have been given separate names. Think about the differences among the following examples:

Example 6.41 *Discipline is important in education. Rousseau opposed discipline, but he was a pervert.*

Example 6.42 *Senator Spohn says we've been too hasty in closing our military bases. But he's got a base in his home state that he's trying to save.*

Example 6.43 *You're telling me I should drink less? You haven't been sober in a year.*

Whereas 6.41 is a straightforward attack on a person's character (calling Rousseau a pervert), 6.42 attacks a person's credibility by suggesting that he has something to gain by getting people to agree with him. These two variations are occasionally referred to by their Latin names: *ad hominem abusive* and *ad hominem circumstantial,* respectively. (*Attacking the person,* in general, is often referred to by the Latin name, *ad hominem.*) Example 6.43 points out that a person has the same fault he is accusing someone else of having. This is called *tu quoque* (Latin) or "you, too." Of the three variations, *ad hominem abusive* relies most heavily on emotion for its persuasiveness. *Ad hominem circumstantial* draws its persuasiveness primarily from its similarity to legitimate attacks on credibility. *Tu quoque* moves a discussion from the arena of critical reasoning to that of a personal contest of dominance and humiliation.

Review

It might be helpful to review the twelve fallacies identified and discussed in these chapters. They are arranged in categories below, with an example of each.

SLEIGHT OF HAND: DISTRACTION

1. *False dilemma.* The arguer claims there are only two alternatives and one is unacceptable, so we should choose the other. But in reality, there are more alternatives than the two stated.
   Example: America—Love it or leave it.

2. *Slippery slope.* The arguer says we shouldn't do P because P probably leads to Q, which probably leads to R, and so forth down the "slippery slope" to a final consequence that is clearly undesirable. But some of these steps are implausible.

Example: Now they want us to register handguns. Next it will be all guns. Then they'll ban guns, and we'll be set up for a police state.

3. *Straw man.* The arguer makes his own position appear strong solely by making the opposing position appear weaker than it really is. He puts a weak argument in his opponent's mouth when stronger arguments are available.

Example: People who believe we should spend less for defense apparently believe that the instability in Eastern Europe poses no threat to our interests.

SLEIGHT OF HAND: COUNTERFEIT

1. *Affirming the consequent.* Any argument that has the following invalid pattern:

If A then B.

B.

_____

A.

Example: If the economy is healthy, unemployment is down. Unemployment is down. So the economy is healthy.

2. *Denying the antecedent.* Any argument that has the following invalid pattern:

If A then B.

Not A.

_____

Not B.

Example: If she loves you, she'll marry you. She doesn't love you. So she won't marry you.

3. *Equivocation.* An argument in which an expression shifts its meaning from one premise to another, making the pattern invalid.

Example: Insane people shouldn't be punished. Someone who commits a murder must be insane. So murderers should not be punished.

4. *Begging the question.* An argument resting on a premise that is either a restatement of the conclusion or that would be doubted for the same reasons that the conclusion would be doubted.
Example: The Bible says God exists. Everything in the Bible is true, since God wrote it. So God does exist.

MOTIVE IN PLACE OF SUPPORT

1. *Appeal to force.* The arguer tries to get you to agree by indicating that *you* will be harmed if you don't agree.
Example: If you want to keep working here, you should reconsider your criticisms of company policy.

2. *Appeal to pity.* The arguer tries to get you to agree by indicating that *she* will be harmed if you don't agree.
Example: I *am* qualified—I have some experience and I really need the money.

3. *Prejudicial language.* The arguer uses language that biases you in favor of his position or against his opponent's position without giving evidence for or against his opponent's position.
Example: I doubt that you would be so naive as to doubt the generally accepted fact that the finest painters were French.

DOUBLE TROUBLE

1. *Appeal to authority.* Appealing to someone whose expertise is not relevant to the issue at hand. Or appealing to someone who is famous or admired, but not an expert on the issue at hand.
(Note: We have just described *fallacious* appeals to authority. There are also *legitimate* appeals to authority—appeals to people who really are experts in the appropriate areas.)
Example of fallacious appeal: A majority of doctors think that the morals of young people have declined.

2. *Attacking the person.* Arguing that a person's point of view should be doubted because the person has bad traits of character or because the person has something to gain by being believed.
(Note: There are legitimate as well as fallacious cases of attacking the person. See text above.)
Example of fallacious attack: Most of the people who want drugs legalized are closet users.

A Note on Terminology

Some of the terms we have used in Chapter 6 on fallacies are terms that are commonly used, while others are terms we invented. The four general category names—sleight of hand: distraction, sleight of hand: counterfeit, motive in place of support, and double trouble—were our own invention. A more common (but in our view less useful) division is into formal and informal fallacies, with such fallacies as affirming the consequent and denying the antecedent included under "formal," and most of the remaining ones included under "informal." All the names for individual fallacies are fairly commonly used, except for "prejudicial language." Fallacies in which language creates prejudice *against* a certain view are commonly called "poisoning the well." We used a broader category name so that we could include cases of prejudice *in favor* of a view.

People often use Latin names for fallacies. We noted these for the variations of *attacking the person* (*ad hominem abusive, circumstantial,* and *tu quoque*). Some other commonly used Latin names are *petitio principii* (petitioning the premises) for *begging the question, ad baculum* (to the stick) for *appeal to force,* and *ad misericordiam* (to misery) for *appeal to pity.* Another commonly used Latin term is *non sequitur.* When someone calls your argument a *non sequitur* she means literally that the conclusion *does not follow,* that is, that the argument is invalid. More specifically, this term is often used to apply to an argument whose conclusion is wildly different from anything suggested by the premises.

Exercise 6.4   **A Comprehensive Review of Fallacies**

---

1. Write an example (of your own creation) of each of the following fallacies introduced in this chapter: appeal to force, appeal to pity, prejudicial language, attacking the person, appeal to authority.

2. The following passages contain fallacies from all the categories we have discussed. For each passage, identify the fallacy or fallacies.
   a. Is gun control legislation justified? Yes. The argument by those who oppose it seems to be that it is a great inconvenience to register guns. But this inconvenience is incidental when you consider the stakes. Either we pass the gun control bill Congress is now considering, or we can watch the violence in our cities continue. Gun control cannot be seen as unconstitutional in these modern times, for the reason that the so-called right to bear arms is completely out of date.

b. So you're thinking of buying a fancy car. I never thought you'd cave in to the crass materialism that has infected our culture.

c. Anyone who serves as president of this organization has a duty to promote its interests—that's written in the charter. Supporting equality of the sexes goes against the interests of this organization. A duty is, by definition, a moral obligation. So as president of this organization, I have a moral obligation to oppose equality of the sexes. Actually, this is an obligation I am happy to fulfill, because I firmly believe that sexual equality is a dangerous idea. You can predict the kind of behavior it will produce in women generally if you look at the angry, hysterical, man-hating females who are leaders of this movement. I would argue that the gentle, ladylike demeanor which is befitting of womankind will all but disappear if the feminists succeed in promoting their cause.

d. As warden, I don't think your complaints about how this penitentiary is run are well-founded. The parole board is not likely to look favorably on the attitude you have been taking. You seem to think that inmates are entitled to dictate the policies of this institution. To me, this is not consistent with the purposes for which you are here. If inmates are made to feel that they have done wrong, they have a chance of becoming reformed. With your proposals, they would not be made to feel they had done wrong. So they wouldn't have a chance of being reformed.

e. Rudi says that the government should provide more jobs for people. He should know. He couldn't get a job on his own if he had to. I had to look for months before I found work. My family even ran low on food. It was humiliating to plead with employers for a job. But I stuck it out and found work, and people like Rudi can do the same.

f. Those animal rights wierdos have really gone around the bend. Now they're saying no one should wear a fur coat. They won't be happy until we're all eating bean sprouts and wearing sackcloth. To them, a weasel is a dog is a human—everything's the same.

g. The idea of promoting the general welfare is firmly planted in our Constitution. How, then, can you oppose welfare programs and claim to uphold our Constitution? If we cut back on welfare programs, people will be put out of jobs, and the poor will not be getting services they need. Resentment toward the system will build up again, and we'll have the same kind of rioting we did in the sixties. I agree with Senator Kennedy—he has always understood the importance of maintaining our welfare programs.

h. COMMISSIONERS IN DEVELOPERS' POCKETS

Editor: The Daily Herald

The County Commissioners want to destroy the country. They are in the pockets of the big land developers. The rezoning decision of last week just proves it. Once multi-unit dwellings are permitted in neighborhoods with single family dwellings, then the sense of community that now exists will be lost. Before you know it we will have strip development as far as the eye can see. Fast-food places will be squeezed between discount stores. If we resist the developers now, then our community will be saved. The voters will remember how the commissioners voted during the next election.

Cynthia Drew
1212 N.W. Breadbasket
City

i. Two congressional committees have issued scathing reports which condemn about every aspect of the cancer insurance industry and the product it offers to the public. One committee recommended that the sale of cancer insurance to the elderly be banned by federal law. . . . Statements in the report of the committees, as quoted in news stories, are too ridiculous to be taken seriously, although a lot of congressmen apparently are not laughing. Neither should the public be laughing because the thrust of this blatant effort to destroy a private business is a new warning that bureaucratic wrath and bureaucratic thirst for power threatens our very freedom of choice and individual preference . . . and isn't it a bit frivolous to have congressional committees, which will BUY just about anything ($660 billion worth a year and climbing), advising the public on how to spend $25 to $75 a year.*

Exercise 6.5   Fallacious or Not?

It is debatable whether any or all of the following passages commit fallacies. Write a brief discussion of each passage, explaining why you think a fallacy is or is not being committed. You may wish to refer back to the relevant sections of the text for help in your deliberations.

---

*Millard Grimes, advertisement for American Family Life Assurance Company, originally published in the Columbus, Georgia, *Sunday Ledger-Enquirer*.

1. The decision of whether to convict this man is more than academic. We are talking about sending a flesh-and-blood human being like you and me into a cage. He is a man with a family—his family is surely innocent of any offense. And yet they will suffer too because of the absence of a breadwinner. These are some of the consequences you will bring about if you decide to convict.

2. I believe the economic issue is the important one in this election. I don't know that much about economics myself, but my mother-in-law teaches economics and my uncle has run a large business for years. I've talked it over with them, and I think that the Republican candidate would probably do a better job of guiding the country's economic policies.

3. Joan thinks that giving money to charities is not really an obligation. She says that giving to the needy is a nice thing to do if you want to, but that you are not doing anything morally wrong if you don't give. She didn't feel this way when she was not so well off. But now that she has come into money this new philosophy of hers is pretty convenient.

4. You can't claim that you have a *right* to free child care, for the reason that neither I nor anyone else has an *obligation* to provide it. What have we done to create such an obligation? You might think that I am merely assuming what I am trying to prove. But by getting you to look at the matter from my point of view I hope you will be less inclined to claim that something you simply desire is your *right*.

5. The company was responsible for sending Bert into the chamber without properly checking for poisonous gases. Clearly, Bert has suffered substantial nerve damage that confines him to his home and makes it difficult for him to carry out even the most mundane activities such as feeding himself. The action of the company has caused him great physical pain and psychological suffering. He deserves compensation.

6. Here you are quoting Franklin on the subject of how one should live his life. But what kind of a life did Franklin himself live? I've read that he was a very difficult man, prone to depression, hard to please, impatient with those around him. When you judge a man's philosophy you have to see how it worked for him.

7. Tina has never had a Teddy Bear. A mother's love. A doll to cuddle. Tina knows nothing of these things. But she does know fear, rejection, and hunger. For just $15 a month, you can help save a child like Tina. Through our "adoption" program you can help provide a child with a better diet, clothes, medical attention, school. And even a toy or two.

But don't wait. There are so many. And somewhere, right now, a child is dying from starvation and neglect.*

8. If you look at a map you'll see that the outline of South America closely parallels that of Africa. This and other similarities between the coast of North America and Europe justify the theory that these continents were at one time part of one supercontinent and have subsequently moved apart. If the geological theory of plate tectonics is correct, then we would expect just such movement.

---

*Adapted from an advertisement for Children, Inc. in *Time Magazine,* Dec. 12, 1979, p. 12, with permission of the advertiser.

CHAPTER SEVEN

Arguments in Context: Understanding More Complicated Passages

Most of the passages we have examined in previous chapters were relatively simple. Even when it was difficult to reconstruct an argument, you were at least told that there was an argument to be reconstructed. In the "real world" of prose passages, you don't find such assurances. This chapter focuses on the task of determining whether a passage contains arguments, and, if so, determining their number and their relationship to one another. You should note at the outset, however, that complicated passages in context can be *interpreted* in several ways. In some cases there may be no one definitive reading. Several alternative reconstructions might be equally plausible. Nevertheless, this does *not* imply that all interpretations are equally acceptable. Even though interpretation is more an art than a science, it is not a mere matter of taste.

Finding an Argument in a Sea of Words

Example 7.1 illustrates the problem that faces you when you try to apply the techniques of reconstruction that we have discussed in previous chapters. It is a short selection consisting of eight sentences (marked S1, S2, etc.) of the kind you might find in a newspaper.

Example 7.1   *ACTIVISTS PIT CIVIL RIGHTS AGAINST FIRST AMENDMENT*

S1 → *Women activists have developed a new strategy in their fight against pornography. They are seeking to use civil rights laws to attack what they consider the exploitation of women that is promoted by pornographic materials.*   ← S2

S3 → *In Minneapolis, Minnesota, these women successfully shepherded a measure through the City Council that would have opened the door for court action against any purveyor of films, magazines, or books that explicitly depict the sexual exploitation of women. Although the mayor ultimately vetoed the proposed ordinance, the movement in Minneapolis and elsewhere in the country is growing as a result of impetus from both the feminist movement on the left and a new, public concern with morality on the right.*   ← S4

S5 → *Opponents argue that the definition of pornography implicit in such laws is a grave threat to First Amendment rights of free expression. These critics point out that ironically enough such ordinances could eliminate so-called Harlequin Romances that are widely purchased by women.*   ← S6

S7 → *The conflict between these two positions is likely to remain unresolved until the U.S. Supreme Court rules on the constitutionality of provisions such as those in the Minneapolis ordinance. Another such case is brewing in Indiana.*   ← S8

Although a headline is provided and the word "argue" is actually included in S5, it is not immediately obvious what argument is being presented or, indeed, whether any argument is being put forward. Many of the sentences (for example, S1, S2, S3, and S8) set the scene by offering a *description* of a state of affairs. Sentence 4 provides some description (namely, the mayor's veto), but it does something else as well: it offers an *explanation* concerning why the movement is growing by pointing to support that extends across the political spectrum.

Sentences 5 and 6 present the most tempting candidates for a deductive argument. They would form the conclusion and premise of a valid argument with the addition of an implicit premise that any law that prohibits widely read books is a threat to First Amendment rights of free expression. But note that the author is not offering this argument herself. It is a *reported argument* from another source, which is not endorsed (or rejected) in the article. Finally S7, although it might seem like a conclusion, is not really argued for in the passage. No direct reasons are given for believing that the conflict will demand Supreme Court action. The statement is *unsupported in the context* of the passage.

What about the headline? Is that a conclusion supported by the article? The passage itself describes a conflict in which one side appeals to civil rights and the other side appeals to the First Amendment. The headline is best construed as a *summary* of the overall content rather than as a conclusion for which reasons are offered.

This example illustrates several roles that statements can play other than as premises or conclusions in arguments. They can be:

descriptions

explanations

reports of arguments

statements unsupported in context

summaries

These are just some of the common tasks performed by sentences in typical passages that you are apt to come across in your search for arguments. We could add a few additional items also encountered frequently:

editorial comments

illustrations, examples, or classifications

analogies

This list of roles statements can play should alert you to an important rule of thumb to guide you when you are looking for an argument in a piece of prose: *Most of what you find in prose passages is not part of an argument.*

Students in informal logic courses are often dismayed when they are asked to move beyond simplified classroom examples to essays, editorials, speeches, and other "real world" passages. They read paragraph after paragraph without finding any arguments. But this should not be surprising when you consider how many roles a statement can play.

More about Description and Explanation

Descriptive uses of language are among the most common items found in prose passages. For example, a person may be described:

Example 7.2   *Mike is a burglar. He is very successful at it. He seldom has to do an honest day's work.*

There are no premises or conclusions in Example 7.2, just three statements describing Mike.

Descriptions can also be given of places and things or abstract objects, such as fields of study.

Example 7.3   *Artificial intelligence is an emerging field of research. It combines elements of computer science, psychology, and even philosophy. Work in the field has been centered at Stanford University, MIT, and Carnegie-Mellon University, but the field is increasingly attracting commercial computer software developers.*

Again, there is no argument in this passage, just three statements describing the new field of artificial intelligence.

Also, a series of events can be described in a narrative.

Example 7.4   *On the very eve of the birth of the Third Reich, a feverish tension gripped Berlin. The Weimar Republic, it seemed obvious to almost everyone, was about to expire. For more than a year it had been crumbling. General Kurt von Schleicher, who like his immediate predecessor, Franz von Papen, cared little for the Republic and less for its democracy, and who, also like him, had ruled as Chancellor by presidential decree without recourse to Parliament, had come to the end of his rope after fifty-seven days in office.*

On Saturday, January 28, 1933, he had been abruptly dismissed by the aging President of the Republic, Field Marshal von Hindenburg. Adolf Hitler, leader of the National Socialists, the largest political party in Germany, was demanding for himself the chancellorship of the democratic Republic he had sworn to destroy.*

Example 7.4 narrates (tells a story about) the end of the Weimar Republic in Germany. It doesn't contain an argument. It is important, however, to remember that descriptions or narrations are often used as premises of an argument.

---

*William L. Shirer, *The Rise and Fall of the Third Reich* (New York: Simon & Schuster, 1960), p. 3. Reprinted with permission.

Example 7.5   *The Weimar Republic was structurally weak. Any democratic state that would permit an opponent of democracy to assume the most powerful position in government lacked a structure of political checks and balances to remain strong. Hitler did just that in 1933.*

In this passage a description of Hitler's assumption of power as that which permitted an opponent of democracy to attain power serves as a premise in a deductive argument leading to the conclusion that the Weimar Republic was structurally weak.

Passages containing explanations raise additional difficulties in interpretation. Even when words that we identified as premise and conclusion indicators (in Chapter 2) are used, they indicate not an argument, but an explanation (or something related to an explanation, a prediction).

Example 7.6   *They were very small and very slow. Consequently, they lost the game badly.*

Example 7.7   *Alice quit taking him out because he was always late.*

These two passages are not offered to convince the reader of a point of view. It is not as though the reader needs to be persuaded that the game was lost or that Alice quit taking him out. These occurrences are presupposed. The passages are aimed at saying *why* these things occurred. This is true of the following more complicated passage as well.

Example 7.8   *The culture shock phenomenon accounts for much of the bewilderment, frustration, and disorientation that plagues Americans in their dealings with other societies. It causes a breakdown in communication, a misreading of reality, an inability to cope. Yet culture shock is relatively mild in comparison with the much more dizzying disorientation brought on by the premature arrival of the future. It may well be the most important disease of tomorrow.**

This passage does not intend to provide an argument to persuade the reader of a particular conclusion. It tries to explain American behavior toward other societies by appeal to a cause, namely, culture shock. Furthermore, it *predicts* that certain unstated but dire consequences are apt to occur as the result of a currently occurring cause, future shock. We will

---

*Alvin Toffler, *Future Shock* (New York: Bantam Books, 1970), p. 11. Copyright © 1970 by Alvin Toffler. Reprinted by permission of Random House, Inc.

discuss causal explanation and prediction and their relationship to empirical theories in Chapters 9 and 10. Explanations and predictions are intimately tied to nondeductive forms of reasoning, although we shall see that there may be some overlap between deductive argument and explanation.

| Exercise 7.1 | **Distinguishing Arguments from Descriptions and Explanations** |

Indicate whether each passage is an argument, an explanation, or mere description. If it is a deductive argument, identify its premises and conclusion.

1. If you're uncoordinated, you can't be a good golfer. You are a good golfer. So, you're coordinated.

2. John is uncoordinated. He has little interest in games. He prefers to read.

3. No one should take pride in having a beautiful face. A beautiful face is an accident of nature. No one should take pride in something that is an accident of nature.

4. My car didn't start this morning because it was very cold and my battery is weak.

5. If Sally goes out with Carl one more time, Carl will think she is serious about him. But she isn't serious about him, and you shouldn't make someone think you are serious when you are not. Sally should stop going out with Carl.

6. Kathy had a good high school education. Dan, Homer, and Edna all had good high school educations and they went to Central High. Kathy must have gone to Central High.

7. Abortion is justified. All societies have the right to establish social policies that provide the greatest amount of social value. Abortion as a social policy provides more social value than any alternative. If all societies have the right to establish social policies that provide for the greatest amount of social value and if abortion as a social policy provides more social value than any alternative, then abortion is justified.

8. Some people have a sense of tact and some do not. Kate is a person who does not.

9. All people need self-esteem. Self-esteem requires doing useful work. All people need to do useful work.

10. Robert will make a poor spouse. Anyone who is unwilling to help with housework will make a poor spouse, and Robert is unwilling to do his share of housework.

11. He never washed the dishes, did the laundry, or cleaned the bathroom. Consequently, she divorced him.

12. Most people cannot produce a well-honed prose essay. For most people, the production of a well-honed essay is possible only if they have an extraordinary grasp of language (that is, are a species of poet) or if they have the discipline to write and rewrite. Most people have neither an extraordinary grasp of language (that is, are a species of poet), nor the discipline to write and rewrite.

Exercise 7.2   Picking the Role of a Statement

Indicate the role or use of each sentence in the following passages. Which are mere descriptions? Which are explanations? Which are (or contain) premises or conclusions of a deductive argument? Indicate, if appropriate, other uses that are played by sentences not fitting into these roles.

1. Pornography is one of the leading triggers of violence against women in U.S. society according to many proponents of stricter laws against the distribution and sale of pornographic materials. Many people are unaware of the nature of much contemporary pornography. It is not just sexually explicit material. It often graphically depicts mutilation or murder and ties it to sexual activities. It is disgusting.

2. The Third Reich, which was born on January 30, 1933, Hitler boasted, would endure for a thousand years, and in Nazi parlance it was often referred to as the "Thousand-Year Reich." It lasted twelve years and four months, but in that flicker of time, as history goes, it caused an eruption on this earth more violent and shattering than any previously experienced, raising the German people to heights of power they had not known in more than a millennium, making them at one time the masters of Europe from the Atlantic to the Volga, from the North Cape to the Mediterranean and then plunging them to the depths of destruction and desolation at the end of a world war which their nation had cold-bloodedly provoked and during which it instituted a reign of terror over the conquered peoples which, in its calculated butchery of human life and the human spirit outdid all the savage oppressions of the previous ages. (Shirer, *The Rise and Fall of the Third Reich*, p. 5.)

3. MEN ARE PAID TWICE WHAT WOMEN MAKE*

Washington (AP)—Men are paid twice what women are paid, and education and seniority are major factors in salary, newly released government statistics confirm.

The highest salaries go to white males between the ages of 45 and 54 with postgraduate college degrees, according to the newly published income figures collected in the 1980 census.

The detailed compilation of salaries paid in 1979 lists earnings of $36,520 for white males between 45 and 54 with five years or more of college.

White women of the same age and education averaged $15,637.

Peak salaries for blacks, in the same age and educational groups, were $25,801 for males and $17,242 for women.

Average salaries vary considerably in the study, according to education, race, gender and age.

For all workers over age 18, men averaged $16,929 during the year while women earned $8,238.

Income grew in parallel with education.

Men with less than eight years of schooling averaged $12,028, while women in that category earned $6,159.

With a high school diploma, male earnings rose to $15,368 and women's to $7,749.

And with a postgraduate college degree men averaged $27,660 and women $13,371.

4. TOO MANY JETS AT RUSH HOURS**

Anyone who travels by commercial airline with any frequency has a repertoire of stories about sitting on runways at major airports in one of a string of jets waiting to take off, or circling in the sky waiting to land. The problem is getting worse.

On a recent day at New York's Kennedy International Airport, one of the nation's busiest, 63 planes were scheduled to arrive in the hour beginning at 3:45 P.M. although the airport's capacity, even in clear weather, is 44 per hour. At nearby La Guardia, 80 airline arrivals and departures have been scheduled for the hour beginning at 8 A.M. though the capacity under optimum conditions is 68.

The Federal Aviation Administration says other airports where overscheduling has become a problem include Chicago's O'Hare, Washington, D.C.'s National, and those in Atlanta, Denver, and St. Louis, the latter three all airline hubs.

---

*Seattle Post-Intelligencer, Thursday, July 26, 1984, p. B11. Reprinted with permission of The Associated Press.
**Seattle Post-Intelligencer, Tuesday, August 14, 1984, p. A6. Reprinted with permission.

What rapidly is approaching crisis dimensions, because of the hazards and inconveniences imposed on the flying public, is the result of deregulation of the airline industry and freedom to schedule flights without restraint. Naturally the airlines tend to concentrate their flights at those times of day most appealing to their customers, usually early in the mornings and in late afternoons.

Legislation was introduced in Congress last week by Reps. Elliott Levitas, D-Ga., and Guy Molinari, R-N.Y., to give the FAA regulatory authority over airline scheduling if the industry fails to solve the problem itself. The bill would give the airlines limited immunity from antitrust laws so they could cooperate in dealing with the problems.

There are signs that the airlines indeed are anxious to resolve the overscheduling dilemma themselves. After all, it's expensive to have a fleet of jets burning fuel while idling on runways and increasing passenger dissatisfaction is not in the industry's self-interest. We believe the airlines are capable of working things out themselves. But if they can't, or won't, then the government is going to have to do it for them in the public interest.

5. DECRIMINALIZATION WILL COME/ William F. Buckley Jr.*

The new quarrel between the administration and the Democratic Party over drug policy has, as usual, to do with money, the anchor position of the Democrats being that a program is only serious to the extent that it is costly. In round figures, President Bush proposes raising his drug budget from $9 billion to $11 billion, while the Democrats want $15 billion.

There is an ancillary argument having to do with the death penalty. In his inaugural address, Bush made a vague statement in which the words "death sentence" occurred, but now he has become specific, asking for a federal bill that would permit the death sentence against drug merchants whose transactions could be directly traced to the death of a tangential figure, whether a bystander who got shot during the transaction, a policeman who got shot or a drug purchaser who died of an overdose.

Rep. Charles Rangel, D-N.Y., who heads the House Committee on Narcotics Abuse and Control, deplores this deviation on the grounds that Bush would be contending against the heavily armed anti-capital punishment lobby and that this would be an unnecessary digression.

Rangel is right for the wrong reasons. The principal objection to asking for a capital punishment bill is that given the judicial structure set up to protect men and women sentenced to death from actually

---

reaching the electric chair, Bush's grandchildren would be on Social Security before capital punishment became a genuine deterrent to drug merchandising. It took 10 years to execute Ted Bundy, who merely murdered, oh, 35 women or whatever the number.

The relative obliquity of the proposed law almost guarantees a lifetime's delay before the Supreme Court got around to saying "Go ahead" to the executioner. What it is, is simply polemical pyrotechnics, designed to evoke a vague worry among drug dealers that they might come within firing distance of the proposed law.

And, as always, we hear from such as the mayor of New York that the government is not doing "enough." This means that the government is not sending enough money to the city of New York to enforce New York's own laws.

Someone should put up a prize for the first mayor or governor of any state in the union who in asking for more money from Washington admits that any money that comes in from Washington has to be raised from his own state in the first instance. This is especially so of the more affluent states.

In hearing commentary on the drug war, in Los Angeles, in Chicago, in New York, one notes a slight but interesting change in attitude. Students of the question are now beginning to admit that the war on drugs is at least as formidable as the war against North Vietnam. These are thoughtful folk who are not yet prepared to explore genuine alternatives, for instance decriminalization combined with hugely increased treatment centers.

What they are saying is reducible to: "Let's give them more time." Let's, in other words, wait another two, three, perhaps five years, and see what the drug warriors come up with. Who knows, maybe we can bribe the drug growers of Bolivia, Peru and Colombia to stop production by making outright cash grants.

Who knows, maybe drug users will become truly afraid of being caught and sent off to jail. Who knows, maybe the drug merchants will suspect that the next client they come upon is another of Mayor Barry's girlfriends, conscripted to duty. And then maybe the whole thing will add up to victory over drugs.

There are those who feel we ought to get on with decriminalization now, rather than after five years of $10 billion, $15 billion, $20 billion spent per year; two, three, four, five hundred thousand more Americans sent to jail; 100, 200 federal judges devoting full time to drug prosecution; and untold tens of thousands of law-abiding citizens mauled and killed on the streets to provide cash for the drug purchasers.

Such as feel this way about the drug war can know how the anti-Vietnam protesters felt along about 1966, 1967, when it became clear to the prescient that the United States was simply not going to come up with the critical firepower to win the war against Vietnam, so why not stop it now?

But the public was not ready to stop it now; there were still prospects of victory, which little by little diminished and ended with the withdrawal of the last GI, followed by the boat people. The prophetic burden. Decriminalization will come, but it is a long way off.

What's the Point? Understanding Complicated Passages

In passages that contain a good deal of argumentative material, it is often surprisingly difficult to determine exactly what point an author is trying to make. You might face obstacles, for instance, in finding the conclusion in the midst of all the other passage statements. In many prose passages, the distinction between explicit and implicit premises and conclusions is not very sharp. A premise or conclusion can be strongly suggested, but not stated precisely. You will seldom be able to copy a series of sentences from a passage and say, "These are the premises and the conclusion."

Even if, using indicator words and seeing the structure of an argument, you find a sentence that plays the role of the conclusion, you might not initially understand what the author means by it and how the premises support it. What does the author mean in the following passage?

Example 7.9   *Social psychologists have rightly held that people who are intermeshed in a network of overlapping, mutually supportive, interpersonal relations and the concomitant commitment to common norms obtain a substantial measure of psychic support. This psychological fortification in turn limits the incidence of self-destructive and other deviant behavior. It follows that individuals with a high degree of involvement with the religious life of their community are less likely to be found on the lists of those who have taken the last fateful step to terminate their sojourn in this vale of tears.*

Looking at the Context   It is often useful, when you are trying to understand an unclear passage, to look at the context in which it appears. Is the passage part of an article whose main point is stated in the title? If so, how is the passage in question related to this point? Is the passage part of a debate in which the participants have clearly indicated which side they are supporting? If so, perhaps the passage is stating premises in support of one of the positions. If the passage in Example 7.9 were from a book, and it occurred in a chapter entitled "Religion and Suicide," you could look for some point about the relation between religion and suicide. This additional information doesn't tell you specifically what the passage means, but it prepares you to focus your attention in a certain direction as you read through it.

Simplifying and Paraphrasing   In order to cut through the net of confusion created by passages such as Example 7.9, it is helpful, after noting the context, to simplify and paraphrase. Once inessential elements are removed or modified, you can more readily grasp the structure of what is being said. Furthermore, a sign of whether you have mastered an argument is your ability to repeat what is meant—not merely the words used. This is a good test of understanding.

The task of simplifying and paraphrasing is not easy. The aim is to change an author's words without distorting the meaning of what was said. It is all the more difficult if you do not clearly understand what the author is saying. A method of *successive approximation* is a useful tactic. Begin with a rough (possibly inaccurate) rendition of the passage. Then, if necessary, modify it in successive versions until it accurately reflects the original. In the process you will "make the author's argument your own" and understand it much better.

A Method of Successive Approximation   The conclusion in Example 7.9 is indicated by the expression "it follows" in the final sentence, but its meaning is far from clear. Once the conclusion is located, a three-step process will help generate a first approximation:

1. *Penetrate the Prose.* Look up the words you don't know in a dictionary; decipher the meaning of metaphors, and of vague, emotional, or flowery language; substitute more precise expressions.
   Sample: The conclusion of the example uses the fancy phrase "those who have taken the last fateful step to terminate their sojourn in this vale of tears" which means roughly "those who committed suicide."

2. *Eliminate the Excess.* Delete all editorial expressions or unnecessary clauses, and rephrase what remains in a straightforward way.
   Sample: The introductory comment, "social psychologists have rightly held" should be removed.

3. *Search Out the Structure.* Figure out which statements provide support for the conclusion. If necessary, sketch the argument in such a way that the structure is clear.

Sample: The argument can be sketched:

(1) People with many friends feel more secure.

(2) Feeling secure makes people less suicidal.

(implicit) *(3) Churchgoers have many friends.*

∴ *So churchgoers are less suicidal.**

When you reconstruct a passage it is important to make a bold beginning. Don't be afraid to produce a very rough approximation. It is better to produce a parody that you truly understand than a parroting of the author's words that you do not. You can always revise your simplified version if you decide that you have weakened or significantly altered what the author is saying.

A Second Approximation So far, we have moved from Example 7.9 to:

First Approximation

(1) People with many friends feel more secure.

(2) Feeling secure makes people less suicidal.

(implicit) *(3) Churchgoers have many friends.*

∴ *Churchgoers are less suicidal.*

This approximation is much clearer than the original, but it is an oversimplification that is probably more open to criticism than the original. For example, it is an overgeneralization to say that churchgoers have many friends, and the passage doesn't make this bold a claim. It was worthwhile to put it this way in the first approximation because it is a simple, clear statement that connects the conclusion with the premises. If we go through our first approximation and qualify each sentence so it is closer to the original (but stated clearly), we arrive at something like the following:

---

*We could go a step further and put these sentences into an if-then pattern, for example, by writing the first premise as *If people have many friends, then they feel more secure than people without many friends.*

Second Approximation

(1) *People who share a network of relationships and norms feel more secure.*

(2) *Feeling secure limits self-destructive behavior.*

(implicit) (3) *People highly involved in religious life are likely to share a network of relationships and norms.*

∴ *People highly involved in religious life are less likely to commit suicide.*

Even though this second approximation is more accurate, it is important to go through the step of *over*simplifying the passage. This helps you penetrate beyond reciting the words of the passage as you would recite words in a poem you have memorized but don't understand. By oversimplifying the passage you take over the thought as if it were your own. You can always go back and qualify.

Exercise 7.3 **Simplification and Paraphrasing: Making a First Approximation**

Simplify and paraphrase the following passages. Try to capture the basic meaning as economically as you can. For the first approximation do not hesitate to substantially rewrite the passage and to eliminate less important elements. The passages need not be read as arguments.

1. Few are the rewards of indolence and many its pains; rich is the harvest of hard work.

2. If you want to get ahead in this world, you've got to be down at the carwash when the fancy cars roll in.

3. Only by cleaving firmly to the bosom of the land can the new pioneer escape the soul-crushing forces of modern, technological society.

4. A full-bodied network of communication is necessary for any office holder if he is to effectively transform his crucial, but unexciting, behind-the-scenes work into the forge that will produce results at the polls.

5. Success in teaching rests on three interrelated factors: (1) A teacher must have that easy familiarity that betokens the true participant in the life of the mind; (2) a teacher must be involved in a give-and-take nexus of communication with the student so that the student is motivated and the teacher is appraised on student needs; and finally (3) a teacher must be able to evaluate both the student's progress and potential

without bias in the light of the teacher's own successes and failures in the classroom.

6. To UNDERSTAND political power right and derive it from its original, we must consider what state all men are naturally in, and that is a state of perfect freedom to order their actions and dispose of their possessions and persons as they think fit, within the bounds of the law of nature, without asking leave or depending upon the will of any other man.*

7. Yet all this bespeaks a dim realization of the truth—the truth that modern man lives under the illusion that he knows what he wants, while he actually wants what he is *supposed* to want. In order to accept this it is necessary to realize that to know what one really wants is not comparatively easy, as most people think, but one of the most difficult problems any human being has to solve. It is a task we frantically try to avoid by accepting ready-made goals as though they were our own.**

(HINT: Does Fromm believe that people really know what they want?)

8. It would seem that the obstacles to generalized thought inherent in the form of language are of minor importance only, and that presumably the language alone would not prevent a people from advancing to more generalized forms of thinking if the general state of their culture should require expression of such thought; that under these conditions the language would be molded rather by the cultural state. It does not seem likely, therefore, that there is any direct relation between the culture of a tribe and the language they speak, except insofar as the form of language will be molded by the state of culture, but not insofar as a certain state of culture is conditioned by morphological traits of the language.†

(HINT: What does Boas say about the relation among language, thought, and culture?)

9. No age in the history of humanity has perhaps so lost touch with this natural *healing* process that implicates *some* of the people whom we label schizophrenic. No age has so devalued it, no age has imposed

---

*John Locke, *The Second Treatise of Government,* ed. Thomas Peardon (New York: Bobbs-Merrill, 1952), p. 4.
**Erich Fromm, *Escape from Freedom* (New York: Avon, 1967), p. 278.
†Franz Boas, *The Mind of Primitive Man* (New York: Collier, 1911), p. 67.

such prohibitions and deterrences against it, as our own. Instead of the mental hospital, a sort of reservicing factory for human breakdowns, we need a place where people who have traveled further and, consequently, may be more lost than psychiatrists and other sane people, can find their way *further* into inner space and time, and back again. Instead of the *degradation* ceremonial of psychiatric examination, diagnosis and prognostication, we need, for those who are ready for it (in psychiatric terminology, often those who are about to go into a schizophrenic breakdown), an *initiation* ceremonial, through which the person will be guided with full social encouragement and sanction into inner space and time, by people who have been there and back again. Psychiatrically, this would appear as ex-patients helping future patients go mad.*

(HINT: Concentrate on the virtue R. D. Laing sees in the alternative rather than the liabilities of traditional psychiatric practice.)

10. If information is power, the ability to distort and control information will be used more often than not to preserve and perpetuate that power. But the national security policy makers, the crisis managers of the nuclear age, are frequently men of considerable intellectual ability who have gone to the right schools. They pride themselves not only on their social graces, but on their rationality and morality. For such men, the preservation of partisan political power would not be a seemly rationale for official deception (although it might be entirely sufficient for the President whom they serve). National security provides the acceptable alternative, the end that justifies all means. . . . The excuse for secrecy and deception most frequently given by those in power is that the American people must sometimes be misled in order to mislead the enemy. This justification is unacceptable on moral and philosophical grounds, and often it simply isn't true. Frequently, the "enemy" knows what is going on, but the American public does not.**

(HINT: According to Wise, how do government officials justify secrecy? Does Wise think this is an acceptable justification?)

---

*R. D. Laing, *The Politics of Experience* (New York: Random House, 1967), pp. 88–89. Copyright © R. D. Laing, 1967. Reprinted with permission of Penguin Books Ltd.

**David Wise, *The Politics of Lying: Government, Deception, Secrecy and Power* (New York: Random House, 1973), p. 501. Reprinted with permission of the publisher.

Fine Tuning: Paraphrase and the Structure of Arguments

In the previous section we concentrated on shortening passages in order to clarify meaning. Although such paraphrasing is helpful as a first step in understanding a variety of prose materials, our primary concern is illuminating arguments that are embedded in complex passages. They are the focus of the remainder of this chapter.

Often, only a small fraction of a passage actually conveys an argument. The remainder may consist of material that is designed to make the audience sympathetic with the position taken, statements intended to clarify the position, support for premises, and so forth. A useful tactic in such a case is to pick out the conclusion, find some statement or statements that seem to support the conclusion most directly, and then add whatever implicit premises are necessary. (Keep in mind the argument patterns.)

We can apply this method to the following passage:

Example 7.10

Well, I insist—and I here follow von Hildebrand—that we parents, we married people, in no way believe sex is dirty, but we believe it is private and intimate. Therefore, it cannot endure being publicized the way mathematics or even the way health is publicized. It is quite tactful for you to go to a party and talk about your tonsils. It is not tactful—not acceptable—for you to go to a party and talk about how your wife makes love to you, not because you think it is dirty, my friends, but because you think it is intimate.*

In looking for the conclusion, the indicator word *therefore* directs our attention to the statement, "It [sex] cannot endure being publicized the way mathematics or even the way health is publicized." We can paraphrase what is essential here in a much simpler way:

Conclusion

Sex should not be publicized.

Now we need to look through the passage to see what is offered as direct support for this conclusion. It is crucial to avoid simply listing all

---

*Quotation cited in Gloria Lentz, *Raping Our Children: The Sex Education Scandal* (New Rochelle, N.Y.: Arlington House Publishing, 1972), p. 76.

the sentences in the passage as though they were premises. Boil the passage down until it can be fit into a structured argument such as those represented by the patterns in Chapters 2 and 4. In the first two lines, the author claims that she does not believe that sex is dirty. We can ignore this material for the purpose of reconstructing the argument, since we want to locate what she *does* believe in support of her conclusion. The third line presents a likely candidate, which we can write as a premise: *It (sex) is private and intimate.* So far, then, we have:

Example 7.11   *(1) Sex is private and intimate.*

∴   *Sex should not be publicized.*

Look at the remainder of the passage. It presents an example of something that may be publicized and claims again (in different words) that sex should not be publicized. None of this adds to the argument. What we need to get from the premise to the conclusion is a *general rule*. With a little thought you can see that the premise the passage leaves implicit is: Whatever is private and intimate should not be publicized. Adding this, we have:

Example 7.12   *(1) Sex is private and intimate.*
(implicit)   *(2) Whatever is private and intimate should not be publicized.*

∴   *Sex should not be publicized.*

For the purpose of reconstructing arguments, first approximations need not be written out in full. You may find it easier to penetrate the prose if you mark up the passage to indicate the central concepts (this might also involve noting whether the same concept is presented in different words). You can eliminate excess by simply crossing out irrelevant elements. And you can focus on argument structure by using some notation to check off "logical words" (such as *if-then, either-or, not, all,* and any indicator words). You can supplement these steps by identifying premises and conclusions. We have done this for the following passage, which offers a view of contemporary American culture.

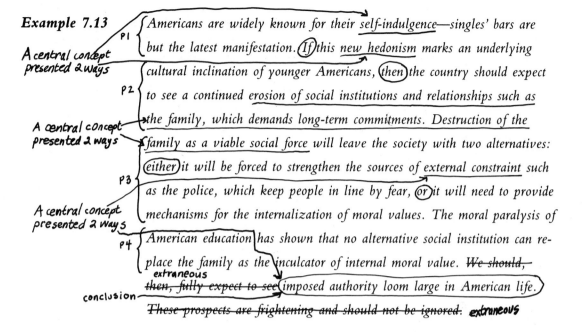

Example 7.13

P1 — *Americans are widely known for their self-indulgence—singles' bars are but the latest manifestation. (If) this new hedonism marks an underlying*

A central concept presented 2 ways

P2 — *cultural inclination of younger Americans, (then) the country should expect to see a continued erosion of social institutions and relationships such as the family, which demands long-term commitments. Destruction of the*

A central concept presented 2 ways

family as a viable social force will leave the society with two alternatives: (either) it will be forced to strengthen the sources of external constraint such

P3 — *as the police, which keep people in line by fear, (or) it will need to provide mechanisms for the internalization of moral values. The moral paralysis of*

A central concept presented 2 ways

P4 — *American education has shown that no alternative social institution can replace the family as the inculcator of internal moral value.* ~~We should,~~
~~extraneous~~
~~then, fully expect to see~~ *imposed authority loom large in American life.*

conclusion — ~~These prospects are frightening and should not be ignored.~~ **extraneous**

Once the passage has been analyzed in this way, it is easier to write out the sketch of the argument. This sketch might use just sentence fragments to display the main links. It is important to keep these elements relatively simple in the first stage of reconstruction so that you can easily understand the general "drift" of the argument.

Example 7.14

Argument Sketch of the Passage about American Culture

(1) Americans are self-indulgent.

(2) If self-indulgent, then erosion of values.

(3) If erosion of values, either internal or external constraint.

(4) No internal constraint.

∴   *External constraint.*

The reconstructions of Examples 7.10 and 7.13 illustrate how passages often demand extensive revision. In reconstructing an argument, as in paraphrasing single sentences, we have two conditions to meet: (1) the reconstruction should capture the apparent meaning of the original and (2) the reconstruction should provide more clarity. For any given argument, these guidelines can be satisfied by a number of different acceptable reconstructions. As for this passage:

Example 7.15   *There are broader reasons for censorship, too. Unless pornographers are restrained, the ethos of society may be eroded. However "pluralistic" or "individualistic" it prides itself on being, any society and all social bonds ultimately rest on a community of shared values. The values shared are different in each society. But unless it holds in common the values important to it, no culture can grow, no society persist. It happens that the values we share with respect to sex are important to us and set limits to the impulse to depict it, which we also share. The boundaries are watched over by censorship. They are changeable of course, and have changed often. So has censorship.**

Different reconstructions may be used to approximate the meaning of the passage.

Example 7.16   RECONSTRUCTION 1

(1) *Protection of (all) shared values is necessary for the continued existence of any society.*

(implicit)   (2) *Whatever is necessary for the continued existence of our society ought to be encouraged.*

(3) *Censorship will protect our shared values concerning the depiction of sex (pornography).*

∴ *Censorship (of pornography) ought to be encouraged.*

RECONSTRUCTION 2

(1) *Either pornography should be censored or social values will be eroded.*

(2) *If social values are eroded, then society cannot persist.*

(implicit)   (3) *Society should persist.*

∴ *Pornography should be censored.*

For this passage, and others more elaborate, reconstructions are possible that treat the passage as consisting of several interrelated arguments. Reconstruction of the argument in these passages may be presented in two different ways: (1) as several distinct arguments or (2) as a composite, continuous argument in which some statements are both a subordinate (or intermediate) conclusion and also a premise.

---

*Ernest Van Den Haag, "Case for Censorship," in *Perspectives on Pornography*, ed. Douglas A. Hughes (New York: St. Martin's Press, 1970), pp. 124–125.

Example 7.17   *(i) A social policy promoting abortion will inevitably lead to greater violations of the rights of the person. (ii) Such a consequence will undermine the mutual respect for the humanity of fellow citizens upon which democratic society is based. (iii) Any policy that destroys social bonds in this way threatens the society that engages in it. (iv) Hence a social policy promoting abortion threatens democratic society.*

This passage can be reconstructed in two ways.

Example 7.18   RECONSTRUCTION 1 *(Two Separate Arguments)*

(from sentence i)   *(1) A social policy promoting abortion will inevitably lead to greater violations of the rights of the person.*

(rewrite of sentence ii)   *(2) A social policy that leads to greater violations of the rights of the person will undermine the mutual respect for humanity of fellow citizens upon which democratic society is based.*

(implicit subordinate conclusion)   ∴   *A social policy promoting abortion will inevitably undermine the mutual respect for humanity of fellow citizens upon which democratic society is based.*

(conclusion from first argument)   *(1) A social policy promoting abortion will inevitably undermine the mutual respect for humanity of fellow citizens upon which democratic society is based.*

(rewrite of sentence iii)   *(2) Any policy that undermines the mutual respect for humanity of fellow citizens upon which democratic society is based threatens the democratic society that practices it.*

(rewrite of sentence iv)   ∴   *A social policy promoting abortion will inevitably threaten the democratic society that practices it.*

RECONSTRUCTION 2 *(Continuous Argument)*

(1) A social policy promoting abortion will inevitably lead to greater violations of the rights of the person.

(2) A social policy that leads to greater violations of the rights of the person will undermine the mutual respect for humanity of fellow citizens upon which democratic society is based.

(subordinate conclusion)   ∴ *(3) A social policy promoting abortion will inevitably undermine the mutual respect for humanity of fellow citizens upon which democratic society is based.*

> *(4) Any policy that undermines the mutual respect for humanity of fellow citizens upon which democratic society is based threatens the democratic society that practices it.*

(main conclusion) ∴ *A social policy promoting abortion will inevitably threaten the democratic society that practices it.*

Whenever we strive to simplify or rewrite what someone else has produced, we run the risk of distorting what that writer said. The method of first approximation is a crude instrument designed to make rough cuts. Once we have discovered the basic structure, we can go back and paraphrase the argument more sensitively, thus capturing some of the subtleties we might have previously ignored. It is too easy for us to be lost in a forest of words when we face a complex passage. Simplification, paraphrase, and argument sketches are means of finding our way through it.

Exercise 7.4	**Putting All This into Practice**

Reconstruct the arguments contained in the following passages. Simplify or paraphrase whenever possible. Add implicit conclusions, or premises, or both, as needed. Some passages contain more than one argument. Select one or two that are important and interesting. Most of the arguments can be reconstructed in several different ways.

1. A woman can now determine early in her pregnancy whether her baby will be a boy or girl. This raises the possibility of having an abortion simply because of the gender of the fetus. But such an action would clearly be wrong. Testing fetuses to determine whether they will become healthy babies is legitimate. But because the information might be misused, doctors should not be allowed to inform the parents of the gender of their fetus.

2. Well, I insist—and I here follow von Hildebrand—that we parents, we married people, in no way believe sex is dirty, but we believe it is private and intimate. Therefore, it cannot endure being publicized the way mathematics or even the way health is publicized. It is quite tactful for you to go to a party and talk about your tonsils. It is not tactful—not acceptable—for you to go to a party and talk about how your wife makes love to you, not because you think it is dirty, my friends, but because you think it is intimate.*

---

*Cited in Gloria Lentz, *Raping Our Children: The Sex Education Scandal* (New Rochelle, N.Y.: Arlington House Publishing, 1972), p. 76.

(HINT: Go beyond the analysis given in the text. Treat this as an argument against sex education classes in the schools.)

3. This touches on another argument presented by parents who are opposed to sex education. They state that sex education robs a child of valuable time that should be spent on basic skills—not to mention the tax dollars that are being poured into sex education.*

(HINT: Use the implicit premise that whatever takes time from teaching basic skills and wastes money should not exist in the schools.)

4. There is a continuity of development from the moment of conception on. There are constant changes in the foetal condition; the foetus is constantly acquiring new structures and characteristics, but there is no one stage which is radically different from any other. Since that is so, there is no one stage in the process of foetal development, after the moment of conception which could plausibly be picked out as the moment at which the foetus becomes a living human being. The moment of conception is, however, different in this respect. It marks the beginning of this continuous process of development and introduces something new which is radically discontinuous with what has come before it. Therefore, the moment of conception, and only it, is a plausible candidate for being that moment at which the foetus becomes a living human being.**

(HINT: Try using the implicit premise that either the fetus becomes human at the moment of conception or it becomes human at some moment thereafter.)

5. LECTURE FRAGMENT

   Plea bargaining (agreeing to plead guilty in exchange for a reduced sentence) generates problems. Innocent defendants who can't afford bail may plead guilty just to avoid jail time waiting for trial. The process makes no presumption of innocence. Guilt is not determined in an adversarial process, it is negotiated. It makes work easier for prosecutors, defense attorneys, and judges, but it sacrifices the interests of society.

   Given these problems, some have suggested that plea bargaining be eliminated. But this might create an even worse problem. Ninety percent of defendants plead guilty, and most of those do plea-bargain. Suppose plea bargaining were eliminated and the percentage of guilty pleas dropped to 80 percent. This would double the number of criminal trials, placing a staggering burden on the criminal justice system.

---

*Lentz, *Raping Our Children*, p. 47.
**Baruch Brody, "On the Humanity of the Foetus," in *Abortion: Pro and Con*, ed., Robert Perkins (Cambridge: Shenkman Publishing, 1974), pp. 70–71.

The experience of Alaska, however, calls this fear into question. Alaska has virtually done away with plea bargaining. There was some increase in the number of trials, but not as much as expected. In the year before elimination of plea bargaining, there were 72 felony trials in Fairbanks. In the year after, there were 90. This is only a 25% increase.

Why was the increase so small? The explanation of why defendants plead guilty could be because most of them are factually guilty; they don't have a viable legal argument for their defense (i.e., they are legally guilty as well), so they believe it is unlikely they would win in a trial. If this is the case, then as Alaska's experience indicates, while it may be difficult to eliminate plea bargaining, it is not impossible.

(Note: There are several arguments in this lecture fragment. After formulating your reconstructions, compare them to those made in Chapter 1, pp. 9–10. Remember that the reconstruction of arguments from longer passages allows for some degree of individual interpretation.)

6. A BAN ON FLAG-BURNING SILENCES NO ONE'S VOICE*

The global quest for freedom continues. Eastern European intellectuals, some of them only recently released from Communist jails, pore over the Federalist Papers, seeking inspiration for the new era. South Africa is moving toward serious discussion of power-sharing among the races. Chinese students struggle to preserve the dream of democracy, sometimes laying their lives on the line for their beliefs.

Meanwhile, back in the U.S.A., a protest group threatens "flag burnings from sea to shining sea" if Congress takes up a constitutional amendment that would protect the U.S. flag from desecration.

Is it any wonder that foreigners sometimes accuse Americans of taking freedom for granted? Here in a land of unmatched liberties, some people can't seem to imagine a political protest that doesn't involve burning one of the leading symbols of those liberties.

The judge who struck down a flag-protection law in the state of Washington said the flag can't endure as a symbol of freedom unless the right to destroy it is protected.

Activist lawyer William Kunstler materialized in the news almost immediately after the decision was announced, pushing his view that a law prohibiting flag-burning would trash the Founding Fathers' attempt to guarantee freedom of speech. Attorneys for other accused flag-burners moved for a dismissal of charges, calling the Washington decision a victory for free speech.

---

*Reprinted with permission of *The Omaha World-Herald*.

Sen. Robert Dole, R-Kan., described the situation more accurately when he said it was a victory for flag-burners. Where is the logic in contending that the flag is cheapened by respect and honored by disrespect?

Flag-burning isn't speech. It's an act. It is a kind of behavior that, like public nudity or the display of anti-Semitic symbols, deeply offends a lot of people. No one's right to express a dissenting view is unreasonably curtailed by laws banning those kinds of behavior, however, just as no one's freedom of speech is denied by a law providing criminal penalties for burning the flag.

The First Amendment freedom of speech allows Americans to say just about anything that comes into their minds. It is the cornerstone of our democracy. What Kuntsler and others are demanding now, in effect, is a constitutional right to perform just about any act that comes into their minds and call it speech. Their crusade reflects the devaluation of ideas that can occur when theater-of-the-streets demonstrations are substituted for rational debate.

(Note: Be sure to distinguish arguments made by the author from those of William Kunstler and Robert Dole, referred to by the author.)

CHAPTER EIGHT

Putting It All Together: Six Steps to Understanding and Evaluating Deductive Arguments

The previous seven chapters have explained parts of a process of understanding and evaluating deductive arguments. Now we can bring these parts together in a sequence of steps illustrated by the flowchart in Figure 8.1.

Much of the earlier discussion of particular steps in reconstructing or evaluating arguments concentrated on short, stylized passages in which each sentence played a role as a premise or conclusion. In Chapter 7, we looked at the task of reconstructing arguments that occur in longer, more complicated passages. We shall now survey the whole six-step procedure represented on the flowchart and adapt it to understanding and evaluating arguments found in longer passages, such as essays and editorials.

The *preliminary step* directs you to read the passage in question carefully. The importance of this step should not be overlooked. As we pointed out in Chapter 7, one of the first things you need to determine is whether a passage does in fact put forth an argument, as opposed to describing, explaining, classifying, and so forth. Consider the context of the passage. Make use of hints such as titles or recurring themes. You can also initially determine (without fully reconstructing any arguments) whether there is one argument or several and how different arguments are related. You might need to read a passage carefully *several times* before you understand it well enough to identify any arguments it contains and to begin a reconstruction of them.

Step 1. You should identify any *explicit* premises or conclusions, but

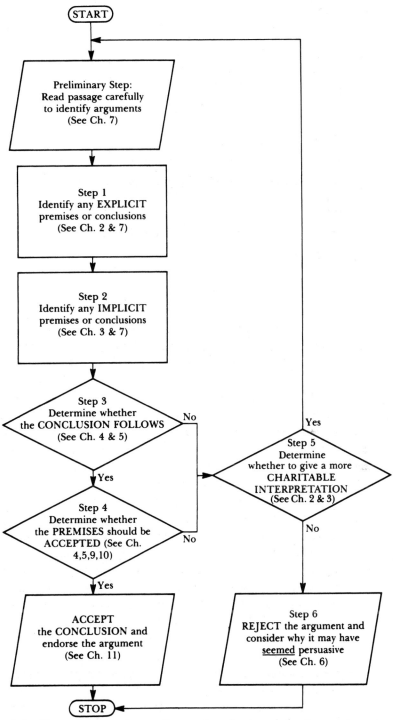

Figure 8.1 Six steps to understanding and evaluating deductive arguments

this doesn't mean copying sentences out of a passage exactly as they are written. More likely, you will paraphrase or restate assertions that are made by the passage. In actual practice, the distinction between identifying explicit and implicit premises is not as sharp as in the stylized passages we dealt with, where whole sentences *could* be copied as premises. But even if no premises can be copied word-for-word from the passage, some premises might be very strongly suggested and easily paraphrased from what is actually written.

Step 2.   We pointed out in Chapter 3 and again in Chapter 7 that the step of identifying *implicit* premises typically amounts to adding any premises that are needed to make the conclusion follow (insofar as this *can* be done without radically distorting the meaning of the passage being interpreted). Adding an implicit conclusion consists of adding a conclusion that *would* follow from the interpreted premises, if the conclusion is not already stated in the passage.

Step 3.   Given what we just said about step 2, determining whether the conclusion follows will often be carried out in the process of adding implicit premises or an implicit conclusion. The premises and conclusion of the argument might have been stated so explicitly, however, that step 2 is unnecessary, and a negative answer to the question in step 3 (Does the conclusion follow?) might be unavoidable. Or (as happens more frequently), the argument might contain an unclear expression that occurs more than once. If so, you will probably make several quick loops through steps 3, 4, and 5, and back through 1 and 2, to determine whether a single meaning that makes all the premises acceptable can be assigned to this expression (see Chapter 5).

Step 4.   Determining whether the premises should be accepted was discussed in Chapters 4 and 5. Techniques for evaluating additional kinds of premises—particularly premises associated with scientific theories—will be investigated in Chapters 9 and 10.

Step 5.   If you find that the conclusion of an argument does not follow or the premises are unacceptable, the flowchart directs you to consider giving a more charitable interpretation of the argument. This procedure is in keeping with the rationale for critical reasoning that has been promoted throughout this book: being presented with an argument should be taken as an opportunity to determine what is reasonable to believe, not as a contest in which the object is to defeat the person who has presented the argument.

If an argument can be interpreted in such a way that the conclusion follows and the premises are acceptable, then the flowchart calls for the conclusion to be accepted. If, on the other hand, there is no reasonable way of interpreting the argument so that it passes these tests, the argument should be rejected.

Step 6. However, if an argument is rejected the flowchart calls for the additional step of considering why the argument may have seemed persuasive. This is a particularly helpful step in a direct exchange with someone who has offered an argument or with an audience that might have been persuaded by it. It is much more likely that you will be able to sell your negative appraisal of the argument if you can explain why the arguer or audience was tempted to accept it in the first place. For this purpose, the discussion of fallacies in Chapter 6 should be helpful, since that analysis was aimed at explaining why people tend to be persuaded by certain kinds of bad arguments. Step 6 can also serve as an occasion to suggest what direction might be taken to improve the argument being examined. Often there is some core of reasonableness that lies behind the argument being offered, but which the presenter of the argument was not able to adequately express. Perhaps even the Principle of Charitable Interpretation won't permit the argument to be revised radically enough to capture this reasonableness. But in the application of the six-step procedure you might have gotten some ideas about how a different but related argument could be constructed that *would* be acceptable.

Sample Application of the Six-Step Procedure

It may be helpful to apply the entire six-step procedure to an argument found in a newspaper editorial. The following discussion is much more detailed than would be appropriate to present in, say, a critical essay. It explains the steps you could go through in your mind in preparing to write about or discuss the argument. An example of a shorter, more tightly organized discussion that could be presented in a critical essay is given later in this chapter.

Suppose you came across the editorial on page 196 and decided to consider it carefully—to attempt to understand it clearly and evaluate its main arguments. How could the six-step procedure be used to carry out this task?

The way you would proceed depends in part upon the particular purpose you had in analyzing the editorial. You might intend to write a reply, discuss the editorial with someone who is interested in the topic of "comparable worth," or simply figure out whether to accept the point of view being advanced by the writer. For many purposes, the following analysis is probably more detailed than you would need to go through, but the steps you would take would be essentially the same.

Pitfalls in Comparable Worth*

1 Some people in a largely female audience objected the other day when . . . economist William Niskanen criticized . . . the concept known as "comparable worth" or "comparable pay." Niskanen called the idea "a truly crazy proposal."

2 Perhaps that wasn't the most diplomatic way Niskanen could have selected for disagreeing with a concept that the National Organization for Women, among other groups and individuals, insists is a matter of justice.

3 But he was right to criticize the idea. . . . There is no good argument for an employer to pay less to women for doing the same job men do simply because they are women. That kind of discrimination is wrong.

4 But that isn't the issue here. The comparable worth concept says men and women in different occupations should receive the same wages if their jobs are "comparable." Advocates of the idea say such a plan is necessary to address the fact that women with full-time jobs are, on the average, paid less than men with full-time jobs.

5 Who decides what is comparable? A study by the State University of New York suggested that a registered nurse was comparable in responsibility and education to a vocational education teacher. Another study ranked dining-hall directors with auto parts handlers and highway maintenance workers with clerk-typists.

6 Such judgments can depend on criteria that are so arbitrary that they are almost worthless. Some people might make a case for the idea that nurses have more responsibility than vocational education teachers and consequently should be paid more.

Or that dining-hall directors ought to be paid more than auto parts handlers.

7 A National Academy of Sciences committee conducted a comparability study based on required skills, level of experience, responsibility, effort, working conditions and other factors. The committee said there are no absolute standards for judging the worth of all jobs.

8 Such efforts raise questions of fairness. How much weight should be given to each of the factors? How about such difficult-to-measure factors as number of interruptions in an employee's working day? Or the degree of danger involved in the job?

9 Even if it were possible to devise a fair system of determining comparability, it would not be a logical basis for determining compensation.

10 The imposition of a comparable pay plan for public employees could place a considerable burden on taxpayers. Obviously, nobody's pay would be reduced. Equalizing would mean raising.

11 A comparable worth system also could disrupt market forces that encourage people to enter occupations where more workers are needed and discourage people from entering fields where there is a surplus of workers.

12 When there is a shortage of nurses, employers ought to be able to offer higher nursing salaries without causing nearby high schools to have to offer higher salaries for vocational education teachers.

13 Niskanen might have been undiplomatic in calling comparable worth a "truly crazy proposal." But the term "voodoo economics" has already been used.

*© 1984 by the *Omaha World-Herald*. Reprinted by permission.

Preliminary Step: Read Passage Carefully to Identify Arguments Even though the main points of this editorial are reasonably clear, a careful reading will lead you to see beyond some surface features that might mislead the casual reader. The beginning and ending attempt to defend a political economist for some remarks he made in a speech, but the body develops the writer's own arguments against the proposal of comparable worth and goes beyond assessing whether the economist's remarks were appropriate.

Paragraph 4 specifies that it is not the issue of men and women getting the same pay for the same jobs that is being discussed, but rather the issue of whether "men and women . . . should receive the same wages if their jobs are 'comparable.' " Clearly, the writer is opposed to such a policy.

What does a careful reading lead us to take as the main arguments of this essay? A major conclusion being supported is that a system of comparable worth should not be implemented. Paragraphs 5 through 8 give one set of related reasons for this conclusion, and paragraphs 10 through 12 give another set of reasons. We can interpret these as two arguments with the same conclusion.

Step 1: Identifying any Explicit Premises or Conclusions As we discussed in Chapter 7, the distinction between explicit and implicit premises and conclusions is not a sharp one when you are reconstructing an argument from a complex prose passage. Nowhere in the essay is it explicitly stated that "a system of comparable worth should not be implemented." But the statements that the economist "was right to criticize the idea" (paragraph 3) and "even if it were possible to devise a fair system of determining comparability, it would not be a logical basis for determining compensation" (paragraph 9) leave no room for doubt that this is what the writer intends.

Picking out premises in the first argument (paragraphs 5 through 8) demands much more interpretation. Paragraphs 5 through 7 assert that different people would judge comparable worth differently, that criteria of comparable worth are arbitrary, and that there are no absolute standards of comparable worth. The way in which the writer moves from one of these assertions to the next, using the same kind of examples in support of each, would suggest that he takes all three to be roughly equivalent. When paragraph 8 moves to the claim that the (unsuccessful) efforts to judge comparable worth objectively "raise questions of fairness," we are led to take two of the premises of the first argument to be:

(1) There are no objective criteria for determining comparable worth.

(2) If there are no objective criteria for determining comparable worth, then comparable worth can't be determined fairly.

Paragraphs containing argument 1

5 Who decides what is comparable? A study by the State University of New York suggested that a registered nurse was comparable in responsibility and education to a vocational education teacher. Another study ranked dining-hall directors with auto parts handlers and highway maintenance workers with clerk-typists.

6 Such judgments can depend on criteria that are so arbitrary that they are almost worthless. Some people might make a case for the idea that nurses have more responsibility than vocational education teachers and consequently should be paid more. Or that dining-hall directors ought to be paid more than auto parts handlers.

7 A National Academy of Sciences committee conducted a comparability study based on required skills, level of experience, responsibility, effort, working conditions and other factors. The committee said there are no absolute standards for judging the worth of all jobs.

8 Such efforts raise questions of fairness. How much weight should be given to each of the factors? How about such difficult-to-measure factors as number of interruptions in an employee's working day? Or the degree of danger involved in the job?

9 Even if it were possible to devise a fair system of determining comparability, it would not be a logical basis for determining compensation.

When the writer states in paragraph 9 that "even if it were possible to devise a fair system of determining comparable worth, it would not be a logical basis for determining compensation," he seems to suggest that the impossibility of determining comparable worth fairly is *one* consideration that would establish that comparable worth shouldn't be implemented, and now he is going to set forth another one. On this interpretation, we assume that the writer has already completed his first argument against comparable worth.

Step 2: Adding an Implicit Premise to the First Argument   Upon reviewing the premises stated above, we can see that we need an implicit premise in order to reach the intended conclusion.

ARGUMENT 1

(suggested by paragraphs 5–8)

(1) There are no objective criteria for determining comparable worth.

(2) If there are no objective criteria for determining comparable worth, then comparable worth can't be determined fairly.

(implicit)

(3) If comparable worth can't be determined fairly, then a system of comparable worth should not be implemented.

∴ *A system of comparable worth should not be implemented.*

Paragraphs containing argument 2

10 The imposition of a comparable pay plan for public employees could place a considerable burden on taxpayers. Obviously, nobody's pay would be reduced. Equalizing would mean raising.

11 A comparable worth system also could disrupt market forces that encourage people to enter occupations where more workers are needed and discourage people from entering fields where there is a surplus of workers.

12 When there is a shortage of nurses, employers ought to be able to offer higher nursing salaries without causing nearby high schools to have to offer higher salaries for vocational education teachers.

Applying Steps 1 and 2 to the Second Argument The second argument is more straightforward. The writer raises two considerations against implementing comparable worth: (1) such a practice for public employees would be burdensome to taxpayers (paragraph 10), and (2) it would disrupt market forces (paragraph 11). The reasoning for the second consideration is interesting enough to be detailed as part of the argument: under a system of comparable worth, if offering higher salaries were necessary in order to counteract a shortage of workers in one field, then higher salaries would also have to be offered in comparable fields. Combining these premises with the obvious implicit premises and keeping the same conclusion as in argument 1, we would have:

ARGUMENT 2

(paraphrase of paragraph 10)
(1) *A system of comparable worth for public employees would be burdensome to taxpayers.*

(paraphrase of paragraph 11)
(2) *If a system of comparable worth were implemented, then higher salaries offered to attract workers to one field would have to be matched by higher salaries in comparable fields.*

(implicit)
(3) *If a policy would be burdensome to taxpayers and would have the consequences for the market described in premise 2, then it shouldn't be implemented.*

∴   *A system of comparable worth shouldn't be implemented.*

Applying Steps 3, 4, and 5 to Argument 1   As will often be the case, we have interpreted these arguments in such a way that the implicit premises we add permit the conclusions to follow from the premises. That is, the conclusions will follow unless there is a shift in the meaning of a word or expression. Noting this for our reconstruction, we can move to step 4. If in our determination of whether to accept the premises we find that their acceptability depends on the meaning of an unclear expression, we can then determine whether there are any shifts in meaning from one premise to another.

Premise 1 states that there are no objective criteria for determining comparable worth. As we noted earlier, the writer seems to interpret this in either of two ways: (1) criteria of comparable worth are arbitrary, or (2) different people would judge comparable worth differently. But it must be remembered that however we interpret this premise, we must use the same interpretation when we consider (in premise 2) whether comparable worth can be determined fairly if there are no objective criteria, if the criteria are arbitrary, or if different people would judge it differently.

With this in mind, we can reject the second interpretation of premise 1 as simply stating that different people would judge comparable worth differently; there are, in fact, many things people would judge differently but which could nevertheless be judged fairly. Different people would judge criminal guilt or innocence differently. They would judge whether a person deserved a promotion differently. They would judge the quality of a dive differently. If we maintain that these are also things that *can't* be judged fairly, we must remember that in premise 3 the failure to be able to judge something fairly will be taken as a reason against implementing it. Should the practices of holding criminal trial, promoting employees, and holding diving contests also be abandoned?

What we are doing at this point is following the flowchart from step 4 to step 5 and back through steps 1, 2, and 3. This is the dialogue-process of interpreting and evaluating that we referred to in Chapter 5. We determined that if a premise is assigned a certain meaning, this will force another premise to be false (or else the argument will become an equivocation and the conclusion will not follow). So we attempted a more charitable interpretation and determined whether this would make the premises acceptable and still allow the conclusion to follow.

In argument 1, we still need to consider the first interpretation of premise 1; that is, we could interpret the claim that there are no objective criteria to mean that all criteria are arbitrary: either no defensible rationale could be given for using one set of criteria rather than another, or after some set of criteria was decided upon, it would yield different results depending upon who applied the criteria. The latter would run into the same difficulties as did "different people would judge comparable worth differently." What about the former?

Could a defensible rationale be given for using one set of criteria for comparable worth rather than another? In determining this we come to some substantive issues that probably lie at the basis of the comparable worth controversy. One approach to the worth or value of a worker would simply be to point to the market for a worker's skill as a gauge of its value. How much people are willing to pay for your work is a measure of how valuable it is to them. But on this interpretation, there can be no problem of comparable worth because (if the market is allowed to operate freely) each person will get exactly what she or he is worth.

Others, however, will estimate the worth of a worker in terms of some notion of what is deserved. Such factors as effort, stress on the job, or education required for the position might be seen as indicating that a person deserves a certain wage, regardless of the market demand for his or her work.

No doubt, the proponents on any side of this issue could give *a* defense of their criteria. But it is likely that none of them will be able to convince all, or even very many of, their opponents. In this sense we can probably accept the claim that there are no objective criteria for determining comparable worth.

Again, we must assign this same interpretation to premise 2 when we ask whether comparable worth can be determined fairly if there are no objective criteria. What if certain criteria are arrived at (by vote, say), even though no one agrees to all of them? If these criteria are applied as uniformly as possible from case to case, then won't comparable worth have been determined fairly? The determination may not satisfy everyone's criteria of *accuracy,* but would the determination be unfair? It may be like the diving example, in which different people might think different factors should be taken into account in judging a dive. But once a set of criteria is decided upon (again by vote), it might well be claimed that the judging could be done fairly.

The implicit premise—if comparable worth can't be determined fairly, then it shouldn't be implemented—would seem to depend on how unfair was the determination of comparable worth and how grievous was the injustice it tried to correct. If it were necessary to spend tax money obtained by a system that has some minimal unfairness in it in order to provide the right to vote to people who had been unjustly excluded from voting, then this would surely not be an overriding consideration against providing this right. The extent to which differences in wages between women and men have been the result of past injustice and the gravity of the injustice would have to be determined.

We have gone to considerable length to interpret and reinterpret the premises of argument 1 so they will be acceptable and the conclusion will follow, but with little success. The point at which we give up this procedure (that is, give a negative answer to step 5) is somewhat arbitrary. Realistically, it depends on how much time and energy we are willing to devote to the argument.

Perhaps it would be adequate for our purposes to suggest a direction that might be taken if the process of reinterpretation were to be carried further. The difficulties raised by the writer with arriving at criteria for judging comparable worth *do* carry some weight as a consideration against implementing a policy of comparable worth. Perhaps the writer did not intend that this consideration alone would be compelling; but that in combination with the problems raised by argument 2, we have adequate reason to reject the idea of comparable worth. A possible direction for further revision could then be to combine argument 1 with argument 2.

Applying Step 6 to Argument 1   To conclude the application of the flowchart to argument 1, we must ask why this argument might have seemed persuasive. The argument doesn't straightforwardly commit any of the common fallacies (unless it is taken as an equivocation). There may be an illegitimate appeal to authority in citing a National Academy of Sciences Committee as having determined that there are no absolute standards for judging comparable worth. (It is questionable whether this issue could be settled by any of the sciences.)

It is undeniable that different people will interpret comparable worth in radically different ways. And it *is* tempting to conclude from this that comparable worth should not be implemented. Why is this? Perhaps it seems unreasonable to enact a public policy when there is very little consensus regarding the criteria upon which it would be based. Perhaps the fact that there is little agreement on criteria raises the possibility that some really inappropriate criteria—ones that should have nothing to do with comparable worth—would be implemented. If this were the case, then it would really seem unjust to implement a comparable worth policy that included inappropriate criteria.

It is likely that the writer is beset by fears such as these, which are not clearly articulated, and that his argument seemed persuasive to him because it captured some of his reasoning and led to the desired conclusion—that comparable worth should not be implemented. It must be remembered that even if the particular argument he presented is not judged to warrant its conclusion, that doesn't mean the conclusion is false. Finally, as we suggested earlier, it could be that argument 1 was intended only as one consideration against comparable worth, with the major consideration set forth in argument 2.

Exercise 8.1   **Applying the Six-Step Procedure**

1. Carry out the remainder of the six-step procedure in evaluating argument 2 from "Pitfalls in Comparable Worth."

2. In Chapter 7 you applied the first two steps of the procedure to the passages in Exercise 7.4. Apply the remainder of the six-step procedure to the arguments from those passages.

3. Apply the entire six-step procedure to the following passages.

   a. STOP SUBSIDIZING THE FUTURE RICH/ John R. Lott Jr.*

   (John R. Lott Jr. is a visiting assistant professor of economics at Texas A & M University.)

   > College Station, Texas—The basic problem with government-subsidized student loans is that they are a subsidy to future high-income people.
   >
   > The loans students receive carry interest rates far below what even the most stable corporations pay.
   >
   > While students, especially those from relatively poor families, do not have a high standard of living during college, they enjoy above-average earnings soon after receiving their degrees. Since the loans are slowly paid off after graduation, during a period of high earnings, subsidized interest rates seem unjustified.

Why should factory workers and secretaries be taxed so would-be managers, lawyers, and doctors can be subsidized?

And subsidized federal loans are only a small part of our educational subsidies. Here at Texas A & M, each student pays only a small percentage of the $10,000-plus it annually costs the state of Texas. The great majority of these students come from relatively well-to-do families. In the cases of those few who do not, the argument about transfers to future high-income earners applies.

It is important to distinguish loans *per se* from the currently heavily subsidized loans.

While *subsidized* loans are unjustified, a weak case can be made for government loan guarantees or possibly loans at unsubsidized rates. This is because of the problems created by current bankruptcy laws, which in some cases have allowed students to rid themselves of educational debt by simply declaring bankruptcy after graduation. Banks may therefore consider student loans too risky.

Unfortunately, these bankruptcy laws probably hurt children from poor families the most. For a student from a poor family, the parents' co-signature does not appreciably reduce the riskiness of the loan, since they do not own enough assets.

The simplest and best solution is to alter the bankruptcy laws to get rid of this problem. Private banks could then handle student loans entirely, with no role played by the federal government.

Evidence provided by Sam Peltzman of the University of Chicago suggests that abolishing subsidized loans will have little effect on the number of people attending higher education. The primary effect will be to end the unjustified taxing of people to subsidize the future wealthy of this country.

b. DON'T ROLL BACK "ROE"/ John R. Silber*

(John R. Silber is president of Boston University.)

Boston—The public debate over abortion, already bitter, is likely to become even more so. Indeed, with state legislatures debating new restrictions made possible by the Supreme Court's decision in Webster v. Reproductive Health Services, consensus looks further away every day.

This bitter debate grows out of widespread confusion between legal issues and moral ones, between religious issues and political

*Copyright © 1990 by the New York Times Company. Reprinted with permission.

ones. We cannot develop a clear understanding of these difficult issues without considering legal and ethical points of view.

I would oppose any law prohibiting abortion in the first two trimesters. That is, I believe that the states should retain the standard set by the Supreme Court in Roe v. Wade even though Webster allows them to restrict it.

It is very doubtful, considering past experience, that restrictive legislation would do more than make presently legal abortions illegal. Some of these abortions, involving technologies that enable laymen to perform abortions safely, would be different from current abortions only in their illegality. Others, performed with coat hangers in back alleys, will be fatal. I could not in conscience recommend legislation having these effects.

But this is not the same as the "pro-choice" position. It is possible to believe that abortion ought to be legal without believing that it is an unconditional right, or even that it is morally justified in more than a limited number of cases.

Nor is the belief that many abortions are immoral the same as the "pro-life" position. There are instances when the taking of human life is justifiable, legally and morally. Homicide is not equivalent to murder. Some homicides are entirely justified, especially those involving self-defense. A woman whose life is threntened by a pregnancy is justified in terminating the pregnancy that might kill or severely injure her.

So, too, when a woman is raped she is under no obligation morally, and should be under no obligation legally, to accept the consequences of an act of sexual intercourse in which she did not voluntarily participate. She has a right to protect herself from the consequences of assault.

But this does not lead me to conclude that abortions are morally justified when the pregnancy does not threaten the life of the mother and follows from sexual intercourse in which she voluntarily participated. Indiscriminate use of abortion is wrong because the indiscriminate taking of human life is wrong.

If abortion were not a supercharged issue, it would be apparent to all parties that a fertilized ovum is, in fact, a living human. Obviously it is not a complete human being. But neither is a fetus in the third trimester or, for that matter, a newborn infant or a child of one or two years of age. The value of the life of an infant is based on its potential to become a fulfilled human being, and that potential exists from the time of conception.

Believing firmly as I do in this moral view of abortion, I think it would be a disastrous error to write it into the statute book.

A free society cannot maintain its unity and order unless there is toleration of diverse opinions on which consensus has not been achieved. Without religious toleration, for example, the unity of the

13 Colonies would have been torn asunder by religious wars of the sort that plagued Europe for centuries. The abortion issue is for many individuals a religious issue, and on such issues we should scrupulously observe the separation of church and state.

By tolerating contrary views, we accept an important fact that is too often overlooked. The instruments of the state and its legal institutions are far too crude and inexact to be used in deciding highly complex issues of personal morality on which persons of good will fundamentally disagree. It is proper to leave such important moral and religious issues to individual moral agents and religious believers.

On the issue of abortion, there is no political, philosophical, moral or religious consensus. I believe abortion is, in general, morally wrong. But I also believe the state should not enact laws to restrict abortion further. This is an issue that cries out for toleration.

Application to Writing

The six-step procedure can be adapted to assist in the writing of a critical essay. The format we recommend can be used to present a critical assessment of almost any discourse that contains an argument—a speech, essay, editorial, letter to the editor, or even a portion of a conversation.

It is often effective to arrange a critical essay into four parts: an introduction, a reconstruction of the argument to be criticized, a critical assessment of the argument, and a conclusion. Although this structure is not a formula to follow blindly, it is a model that can be adapted to a variety of writing tasks.

The *introduction* should convey the importance of the critical discussion to follow. A good way of doing this is to relate the particular essay, speech, or whatever to some broader issue on which the argument at hand has some bearing. One way of unifying your essay is to move in the introduction from a broad topic of concern to the particular issue at hand, and then to move back to the broad area of concern in your conclusion.

The *reconstruction of the argument* should begin with a paraphrase (or quotation) conveying the argument in unreconstructed form. This paraphrase should be done as succinctly as possible to avoid losing the flow of the essay at this point. Then, you should introduce any necessary implicit statements and give the complete argument. For purposes of the essay assigned at the end of this section, you may use technical terms such as *standard form* or *implicit premise*. But in general, suit your terminology to the audience for whom you are writing.

The *critical assessment* should begin with a statement of whether the conclusion of the argument follows from the premises. If it doesn't, demonstrate this to the reader as clearly as possible. (Refer to Chapter 4 for tips on showing invalidity.) If the argument can be made valid by adding more premises, discuss this in either the reconstruction or the critical portion. Next, discuss whether the premises are acceptable. Remember to criticize specific premises, one at a time. If you decide that the premises are acceptable, you should still try to raise criticisms you think might be made by an intelligent reader and reply to these criticisms on behalf of the argument. If a vague or ambiguous term occurs in more than one place in the argument, use the techniques described in Chapter 5 to explain how different interpretations of the meaning of this term will affect the argument.

The *conclusion* should restate briefly your final assessment of the argument. If you reject the argument, you could attempt to explain here why the arguer might have been persuaded by it even though it is a bad argument. You could also return in your conclusion to the broader concerns you raised in your introduction—the importance of the issue, what position now seems reasonable in regard to it, and so forth.

To get a better idea of how this format can be used, read the following excerpt from a speech on the subject of crime and its causes and the sample critical essay that follows it. The sample essay criticizes an argument from the speech.

OUR PERMISSIVE SYSTEM OF CRIMINAL JUSTICE

Violence is no longer the manufactured melodrama of the theatrical arts. It has become part of our everyday life—gruesome tragedies, perpetrated against our next-door neighbor, our family and our friends, personally touching each of us. Mathematically, one out of every five families will have a major crime committed against some member of that family.

Crime is the product of flesh and blood individuals—individuals who choose to satisfy their carnal, fiscal and physical desires by denying the rights of others . . . individuals who willfully choose to assault the person or take over the property of other human beings.

Aided, I might add, by accomplices. Accomplices who have contributed to the rise in crime. These friends of the felon are the professional apologists, the excuse makers, the contemporary environmentalists, the behaviorists . . . those people who are more interested in bleeding hearts than bleeding victims. They are the ones who blame everybody and everything, except the responsible individual.

Advocates of this philosophy reside in the present Department of Corrections, including its Division of Parole, and also within the probation departments of our counties. It is taught in our universities and colleges as mod-

ern penology and promoted as fact, not theory. This social philosophy is especially attractive to those who dislike the competition of the American way of life—the kind of life where a man is responsible for his own actions. The concept that man controls his own destiny and is accountable is anathema to the Socialist mind.

One point that apologists rarely explain away is why, for every criminal who comes from a slum area, are there thousands from the same area who hold jobs? Why, for every under-educated criminal, are there thousands of successful individuals who made it with less education? Why, for every unemployed criminal, are there thousands who never had to resort to crime as a means of survival?

I was raised in a factory town on the south side of Chicago. A tough neighborhood, what some would call an economically deprived area by today's standards. I dropped out of high school after only two years and joined the Navy to fight for my country in the Second World War. I also came from a broken home. So, I was a high school drop-out, from an economically deprived area and a broken home. I must assume that all those with the same background will grow up to be senators.

It isn't society nor environment that commits crimes. Criminals commit crimes . . . individuals. Criminal individuals commit crimes.*

IS THE ENVIRONMENT THE CAUSE OF CRIME?

In his speech, "Our Permissive System of Criminal Justice," Senator H. L. Richardson expresses his anger toward those who claim that the environment, rather than the individual criminal, is responsible for crime. He believes not only that this theory is false, but also that people who propose it have aided criminals and helped crime to flourish. It can be questioned whether this theory has really contributed to a rise in crime, but I will limit this essay to the question of whether Richardson has given us grounds for believing that the environment is not the cause of crime.

Richardson's argument is essentially that not everyone from a "slum area" is a criminal, so it is not the slum area that is the cause of crime. This argument contains the implicit premise that if slum areas did cause crime, then everyone from a slum area would be a criminal. If we add this premise, the argument can be stated like this:

---

*Excerpts from a speech by California Senator H. L. Richardson, "Time to Reaffirm Basic Truths about Crime," *Human Events*, August 31, 1974, pp. 18–19. Reprinted with permission of the publisher.

1. If slum areas caused crime, then everyone from a slum area would be a criminal.
2. Not everyone from a slum area is a criminal.

∴ Slum areas do not cause crime.

Supposedly, Richardson would make this same argument about other environments besides slum areas, which might be thought to cause crime. Otherwise, he could not come to his *general* conclusion that the environment does not cause crime. If we put his argument in this more general way, it would look like this:

1. Given any environment, if that environment caused crime, then everyone from that environment would be a criminal.
2. Given any environment, not everyone from that environment is a criminal.

∴ No environment causes crime.

Both of these arguments are valid, but it is doubtful that all their premises are true. Consider Premise 1 of either argument—that if slum areas (or some other environment) caused crime, then everyone from that area would be a criminal. There is a sense of "cause" in which we would say that one thing caused another even if it did not <u>always</u> produce this effect. For example, we say that drunken driving causes accidents even though people sometimes drive while drunk without having an accident. Similarly, those who say that slum areas cause crime might mean that these areas tend to produce criminals, and are therefore at least partially responsible for crime. It would not follow that everyone from a slum area must be a criminal.

As was stated earlier, Richardson must make his argument a general one about *any* environment if he wishes to come to the general conclusion that no environment causes crime. The second premise of this general argument is: <u>Given any environment, not everyone from that environment is a criminal.</u> It is not at all obvious that this premise is true. Suppose we take a poor neighborhood as an example of an environment. Many people from this environment will not be criminals. But suppose we narrow down the environment further by considering only the homes of male teenagers who have friends who commit crimes regularly. Now a larger percentage of the people from this environment will be criminals like their friends. And we could continue to narrow down the environment to include only teenagers who had been treated brutally as young children, and so on. It is at least possible that we would end up describing an environment that always produced criminals.

The issue of whether the environment is the cause of crime is an important one. The attitude we take regarding it affects the course of action we would recommend in combatting crime. There may be grounds, other than those that Richardson provides, for believing that the environment is *not* responsible for crime. It is also possible, as our first criticism suggests, that Richardson has presented us (and himself) with a false dilemma in assuming that either the environment is wholly responsible or the individual is wholly responsible. Perhaps it was his eagerness not to let individual criminals "off the hook" that prompted him to argue that the environment has no causal role in producing criminals. This essay has shown that whatever his motive for advancing it, Richardson has not given us sufficient reason to accept his conclusion.

Exercise 8.2	**Writing a Critical Essay**

Following the recommended format, write an essay criticizing one of the following essays (or another appropriate editorial or essay). There are a number of arguments presented here, but most of the premises and conclusions are unstated or not clearly stated. Read the editorial carefully several times before you attempt to reconstruct an argument from it.

1. LEGAL DRUGS UNLIKELY TO FOSTER NATION OF ZOMBIES/ Stephen Chapman*

   There is good news and bad news about cocaine. The bad news is that captive monkeys given unlimited access to the stuff will spurn everything else to get high, until they die of starvation.

---

*Copyright 1990 by Stephen Chapman. Reprinted by permission.

The good news is you're not a monkey.

In a society of lower primates, which are incapable of prudent restraint in the use of mind-altering substances, legalizing cocaine and other illicit drugs would probably be a bad idea. When it comes to humans, the issue looks a bit different.

We know that a 20-year government effort to stamp out illicit drug use has been a colossal failure. We know it has swallowed vast amounts of money, prison space and police time. We know it has spawned epidemics of violent crime in the inner city, much as Prohibition sparked gangland wars.

What we don't know is what would happen if drugs were legal. Would we become a nation of zombies—a "citizenry that is perpetually in a drug-induced haze," as drug czar William Bennett predicts?

Bennett says we don't have to try legalization to know how horrible it would be: "We have just undergone a kind of cruel national experiment in which drugs became cheap and widely available: That experiment is called the crack epidemic."

But what keeps clean-living citizens like Bennett from becoming crackheads? Is it the fear of jail? If crack were sold at a legal outlet around the corner, would he pick up a case? Would Miss America? Would you?

Not likely. A poll sponsored by the Drug Policy Foundation asked Americans if they would try illicit drugs if they were legal. Of those who had never tried marijuana before, only 4.2 percent of those questioned said they would try it. Fewer than 1 percent of those who had never used cocaine said they'd take it out for a test drive.

That 1 percent can be mightily grateful to Bill Bennett for deterring them. The other 99 percent gain essentially nothing from the drug war. In fact, if they live in the inner city, the drug war puts them in danger every day by reserving the business for violent people with lots of guns and ammo.

The poll confirms the few experiments with drug tolerance. After the Netherlands practically legalized marijuana in 1976, its use declined. In the various U.S. states that decriminalized marijuana in the 1970s, pot grew less popular.

Even if everyone were tempted to sample the newly legal drugs, very few would imitate monkeys. The government's National Institute on Drug Abuse says 22 million Americans have used cocaine at least once. Of these, 8.2 million have used it in the last year. Just 862,000 use it every week. That doesn't sound like a ferociously addictive drug.

When it comes to crack, a smokable form of cocaine which is allegedly more tenacious in its hold, no one knows exactly how many addicts there are. But NIDA says fewer than one in every five of the 2.5 million people who have tried it are regular users, blasting off at least once a month. Bennett's "epidemic" has afflicted no more than one American in every 500.

Crack is supposed to be uniquely destructive because of the severe damage it does to fetuses. Propagandists for the drug war claim that 375,000 "crack babies" are born every year, requiring billions of dollars in extra medical care. But the government says there are fewer than half a million people who smoke crack regularly. Apparently we're supposed to believe that four out of every five of them give birth each year.

In fact, despite being cheap and widely available, crack hasn't produced mass addiction. Why not?

The best explanation comes from Dartmouth neuroscientist Michael Gazzaniga in a recent interview in National Review magazine. Only a small portion of the population is inclined to abuse drugs (including alcohol), and these people will systematically wreck themselves with whatever is at hand, he says. But those who aren't prone to abuse won't become addicts regardless of what drugs are legally available.

"In our culture alone," said Gazzaniga, "70 percent to 80 percent of us use alcohol, and the abuse rate is now estimated at 5 percent to 6 percent. We see at work here a major feature of the human response to drug availability, namely, the inclination to moderation." People allowed to make free choices generally make sound ones.

But a recognition that humans can use freedom wisely is not one of the distinguishing traits of those behind the drug war who can imagine all sorts of costs from legalization but can't see the real ones from prohibition. If the citizenry ever emerges from the haze produced by the drug war, it may realize that the greatest harms are the ones we've already got.

2. DRUG LEGALIZATION: ASKING FOR TROUBLE/ Robert L. DuPont and Ronald L. Goldfarb*

(Robert L. DuPont, a psychiatrist, has directed the National Institute on Drug Abuse. Ronald L. Goldfarb is a former Justice Department prosecutor.)

The world's most reasonable-sounding but dumb idea is the one that advocates solving the country's drug problem by legalizing drugs.

Its fundamental flaw is the premise that the drug problem is not one of drug use but of drug prohibition. The reality is otherwise: drug use is the core drug problem. Legalization cures the problem of prohibition at the cost of more drug use.

Legalization advocates emphasize the high cost of maintaining the

---

prohibition of such drugs as marijuana, cocaine, PCP and heroin. The costs of prohibition are high and rising. But the debates about legalization generally overlook the costs attributed to drug use itself—the lost potential and the lost lives. A few people die now in America because they cannot get drugs cheaply. Far more die and suffer because they can, despite prohibition. Fourteen million Americans now pay $100 billion a year for illicit drugs. How many more Americans would consume how much more if drug prices were cut by 90 percent or more as the legalization advocates propose?

The litmus test of any legalization plan is what to do with dangerous drugs such as crack and PCP. Crack, or smokable cocaine, is the only drug problem that is getting worse in the United States. Legalizing limited use of small quantities of marijuana or giving IV drug users sterile needles will not dent the crack problem.

Watch what happens when you ask advocates of legalization how their scheme would work: they turn silent, or they talk about how bad prohibition is. Which drugs would be legalized, in what forms, at what potencies and for whom? Imagine your junior high school—or college-age—son or daughter, or your neighbor, dropping into the local, government-run package store. "A packet of crack, please, some PCP for my date and a little heroin for the weekend."

"Yes, sir. Will that be cash or charge?"

Some legalizers have talked about doctors writing prescriptions for legalized cocaine, heroin or other drugs. This idea is ridiculous. Doctors don't and shouldn't write prescriptions for chemical parties.

Drug abuse treatment, both public and private, is expensive and a growth industry because of the national drug epidemic, not because of drug prohibition. Using drugs such as methadone in the treatment of heroin addiction is a far cry from legalization, because methadone is only available in tightly controlled settings and only for therapeutic purposes. This fits with the long-standing U.S. approach, which allows dependence-producing substances to be used in medical practice to treat diseases but not outside medical settings and not for recreational purposes.

Advocates of legalization point to the "failure" of Prohibition. But during Prohibition—of manufacture, not use, of alcohol—consumption did decline drastically, and alcohol-related arrests dropped by half. Thus, laws do cut drug consumption, prevent new users and decrease casualties. Correctly or not, society seems to have made a costly, special deal with recreational drinking.

The most recent National Institute on Drug Abuse survey of Americans over the age of 12 showed that in 1988 there were 106 million alcohol users, 57 million cigarette smokers, but only 12 million users of marijuana and 3 million users of cocaine. All four numbers were down from 1985 levels. Alcohol use dropped 6 percent, cigarette use dropped 5 percent, marijuana use dropped 33 percent, and cocaine use dropped 50 percent. It is not easy to look at these numbers and conclude that prohibition of illegal drugs is not working to reduce use or that we are losing the war on drugs.

The best way to cut the drug market is to decrease society's tolerance for illicit drug use. That means creating painful consequences for illicit drug use to help the non-user stay clean. There need to be more and better programs to help the current drug users get clean. This country needs less debate on the legalization of drugs and more discussion about how best to deter drug users and provide drug treatment.

Law enforcement aimed at the supply of drugs is an important but small part of the solution. We do not believe that the drug problem will be solved by criminal sanction. No social problems are. We agree with the Harlem barbershop owner who said the idea that jails stop drugs is "like saying cemeteries stop death." Along with deterring use and punishing sales, we also must learn more about causes and prevention of drug use.

The battle to end the drug abuse epidemic is likely to be won or lost in families and neighborhoods, in workplaces and schools. Do we, individually and collectively, tolerate or do we reject illicit drug use? The debate about legalization simply delays the important commitment to reject the use of illicit drugs. It also demoralizes the people most committed to ending the drug problem by raising questions about national support for their vital efforts.

Debating legalization is a dangerous delusion. Why now, when only a few months ago the federal government released new statistics that showed a 37 percent decline in the regular use of illicit drugs in America, a fall that included every region in the nation, all races, both sexes and all social classes? With that sort of progress in the war on drugs, this is a particularly odd time to give up a battle.

The problem with drugs is drug use. Every proposed reform that makes drugs more available or acceptable is going to increase drug use. It would also increase the suffering and unhappiness that flows from drug use for both users and non-users of drugs.

Exercise 8.3   Participating in a Critical Exchange

A good exercise for displaying your reasoning skills orally, rather than in writing, is a structured, critical exchange on an important issue such as whether a woman should have the right to have an abortion, whether capital punishment is ever justified, whether casual sexual relationships are worth pursuing, whether a woman should take her husband's name when she marries, or whether drugs should be legalized.

A structured, critical exchange is similar to a formal debate, except for a few crucial features. Most important, the object is not to win but to join with those participating in the exchange to determine what position is most reasonable to hold regarding the issue in question. In order to build this goal into the structure of the exchange, a period of time should be allowed, after the participants take the roles of advocation on one side of the issue or the other, for each person to explain where she or he really stands on the issue, having considered all the arguments and criticisms that have been raised.

In addition, the arguments presented should be developed cooperatively in advance of the presentation of the exchange, so that the participants representing each side can help make all the arguments (including those they will be criticizing) as strong and worthy of consideration as possible.

Here is a format for a critical exchange involving four people that can be used in an hour-long class period and that allows time for questions and comments from the audience. The format incorporates the features mentioned above, which are aimed at minimizing competition and maximizing insight.

Preparation for the Exchange

1. Meet as a four-person team to decide on a topic. (You can use any of those listed above or another that is of interest to the team.)

2. Decide which two members will take the affirmative side and which two the negative side in presenting arguments on the issue. It is not necessary to take the side that you feel initially inclined to support. Sometimes it is a better learning experience to argue for the other side.

3. After some brainstorming and background reading, the team should develop two arguments on the affirmative side and two arguments on the negative side. The arguments should be briefly stated and tightly structured, so that they can be written on the blackboard or on a hand-out sheet for the audience.

4. As a team, discuss possible criticisms of the arguments. Obvious flaws in the arguments can be spotted at this time, and the arguments can be rewritten.

Presentation of the Exchange

1. Affirmative team: Each member takes about three minutes to present one argument in favor of the proposition being discussed. (An example of an argument might be: "A woman has the right to do whatever she wants with her body. A fetus is a part of a pregnant woman's body. Therefore a woman has the right to have an abortion if she wants.")

Explain what is meant by each premise and why it is reasonable to believe that premise.

2. Negative team: Each member takes about three minutes to criticize the arguments that have been presented, applying the techniques of criticism that have been learned in class.

3. Negative team: Each member presents an argument opposing the proposition in question (three minutes each).

4. Affirmative team: Each member criticizes the negative team's arguments (three minutes each).

5. Concluding presentations: Having considered all arguments and criticisms, each member states where she or he really stands on the issue. Replies to criticisms and additional reasons can be brought up at this time.

6. Class comments: Class members who have been listening to the exchange are allowed to make comments or address questions to the participants.

CHAPTER NINE

Induction and Empirical Generalization

The arguments we have discussed thus far have traditionally been called *deductive*. We now turn to a different kind of argument. Suppose Jake examines the top two layers in a container of strawberries at his local market and finds most of them delightfully ripe. He concludes that probably most of the berries in the *whole* container are ripe. It is useful to place arguments like this in another category. We reconstruct them somewhat differently, apply specifically tailored criticisms, and also employ different criteria for their success. For example, we might accept Jake's argument as successful even though we acknowledged that, however unlikely, it is still possible that his conclusion is false.

In this chapter we are going to discuss two primary kinds of nondeductive or "inductive" arguments. Jake's argument about the strawberries is an example of the first kind, which moves from premises that describe particular observations ("Berries in the first two layers are mostly ripe") to a more general conclusion that goes beyond what is observed ("Most of the berries in the whole container are ripe"). A second kind of nondeductive argument moves from a general premise to a particular conclusion. An example is the argument: Most teachers enjoy talking, and Mario is a teacher. So Mario probably enjoys talking.

In addition, we will examine two other types of nondeductive reasoning: *causal reasoning*, which resembles the particular-to-general, and *analogical reasoning*, which resembles the general-to-particular.

Two Major Types of Nondeductive Arguments

Inductive arguments with true premises are typically judged successful if the truth of the premises makes it *unlikely* for the conclusion to be false.* Nevertheless, the possibility (however slim) remains that the conclusion might have to be rejected on the basis of additional investigation. For this reason, scientific statements, which often rest on inductive techniques, are frequently treated as tentative hypotheses or conjectures that are open to revision.

Jake's reasoning about strawberries can be represented as consisting of two premises that cite evidence about the particular strawberries he observed and a conclusion that applies not only to specific layers but to the unexamined layers as well.

Example 9.1   *(1) The first layer of strawberries contains many ripe ones.*

(2) The second layer of strawberries contains many ripe ones.

(likely)** All layers of strawberries contain many ripe ones.

A less obvious version of this argument pattern moves from evidence about the past to a conclusion that applies not only to the past but also to the future.

Example 9.2   *(1) In the 1960s measures to combat inflation led to increased unemployment.*

(2) In the 1970s measures to combat inflation led to increased unemployment.

(3) In the 1980s measures to combat inflation led to increased unemployment.

(likely) Measures to combat inflation will always lead to increased unemployment.

---

*By contrast, as we have seen in Chapter 4, in a sound deductive argument, the truth of the premises makes it *impossible* for the conclusion to be false.

**The conclusion is asserted to be *likely* relative to the evidence provided in the premises. Against a wider background of evidence, the conclusion may be unlikely.

As in the previous example, the argument generalizes from information about a certain sample of cases to a conclusion that goes beyond the evidence.

The conclusion of such inductive arguments is called an *inductive* or *empirical generalization.** It is important to notice that there is a *leap* made from premises (evidence) about particular cases to a conclusion that applies *generally*—not just to these specific instances. Not all such leaps are equally justified, and we will discuss techniques later in this chapter for criticizing inductive arguments that make them.

A second feature of Jake's reasoning about the strawberries is that his "premises" reflect his observation or experience with the top layers of the container. An *empirical generalization* results from reasoning that relies on experience, particularly observational experience. The scientific *experiment* is one of the most conspicuous examples of this type of reasoning. The observed results of a particular experiment are generalized to events outside the laboratory.

Both of the examples of inductive reasoning we have just considered move from *particular to general,* that is, statements about particular instances (particular layers of strawberries or particular decades) to a generalization based on them. But some nondeductive arguments move from *general to particular.* They contain an empirical generalization as a premise that is "statistical."** The argument applies this generalization to a particular person or situation and reaches a conclusion about them or it.

Example 9.3

(1) Most 103-year-old persons who have major surgery suffer serious complications.

(2) Didi is a 103-year-old person who has had major surgery.

(likely) Didi will suffer serious complications.

---

*The process of moving from statements about particulars to a statement about a whole that contains them is called "generalizing." To call a statement "general" means that it applies to a number of individuals rather than to particular, or specific, cases. Generalizations can apply to all cases, such as: *all animals with hearts have kidneys.* (These are also called "universal empirical generalizations.") But in some contexts, generalizations can also speak of some, a few, or a certain percentage of cases—for example, *30 percent of adult Americans are overweight; some stocks are too speculative; a few TV programs are worthwhile.*

**The term *statistical* is used broadly to include not only those cases in which some specific percentage is mentioned, but also premises that include such unspecific statistical terms as *many, most, a few, seldom,* and so on, in contrast to the universal empirical generalizations that contain terms such as *all, every, always, no, none,* and *never.*

Assuming the truth of the premises, this argument provides good reasons for believing the conclusion. It may be called inductive because, like the examples discussed earlier, the truth of the premises doesn't guarantee that the conclusion will be true, but only makes it likely.

Inductive Versus Deductive Arguments

In previous chapters we indicated that a sound deductive argument has two principal properties.*

1. The conclusion follows from the premises. (If all the premises are true, it is impossible for the conclusion to be false.)

2. The premises are true.

As we have indicated, for inductive arguments the requirements for success are somewhat different. A fully successful inductive argument has true premises, but the connection between premises and conclusion is not as strong. If the premises are true, then it is improbable or unlikely that the conclusion is false. For a deductive argument the truth of the premises assures us of the truth of the conclusion; for an inductive argument the truth of the premises makes the conclusion likely or probable—although there is always the possibility that the premises are true and (unlikely as it seems) the conclusion is false. Compare these two candidates, one billing itself as a deductive argument, the other as an inductive argument:

	DEDUCTIVE	INDUCTIVE
Example 9.4	*(1) All God's creatures need potassium in their diets.*	*(1) Most adults can tolerate moderate amounts of sugar in their diets.*
	(2) Alvin is one of God's creatures.	*(2) Alvin is an adult.*
	∴ *Alvin needs potassium in his diet.*	*(likely) Alvin can tolerate moderate amounts of sugar in his diet.*

*In addition, it needs to be *legitimately* persuasive to be fully successful as indicated in Chapter 4.

The principal difference is that if the premises of the deductive argument are true, then the conclusion *must* be true. But the premises of the inductive argument may both be true and the conclusion false. For example, if Alvin is diabetic, then the conclusion of the inductive argument is false, even though both premises are true.*

Sometimes it is fairly easy to determine whether an argument is best construed as inductive rather than deductive. You can look for indicator words such as *probably* or *likely,* associated with the conclusion. Similarly, as we shall see, the language of sampling or polling again suggests induction. But on some occasions it is difficult to determine whether the conclusion of an argument is *presented by the arguer* as only made probable by the premises, or whether the conclusion is *presented* as guaranteeing the truth of the conclusion. For example,

Example 9.5

Fred must be pretty well off. Volvo owners have higher than average incomes and Fred owns a Volvo.

DEDUCTIVE VERSION

(1) All Volvo owners have higher than average incomes.

(2) Fred is a Volvo owner.

∴ Fred has a higher than average income.

INDUCTIVE VERSION

(1) Most Volvo owners have higher than average incomes.

(2) Fred is a Volvo owner.

(likely) Fred has a higher than average income.

There is no direct clue in the passage to suggest which version is intended by the arguer. If it were in an advertising brochure in a section entitled, Volvo Owners Tend to Be Brighter and Wealthier, the inductive version would be more clearly indicated because of the word *tend*. Reference to

---

*A common misconception distinguishes *inductive* from *deductive* reasoning by holding that induction moves from particular to general and deduction from general to particular. As Examples 9.3 and 9.4 demonstrate, *inductive* arguments can move from *general to particular*. And we can construct *deductive* reasoning that seems to go from particular to general—for instance, "If Jerry can do it, then anybody can do it. Jerry can do it. So anybody can do it."

tendencies in this and related contexts suggests something often (but not always) takes place. In the absence of even this type of clue, we are left only with an application of the Principle of Charitable Interpretation, which asks us to interpret the argument so that the premises support the conclusion. In the *deductive version,* the first premise would be hard to accept. It is difficult to believe that every single Volvo owner is well off. Some older Volvos are no doubt owned by students with relatively low incomes. To treat the passage as containing an obviously unsound deductive argument, rather than a much more plausible inductive argument, would be uncharitable. The charitable course, other things being equal, is to interpret an argumentative passage as a plausible inductive argument (one with no obvious faults) rather than as an unsuccessful (unsound) deductive argument. The author, of course, is ultimately responsible for guiding the interpretation of an argument. In some contexts you might not be able to tell whether the author intended to present a weak deductive argument or a somewhat less weak inductive argument. In either instance, however, the argument is open to criticism.

More Complex Passages

More complex examples of empirical reasoning may include both types of inductive arguments: particular-to-general arguments and general-to-particular arguments as illustrated in the following passage and reconstruction.

Example 9.6   *A recent poll of a random sample of Americans of voting age indicated that 68 percent favored a constitutional amendment aimed at assuring a balanced budget. With such a large approval rating, it is only a matter of time before a balanced budget amendment is ultimately passed into law since most proposed additions to the Constitution, with substantial public support, ultimately gain ratification.*

Reconstruction   *PARTICULAR-TO-GENERAL (Implicit)*

(1) Sixty-eight percent of the eligible voters sampled in the poll favored a balanced budget amendment.

_____

(likely) About 68 percent of the eligible voters in America favor the principle of a balanced budget amendment.

GENERAL-TO-PARTICULAR (Implicit)

(1) About 68 percent of the eligible voters in America favor the principle of a balanced budget amendment.

(2) Most measures supported by a large portion of the American electorate are ultimately passed into law.

(likely) A balanced budget amendment will ultimately be ratified.

This passage makes a prediction—a balanced budget amendment will ultimately be ratified. The conclusion of the first reconstructed argument is the premise of the second. Further, the reasoning includes premises that are "statistical" in form, namely, they talk about "most" rather than "all."

But the category of inductive or empirical reasoning is even broader. One especially important kind of inductive argument leads to conclusions about *cause*—for example, that the feminist movement caused the recent resurgence of attacks on pornography or that the entry of nontraditional students into college accounted for (that is, caused) the decrease in College Board examination scores during the 1960s and the 1970s. Such *causal reasoning* can be represented as a move from "correlation" to "cause."

Example 9.7 *(1) The growth of the feminist movement occurred at the same time as the resurgence of attacks on pornography.*

(likely) The growth of the feminist movement caused the resurgence of attacks on pornography.

Example 9.8 *(1) The decline in College Board examination scores occurred at about the same time as the number of nontraditional students taking the test increased.*

(likely) The decline in College Board examination scores occurred because of the increase in the number of nontraditional students taking the test.

As they stand, these leaps from correlation or association to conclusions about a cause need more justification. Later in this chapter we will discuss how such arguments can be supported and when they can be criticized.

In addition to these more narrowly focused cases, inductive inference occurs more broadly in passages that advance a *theory* or pattern of hypotheses or use such a theory to *explain* phenomena of interest to us. For instance, a theory about the transformation of American childraising practices might be used to explain changes in the College Board scores. More indulgent parents might be seen as producing less studious children. Such a theory gains in plausibility to the extent that it helps us understand not only the change in test scores but a host of other features of modern American life. We will examine inductive reasoning involving *empirical theories* and techniques for criticizing them in Chapter 10. In this chapter we will look at narrower examples of induction.

Exercise 9.1   Generalizations, Descriptions of Particulars, and Inductive Arguments

1. The previous section distinguished several kinds of statements. In order to practice seeing differences among them, determine which of the following statements are generalizations and which are descriptions of particular states of affairs. Indicate which of the generalizations are universal and which are statistical. Remember that statistical generalizations can include terms such as *most, many, few*, as well as numerical expressions. It might be debated whether some statements are general or particular. Provide a brief justification of your choice in these cases.

   a. Alvin bought the strawberries on June 15.
   b. Most people don't trust government.
   c. Seventy percent of the people who live in Texas like chili.
   d. Jerry parties on Friday nights.
   e. Smoking is hazardous to your health.
   f. Nobody gets everything he likes.
   g. Frankie and Johnny are lovers.
   h. Few people enjoy having their gallbladder removed.
   i. Alice will not go out to dinner tonight.
   j. Every animal with a heart is an animal with kidneys.
   k. Children always suffer in a divorce.
   l. Brenda voted Republican and Mike voted Democratic.
   m. Man does not live by bread alone.

2. Reconstruct the argument(s) in the following passages. Label them *deductive* or *inductive*. (One passage contains both kinds of argument.) Among the inductive, note which are *particular-to-general* arguments, which are *general-to-particular* arguments, and which are both.

   a. Most people under thirty-five can jog without special precautions. Debra is young, so she can begin running right away.

b. The outlook for education in America is bleak. Educational disaster will be avoided only if people give up their selfishness. But Americans are not willing to do that.

c. A reporter is seldom able to get a politician to admit his or her real motives. *The Daily Herald* story about the mayor doesn't tell the whole story.

d. Alvin should pay at least half his income in taxes because everybody who has more than $1 million income, whether from wages or some other source, should pay at least 50 percent in taxes no matter what his or her deductions.

e. You should buy a Chevy. Jerry and David each had one and they were great cars.

f. Any time population increases in a state, the housing demand increases as well. Population has been increasing in Oregon, Washington, and California. So we can expect the demand for housing to increase in those states.

g. The mayor really doesn't care about the poor in spite of her pious pronouncements. If she were truly interested, she would be actively seeking to bring more jobs into the city.

h. Willy was late on Monday and late on Tuesday. We shouldn't expect him to be on time today.

i. It is decision time at Widget, Inc. The company president says: "Our market research department has just completed a test of the New and Improved Widget in three test market areas: Dallas, Detroit, and Denver. In all three cities the consumers preferred the New Widget over the old two to one. I think we should go for it.

j. America is a democracy, and most democracies will not long permit substantial differences in wealth. Since, as recent survey data indicate, roughly 30 percent of America's wealth is owned by 2 percent of the population, it is likely that legislation to alter this distribution, at least somewhat, will be produced.

k. Most Americans are shocked by the rapid deterioration of basic industries such as steel and automobiles. They are also coming to understand that a "strong dollar" raises prices of American goods overseas and decreases the cost of foreign goods in the United States. If so, most Americans should support measures to "weaken" the dollar.

l. A recent survey indicated that the top 2 percent of the population controls 30 percent of the country's wealth. If so, a targeted marketing campaign designed to induce these individuals to buy Widgets should improve the bottom line for Widget, Inc.

Criticizing Arguments
That Generalize

Arguments that move from particular pieces of evidence or samples to general statements can be criticized in three ways. As in the case of deductive arguments, such pieces of inductive reasoning may be shown unsuccessful (1) by indicating that some of the premises are false, that is, by *disputing the data;* (2) by showing that the pattern of reasoning is faulty. In addition, it is also appropriate at times to (3) attack the conclusion directly (independently of any argument that might be put forward to support it) by offering a *counterinstance* or *counterevidence.*

Disputing the Data   The most straightforward means of criticizing an argument that generalizes is by *disputing the data,* that is, showing that the "evidence" used as a basis for the generalization does not really exist or has been misinterpreted. Recall the example of Jake and the strawberries. Jake examined two layers of strawberries in a container and found many of them ripe. He generalized that many of the berries in the whole container were ripe. A person versed in new horticultural technologies could criticize his reasoning by pointing out that these berries might be the newly developed hybrid California Red strawberries that have the red color of the ripe, traditional berry even when they are hard and undeveloped. This horticultural commentator is disputing Jake's interpretation of the evidence used in support of his generalization (the berries look ripe but weren't). Of course Jake might be suspicious of such an improbable story. Observing berries more carefully to see how hard they were might resolve the issue. The technique of criticism employed by the commentator is similar to questioning the soundness of a deductive argument by challenging the truth of a premise.*

Questioning the Representativeness of the Sample   Even if we accept the data, we can challenge some generalizations by pointing out that illegitimate reasoning is involved. Typically, generalizations go beyond the data used to support them in order to make claims that apply to a wider class of cases. This type of reasoning is an instance of *sampling:* the evidence about an observed sample is generalized to a larger population.

---

*Perhaps a more plausible criticism of Jake's reasoning could be given by a cynical consumer advocate who might point out that fruit vendors sometimes put the unripe, green fruit at the bottom of the container. Such a comment concerns whether the top layers are representative of the whole container. The next section considers this kind of criticism.

One of the most familiar instances of sampling is the political poll. Prominent pollsters, such as the Gallup or Harris organizations, try to make generalizations about the beliefs of large numbers of people. It would be very time-consuming and expensive (indeed virtually impossible) to question all the people who might vote in an election. Instead, the polling organization looks at a much smaller group (the *sample*), which it expects to represent the beliefs of a much larger group (the *population* of prospective voters). Just before the election 1,500 people might be polled about their presidential preferences. Let's say that 45 percent of the people who say that they are planning to vote prefer candidate A, 47 percent prefer candidate B, and 8 percent are undecided. The polling organization would be prepared to generalize from its sample to the whole voting population (perhaps 100 million people).*

The move from sample to population is justified if we can be assured that the sample is *representative* of the population from which it is taken. Two factors are important in judging whether a particular sample is representative: its *size* and whether it was selected in an *unbiased* or *random* fashion.

Suppose that a young man has arrived at a Woody Allen view of life (that women will always reject him) on the basis of unsuccessful dates with only two women, and he uses this two-case sample to generalize to all women. The generalization that all women will reject him can be criticized by pointing out that the sample (two cases) is not sufficiently large to justify the inference to the whole population of all women whom he might date. This criticism should be used sparingly, however, because properly constituted samples need not be excessively large. A sample of 1,500 is often used by social scientists to support generalizations about the entire American population, and a sample of millions may be unrepresentative of the whole country if it is selected from a restricted geographical region or limited to a certain income group. For purposes of certain statistical tests, though, a sample of less than thirty is especially suspect because it may distort the findings.

Ordinarily, there is a trade-off among three factors: (1) the *size* of the

---

*Typically, polling organizations hedge their bets by announcing a margin of error (with the usual Gallup poll, 1,000–1,500 people constitute the sample, and the margin of error is considered to be 3 percent). If we use a 3 percent error in our example, the pollster might assert that in 95 percent of the cases, the actual percentage of the population is within 3 percent of the number listed: between 42 percent and 48 percent favoring candidate A, 44–50 percent favoring candidate B. The larger the sample, in general, the lower the margin of error. Statistical theory can be used to determine the interval in which we can have this confidence.

sample required, (2) the *margin of error* that is acceptable, and (3) the *level of confidence* that can be placed in the generalization. So, for example, if the pollster is prepared to live with a larger margin of error, she may use a smaller sample size. Indeed, if she were willing to say that candidate A is the choice of 45 percent plus or minus 20 percent, she could use a sample as small as thirty and still generalize to the American electorate.

Similarly, if the pollster (or the public) is willing to live with a confidence level lower than the customary 95 percent, she could get by with a smaller sample and retain the same margin of error. But the price here is a greater chance that the sample does not adequately represent the population. At the 95 percent confidence level, statistical theory tells us that the sample will accurately represent the population within the margin of error 95 percent of the time (19 samples out of 20). Sampling in the remaining 5 percent of the cases (1 sample in 20) will be inaccurate. If we drop the level to 90 percent, then we must be willing to accept a greater chance of error. We should expect to be accurate nine times out of ten, but that means being wrong in 10 percent of our polls.

There is no set formula for deciding among these trade-offs. How big a margin of error should we have? To know that 45 percent of the prospective voters prefer a candidate with a range of plus or minus 30 percent is not much help in predicting a close election. But we might be willing to live with a range of plus or minus 5 percent, or 4 percent in some circumstances. In others, we could demand even tighter boundaries, in which case we would need a larger sample. What level of confidence should we expect? Again, it depends on the reasoning involved. The level for a largely academic piece of research might be as low as 90 percent; that is, we might be willing to live with the likelihood of being wrong one time in ten. In medical research where a life might depend on our reasoning, we could demand a 99.9 percent level (incorrect findings of only one in 1,000).

Even if our sample is large enough, it still might not be representative. In order to be justified in going from data obtained about a sample to a conclusion about the larger population, the sample must resemble the population in terms of the characteristics measured. But a person doing sampling can't directly know whether the sample is representative.* One way to improve the likelihood that it is representative is to select the sample on a random basis. Random sampling helps eliminate sources of systematic bias that over- or underestimate certain parts of the population and thereby helps ensure a sample with greater odds of being significantly like the population from which it was selected.

---

*Direct knowledge that a sample is representative would involve comparison of the sample with the population. But this would defeat the whole purpose of sampling. A sample is used because it is impossible or impractical to measure the whole population.

Drawing a random sample is not as easy as might first be imagined. Picking numbers out of a telephone directory in what might seem to you to be a random pattern will not do (fatigue, for instance, might result in an underselection of people with numbers near the end of the book). A more respectable technique uses a computer or a table of random numbers to pick out the sample.* Other more elaborate methods of sampling have been developed to produce a sample that is as representative as possible in a number of different situations. One common variant is a stratified random sample, which tries to ensure that certain characteristics known to hold for the whole population, such as distribution of sex, age, or race, get replicated within the sample. If 20 percent of the population is between thirty and forty years old, then approximately 20 percent of the sample should also be between thirty and forty years old. Selection of individuals within each of the strata remains random. Of course, for such a procedure to work, we need to know the distribution of age or other stratifying characteristic in the population as a whole.

An argument based on a sample that is too small or that is selected in a biased way is open to criticism. But how do we know whether the size is adequate or the sample, unbiased? The answer depends on background knowledge. A biologist might be prepared to generalize about some characteristics from a sample of one or two members of a newly discovered species to a conclusion about the whole species because she knows that some characteristics—number of chambers in the heart, for instance—vary little among members of the same species. Similarly, if a political scientist believes that attitudes about economic matters do not vary widely among Republicans, he may be able to determine Republican attitudes toward a new economic proposal from a relatively small sample.

Conversely, a large sample may be needed if we seek information that is strongly influenced by narrow geographical or regional considerations. Whether there is much or little variation in a given characteristic is often a matter of expert knowledge.** Sometimes our common knowledge is sufficient to call a generalization into question because it is based on too small a sample, as in the case of the young man who generalized from two dates to all women. Notice, however, that the size of the sample we demand depends on the nature of the case. Suppose that instead of basing a judgment about his prospects on dating two women, we were considering

---

*A table of random numbers can be used to generate telephone numbers. Such random digit dialing has the advantage over selection from a directory because unlisted numbers are polled: but such a method will still be somewhat biased—people without phones or people who spend large amounts of time away from home will not be adequately represented.
**Given assumptions about this variability, statistical theory can give a precise answer to the question how large the sample must be to produce a result with a given error factor.

a judgment about a person's suitability for marriage on the basis of two unsuccessful marriages. Here, we might expect relatively little variation. Two failed marriages might indeed be good evidence that the person has difficulties in maintaining the sustained commitment required of a lasting marriage.

Background knowledge is also relevant to questions about the representativeness of a sample. If we have a complete listing of all the individuals in a population being examined, then it is relatively easy to pick out a random or scientific sample using a table of random numbers, but such a complete list (sampling frame) is often unavailable. In its absence, we are forced to rely on our judgment about factors that might distort the results. Suppose we were sampling by randomly selecting telephone numbers out of a directory and conducting a phone interview. As we stated earlier, we would miss people without phones and those with unlisted numbers. We need additional knowledge to estimate how many people were left out of our sampling frame. The results of other surveys and telephone company figures would be helpful in determining how significant this number is. The importance of such background knowledge or speculation is even more conspicuous for stratified random sampling. If we are unsure about the racial makeup of a community, then a stratified sample that attempts to reflect a certain racial distribution will also be suspect.

Criticizing an argument by questioning the representativeness of the sample on which it is based might sometimes demand expert knowledge, but in other situations the nonexpert has background enough. Conclusions about community attitudes drawn exclusively from interviews at noon in the financial district or, alternatively, at 5:30 in a tavern near the docks, are suspect even if the number of people interviewed is quite large. It is common knowledge that the people present at those times and in those places are not likely to be representative of the community as a whole. An argument that assumes they are is unsuccessful.

Challenging the Truth of the Conclusion*   Even when we are not in a position to question the sample size or its representativeness, we may be able to undermine an argument that leads to a generalization by directly challenging the generalization itself, irrespective of the argument offered in its behalf. The most effective way of doing so is to show that the alleged regularity described by the generalization does not exist. If some-

---

*Note that attacking the conclusion is appropriate only for inductive arguments. The ineffectiveness of doing so for deductive arguments was explained in Chapter 4.

one with a psychological bent propounds the universal generalization that all men who have dominating mothers and weak fathers remain bachelors (perhaps citing the evidence of a few conspicuous cases), we can criticize him by finding a *counterinstance,* that is, at least one man who has a strong and dominating mother and a weak father but who did not remain a bachelor. This criticism is most appropriate when the generalization in question makes strong assertions about *all* cases or *no* cases.

If a generalization does not make such a universal claim but is, rather, statistical in form, that is, it makes a claim about most (a few or a certain percentage of) cases, it may still be criticized, but a single (or even a few) counterinstances are not enough. What is needed is *counterevidence* in the form of a census (an examination of all) or an adequate sample of the population being generalized about. For example, if the generalization is put forward that *most* homeowners in Hot-tub Acres prefer a dog-leash ordinance, it can be criticized by pointing to a census of all homeowners which indicates that less than one quarter favor the dog-leash ordinance.* A similar counterargument could have been offered even if we didn't have a complete census, if our sample was sufficiently large and representative and we got similar results.

Summary In this section we have discussed the following types of criticism that are appropriate to arguments with generalizations as conclusions. Successful criticism depends in part on our background knowledge, but often the amateur knows enough to advance a compelling objection.

CRITICISMS OF ARGUMENTS THAT GENERALIZE

1. Disputing the premises: Is the evidence cited in the premises true or can the data be disputed?

2. Questioning the representativeness of the sample:**
   a. Size of sample: Is the sample large enough (given variability of factors being generalized)?
   b. Sample selection: Is the sample characteristic of the population, or is it likely to be biased in such a way as to over- or underestimate some significant segment of the population? What was done to

---

*If the census indicated that, say, 53 percent favored the ordinance, then the counterevidence is less unequivocal. Is 53 percent *most* of the homeowners?

**Arguments that generalize on the basis of unrepresentative samples (particularly those that are too small or selected without appropriate randomization or appropriate sampling frames) are sometimes held guilty of the *fallacy of hasty generalization.*

ensure representativeness? What are the potential biases that might affect the results? Are there alternative sampling frames that might have produced a more representative sample?

3. Challenging the truth of the conclusion: Is the generalization presented in the conclusion made doubtful by counterinstances or counterevidence?

Exercise 9.2   Criticizing Empirical Generalizations

---

1. The following passages describe situations in which a generalization is made on the basis of sample. For each case, (1) reconstruct the argument. The premise(s) will report an observation of a sample. The conclusion will be a generalization about a larger population. (2) Criticize any faulty reasoning exhibited in the passages, and (3) describe how a more appropriate sample might be obtained. Note that the same type of case (or "unit of analysis," as it is sometimes called) must apply in both premise and conclusion. For example, the city newspaper indicates that 23 high schools in a sample of 25 high schools in the region had a decline in dropouts and concludes on that basis that most high schools in the region had a decline in dropouts. In this instance, the case or unit of analysis is the high school, so both the premise and the conclusion are "about" high schools.

(1) 23 of 25 high schools in the region (sampled) had a decline in dropouts.

(likely) Most high schools in the region had a decline in dropouts.

In this example, we are not told whether the sample was random or not. If not, the reasoning could be faulted.

a. A student has taken three courses at the university. All her teachers were men. She assumes that most university teachers are men.

b. A quality control engineer closely examines a random sample of automobiles produced on Tuesdays and Wednesdays at the Youngstown plant. He finds that only 3 percent of all the cars produced at this plant are faulty.

c. In 1936 the *Literary Digest,* a popular magazine among the well-to-do and well educated, conducted a poll. The people surveyed were selected from among those included on their subscription records, in telephone books, and on automobile registration lists. They got responses from almost 2 million people and concluded that Franklin Roosevelt would not be elected.

d. Bruce examined records of several countries and determined that in the United States, Canada, and France males live considerably longer than females. He concluded that most males live longer than females.

e. The record book shows that the National Football Conference in recent years has won more cross-conference games and the Super Bowl more often than the American Conference. The NFC will continue to dominate.

f. A student newspaper conducted a survey by asking students a series of questions. The survey was conducted at noon in front of the student center and involved 250 students out of a student body of 8,000. The interviewers were careful to get a sample with a racial, sexual, and religious breakdown similar to that of the university as a whole. In the survey 53 percent of the students interviewed said they opposed abortion. The newspaper presented the results of its survey in an article that was headlined "Majority of student body opposes abortion."

g. A San Francisco area survey of randomly selected individuals seeking treatment for gout indicated that contrary to tradition, most gout sufferers are not addicts of rich gourmet food and beverages.

h. Al had trouble in high school math and didn't do a very good job in college algebra. He'll never make it as a math major.

i. All bachelors are unhappy. They just interviewed the guys down at the Beta fraternity house and they turned out to be unhappy. They got the same results down at Bernie's Disco.

j. Ten years have made a difference. After Three Mile Island (TMI), the nuclear industry created the Institute of Nuclear Power Operations (INPO). Teams of experts regularly evaluate U.S. nuclear plants. The INPO analyzed information about reactors all over the world—updating operating companies through a computer network. It also created a National Academy Training. The result is an impressive improvement in all aspects of operations and safety. In a recent Gallup poll, 6 in 10 people said nuclear power was safer than 10 years ago. In that same poll, 8 in 10 rated nuclear energy as important and somewhat important in meeting electricity needs in the years ahead.*

*Michael Fox, "Don't Judge Nuclear Energy by Accident 10 years ago," *The Daily Olympian,* March 26, 1989, p. 11A.

k. SEX WAS FORCED ON US, 19 PERCENT SAY IN COLLEGE POLL*

Boston (AP)—A fifth of some 1,500 undergraduate women surveyed at Harvard said they had been forced into sexual activity they didn't want, according to a report published yesterday.

Fifty-seven percent of the women polled also said they consider themselves sexually active, The Boston Globe reported.

Nearly 1,500 women undergraduates, or 54 percent of the female undergraduate population, answered the questionnaire passed out in September 1983, the Globe reported. University Health Services and Radcliffe College sponsored the Women's Health and Sexuality Survey.

Nineteen percent of respondents answered yes to the question, "Have you ever been forced into any sexual activity you didn't want?"

That percentage was "frighteningly high," said the survey's author, Michelle J. Orza. "These are young women. How many will answer yes when they are 30?"

Seven percent of the respondents answered yes to the question, "Since you have been at Harvard, have you ever been the recipient of undue and/or unwanted personal attention from a faculty member, teaching fellow or administrative officer of the university?" the Globe said.

Forty percent of women undergraduates answered yes to a similar question in a study last year, the Globe reported.

l. POISONOUS LEAD IN BLOOD DECLINES**

Boston (AP)—The amount of poisonous lead in people's blood fell dramatically during the late 1970s, probably because of declining use of leaded gasoline, a federal study concludes.

High levels of lead in the body are associated with learning problems and low intelligence, and some researchers fear that lesser amounts may also be dangerous.

The survey shows that average blood lead levels across the United States dropped about 37 percent between 1976 and 1980. The decline was so sharp that the researchers at first feared they had made a mistake.

Changes in the amount of two other possible sources of the substance—lead-based paint and lead tainted food—could not account for so great a drop, the researchers said. They concluded that "the most likely explanation for the fall in blood lead levels is a reduction in the lead content of gasoline during this period."

About 90 percent of all the lead in the air comes from gasoline, they noted.

---

*Associated Press in *Seattle Post-Intelligencer*, November 18, 1984. Reprinted by permission.
**Associated Press in *Seattle Post-Intelligencer*, November 18, 1984. Reprinted by permission.

INDUCTION AND EMPIRICAL GENERALIZATION 235

2. Design a sampling procedure that can serve as a basis for successful arguments leading to generalizations on the following topics. Indicate what techniques you are doing to use to ensure representativeness. List some of the factors that might contribute to a bias in sampling. If possible indicate how to set up a sampling frame (a comprehensive list) from which to draw the sample.

   a. The number of minority group members living in the United States.
   b. The attitude toward the budget deficit at your school.
   c. The attitude toward abortion in your neighborhood.
   d. The number of people in a class using this book who have used illegal drugs.
   e. The amount of air pollution in your city.

A Special Case: Causal Generalization

Causal generalizations are of special interest because they often play a central role in a debate about what should be done. We want to know whether smoking, exposure to asbestos, or consumption of diet beverages *causes* cancer, not merely for the sake of the knowledge itself but also because knowledge of cause provides a basis for *control*. If we know that exposure to asbestos is the major cause of mesothelial cancer, then we can prevent or limit this cancer by intervening to control exposure to asbestos.*

Causal generalizations are typically justified by using sampling procedures. For example, a sample of individuals suffering from mesothelial cancer might be examined to determine whether they had had exposure to asbestos. If our sample is large enough and is representative of those having this form of cancer, then we might be justified in asserting that most victims of mesothelial cancer have had exposure to asbestos. But note that

---

*Mesothelial cancer is a particularly rare form that attacks the lining of the lung, heart sack, and some tissues on the inside of the abdomen. A number of studies have indicated that a majority, and perhaps as many as 72 percent, of the victims have had substantial exposure to asbestos particles. Of even greater significance is the fact that about 10 percent of the workers in the asbestos insulating industry contract the disease. International Labour Office, *Asbestos: Health Risks and Their Prevention* (Geneva: International Labour Office, 1974), pp. 6, 37.

even though we might be justified in holding that most victims have had exposure to asbestos in the population as a whole, we still have not established that asbestos causes the cancer. This point is often made by saying that at best the process of statistical generalization establishes an *association* or *correlation* (that is, that two or more features are characteristically found together in a set of cases), but that correlations do not necessarily indicate causes.*

The special problems about interpreting and criticizing causal arguments are illustrated by an argument once offered in a television interview by a critic of experimental education. This critic wished to discredit efforts to provide sex education in the public schools. She maintained that increases in the amount of sex education offered in the high school curriculum were strongly correlated with increases in the rate of venereal diseases.

She was correct in asserting that rates of VD (at least of gonorrhea) have increased dramatically since 1960. But accurate information about the nature and extent of sex education programs in U.S. high schools is difficult to obtain and, unfortunately, she did not provide any sources. For purposes of illustration we can use a graph to display the actual increase in gonorrhea as estimated in the *U.S. Statistical Abstract,* along with some largely fictional data that will support the critic's claim about a strong correlation.**

The data that underlie this example do support the generalization that increases in the number of gonorrhea cases are correlated with increases in the number of students in high schools with sex education programs. This is shown visually by the roughly parallel lines in Figure 9.1.

Obviously, however, the critic was concerned to assert more than the mere correlation of sex education and gonorrhea. She is interested in showing that sex education courses are a major causal factor in the spread of venereal diseases and that we can control the incidence of the disease by eliminating sex education from the schools. But such a jump from correlation to cause is at best suspect.

---

*Sometimes we are prepared to assert a causal generalization even without knowledge of a widespread correlation. You may believe that Frank's Finnish potato salad causes food poisoning from your own case, even before you determine that it affected other people as well. This indicates that the actual sequence of steps in discovering a causal relation need not always involve a move from correlation to cause.

**An unpublished National Institute of Education study suggests that perhaps 36 percent of the schools offered sex education programs in the mid-1970s, according to Douglas Kirby et al., *An Analysis of U.S. Sex Education Programs and Evaluation Methods* (Bethesda, Md.: Mathtech, Inc., 1979).

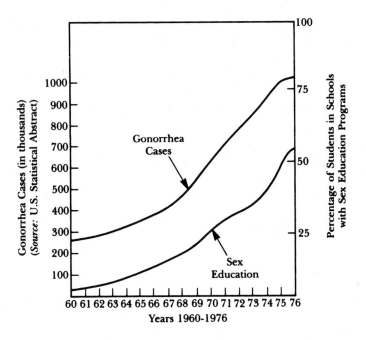

Figure 9.1 Number of gonorrhea cases (actual estimates) and percentage of students (largely fictional estimates) in high schools with sex education programs

---

Five Common Criticisms of Causal Reasoning

Five types of criticism are appropriate to simple causal arguments like the one just stated.*

---

*These criticisms go beyond those considered in the previous section. We are *not* concerned here with the sampling procedures that established the generalization that asserts the correlation, although they might be faulty as well. Rather, we are dealing with the argument:

> *(1)   Increases in sex education courses are correlated with increases in gonorrhea (in the United States, 1960–1976).*

> *(likely)   Increases in sex education courses caused increases in gonorrhea (in the United States, 1960–1976).*

1. The correlation may be coincidental. The two characteristics might be accidentally correlated rather than genuinely connected. Increase in the national debt is also correlated with increases in gonorrhea but few are tempted to say that increases in the debt caused the increase in gonorrhea. The correlation between sex education and gonorrhea might be similarly coincidental.

2. The items might be correlated because they are *both effects of the same underlying cause,* that is, the apparent relation is *spurious.* Both the increase in gonorrhea and the increase in sex education courses might have been caused by changes in the sexual attitudes of the young. Increased sexual activity might have spread the disease and simultaneously moved school officials to develop sex education programs.

3. The causal relation might be genuine but *insignificant.* Sex education courses might have induced only a few people to engage in the sexual activity that led to the transmission of gonorrhea. In this case, sex education would be *a* causal factor, but it would not be a major causal factor in the sense that eliminating it would significantly control the spread of gonorrhea.

4. The causal relation might be in the *wrong direction.* Perhaps the increase in gonorrhea, and other factors, caused the increase in sex education courses by alarming parents and school officials, rather than the other way around. (Remember, to say that A is correlated with B implies that B is also correlated with A. So correlation does not tell us the direction of causation.)

5. The causal relation might be *complex.* Increase in sex education might have caused changes in sexual attitudes that led to increased sexual activity and, ultimately, to the spread of gonorrhea. But increases in gonorrhea might have simultaneously caused the development of expanded programs of sex education.

An argument that moves from correlation to cause is never adequate unless it is offered in a context that rules out these considerations.* What then are the requirements necessary to establish causation?

---

*When these factors are not taken into account, the move from correlation to cause can be deceptive. The author of the argument is sometimes said to be guilty of the *fallacy of post hoc, ergo propter hoc,* which, roughly translated, means "before this, therefore because of this."

It is difficult to list the requirements in an enlightening definition of *cause*. Philosophers have long debated about what, if anything, is meant by saying that one thing causes another other than that they are correlated in certain ways. To determine whether something is a cause in the sense of a controlling factor, we characterize it as *a condition without which the effect would not have occurred*. Treated in this way, the connection between judgments of causation and questions of control is made more manifest. If an effect would not have occurred without the cause, then, in principle, one way of controlling the effect is (or would have been) to eliminate the cause.*

In practice, of course, it might be impossible to control an effect even if we know the cause. We know that nuclear fusion causes radiation from the sun and other stars, but it is unlikely that we will be able to control, or prevent, solar radiation. Consequently, it is a mistake to think that merely establishing a cause permits us to control the effect in all or even most cases.

Our purpose in this section is to examine how causal generalizations may be justified and how arguments that support them may be criticized. By concentrating on causal arguments themselves rather than on any attempt to formally define causality, we can avoid many of the issues that have complicated the philosophical debate on this subject.

The Controlled Experiment: Handling the X-Factor

It is helpful to see the task of establishing and criticizing causal generalizations as part of the dialogue-process we discussed in Chapter 5. The basic form of a causal argument displays a move from a statement of correlation or association to a statement of cause.

---

*Although this characterization will serve the purpose of dealing with arguments from correlation to cause, it is inadequate as a general characterization of cause. It could be objected, for example, that smoke inhalation might cause a person's death even though he would have died from his burns anyway. So our rough characterization needs refinement. We might say that the death would not have occurred *at the time* it did without smoke inhalation.

Example 9.9*   *(1) A is correlated with B.*

(likely) A causes B.

The "burden of responsibility to respond" shifts to one or another parties in the dialogue**—proponent or critic of the causal generalization—depending on the background or context in which the generalization is advanced. The "bare argument" of the form displayed in Example 9.9 is open to the general criticism that the correlation is coincidental. The *burden is on the proponent* of the causal conclusion to counter the claim that some other factor, X (also associated with B), is in fact the major cause of B. The first task in constructing an adequate causal argument is to handle the X-factor, and an argument that doesn't is open to criticism.

The classical way of eliminating the X-factor is by the *controlled experiment.* If properly carried out, such an experiment forms a background context that shifts the burden of responsibility from the proponent to the opponent or critic. Such experiments use *random* assignment procedures and close monitoring of possible interfering factors in order to blunt possible criticism. The virtue of the controlled experiment is that it transfers the onus of responsibility to the critic, who must now provide some reason (knowledge) why it is plausible that an X-factor is at work. Causal arguments that move from correlation to cause without any further support are weak, and the critic has the upper hand. But if the correlation is established by a controlled experiment, the critic must do more. It is not enough to suggest that there might be an X-factor; some attempt must be made to establish its existence.

To illustrate the controlled experiment, suppose we wish to establish that a new acne medicine (AcneX) taken in a certain dosage over a certain period of time causes a reduction in acne-related skin prob-

---

*More elaborate versions of this basic model refer to several studies that indicate the correlation:

(1) A is correlated with B (in study 1).

(2) A is correlated with B (in study 2).

(3) Etc.

(likely) A causes B.

**Although the discussion is cast in terms of a dialogue between individuals, the same issues arise when an investigator has a "dialogue" with herself about causal generalization.

lems.* To do so, we randomly assign test subjects from some sampling list (say, adolescents) to one to two groups: the experimental group or the control group against which it is compared. The initial skin conditions of all the participants in both groups are determined. The experimental group is then treated with the new medicine in the required dosage, and the control group is not. If after the designated period of time the experimental group has fewer skin problems than the control group, we would be tempted to generalize the results by saying that the new acne medicine *caused* the reduction in acne-related skin problems. Our confidence in this causal generalization will be increased even more if the results can be duplicated in other studies.

The argument moves from a statement about association or correlation in a sample to a causal generalization as a conclusion.

Example 9.10

(1) Treatment with AcneX is correlated with reduced acne-related skin problems.

(likely) Treatment with AcneX caused reduction in acne-related skin problems.

The basic model for the controlled experiment as illustrated by this example can be depicted as follows:

Example 9.11 *Controlled "True" Experiment (before-after design)***

	Initial Examination (pre-test)	Experimental Intervention	Outcome Examination (post-test)
Experimental group (randomly assigned)	Condition of skin determined	Treatment with AcneX	Reduced acne-related skin conditions
Control or comparison group (randomly assigned)	Condition of skin determined	No treatment	No change in acne-related skin conditions

---

*Such a controlled experiment assumes that we can accurately measure the degree or amount of acne-related skin conditions, e.g., the number of eruptions or percent of the body covered by irritations. A precise statement of what would count as such a condition is sometimes called an "operational definition." We defined or specified operations such as counting the number of eruptions or measuring the irritated area.

**This is called a "before-after" design because it measures the experimental and control groups both before and after the intervention (in contrast to an "after-only" design that only examines the groups after the intervention).

Random assignment strengthens the case for the causal generalization because it rules out a number of possible criticisms against it. These *threats to the causal claim* include the following:*

maturation

historical circumstance

moderation of extreme conditions

We know that acne tends to lessen as part of the normal human developmental process as people get older. *Maturation* could account for the experimental differences if the experimental group were significantly older than the comparison group. We know that people who volunteer to take an experimental drug are apt to be different from those that do not. The volunteers might be especially concerned with treating acne and as a consequence, they might be influenced by *historical circumstance* (advertisements or education programs) to take better care of their skin or might be willing to change their diet more readily than people in a comparison group who were not as eager to participate. In such a case, it is incidental advertisements and education, not the new drug, that account for the improvement in the skin of the experimental group. Finally, we know that if people are suffering from a particularly severe episode of acne it is likely that their condition will moderate even without special medication, given the ebb and flow of the disorder. If people were selected for the program (or self-selected) because of an especially severe episode, then we would expect a *moderation of extreme conditions* even if the test medication had no effect.**

Random assignment of individuals to the experimental and control groups makes it very unlikely that these threats to the causal claim apply. Of course, it is still possible that in spite of random assignment, those who are older, more eager, or suffering from an especially acute episode will be selected, by chance, for the experimental group and those without these conditions will fall into the comparison group. But this is very unlikely. Unless the opponent has *specific reason* for believing that this is the case, his criticism amounts to little more than the weak assertion that it is *possible* that some X-factor exists. The burden of responsibility shifts to the critic to show some specific and significant differences between the experimental and control groups.

---

*Social scientists call them "threats to internal validity." The concept of validity is used differently here than in discussing deductive arguments. A longer list can be developed but these three are important and illustrative.
**Social scientists call this "regression toward the mean."

Even though random assignment handles certain threats, it does not handle all of them. It remains possible that expectations *bias* observation of results. Determining whether a particular patch of irritated skin is an acne-related skin disorder might not always be easy. Judgment calls need to be made, and even a conscientious investigator might be subtly biased if she expected reduction of acne in the experimental group and no reduction in the control group. To handle this possibility, "double-blind" experiments are conducted in which neither the person treated nor the judge of pre- and post-test results is aware of whether medicine has actually been given. To attain this state, a placebo (often a sugar pill) that looks like the real medication is given to those in the control group.* The use of a placebo is not possible in many "social experiments"—students in a new type of educational program typically know they are being "treated" though testers could be kept ignorant of whether they were.

Special problems arise in experiments with human subjects. The pre-test might affect them in a way that influences the outcome. Measuring the acne in the control group might cause its members to take better care of their acne and thus lead to an underestimation of the effect of the new medicine. In some cases, it is possible to rule out this threat by having two more groups—another experimental and another control group that get only a post-test.** If these precautions are taken, the move from association or correlation to cause is even more strongly entrenched, and the task for the critic even more demanding.

What Happens if Control Is Limited?

The fully controlled experiment is difficult to carry out in many circumstances. Since acne is not life threatening and the medicine in question is not (we can assume) likely to have serious side effects, we can administer or withhold the medicine with few qualms. But consider the case of mesothelial cancer and asbestos cited earlier. Even if practical problems concerning the length of onset of the cancer could be handled by having a

---

*An even more elaborate extension of this design is the "double blind with crossover." In this version, sometime during the experiment treatment is withheld from the experimental group and initiated for the control group. If the medicine works, the experimental group should improve and then return to the initial state; the control group should remain the same, and then improve.

**This is sometimes called a "Soloman Four-Group Design."

long-term experiment, further obstacles would remain. We could not morally or practically subject a sufficiently large random sample of people to asbestos exposure in order to determine whether they develop significantly more mesothelial cancer than a control group not so exposed. Rather, we have to rely on a so-called natural experiment. Nobody exposed people to asbestos to determine whether it had adverse health effects. But given that this exposure (the "intervention") actually occurred, we can investigate the health consequences. To do so it is necessary to compare the rate of mesothelial cancer among those exposed to those who have not been exposed.

Example 9.12   *Design of a "Natural" Experiment*

	"Natural" intervention	*Outcome examination*
"Experimental" group: Asbestos insulation workers	*Prolonged, heavy exposure to asbestos insulation*	*10% incidence* of mesothelial cancer*
Control group: People not exposed to asbestos	*No exposure to asbestos insulation*	*0% incidence** of mesothelial cancer*

Research into mesothelial cancer also differs from the acne case in that members of the experimental group are not randomly selected (though members of the control group might be). As a consequence, it is somewhat more likely that an X-factor exists that is systematically responsible for the outcome—perhaps some other material commonly found in the workplace.

Even so, unless there is some other identifiable factor plausibly attributed to the experimental, but not the comparison group, the response of the critic will be relatively weak.

The critic is in a stronger position when there is *no* random assignment to the experimental and control group.[†] Suppose there is a new method of

---

*International Labour Office, *Asbestos*.

**The figure is virtually zero because mesothelial cancer is extremely rare. This is an unusual situation. More common is that faced by researchers looking into smoking and lung cancer. Nonsmokers do get lung cancer, but the importance of cigarettes as a causal factor is indicated by the substantially higher incidence of lung cancer among heavy smokers. Further evidence is provided if we consider a second experimental group of moderate smokers. Their lung cancer rate is intermediate between that of the nonsmoker and the heavy smoker.

[†]This design is sometimes called "quasi-experimental." It provides more support than a *non*experimental design that merely compares outcome scores and in which the experimental group might have begun with higher scores. It is not as resistant to criticism as the "true" experiment with random assignment.

producing reading improvement. Instead of the traditional classroom divided into poor, average, and good readers, a system is introduced for using interactive computer terminals for self-paced, individualized instruction. An appropriate evaluation of the success of this experimental alternative to the traditional method would employ an argument along these lines.

Example 9.13   *(1) Exposure to computer-assisted reading instruction is correlated with improvement in reading.*

(likely) Computer-assisted reading instruction causes improvement in reading.

Imagine that this inference is backed up by the following research design.

Example 9.14   ***Controlled Experiment without Random Assignment***

	Initial examination (pre-test)	*Intervention*	*Outcome examination (post-test)*
Experimental group: Self-selected from available subjects	*Reading score on a standardized test—measurement of other relevant factors*	*Computer-assisted instruction in reading*	*Reading score on an equivalent standardized test—measurement of other relevant factors*
Control group: Self-selected from available subjects	*Reading score on a standardized test—measurement of other relevant factors*	*No special instruction—traditional methods*	*Reading score on an equivalent standardized test—measurement of other relevant factors*

Given that the experimental group was self-selected and given our knowledge about possible factors associated with willingness to participate, the burden of responsibility shifts to the proponent of the causal generalization who has to rule out the possibility that change is really the result of some other factor, such as intelligence or parental involvement. If further information is available to rule out these factors, the burden shifts back to the critic to produce some additional reasons for rejecting the inference. The more knowledge we have about the case, the better position we are in to confidently accept or reject the inference. The advantage of a fully controlled ("true") experiment is that it allows us to get by without much specific, additional knowledge about the experimental and control groups.

Even if we can be confident, however, that the intervention is causally related to the outcome in a particular case, we may not be able to generalize as broadly as we would like. A particular drug rehabilitation program that worked for clients in Des Moines, Iowa, might not work for clients in New York City. In order to generalize to broader contexts, it is necessary not only to have random assignment to experimental and control groups, but also random selection from the population to which we want to generalize.*

For instance, the program might work not because of its nontraditional structure, but because of the special characteristics of the administering staff. Thus, although a controlled experiment might show that the *program* had a causal impact in curbing continued drug abuse among those randomly assigned to it, we aren't justified in concluding that programs with that nontraditional structure *cause* rehabilitation by virtue of their structure. Similarly, in Example 9.13, any claims that the intervention of computer-assisted instruction is the sole cause of the change depends on background assumptions. It is presupposed, for example, that any difference in the amount of improvement results solely from computer-assisted instruction without regard to unknown factors. If it produces results only when some other unexpected factor is operating, then clearly we would be mistaken in predicting that it will work in the future, for this unknown factor might no longer be present. For instance, computer-assisted instruction using a TV screen as a terminal might work only in a culture in which there is a great deal of recreational TV watching as well. As long as the control and the experimental groups are both drawn from a population that has had massive exposure to TV we are apt to miss this connection. Of course, the greater our understanding of the factors affecting learning, that is, the better our theories, the better we will be able to determine whether the control and experimental groups are alike in relevant respects. Only by having an adequate theory can we minimize the possibility that there is some X-factor affecting our results.

There is a second way that theory is assumed when causal inferences are made. The outcome or effect must be measured, and this measurement often relies on a theory that justifies the measuring "instrument." It is assumed in the computer-assisted instruction example, for instance, that

---

*If you select from an appropriate population, then your results are said to have "external" validity.

the standardized reading test is a good measure of reading ability. Such background assumptions about "instruments" or techniques of measurement are commonplace in the natural sciences, as for example when a spectrophotometer—an instrument for measuring the wavelength of emitted light—is routinely used in the course of some laboratory experiment. Unless there is a reason for believing the apparatus is broken, the scientist assumes that the spectrophotometer is accurately measuring wavelength.

These assumptions about the measuring instrument depend on appeal to a theory concerning its operation that is often well known and well accepted. And generalizations that rely on experiments employing such instruments presuppose the adequacy of these underlying theories. When doubt can be raised about measuring "instruments" such as a survey research questionnaire or an IQ test, it may be difficult to justify a generalization based on their use.*

Chapter 10 contains a detailed discussion of empirical theories of the type that are often assumed by causal inferences. Unless a causal generalization is backed up by appropriate controlled experiments and acceptable theories about relevant factors and instruments, it remains open to question. An argument that blithely moves from correlation to cause may always be criticized. The most impressive criticism will at least sketch out how the correlation could be obtained even though there is no causal relationship.

In review, there are five ways in which such criticism may be launched without considering more extensive issues about theory:

1. *Coincidental correlation.* Some unsuspected factor is shown to be the genuine cause, and the correlation is thereby shown to be purely accidental.

2. *Joint effect of an underlying cause.* Some underlying factor is shown to be directly or indirectly responsible for the items correlated. That is, the apparent relation is spurious.

3. *Genuine but insignificant cause.* Other factors are shown to be of greater importance in producing the effect in question.

4. *Wrong direction.* The correlation is shown to support a causal inference in which cause and effect are the opposite of what has been claimed.

---

*Further, even if we establish that some intervention actually causes some change in a population, we have not yet established whether the *amount* of change is significant. Suppose, for instance, that the acne medicine we described earlier reduced skin problems, on average, one-quarter of a skin eruption per person per month. Is that significant enough to take the medicine? Probably not.

5. *Causal complexity*. It is shown that factors correlated are not related to each other in a straightforward way.

Exercise 9.3   **The Faulty Move from Correlation to Cause**

Indicate whether these passages contain a faulty move from correlation to cause. If so, state your criticism.

1. There is a correlation between heavy consumption of coffee and heart attacks. So coffee drinking causes heart attacks.

2. There is a correlation between the increase in the number of sex education courses during the 1960s and the increase in the venereal disease rate, so sex education was an important factor in the increase in the venereal disease rate.

3. There is a significant correlation between going to the hospital and dying, so hospitals are important causal factors in the occurrence of deaths.

4. There is a significant correlation between the increase in the number of hours children watch TV and a decrease in the college admission test scores, so TV watching caused the lower scores.

5. There is correlation between smoking and lung cancer, so smoking causes lung cancer.

6. A survey by the Sleep Disorder Clinic of the VA hospital in La Jolla, California (involving more than one million people) revealed that people who sleep more than ten hours a night have a death rate 80 percent higher than those who sleep only seven or eight hours. Men who sleep less than four hours a night have a death rate 180 percent higher, and women with less sleep have a rate 40 percent higher. This might be taken as indicating that too much and too little sleep cause death.

7. STUDY LINKS HOMICIDE WITH TV USE*

    SEATTLE (AP)—Television viewing "is a factor" in about half of the 20,000 homicides and many other violent crimes that occur each year in the United States, according to a psychiatrist who studied statistical links between homicides and the rise in television ownership.

---

*Associated Press in *Daily Olympian*, April 5, 1989. Printed with permission.

The study, published Tuesday in the April issue of the American Journal of Epidemiology, is billed by the University of Washington as the first study ever to look at the statistical relationships between exposure to television and acts of violence for the entire country.

The study by Dr. Brandon Centerwall, a member of the psychiatry faculty at the University of Washington School of Medicine, also indicates that as many as half of other violent crimes—including rapes and assaults—are related to exposure to television.

"Television is a factor in approximately 10,000 homicides each year in the United States," Centerwall told a news conference Tuesday.

"While television clearly is not the sole cause of violence in our society, and there are many other contributing factors, hypothetically if television did not exist there would be 10,000 fewer homicides a year."

To arrive at this conclusion, Centerwall studied the white population of South Africa, where television was not introduced until 1975. Using statistics from 1945 to 1974, he compared homicide rates among South African whites to the rates among U.S. whites and the entire Canadian population.

He found that homicides remained roughly flat in South Africa before television was introduced. In the United States and Canada, however, homicide rates doubled within 20 years after the widespread introduction of television, Centerwall said.

It took Centerwall seven years to complete his study.

Centerwall said he hypothesized that if television ownership is followed by an increase in violence, then those populations that had television earlier should have had an earlier increase in violence.

He tested his theory by comparing the change in homicide rates among white and minority populations in the United States. According to Centerwall, televisions were widespread in American white households about five years before they appeared in minority homes. Accordingly, homicide rates among minorities rose four years after the rates went up among whites, he said.

Centerwall said regions of the United States that had widespread television before the rest of the country also saw earlier increases in homicide rates.

"There is a strong relationship between when a region acquired television and when its homicide rates went up," he said.

According to Centerwall, the homicide rates among South African whites in 1983—the last year for which statistics were available—were 56 percent higher than in 1974—the year before the introduction of television, indicating a trend similar to what occurred in the United States after the introduction of television.

In addition to the fact that South Africa did not introduce television until as late as the mid-1970s, it was an appropriate country to choose for the study because it is a prosperous, industrialized Western country similar in many respects to the United States, Centerwall said. He limited his study to South African whites because South African blacks and other minorities live under very different conditions.

Centerwall said he found there was a lag of 10 to 15 years between the time television was introduced in the United States and the rapid increase in homicide rates. He explained that other studies have determined that children are most likely to be strongly influenced by television. Homicide, however, is generally an adult crime, so the initial "television generation" would have had to age 10 to 15 years before it would have been old enough to affect the homicide rate, he said.

8. EAR HAIR LINKED TO HEART ATTACKS*

Boston (UPI)—Dark hair in and around the hole leading into a person's inner ear indicates they may be at greater risk of having a heart attack, a Boston University doctor said yesterday.

A study of 43 men and 20 women found that those people with ear hair often had heart attacks. The findings were published as a letter to the editor in the New England Journal of Medicine.

People with a crease running across their ear lobe, it had been shown in earlier studies, also may be more likely to have heart attacks. The latest study found 90 percent of all people studied with both traits have had a heart attack.

(HINT: What might the "X-factor" be?)

9. TYPE A'S MUST CHANGE TO AVOID HEART ATTACKS**

Miami Beach, Fla.—Teaching heart attack victims to conquer their hostility and impatience, hallmarks of Type A personality behavior, cuts their risk of suffering another seizure by half, a researcher has reported.

"I think that when this is confirmed, it will almost be considered malpractice not to try to alter Type A behavior in the patient who has already had a coronary," said Dr. Meyer Friedman, of Mount Zion Hospital and Medical Center in San Francisco. He released his findings at a meeting of the American Heart Association.

People with Type A behavior tend to approach life with a sense of urgency. They are impatient, aggressive and often hostile.

About three-quarters of all Americans are said to show some degree of Type A behavior. However, the link between this kind of personality and heart disease is still controversial.

---

*United Press International in *Seattle Post-Intelligencer,* November 14, 1984. Reprinted with permission.
**Associated Press in *Seattle Post-Intelligencer,* November 18, 1984. Reprinted with permission.

In the latest study, doctors randomly assigned 891 heart attack survivors to two groups. Some received ordinary cardiac care, while the rest also were counseled by psychiatrists in an effort to change their behavior.

After three years, 9 percent of those who stuck with the counseling program had suffered new heart attacks, compared with 20 percent of the people who had received medical care alone. And of those who dropped out of the behavior training, 26 percent had heart attacks.

"What a person feels and thinks may be as important as what he eats or inhales in respect to heart disease," Friedman said.

10. Chicago* (AP)—Cigarettes are powerfully addictive and cause more than 350,000 deaths a year, but if people kick the habit even after decades of smoking they can greatly reduce the risk of fatal heart disease, researchers say.

Doctors who conducted a five-year study suggest that even among people who have smoked for as long as 50 years, the effects are at least partly reversible within one to five years after quitting.

"It's never too late to quit. That's the message," said Dr. Adrian Ostfield, one of the study's authors.

The study of 2,674 poorer, urban residents in Cook County—ranging from 65- to 74-years-old—found the risk of heart disease death was 52 percent higher among current cigarette smokers than non-smokers and ex-smokers alike.

Among people younger than 65, that risk is nearly 100 percent greater when comparing heavy smokers—a pack or more a day—to non-smokers, said Ostfeld, professor of epidemiology and public health at the Yale University School of Medicine.

The study said some doctors may be reluctant to urge elderly patients to stop smoking because they believe another few years isn't likely to add to the risk created by a lifetime of smoking.

But Ostfeld said even "if you've been smoking 40 or 50 years, it still appears reasonable to quit," and those who do can expect to lose their cigarette cough, find it easier to walk up stairs and be less prone to heart attacks.

Ostfeld's study is one of several dealing with smoking and tobacco in today's Journal of the American Medical Association.

Smoking is the single largest preventable cause of death in America and because of recent advances in understanding addiction, the medical field has an "unparalleled opportunity" to fulfill its primary responsibility of reducing suffering and death, Dr. William Pollin wrote in an editorial in the journal.

---

*Associated Press in *Seattle Post-Intelligencer,* November 20, 1984. Reprinted with permission.

11. WHY SEX IS LIKE SNAKE OIL/ Lawrence Shornack*

(The writer is associate professor of sociology at North Carolina Agricultural and Technical State University.)

To the Editor:

Walter A. Sheldon (letter, Oct. 4) criticizes abortion opponents for hypocrisy in not also advocating sex education, which would reduce teenage pregnancies.

While most research fails to find that information results in contraceptive use, sex educators continue to sell the public on the notion that the problem lies in lack of information.

Although parents endorse factual sex education in polls, sex educators deride facts as "plumbing," and textbooks promote sexual permissiveness beyond traditional values.

When contraceptive use increases but pregnancies continue to climb, researchers explain that teens are using the wrong contraceptives.

When research repeatedly shows that sex education does not have the desired effect, sex educators simply change the packaging; the latest version, called "sexual decision-making," somehow is to prepare girls in grade school for the sexual rush they will encounter in adolescence.

Hypocrisy is not the best word to describe refusing to recommend snake oil to the public.

12. SEX EDUCATION IS NOT LIKE SNAKE OIL/ Jo Ann S. Putnam-Scholes**

(The writer has taught sex education in public high schools for 25 years.)

To the Editor:

Lawrence Shornack (letter, Oct. 14) speaks with a forked tongue when he compares sex education to snake oil, saying research indicates no benefits from such programs. Research can argue both sides, but United States Census figures are more telling. Births to teens 14–19 peaked in 1957 and today are down by over 45 percent.

This sharp, steady decline paralleled the advent of the Pill in 1960, and the doubling of birth control clinics nationwide during that decade. More importantly, this reduction in births to teens began 13 years before abortion was legalized. Conclusion: access to effective birth control significantly reduces births to teens.

But surprisingly Mr. Shornack says teens are prompted to sexual activity by textbooks! To test this, the 1950's are a good control group, for teens then had little if any sex education textbooks or courses, the Pill was not available, and teens knew the strict code prohibiting their sexual activity. Yet their very high rate of births dispels the myth that those restrictive conditions of the 50's promoted sexual decorum. Nostalgia prevents us from learning from the past.

While it may be difficult for the public to resist the unfounded sociological smorgasbord (permissive parents, society, textbooks, and the stand-bys: sex, drugs and rock n'roll) offered to account for so-called teen sexual irresponsibility today, as a trained sociologist, Mr. Shornack ought to resist such tempting oversimplifications.

Widespread access to modern contraceptives is barely 25 years old, a brief time indeed to expect profound changes in so complex a realm as sexual behavior. We don't expect children to master math or history with a single-course exposure at age 13 or 15; why are we disappointed and angry if they fail to master sexual responsibility in so short a time?

But change does occur with long-term, sequential education, and when schools at every grade-level help youngsters develop self-esteem, individual responsibility, and respect for personal, family, and societal goals. And if that's snake oil, I'll take a dozen bottles, please.

Criticizing Arguments with "Statistical" Premises

The second type of nondeductive argument we introduced in this chapter moves from general to particular. This type contains statistical premises—those with *most, many, few, a certain percentage of cases,* rather than *all* or *none.* Unfortunately, no one has produced a theory that does for them what the theory of validity does for deductive arguments. No limited set of rules or techniques allows us to demarcate, in a foolproof way, good and bad patterns of reasoning for these cases. The basis for this difficulty lies at the very foundation of empirical reasoning. Our judgments about them rely on our background knowledge in a crucial way. We have already seen that background knowledge is important in arguments that generalize. It is also important for arguments that contain statistical premises.

Three criticisms apply to arguments with statistical premises; two are only occasionally applicable, the third is more widely useful. (1) As in the case of deductive arguments and inductive arguments that move from the particular to the general, you can simply call one or more of the premises into doubt. (2) Sometimes, even when all the premises are true, arguments with statistical premises can be dismissed without recourse to background knowledge, as when the conclusion is *just not made more likely* by the premises. Opportunity to criticize such structurally faulty arguments is likely to arise, however, only when the arguments are complex.

Example 9.15   *(1) Many air traffic controllers are under great stress.*

(2) Many people under stress are heavy drinkers.

(3) Many heavy drinkers lose their driver's licenses.

(4) Many people who lose their license are bad insurance risks.

(5) Many people who are bad insurance risks live in New York City.

(6) Fran is an air traffic controller.

(likely) Fran lives in New York City.

This string of premises does not make the conclusion more likely, and the longer the series of such connections, the more questionable the inference. (3) The principal method of criticizing arguments with statistical premises can best be put in focus by noting that two arguments of this type can have all their premises true and yet yield incompatible conclusions.

(A)	(B)

Example 9.16

(A)	(B)
(1) Most people who have their gallbladder removed recover without serious complications.	*(1) Most 103-year-old persons who have major surgery suffer serious complications.*
(2) Didi is about to have her gallbladder removed.	*(2) Didi is a 103-year-old person about to have major surgery for gallbladder removal.*
(likely) Didi will recover without serious complications.	*(likely) Didi will suffer serious complications.*

Background knowledge is important in this case. If all we know about Didi is that she is about to have her gallbladder removed, then argument (A) seems successful (given the truth of both premises); however, given the additional knowledge that she is 103 years old, we can produce a *counterargument* (B) that leads to the incompatible conclusion that Didi will suffer serious complications.* This counterargument provides more specific information that points out that the case is an exception to a statistical premise. Given our common knowledge about surgery for the elderly, Didi's age makes her a plausible exception to the premise that most people who have their gallbladder removed recover without serious complication.

Similar considerations apply to some arguments that present "shocking statistics." Somebody says to Big Mike, "Do you realize that a murder is committed every 25 minutes? So be careful, you are in danger of being murdered."** Given appropriate knowledge of Big Mike's circumstances we can produce a counterargument.

Example 9.17

ARGUMENT CRITICIZED	COUNTERARGUMENT
(1) A murder is committed in the United States every 25 minutes (that is, murder is frequent in the United States).	*(1) A murder has never been committed in Serenityville.*
(2) Big Mike lives in the United States.	*(2) Big Mike lives in Serenityville.*
(likely) Big Mike is in danger of being murdered.†	*(likely) Big Mike is in no danger of being murdered.*

Here again the counterargument introduces more specific information that suggests that a premise in the argument being criticized does not directly apply.

Our commonsense background knowledge sometimes provides us with the appropriate materials needed to construct a counterargument, but in other cases arguments can be challenged (if at all) only on the basis of expert knowledge. Consider the following argument.

Example 9.17

(1) Most long-time, heavy smokers suffer from smoking-related health problems.

(2) Bruce is a long-time, heavy smoker.

(likely) Bruce will suffer from smoking-related health problems.

---

*This situation has no analogue in the case of deductive arguments. Two deductively sound arguments cannot come to incompatible conclusions. In this case, we have arguments with true premises in which the conclusion of each is likely *relative to the premises,* but which have incompatible conclusions.

**Murder rate based on 1988 FBI *Uniform Crime Report* figure of 20,675 murders nationwide.

†We could raise a question about whether Big Mike was in danger of being murdered even if he lived in an area in which murders did occur every 25 minutes. The number of people in the area surely constitutes another relevant consideration.

Given the results of numerous scientific studies that have been cited by the surgeon general of the United States, such an argument might seem conclusive (assuming that the premise about Bruce is true). But perhaps Bruce has a rare genetic makeup that enables his body to resist the health-destroying effects of heavy cigarette smoking. Should this be the case, a sophisticated scientist supported by the Tobacco Institue might be about to launch a counterargument along the following lines.

Example 9.19

(1) *Most people with the "lucky" gene configuration will resist the health-sapping consequences of smoking.*

(2) *Bruce has the "lucky" gene configuration.*

(likely) Bruce will resist the health-sapping consequences of smoking.

The important point here is that the criticism of arguments with statistical premises may depend on expert knowledge. The mere possibility that an expert might ultimately discover some new, relevant information is not in itself a reason for rejecting an argument that is otherwise acceptable. In a sense these arguments are always open to question because additional evidence can always be made available *in principle*. But we can strengthen an argument that has statistical premises by using all available, relevant evidence. If we don't have the time or energy to marshal *all* available evidence, we can still bring the conclusion within an acceptable margin of error. We can do this more readily if we believe that additional evidence is only minimally important and that additional factors are unlikely to appear. If an argument does not live up to the requirement of using all *available, relevant evidence,* it is open to criticism.

In this section we considered three criticisms appropriate to arguments with statistical premises:

1. Call at least one of the premises into doubt.

2. Indicate that the premises do not make the conclusion more likely.

3. Develop a counterargument.

The first technique is appropriate to deductive and nondeductive arguments alike. The third is especially appropriate for arguments with statistical premises.

Exercise 9.4   **Criticizing Arguments with Statistical Premises**

Which of the following arguments are acceptable? If none, sketch out your criticism. Use information either provided in the premises or taken from your own background knowledge to develop any appropriate counter-arguments.

1. *(1) Most auto fatalities are the result of the drinking driver.*

   (2) Armand was an auto fatality at 9:30 on Sunday morning.

   (likely) Armand's death was the result of the drinking driver.

2. *(1) Most sexually active women who take birth control pills according to directions do not conceive.*

   (2) Edna is a sexually active woman who takes birth control pills according to directions.

   (likely) Edna will not conceive.

3. *(1) Most areas with low unemployment rates have higher wages.*

   (2) American cities with a strong service economy have low unemployment.

   (likely) American cities with a strong service economy have higher wages.

4. *(1) Most incumbents are reelected in the United States if they decide to run.*

   (2) Mayor Armwrestler is an incumbent running for reelection who has long stood for increasing expenditures on social programs.

   (likely) Mayor Armwrestler will be reelected.

5. *(1) Most students will benefit materially from their college education.*

   (2) Bruce is a college student studying Greek and Latin.

   (likely) Bruce will benefit materially from his college education.

Another Special Case: Arguments from Analogy

There is a common kind of argument, called an *argument from analogy,* that rests on a comparison of two things. For example, it has been argued that the universe is like a clock. Both, it is claimed, are systems of moving parts, set in a precise order, balanced, and having repeated, uniform motion. The argument concludes that since clocks have makers, it is likely that the universe had a maker.

Arguments like this are not deductive, since being similar in some respects does not guarantee that things will be similar in other respects. At most, the premises make the conclusion *likely*. Of the two kinds of nondeductive arguments we have discussed, arguments from analogy are more like those that move from a generalization to a particular instance. Typically, an argument from analogy claims that two kinds of things are alike in many respects (this is the general premise), and that the first has some further characteristic. It then moves to the claim that the second thing shares this characteristic (this is the particular conclusion).

How can an argument from analogy be criticized? Let's begin with a simple example. A U.S. vice president once claimed that he never expressed disagreement with the president's policies because "You don't tackle your own quarterback." His argument rested on an analogy between presidential administrations and football teams, in which the role of the president is parallel to that of quarterback. As with many arguments from analogy, it is left to the audience to think of other ways these two kinds of organizations are similar. We might note, for example, that both "teams" include members who perform specialized tasks, and whose actions must be coordinated; and that both teams are often required to respond to situations quickly and decisively. We might incorporate such considerations into an argument along the following lines:

Example 9.20

(1) *Organizations like presidential administrations and football teams have common characteristics a, b, c. . . .*

(2) *A football team has the additional characteristic that it functions best if the leader is obeyed uncritically.*

(likely) A presidential administration functions best if the leader is obeyed uncritically.

Generally, arguments from analogy have the form:

Example 9.21

(1) *Things like A and B have characteristics a, b, c. . . .*

(2) *A has the additional characteristic z.*

(likely) B has characteristic z.

Note, however, that it is not the number of characteristics the two things have in common that will strengthen an argument from analogy. A stuffed animal and a real animal can have countless trivial similarities—color, shape, size, number and proportion of limbs, and so on. But these similarities don't make it more likely that since the real animal has a brain, the stuffed animal has a brain also. There must be a genuine connection between the shared characteristics and the additional characteristic in question.*

We must keep a similar point in mind when we criticize an argument from analogy. It might seem that we can criticize this kind of argument by simply pointing out a large number of ways in which the two objects in question are *not similar*. The problem, however, is that some dissimilarities are relevant but others are not. In attacking the analogy between the presidential administration and a football team, it is surely irrelevant to point out that there are more people in a presidential administration than there are members of a football team. But it *is* relevant to point out that there is no close similarity between winning a football game and some function or purpose of a presidential administration. What makes the latter a relevant criticism but not the former?

Basically a dissimilarity is relevant if it makes *less likely* the particular similarity asserted in the conclusion of the argument. The fact that a football team has fewer members than the administration doesn't make it less likely that the quarterback and the president should both be uncritically obeyed. But the fact that the administration aims (or *should* aim) at making wise policy decisions rather than winning contests *is* relevant. Whereas tackling the quarterback is obviously detrimental (normally) to winning football games, criticizing the president might actually play a helpful role in arriving at wise policy decisions.

Such considerations lead to a counterargument to the argument from analogy in Example 9.20.

Example 9.22

    (1) Most activities that aim at making wise policy decisions demand critical consultation.

    (2) A presidential administration aims at making wise policy decisions.

(likely) A presidential administration demands critical consultation.

---

*The nature of this connection is a very complicated matter to explore thoroughly. In biology, for example, where analogies are drawn between one biological system and another, certain important characteristics are seen as serving a necessary function in the preservation of the whole. These characteristics can be seen as genuinely connected in our special sense in that they cannot be eliminated without substantially affecting each other. For example, food intake and locomotion are connected in this way. Roughly speaking, if two systems are of the same type, then any characteristics that serve a necessary function in one will have an equivalent in the other. The football analogy treats both the football team and the presidential administration as instances of a certain kind of system and holds that uncritical obedience to the person serving the leadership function is essential to maintaining the strength and effectiveness of the group.

Another approach to criticizing an argument from analogy is to *challenge the premises*. As we have construed such arguments, the premises are of two kinds: one cites similarities between objects; the other attributes a certain additional characteristic to one of the objects. To challenge the first kind of premise, you can simply raise the question of whether the supposed similarities really hold.* Concerning the "universe-as-clock" analogy, you might ask whether the universe really has the kind of precise order and uniform motion that a clock has, or whether it is not in fact much more chaotic.

The second kind of premise, which attributes an additional characteristic to one of the objects (as in "You don't tackle your own quarterback"), might also be subject to doubt. Tackling your own quarterback is just the thing to do if he is running in the wrong direction. In such a criticism, we *accept the basic analogy but maintain that it needs to be extended in another way*. We point out that if the analogy is developed properly, we can justify criticizing the president in certain extreme circumstances. Such criticism not only takes support away from the conclusion of the argument, it can actually make the conclusion unlikely. For if the analogy between the two objects holds, and if it *is* sometimes justified to tackle your own quarterback, then it is probably justified also for a vice president to criticize the president. This would be the case if the president were working against the proper goals of the administration.

Criticizing a sophisticated analogy may take some ingenuity, particularly when you attempt to point out a relevant dissimilarity between the objects that have been compared. We have not attempted to point out, in the "universe-as-clock" analogy, any relevant dissimilarities that would make it less likely that the universe had a maker. We leave this as a problem in Exercise 9.5 to test your ingenuity.

Finally, analogies can be usefully employed in the reasoning process even when analogical arguments based on them are open to criticism. Through most of the text, we have concentrated on criticism. We have said little about creating arguments or, more generally, coming up with new and interesting ideas. It is in the discovery or creating phase of reasoning that analogies might be most important. Often we can get insight into new domains by seeing them as analogous to more familiar territory. We might, for instance, get insight into special features of human memory by seeing it as analogous to computer memory, which at least the computer scientist understands well. But this insight might only be a starting point.

---

*Arguments that depend on appropriate similarities that don't hold are sometimes treated as falling prey to the *fallacy of faulty analogy*.

Even if the analogical argument in itself is unconvincing, the analogy might suggest a new hypothesis or theory about human memory. This hypothesis might not be defensible by appeal to the analogy alone but could be *independently tested* by carefully studying human memory. Because analogies can play this role in creative thinking, the best analogies are often held to be those that are *most fruitful* in generating new, interesting, and unexpected connections.

Exercise 9.5	Criticizing Arguments from Analogy

Criticize the following arguments from analogy.

1. A country is like a ship with the president as captain. Just as a captain should be obeyed without question during a storm, the president should be given special powers in periods of crisis.

2. In the politics of confrontation the rules of poker apply. Once you begin to run a bluff, never show the slightest hesitation.

3. The finances of a government are like the finances of a family. A family can't go on spending more than it takes in.

4. In life as in basketball you cheat if you can get away with it—that way you have a better chance of winning.

5. An analogy is like a rented tuxedo. It never quite fits.

6. Spending a great deal of money to provide medical care for the aged is like wasting money on a car. When a car is all worn out, needs a new engine, transmission, and body work, it's just better to junk it. The same goes for people.

7. The vice president is the spare tire on the automobile of government.*

8. Just as it is rational for a single individual to maximize his happiness, so it is rational for the entire body of society to maximize the happiness of the whole.

9. The human mind is like a computer. It slows down when it has to confront too many alternatives.

---

*Douglas R. Hofstadter. *Gödel, Escher, Bach: An Eternal Golden Braid* (New York, N.Y. Basic Books, 1979), p. 670.

10. The universe is like a clock. Both are systems of moving parts, set in a precise order, balanced, and having repeated, uniform motion. Since clocks have makers, it is likely that the universe had a maker.

11. No one knows where the borderline between non-intelligent behavior and intelligent behavior lies; in fact, to suggest that a sharp borderline exists is probably silly. But essential abilities for intelligence are certainly:

to respond to situations very flexibly;

to take advantage of fortuitous circumstances;

to make sense out of ambiguous or contradictory messages;

to recognize the relative importance of different elements of a situation;

to find similarities between situations despite differences which may separate them;

to draw distinctions between situations despite similarities which may link them;

to synthesize new concepts by taking old concepts and putting them together in new ways;

to come up with ideas that are novel.

Here one runs up against a seeming paradox. Computers by their very nature are the most inflexible, desireless, rule-following of beasts. Fast though they may be, they are nonetheless the epitome of unconsciousness. How, then, can intelligent behavior be programmed? Isn't this the most blatant of contradictions in terms? One of the major theses of this book is that it is not a contradiction at all. One of the major purposes of this book is to urge each reader to confront the apparent contradiction head on, to savor it, to turn it over, to take it apart, to wallow in it, so that in the end the reader might emerge with new insights into the seemingly unbreachable gulf between the formal and the informal, the animate and the inanimate, the flexible and the inflexible.

This is what Artificial Intelligence (AI) research is all about. And the strange flavor of AI work is that people try to put together long sets of rules in strict formalisms which tell inflexible machines how to be flexible.

What sorts of "rules" could possibly capture all of what we think of as intelligent behavior, however? Certainly there must be rules on all sorts of different levels. There must be many "just plain" rules. There must be "metarules" to modify the "just plain" rules; then "meta-

metarules" to modify the metarules, and so on. The flexibility of intelligence comes from the enormous number of different rules, and levels of rules. The reason that so many rules on so many different levels must exist is that in life, a creature is faced with millions of situations of completely different types. In some situations, there are stereotyped responses which require "just plain" rules. Some situations are mixtures of stereotyped situations—thus they require rules for deciding which of the "just plain" rules to apply. Some situations cannot be classified—thus there must exist rules for inventing new rules . . . and on and on. Without doubt, Strange Loops involving rules that change themselves, directly or indirectly, are at the core of intelligence. Sometimes the complexity of our minds seems so overwhelming that one feels that there can be no solution to the problem of understanding intelligence— that it is wrong to think that rules of any sort govern a creature's behavior even if one takes "rule" in the multilevel sense described above.*

*From *Gödel, Escher, Bach: An Eternal Golden Braid* by Douglas R. Hofstadter. © 1979 by Basic Books, Inc., Publishers. Reprinted by permission of the publisher.

CHAPTER TEN

Explanation and the Criticism of Theories

Chapter 9 concentrated largely on reasoning that moved from evidence about particular cases to broader generalizations. Sampling might be used to support the conclusion that most Americans favor laws permitting abortion. The results of a controlled experiment might be used to support the *causal* generalization that farming without extensive plowing causes soil erosion to decrease. We might call this "bottom-up" reasoning. It goes from a large base of evidence to a conclusion that sees these data as a part of a single pattern. We also introduced simple general-to-particular arguments that illustrate "top-down" reasoning, for example, arguing from a premise stating that most widely supported measures are ratified to the conclusion that it is likely that a balanced budget amendment in particular will ultimately be ratified.

This chapter is concerned with expanding the discussion of top-down reasoning by examining *explanation*. We will focus on reasoning that tries to explain why generalizations hold and patterns occur, or how cause is related to effect, by appeal to what we will call a "theory."* Consider the

---

*This is one kind of theory; it differs in part from what we called a "conceptual theory" in Chapter 5 because of how it is typically used. Conceptual theories illuminate the meaning of concepts and provide an interpretation for the terms expressing them. The empirical theories we discuss in this chapter often explain or predict events or patterns of events.

generalization that lack of hygiene causes the spread of disease. Why does this relationship hold? At one time in human history people believed that there was no special connection between cleanliness and health. Disease was explained by appeal to an act of God or correlatively to the moral fault of those who became sick. We might call these the Divine Intervention or Moral Fault theories of disease. Most of us today embrace another theory—the Germ Theory—of disease (at least for a wide variety of diseases).* According to this theory, disease symptoms are typically caused by the presence of large numbers of germs (viruses, bacteria). Such a theory allows us to explain why lack of hygiene causes disease. Lack of hygiene promotes the transmission of germs from one person to another causing the spread of the disease caused by these germs.

These, then, are examples of theories—good and bad—that might be offered to explain why certain patterns occur or why certain generalizations hold. Our aim in this chapter is to improve your ability to identify such theories and to understand and apply techniques for criticizing them. Criticism of theories, particularly theories well developed by scientific research, demands expertise or at least special sustained efforts that few of us are able to marshal. Nevertheless, we are regaled on a regular basis by less well-developed theories about which we possess sufficient expertise or knowledge. This chapter focuses on theories of this sort, although even in more sophisticated theorizing, we need to consider possible criticisms to really understand the theory.

Picking Out Theories

Actual passages containing theories and explanations using them are not always easy to interpret. The general tactic for finding theories in such passages is to find *what is explained* and *what does the explaining*. Theories do the explaining; they typically answer the question "Why?" But sometimes it is difficult to pick out what is explained and what does the explaining. In such cases, four additional aids might be useful.

1. Indicator words such as "explains," "accounts for," and "because" often mark off elements in an explanation.

---

*It remains unclear whether *diseases* such as cancer and heart conditions are caused, even in part, by "germs."

2. Theories typically have a broader scope than that which they explain; many regularities are explained by the same theory.

3. Theories are customarily more remote from direct evidence than the events or processes they explain.

4. Theories commonly use specialized or technical language.

Use of Indicator Words   As with deductive arguments, we might be given clues about the structure of a passage through the occurrence of indicator words. Of these, "because," "accounts for," and "explain" are probably the most commonly used.

Example 10.1

The political boss and his political machine flourished in cities like Chicago even after the age of reform in the early part of this century, as Robert Merton suggests, because political patronage served to integrate new immigrants into American life. After the New Deal programs of the 1930s, this function was less important, and the political boss and his machine gradually died out though vestiges remained until the 1970s.

Here the expression "because" indicates that what precedes it is explained by what follows it. The success of the institution of political bossism in American cities is explained by the theory that political bosses served an essential function in maintaining the social life of the country, namely, introducing and socializing new members.

Another very common device for calling attention to theories is the explicit use of the Why? question. The answer to the question presents a theory.

Example 10.2

Why did the political bosses continue to have power in American cities long after the Progressive Era that brought reform to many other aspects of American government? Quite simply, they served an essential function in bringing new immigrants into the social life of the country in a period that had no other social welfare programs.

Theories Have Broader Scope   Even when a passage doesn't contain indicator words, we can often pick out the theory by noting that it provides an explanation for more than one pattern or regularity. The Germ Theory accounts for the transmission of such diverse diseases as syphilis, stomach flu, leprosy, and athlete's foot. Newton's laws (theory) of motion helped explain phenomena as disparate as the movement of the planets, the falling of objects like apples, the trajectory of cannonballs, and the swing of clock pendulums. Such theories have especially wide scope; they explain a wide range of phenomena. This feature helps us identify the theory in more complex passages.

Example 10.3   *People living alone are more likely to commit suicide than those living with others, as the great French sociologist Emile Durkheim recognized many years ago. Social support helps a person overcome the stress and pain that all people confront in life. This relief is not available to people living alone. Similarly, religions like Catholicism that promote community have a lower suicide rate than Protestant faiths such as Lutheranism that are less community-oriented.*

Here the theory that *social support* helps overcome stress can be identified by virtue of its scope. It applies to both the suicide rate of people living alone *and* to the suicide rate of members of certain religions. Further, such a theory of social support would apply, presumably, not merely to suicide but to a variety of other psychological effects.

Theories Are More Remote From Evidence   Germs (bacteria and viruses) are unobservable to the unaided sense, while the symptoms—high fever, headache, vomiting, and so on—that they explain can be observed directly. This is a natural consequence of the fact that the theories are constructed to explain events or processes whose occurrence is puzzling to us; we theorize in the first place by trying to get at what is "behind" the evident symptoms or effects, since their explanation is not evident on the surface. One reason that theories can have broader scope than that which they explain is because they use concepts less closely tied to observation or other concrete,* direct evidence. In Example 10.3, social support is more remote from direct evidence than instances of commiting suicide, living alone, or practicing Protestantism (although in any given case it might be difficult to determine whether a death was a suicide or if the person was a Protestant). Even the concept of stress might be somewhat more remote from direct evidence if we allow for the possibility of unrecognized stress that was not consciously felt. It is often difficult to determine whether one concept is more remote from direct evidence than another, but the flavor of this distinction can be illustrated by some cases. Imagine a person interested in voting behavior who is somehow able to watch Calvin's activities on election day. This observer might describe Calvin's behavior in a number of ways.

---

*Some might prefer to mark this distinction by contrasting more *abstract* or theoretical concepts with more concrete or more observational ones. In addition, what counts as observable is relative to the capabilities of the observer.

Example 10.4
(1) *The movement of Calvin's hand brought it about that the ballot was marked.*

(2) *Calvin cast a ballot.*

(3) *Calvin voted for his candidate.*

(4) *Calvin expressed his faith in the political process.*

(5) *Calvin exercised his political rights.*

(6) *Calvin overcame his political alienation.*

Such a list is arranged according to proximity to direct evidence. The most observable (directly evidential) statement is (1). Statement (6) is the most remote from direct evidence. One way of characterizing this range is to say that, as the statements become increasingly remote from direct evidence, they become more prone to error. Movement of the hand is readily detectable (at least to our well-placed observer). Casting a ballot might not be so readily apparent. After all, Calvin could be testing the marking equipment. Even if he is casting his ballot, he might not be voting, if by *vote* we mean "cast a ballot that is officially counted, for the person he intended." After all, if Calvin "mismarked" his ballot or some corrupt official discarded it, he *didn't* really vote for his candidate.

As we move even further down the list, the possibility of error or disagreement among similarly placed observers increases. More remote, or as they are sometimes called, more "theoretical" concepts are more subject to dispute. We could probably get agreement about whether Calvin was expressing faith in the political process (although this might be complicated) more readily than whether he overcame alienation. A person's testimony about his faith in the process would count as evidence of the former, but a person might not be aware of his alienation.

As we move down the list, notice as well that the concepts cover an increasing variety of cases. There are ways of casting a ballot other than marking it (we could use a voting machine or punch card). And there are ways of voting other than using a ballot (voice voting or raising hands); other ways of expressing faith in the political process (working on a transition team); other ways of exercising political rights (picketing); other ways of overcoming political alienation (working with a group to change a party platform). The use of concepts more remote from direct evidence enables statements of a theory to have a broader scope.

Theories Use Specialized or Technical Language   Another clue to concepts in theory is the use of specialized, technical or "theoretical" language. In creating or broadening a theory we often need to coin new terms to describe the range of objects, processes, or events we are grouping under the theory. This is most conspicuous in the natural sciences, where new terms are often created or old ones more precisely specified. Such terms are needed because no expression in the existing language has the scope required or because the language community has not developed a term for something so remote from direct evidence. It is sometimes possible to identify elements in the theory by finding such language.

Example 10.5   *Automobile engine blocks are apt to crack in very cold weather unless antifreeze is added to the radiator fluid. A block cracks when the pressure exerted by expanded ice exceeds the ultimate tensile strength of the metal out of which it is constructed. Antifreeze (usually ethylene glycol) freezes at much lower temperatures than water.*

In Example 10.5, the cracking of engine blocks is explained by a theory of sorts. The theory uses technical or "theoretical" expressions, such as "tensile strength" and "ethylene glycol"; whereas what it explains is characterized by more everyday terms, such as "engine block," "cold weather," and "antifreeze," which are less remote from observational evidence. Even here, however, the term "engine block" is more specialized and technical than the expression "cold weather."

Levels of Explanation   Thus far we have looked at explanations for patterns of regularities. But we are often interested in explaining particular conditions. Why has John, in particular, remained a bachelor? Sometimes we answer questions like this with an *explanatory argument* of the general-to-particular inductive form. Our purpose, however, is not to establish the *truth* of the conclusion, which we already know, but to see that the event "follows from" a description of a regular pattern of events. Suppose you have a friend John who has remained a bachelor. We might attempt to explain John's condition by considering events in his childhood and how they fit into a more general pattern of regularities concerning families:

Example 10.6   *Regularity*   *(1) Most men who have dominating mothers and weak fathers remain bachelors.*

Observed data   *(2) John had a dominating mother and a weak father.*

(likely) John is a bachelor.

Such an explanatory argument helps us understand John's condition by treating it as an instance of a general pattern. But we can also ask why this general pattern exists.

We might explain why the regularity in question occurs by appeal to some psychological theory. Sigmund Freud, for instance, might be taken as suggesting that strong mothers and weak fathers produce a situation in which the male child's attraction to his mother is not fully resolved, resulting in a condition in which the child grows up having difficulties relating to women.* This theory purports to explain why a certain family situation is likely to produce an adult who does not marry. This regularity in turn would help us understand and explain particular features of the world, such as why John is a bachelor.

This very rough version of Freudian theory can be formulated more fully:

Example 10.7

(T₁) All male children have a strong, positive emotional attachment to their mothers and a hostile reaction to their fathers (this is called the Oedipus complex).

(T₂) The Oedipus complex produces anxiety in male children.

(T₃) In normal personality development, the male child identifies with his father. This identifying reduces the anxiety caused by the Oedipus complex and allows the child to develop satisfactory relations with women later in life.

(T₄) If the mother is especially dominating and the father is weak, the child does not identify with the father, and the anxiety caused by the Oedipus complex is not reduced. As a result the child does not develop satisfactory relations with women in later life.

(T₅) Bachelorhood (in our society) is often a sign of the inability to establish satisfactory relationships with women.

We have at least two levels of explanation in Examples 10.6 and 10.7. In the former, a particular event is explained by appeal to a regularity captured by an empirical generalization. We might call this a theory of very narrow range—a theory about bachelors and their parents. This regularity or pattern is in turn explained by the latter, broader Freudian theory. We are not endorsing this Freudian theory as adequate (or indeed, even as an accurate representation of Freud's view), but it does illustrate how a more

---

*Sigmund Freud, 1856–1939, Austrian neurologist and founder of psychoanalysis, has suggested such an explanation with his theory of the Oedipus complex.

narrow explanation of particular events fits into a larger scheme of explanation by theory.

The Freudian theory in Example 10.7 has only two "levels" of explanation. In more complex cases there may be many levels of explanation and hence many levels of theory. These correspond to increasingly broad answers to the question Why? as in the series in Example 10.8.

Example 10.8   *Why did Bruce's engine block crack?*
The water in it expanded when it froze.
Why does water expand when it freezes?
It forms a crystalline structure that occupies greater volume than water in the liquid phase.

Why does water form such a crystalline structure?
*It consists of a number of molecules of H_2O that have an angle of 105°
between the two hydrogen atoms.*

Why does the H_2O molecule have this form?
Quantum mechanics tells us . . .

This series of questions and responses provides explanation at increasingly higher levels of abstraction. We move from concrete notions, such as an engine block cracking, through a theory of water freezing, to a chemical theory of the hydrogen and oxygen atoms in a crystal, and ultimately to quantum mechanics and atomic physics. At each level a theory of broader scope with more abstract concepts helps explain a theory that was narrower, less abstract, and less remote from evidence.

Exercise 10.1   Finding Explanations

As we have indicated, the mark of empirical theories is that they explain. The statements that make up the theory can often be recognized in prose passages by certain clues: (1) the presence of indicator words, (2) a broader scope, (3) remoteness from direct evidence, and (4) specialized or technical language.

Use these techniques to analyze the following passages, pick out what is explained, and indicate the broader theory that does the explaining. Note that a theory in a given passage may consist of several statements and may be used to explain several things.

1. During the 1980s, numerous banks and savings and loans in the United States have failed. Between 1981 and 1984, over 150 failed, and the

number has increased since that time. Before that time, since the Great Depression, the number of bank failures for a typical three-year period has been much lower than 150. Why this recent increase in failures? One reason that has been suggested is that banks have been largely deregulated, resulting in less-conservative practices by bankers willing to take risks.

2. Bruce poured some sulfuric acid over some zinc in the chemistry lab and hydrogen gas was released. This reaction is captured by the formula:

$$H_2SO_4 + Zn \rightarrow ZnSO_4 + H_2$$

sulfuric acid + zinc yields zinc sulfate + hydrogen gas

3. President Bush was able to win decisively the 1988 election because he was able to hold the South and West for the Republicans and to discredit his opponent in the traditionally Democratic areas of the Midwest and East.

4. The [U.S.] Constitution survived only because it was frequently adapted to fit the changing social balance of power. Measured by the society that followed, the [U.S.] Constitution envisaged by the men at the [constitutional] Convention distributed its benefits and handicaps to the wrong groups. Fortunately, when the social balance of power they anticipated proved to be illusory, the constitutional system was altered to confer benefits and handicaps more in harmony with social balance of power.*

5. The struggle for civil rights temporarily submerged the potential conflict between the two principles. All that black Americans needed, some thought, was an equal chance. When experience revealed that decades of deprivation had taken their toll, so that those disadvantaged before needed more than an equal chance now, the demands shifted to equal results for black people as a group. It was no longer enough to be allowed to run in the race; it became necessary for a proportionate number of blacks to win. Racial quotas, which had been anathema, became acceptable. From this shift in the paradigm of equality flowed a sequence of important consequences. First, white, liberal support split into factions, one favoring "opportunity" and one favoring "results." Second, civil rights groups such as the Congress of Racial Equality (CORE) and the Student Nonviolent Coordinating Committee

---

*Robert Dahl, *A Preface to Democratic Theory* (Chicago: University of Chicago Press, 1956), p. 143.

(SNCC), rejected white leadership. Thus a cadre of white activists, accustomed to leadership and trained to represent deprived groups, was left out of work and free to lead the fight against risks perpetrated by giant corporations and big government on the public at large. The major manifestation of their leadership became the public interest group.*

6. My assumption is that territorial behavior is partly or originally caused by home ranges and groups that become familiar and thus attractive. It is supported first by psychological data showing that attraction usually increases with familiarity. In addition, there are two species of primates which perform certain elements of territorial behavior, but only in areas where their home ranges are unusually small.**

(HINT: Why did territorial behavior develop according to Kummer?)

7. Our curiosity is naturally prompted to inquire by what means the Christian faith obtained so remarkable a victory over the established religions of the earth. To this inquiry an obvious but satisfactory answer may be returned, that it was owing to the convincing evidence of the doctrine itself and to the ruling providence of its great Author. But as truth and reason seldom find so favourable a reception in the world, and as the wisdom of Providence frequently condescends to use the passions of mankind as instruments to execute its purpose, we may still be permitted (though with becoming submission) to ask, not indeed what were the first, but what were the secondary causes of the rapid growth of the Christian Church? It will, perhaps, appear that it was most effectually favoured and assisted by five following causes: (i) The inflexible and, if we may use the expression, the intolerant zeal of the Christian—derived it is true, from the Jewish religion but purified from the narrow and unsocial spirit which, instead of inviting, had deterred the Gentiles from embracing the law of Moses. (ii) The doctrine of a future life, improved by every additional circumstance which could give weight and efficacy to that important truth. (iii) The miraculous powers ascribed to the primitive church. (iv) The pure and austere morals of the Christians. (v) The union and discipline of the Christian republic, which gradually formed

---

*Mary Douglas and Aaron Wildavsky, *Risk and Culture* (Berkeley: University of California Press, 1983), p. 164. Reprinted with permission.
**Hans Kummer, *Primate Societies* (Chicago: Aldine, 1971), p. 74.

an independent and increasing state in the heart of the Roman Empire.*

8. The impact of smoking on health is reflected by data in two areas: the longer you smoke the more likely you are to die, and the more you smoke per day the more likely you are to die. Overall mortality ratios** increase with the duration of the smoking habit. . . . The mortality ratios remain quite low, only slightly above the rates for nonsmokers for the first 5 to 15 years of the smoking habit, and then increase more rapidly. . . . Smokers of more than two packs of cigarettes a day have an overall mortality ratio that varies from 1.83 to 2.23. Similarly, mortality ratios increase with the amount smoked, as indicated in the following table.

Mortality ratios for males currently smoking cigarettes only, by amount smoked

Number of cigarettes per day	Results for the study of various groups							
	British doctors	Males in 25 states	U.S. veterans	Japanese	Canadian pensioners	Males in 9 states	California occupations	Swedish
Nonsmokers	1.00	1.00	1.00	1.00	1.00	1.00	1.00	1.00
1–9	1.41 (1–15)	1.45	1.25		1.41	1.34	1.44	1.20 (1–7)
10–20	1.57 (16–25)	1.75	1.51		1.56	1.70	1.79	1.40 (8–15)
21–39	2.16 (>25)	1.90	1.69		1.65 (>20)	1.96	2.27	1.80 (>16)
40+		2.20	1.89			2.23	1.83	
All smokers	1.63	1.83	1.55	1.25	1.54	1.74	1.78	1.58

Source: *Smoking and Health: A Report of the Surgeon General*, U.S. Department of Health, Education and Welfare (Washington, D.C.: U.S. Government Printing Office, 1979), pp. 2–17.

(HINT: What accounts for the mortality ratios listed in the chart?)

9. Berkson suggests three explanations for the association [of smoking and the death rate from disease]. The first is that "the observed associations are spurious, that is they have no biological significance but are

---

*Edward Gibbon, *The Decline and Fall of the Roman Empire*, first published between 1776 and 1788, as presented in *The Portable Gibbon*, ed. Deros Saunders (New York: Viking, 1952), pp. 261–262. Reprinted with the permission of the publisher.

**Mortality ratios were obtained by dividing the death rate of a group of smokers by the death rate of a group of nonsmokers. For example, if 20 smokers out of 10,000 died and 10 nonsmokers out of 10,000 died, the mortality rate would be 2 (20 divided by 10).

the result of interplay of various subtle and complicated biases." The second . . . is that . . . "Persons who are nonsmokers, or relatively light smokers, are the kind of people who are biologically self-protective, and biologically this is correlated with robustness in meeting normal stress from disease generally." The third . . . is that smoking increases the "rate of living" . . . smokers at a given age are, biologically . . . older than their chronological age. "As a result, smokers (in particular, heavy smokers), are subject to the death rates of nonsmokers or relatively light smokers who are chronologically older. Diseases like cancer and heart disease, the death rates for which [increase with age] . . . will be considerably more prominent in heavy smokers than in nonsmokers or relatively light smokers of the same age."*

10. Select an explanatory passage from a textbook or other source. Clearly state the theory by listing in your own words the more theoretical statements that do the explaining. Provide as well the statements describing the regularities or observations that are explained.

Criticism of Theories

Selecting empirical theories and the explanations in which they play a role is only the first step toward the greater objective of critically evaluating them. We will discuss four kinds of criticism that have widespread applicability. You should be aware, however, that even if a theory survives these four criticisms, it may suffer from additional faults that demand special expertise to discover.

1. *Subverting support.* Expected regularities or patterns do not occur or are questionable.

2. *Noting nonsupport.* (a) There is a lack of evidence that predicted that such regularities do occur, or (b) the defense against damaging evidence is ad hoc.

3. *Unveiling untestability.* Concepts of the theory lack empirical content and cannot be operationalized.

4. *Offering an alternative.* An alternative theory is more plausible.

---

*H. J. Eysenck, *The Causes and Effects of Smoking* (Beverly Hills, California: Sage Publications, 1980), p. 23.

There is some similarity between the criticism of empirical theories and the criticism of arguments. Just as it is ineffective to simply deny the conclusion of an argument, so also is it ineffective to simply deny a theoretical statement (though this may be tempting). This ineffectiveness is particularly true of empirical theories because one feature of such theories is that they are only indirectly testable by observation. This accounts for the rather indirect nature of the criticisms just listed. It would be ineffective, for instance, to simply deny that male children have an Oedipus complex because many male children act affectionately toward their fathers. If the claim concerning the Oedipus complex had to do with such superficial behavior as this, it would not have the status of theory. Consequently, the critic has to provide grounds for her criticism—but theoretical statements are not immune from criticism.

Subverting Support   The first technique of criticism is to show that regularities upon which a theory is based or which it predicts do not occur or are questionable. The techniques for criticizing empirical generalizations discussed in Chapter 9 are applicable here. (1) We could *find a counterinstance* to some universal generalization that states a regularity. (2) We could *challenge the sampling* procedure involved in establishing a generalization actually offered in support of the theory. And even if we can't directly refute the generalization, (3) we might *provide counterevidence,* that is, observational data that would establish the existence of a regularity incompatible with the theory.

An instance of subverting the support can be illustrated if we reconsider the example of a quasi-Freudian theory concerning bachelorhood presented earlier in this chapter. This theory was supported by the regularity that most men who have dominating mothers and weak fathers remain bachelors. If we show that the alleged regularity expressed in this generalization does not occur, then we have taken some steps toward falsifying the theory (or elements of it).

Alternatively, we could look for a regularity that the theory predicts but that does not occur. We could attempt to get observational data about men who come from broken homes. Suppose we found that men from broken homes marry at the same rate as men from other backgrounds, including those with a strong father-figure. This generalization asserts the existence of a pattern that is incompatible with the theory and gives grounds for rejecting it. This technique can be extended. We can think imaginatively about what regularities follow from the theory and whether it is plausible to maintain that they exist. If these implications are dubious, support for the theory is undermined.

Because theories are only indirectly connected to possible observations and observable patterns, the falsity of particular generalizations does not often *conclusively* falsify the theory.* For example, someone holding the theory we have been discussing might claim that even if we find that a large number of men who had strong mothers and weak fathers become married, this doesn't conclusively discredit the theory because these men could be getting married due to social pressures for conformity even though they do not have satisfactory relations with women. But the point can be pressed by the critic that unless the theory is really without meaningful content, it should lead us to expect *some* kind of regularity. Perhaps it is a tentative and uncertain process determining precisely what these regularities are. But to the extent that we can reasonably determine that certain regularities are to be expected, but we find that these do not in fact occur, we have at least strong tentative grounds for rejecting the theory.

Noting Nonsupport   We have stated the second kind of criticism in two parts. We can point out that: (1) There is a lack of evidence that expected regularities do occur, or (2) the defense against damaging evidence is ad hoc. It is probably unclear initially why (1) and (2) are said to be criticisms of the same kind, but this should become evident after each part is explained.

Criticism (1) is that there is no evidence that expected regularities *do* occur. This is not grounds for rejecting a theory, but it is grounds for withholding acceptance of it. Suppose someone notices among his friends that those who are careful about their diets are usually happy in the morning, whereas those who aren't are usually grumpy. He speculates— that is, offers a theory to explain—that this difference is the result of a difference in some dietary factor (perhaps a vitamin) that chemically affects the region of the brain controlling emotions. In this case no special evidence has been offered to support the view that care about diet is regularly associated with a sunny attitude in the morning, or for believing that morning grumpiness is the result of a dietary (vitamin) deficiency. This is not to say that the theory is wrong. It can be criticized because it is mere speculation—there is very little in its favor, except the finding that in *some* cases diet is connected with behavior.

---

*Thomas Kuhn and other historians of science have pointed out that embarrassing results, even apparent exceptions or anomalies, for a theory can be known, yet scientists not be forced to reject it. They may have grounds for assuming them to be unimportant or for believing that they may ultimately be explained away.

Criticism (2)—showing that the defense against damaging evidence is ad hoc—is actually a special case of showing that there is lack of evidence in support of a theory. The charge that a defense is ad hoc is usually made when someone has altered his theory to accommodate some embarrassing counterevidence. For example, imagine a college professor who believes (theorizes) that he has done an especially good job teaching during the course of the year. He expects a certain regularity, namely, a high rating on the student evaluations in all his classes (say he expects a rating mostly of 5's with a few 4's on a 5-point scale). Instead he gets just the opposite result, mostly 1's with a few 2's. Faced with this counterevidence, he could give up his theory that he did a good job of teaching. But suppose instead that he alters his theory. He continues to hold that he did a good job, but adds that the students systematically misread the directions. They erroneously thought that 1 rather than 5 was the highest rating. There is no special evidence to suppose that students did make this mistake. Since the alterations were put forward to save the initial theory, we can criticize it as being ad hoc, that is, designed to fit just *this* circumstance. Because scientists are sometimes justified in modifying their theories in the face of counterevidence, we should be careful to restrict use of this criticism to cases in which a theory is modified or complicated *just to avoid* particular counterevidence.

Another example of this ad hoc move is the defense of the divine creation theory of the origin of animal and plant species that was offered to escape the apparently conflicting evidence presented by Charles Darwin and other evolutionists that different species evolved over a period of millions of years. In the face of the evidence that fossils of simpler animals and plants were generally located in rock strata farther from the surface than the fossils of more complex creatures, some creationists replied that fossils had apparently been planted by the devil in order to tempt people away from their faith. If it were not for the way in which the existence of fossils threatened his theory, the creationist would have no reason to claim this. In cases of ad hoc defense such as these, there is *no evidence* to support the claim the defender wishes to make. This is what makes the criticism of an ad hoc defense a particular instance of the criticism that there is a lack of evidence supporting a theory.

Unveiling Untestability   A third variety of criticism focuses on the requirement that at least some of the statements in an empirical theory be connected with possible observation (albeit indirectly). If the concepts or statements of a theory cannot be connected to possible observational experience even indirectly, then they have no empirical content. If they have no such content, then they are not really empirical statements and only pretend to be. The process of providing the connection between the concepts and statements in a theory and possible observations is often called "operationalization" (particularly in the social sciences). We can criticize a theory if its statements are not connected to operations that allow us to test them.*

As an illustration of this kind of criticism consider someone who attempts to account for a pattern of plane and ship disappearances in the Bermuda Triangle (an area of ocean between Florida and Bermuda) by theorizing that they were caused by a mysterious force. When pressed, the person holds that this force may be so subtle that we may never be able to detect it. In such a case, we can criticize the theory on the grounds that the concept of a mysterious force is without substantial empirical content. How can we test whether it produced the pattern unless we can somehow detect it?

More sophisticated theories may also be criticized along these lines by pointing out that although they may have some connection with possible observational regularities, they do not make very precise predictions. A psychic healer might explain why many of the people who see her feel better by postulating that psychic energy that moves between the healer and the patient has been liberated. How do we measure the flow of this energy? Precisely what kind of improvement in health is required? Does the theory count as a *cure* in cases in which a person with a psychosomatic disorder is made to feel better by verbal assurance? Is "liberating psychic energy" involved in psychosomatic "cures"? The theory is open to criticism unless it can answer some of these questions.

A similar criticism has been advanced against Freudian theory. Some have held that it does not indicate precisely enough what regularities support it and what count against it. The question of whether this criticism is justified goes beyond the scope of this text, but it should be noted that a much more elaborate version of Freudian theory than the rough sketch we have used as an example is necessary for precise testing.

Offering Alternatives The final type of criticism applies to cases in which a theory has survived the previous objections. Even if a theory faces

*Theories may also be criticized if they lack what social scientists call "construct validity," that is, they do not measure what they are supposed to measure. Some people have argued, for instance, that IQ tests don't really measure intelligence. Insofar as this issue is in part about the *concept* of intelligence, many of the considerations of Chapter 5 will apply.

no grounds for rejection and has support and empirical content, it may still be criticized if there is a more plausible alternative.

We can use this criticism against the theory that the Republican presidential victory in the 1984 election represents a shift of ideology on the part of the American electorate. Such a theory would point to the 1980 election of Reagan and the acceptance of his economic policies by Congress as additional evidence that the United States had undergone a political transformation. An alternative theory could point to the special personality of President Reagan and his impressive ability to use the TV medium as an explanation for his success. Such an alternative would be compatible with his having short "coat tails" in 1984, that is, with the inability of Republicans to gain a substantial number of victories in closely contested House and Senate races.

Offering such an alternative does not in itself discredit the original theory under consideration. It merely establishes that the regularities offered as evidence do not rule out all plausible alternatives. Faced with an objection of this sort, the thoughtful theoretician should try to provide observational evidence that will distinguish his approach from alternatives. Often this process involves the expertise of the specialist—the person who is able to conduct tests or experiments that will tease out the subtle differences needed to distinguish between two alternative empirical theories.

To summarize, four kinds of criticisms are appropriate to empirical theories.

1. *Subverting Support.* Showing that expected regularities or patterns do not occur or are questionable.

2. *Noting Nonsupport.* Indicating lack of evidence in support of regularities or pointing out ad hoc moves.

3. *Unveiling Untestability.* Revealing that a theory lacks empirical content.

4. *Offering an Alternative.* Handling the same regularities in a more plausible way.

Putting These Techniques into Practice   In order to apply the techniques of criticism effectively, it is useful to reconstruct the passage in order to clearly isolate the theory involved and identify that which it aims to explain. Consider the following passage.

Example 10.9
A Sample
Theory

In the suburban American family the roles are clearly drawn. The husband and father is career-oriented and measures himself in terms of success in the competitive business world. The wife and mother is consigned to the home and is given responsibility for raising the children. She is forced to give up whatever ambitions she may have had in order to assume the posture of domesticity. This situation fosters an unsatisfying marriage in which both parents stay together only for the sake of their children. Social convention limits the resentment they can direct toward their own children, but it is not surprising that parents from middle America reacted so strongly to the youth culture of the 1960s. Youth hatred and overreaction to hippies can be understood as a manifestation of the underlying tensions in the middle American family.*

This theory of the middle-class American family can be reconstructed by first picking out the regularity upon which the passage is focused. The passage seeks to explain a pattern of strong, hostile reaction of middle-class, suburban Americans to the youth culture—in particular, to hippies. We should concentrate on the theory that is used to explain this social phenomenon or regularity. The author of the passages believes that the middle-class, suburban American family has a characteristic structure that produces the attitude of resentment of the children. The theory also maintains that in the social environment this resentment is transferred to young people in general, especially the hippies (whom we may suppose to embody the youth culture most dramatically).

As with previous kinds of reconstructions, it is important that you rework the actual text to provide the clearest reading you can that is compatible with what the author says. We can make this reconstruction explicit by listing the relevant theoretical statements and the narrower regularities they explain. For example, Slater's theory of the middle-class American family could be reconstructed as follows:

Example 10.10
The Theory:

(T_1) In the suburban middle-class American family, the husband/father is career-oriented.

(T_2) In the suburban middle-class American family, the wife/mother is overly domesticated.

(T_3) In the suburban middle-class American family, the roles of husband/father and wife/mother create resentment of the children.

---

*Adapted from *The Pursuit of Loneliness* by Philip Slater (Boston: Beacon Press, 1976).

(T₄) In the suburban middle-class American family, resentment toward children cannot be directly expressed but becomes transferred toward youth in general.

**The Regularity
or
Pattern:**

(T₅) The hippies are symbolic representatives of the youth culture.

(R₁) The suburban middle-class American reacts very strongly to youth in general and hippies in particular.

Note that this presentation assumes that the terms that occur in the statement of regularity *(react strongly, hippies)* are relatively easy to apply, that is, that most people will agree on whether there was a strong reaction or whether a person is a hippie. The central terms of the theoretical statement are considered more abstract: *career-oriented, overly domesticated, transfer of resentment, symbolic representative of the youth culture.*

Note as well that this reconstruction can be extended. We might, for example, try to supply further regularities that would be predicted by the theory. For instance:

(R₂) The husband/father in the suburban middle-class American family believed that success in his job is the most important part of his life.

(R₃) The wife/mother in the suburban middle-class American family believes that her place is in the home.

This theory is open to many of the types of criticism we have considered in this section.

1. We could *subvert support* for the theory by noting that the regularity R₁ is, at best, applied to a particular period of history—the 1960s. Middle-class Americans no longer seem to be reacting strongly to youth in general and hippies in particular (but extremes in style and behavior still evoke negative reactions). It is unclear whether the strong reaction to hippies in the late 1960s and the early 1970s applied to youth in general.

2. We could *note nonsupport* for R₂ and R₃ especially as they apply today with our altered and changing attitudes about the roles of men and women in the family.

3. We could *unveil the untestability* of notions such as "symbolic representation" in T₅ or "transference of resentment" in T₄.

4. Or most effectively, we could *offer an alternative* theory to explain the patterns or regularities. One promising alternative is to see reaction of middle-class Americans toward hippies during the late '60s and early

'70s as based on political and economic values rather than on family structure. The hippie life-style promoted economic values deeply at odds with the attitude toward work found among the middle class. Further, the opposition to the Vietnam War that was centered among the young was also threatening to middle-class support of that venture. Additionally, hostility may have sprung from the recognition that the young, as members of the "baby boom" generation born between 1945 and 1960, were exceptionally numerous and hence a potentially very powerful, political and economic force, should they become united in values and politics. These equally plausible alternative theories would explain R_1 without introducing a theory involving the stereotyped roles of mother and father in the suburban American family.

Incorporating Induction and Theories into the Six Step Procedure   In Chapter 8 we presented a flowchart (see p. 193) to help you in reconstructing complex passages, particularly those containing deductive arguments. In Chapter 9 we discussed induction and related causal and analogical arguments, and here in Chapter 10 we have considered empirical theories and explanation. These forms of reasoning can be found on their own in complex passages, but they can also fit into a wider deductive framework. Consequently, they can be incorporated into an expanded version of the six-step process presented in the flowchart. If you return to the flowchart in Chapter 8, you will notice that steps 3 and 4, repeated in Figure 10.1, can be interpreted in the light of our discussion of induction and empirical theories.

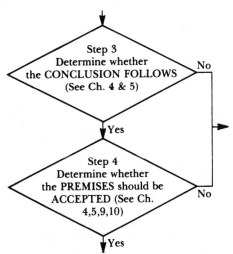

Figure 10.1   Relevant sections from the flowchart for the six-step procedure

The techniques discussed in Chapter 9 help us determine whether a conclusion is an inductive argument *follows* from the premises as suggested in step 3. Furthermore, inductive arguments and related causal or analogical arguments can be used in step 4 to justify the premises themselves, that is, premises in an argument might themselves be conclusions of a further argument based on inductive reasoning. In addition, statements within a theory that has withstood criticism and predictions that flow from them can be used as well in a broader argumentative context. Of course, if these supportive inductive arguments or empirical theories are open to criticism, then arguments that rest premises on them are thereby weakened.

Exercise 10.2 **Criticizing Empirical Theories**

The following are nine selections ranging in length from a single paragraph to many pages. Each contains at least one empirical theory. In each case you should undertake these tasks.

(i) List the most important aspects of the theory (that which is put forward in the passage to provide explanation) as well as any significant regularities or patterns that are explained or predicted by the theory.

(ii) Sketch criticisms of the theory using the techniques discussed in this chapter.

(iii) (Optional) If appropriate, use the expanded version of the six-step process to assess some of the arguments in the passages.

(iv) (Optional) Write a full essay presenting the relevant parts of the theory and the appropriate regularities it explains. Then provide as strong a criticism as you can. Your essay should have the following parts:

An **introduction** that states *your* thesis, that is, what *you* are claiming in the essay.

A succinct **presentation** of the aspects of the theory relevant to your criticism (for a complex theory this section may consist of several paragraphs).

A **criticism** section employing one or more of the types of criticism discussed in the text (again this may consist of several paragraphs).

A **conclusion** that may be merely a brief summary of your position and a presentation of positive comments about the theory or aspects of it, or further comments about an alternative theory.

Passage 1

It is well known that black Americans and members of labor unions tend to vote for Democratic candidates, and that business people and religious fundamentalists tend to vote for Republican candidates. The reason is not difficult to find. In America people see themselves as primarily members of one group or another. When they go to vote they tend to choose parties that historically represent the interests of the groups of which they are a member and which have an ideology similar to theirs.

Passage 2

If we look at the history of colonialism in Africa and Asia we find that the earliest revolts against colonialism took place in the countries with the best, not the worst, social and economic conditions. Similarly, if we look at the history of riots in the United States, those springing from both racial conflict and labor disputes, we find that disorder occurred much more often in places where the social and economic conditions were better rather than where they are worse. These counterintuitive results can be explained when we realize that the violence results not from oppression alone, but from the perception that better conditions are possible. Frustration comes when people first have their expectations increased, and then realize that these new higher aims cannot be immediately satisfied.

Passage 3

The French sociologist, Emile Durkheim, undertook a study of suicide. Included among his data was evidence from various European countries about the relationship of suicide to marital status and religion. For example, the recorded suicides for Catholics in Austria for 1852–1859 were 51.3 per million persons and for Protestants 79.5 per million. Similarly, in Prussia for the years 1849–1855 the recorded suicides were 49.6 per million for Catholics and 159.9 per million for Protestants. He also found that during this period the recorded suicides for unmarried men were 975 per million, while there were only 336 per million for men with children. He used this and other evidence to support the view that in general Catholics have a lower recorded suicide rate than Protestants and that married persons living with spouses have a lower recorded suicide rate than single persons living alone. Why? He believed that suicide rates are a function of *unrelieved* anxieties and stress. Being a member of a closely knit group, like the Catholic community or a strong family, provided a measure of social cohesion that gave psychic support to group members subjected to acute stress and anxieties. Durkheim's theory of suicide is another instance that shows that we can "get by with a little help from our friends!"

Passage 4

The millionaires are a product of natural selection acting on the whole body of men to pick out those who can meet the requirement of certain work to be done. . . . It is because they are thus selected that wealth—both their own and that entrusted to them—aggregates under their hands. . . . They may fairly be regarded as the naturally selected agents of society for certain work. They get high wages and live in luxury, but the bargain is a good one for society. There is the most intense competition for their place and occupation. This assures us that all who are competent for this function will be employed in it, so that the cost of it will be reduced to the lowest terms.*

Passage 5.   Science, Proof, and the Ancient Astronaut Hypothesis**

The Case for von Däniken

It is common knowledge that it is both possible and probable that intelligent beings exist elsewhere in the universe. Even Carl Sagan admits that. To assume otherwise is to regress to the Middle Ages, when it was believed that the earth was the center of the universe and man the supreme creation.

Historian Will Durant, in his *Story of Civilization,* suggests that we are not necessarily the descendants of the primitive cultures to which archaeologists and anthropologists like to attribute our ancestry. His thesis, and the mysteries that science has not explained, suggest the possibility that ancient space travelers visited earth. No argument based on such data as problems of intergalactic travel and the vastness of space has yet proved that superior intelligence could not accomplish what we, with our few centuries of limited scientific technology and theory, believe to be impossible.

It is both possible and probable that ancient astronauts did visit earth. This cannot be denied unless one holds that evolution is impossible, or that there is no evolution and God created only us (a point that raises questions on which *no* evidence could be brought to bear), or that such evolution as there has been took place only on earth, or that except for us, there are no astronauts or other in-

---

*William Sumner, *Earth-Hunger and Other Essays* (New Haven: Yale University Press, 1913), p. 3, as quoted in Richard Hofstadter, *Social Darwinism in American Thought* (Boston: Beacon Press, 1955), p. 58.

**Adapted from Pasqual S. Schievella, "Science, Proof, and the Ancient Astronaut Hypothesis," in *Philosophy of Science and the Occult,* ed. Patrick Grim (Albany, New York: State University of New York Press, 1982), pp. 268–270. Reprinted with permission of the author.

telligences in the universe, or that the evidence is all in as to our origin, or that we have *absolute* knowledge about these things, and the like. Surely no enlightened person could hold such medieval ideas.

Unless we deny the possibility of evolution elsewhere in the universe or pretend to be an absolute knowledge regarding our past, we must recognize at least the *possibility* that technologically advanced civilizations may have arisen elsewhere and that they may have visited us in the remote past.

The ancient astronaut hypothesis, then, is at least possible. As to proof of von Däniken's theories, it must be noted that the ancient astronaut hypothesis cannot be expected to follow the rigid rules and standards of proof set for natural science. Its modes of proof are primarily like those in the social sciences, such as psychology, sociology, and anthropology. To expect formal rigidity in such informal disciplines is to demand what cannot be. Nevertheless, one would expect scientists to permit von Däniken to extrapolate from his data, since they themselves accept extrapolation as a kind of evidence permitting further advances in science.

What *could* constitute proof for the ancient astronaut hypothesis? We are not likely to find an ancient astronaut. As von Däniken points out, "crashed" spaceships from the distant past would probably long ago have disintegrated or possibly have been carried away piecemeal. What then?

Von Däniken's thesis explains hitherto inexplicable mysteries none of which has received any elucidation from academic minds fettered by prejudices and preconceptions. It is not fatal to the hypothesis that critics find errors. Taken as a whole, von Däniken's findings point convincingly to the likelihood of extraterrestrial interference in man's distant past. That is not to deny that von Däniken manipulates many of his facts to adapt them to the ancient astronaut hypothesis. But what scientist does not do this when he formulates a theory?

The ancient astronaut hypothesis is little different from most of recorded history. The hypothesis requires only "validation" of the reported data through correlation of those data with the unexplained and wondrous technical artifacts of the distant past. The proofs of the ancient astronaut hypothesis can be found in the logic of both possible and probable events, in the historical, even though predominantly religious, documents that are held in such high historical esteem throughout the world, and in the ancient artifacts that cannot be explained in terms of the supposed knowledge and capabilities of antiquity. Any mythologist will readily insist that much of mythology is but disguised history. There remains only to break the code of the expressions of antiquity and to translate them into the speech patterns of a space-age language. As George Sassoon explained, even the word "Glory" in the scriptures turns out to be a highly probable reference to a space craft. All these, studied as a body of coherently describable data, point to extraterrestrial intervention. Furthermore, the descriptions in ancient documents, when *coupled* with empirical data, considerably weaken the argument that *terrestrials* are responsible for those artifacts which obviously were beyond their linguistic, conceptual, and technical abilities. Let us consider some of those wonders. A few should suffice.

At the Bay of Pisco, south of Lima, Peru, there is an enormous trident engraved on the side of a hill pointing (we can now say with accuracy, thanks to the intensive research of Josef Blumrich) directly at a small island by the name of Isla Blanca. In addition, not far from the small city of Nazca, Peru, one can find what are now called the Nazca ground drawings. Inscribed on approximately thirty square miles of arid Nazca pampas are huge drawings of a spider, a monkey, a hummingbird, and the like. They are so large that they can be recognized only from the air. Other drawings could easily be mistaken for aircraft landing strips. Some are merely straight (often parallel) lines running across rough terrain and up mountainsides, appearing to deviate not an inch—sometimes almost ten kilometers (6.21 miles) long, as if cut by a laser beam from on high. As to their source and meanings, there are no accepted explanations. A NASA engineer, Robert Earle, claims to have determined that most of the lines point to important geographic locations on the earth.

Another unexplained mystery is that of the Terraces of Baalbek in Lebanon where huge stone blocks sixty feet long and said to weigh 2,000 tons have been moved into place. They are so massive that even our modern technology could not handle them.

Then there are the so-called "fortress" walls at Sacsayhuaman, outside the city of Cusco in Peru. There are thousands of enormous irregularly shaped stones, many tons in weight, fitting together as closely and as neatly as the pieces of a jigsaw puzzle, without any kind of connecting adhesive. The thin edge of a sheet of paper could not be inserted between them.

Another marvel is the recessed quadrangular wall at Tiahuanacu, outside of La Paz, Bolivia. The inside surface is studded with sculptured faces apparently representing every racial type on earth. There are many hundreds of other unexplained mysteries which most scientists show no inclination to investigate. I shall mention only one more: the mystery of the existence of models of sophisticated aircraft. Some of these models show a separation space indicating the possible existence of nuclear engines. Such models, which are in museums throughout the world, have been tested and found to be aerodynamically accurate in design. They are amazingly interesting artifacts because they correlate so well with the many scriptural descriptions of flying machines emitting smoke, fire, and thunderous noise.

Even if we accept the claim that all these things originated with terrestrial beings, we would be hard-pressed to explain the disappearance of such superior civilizations. We have found no documentary *evidence* or, indeed, evidence of any kind to support a terrestrial origin for such technological achievements.

It seems, then, as von Däniken reiterates, that it is time to bring to bear upon these fascinating mysteries, and the descriptions of them in the languages of antiquity, new perspectives and viable hypotheses made possible by the more sophisticated language and knowledge of our day.

If scientific and religious institutions would allow it, and if governments or foundations would advance funds to support it, researchers could feed data from all over the world into computers to determine the comparative similarities among empirical descriptions of "gods from space" and to determine whether these descriptions are, as the critics prefer to believe, nothing more than the creations of insane minds or over-fertile imaginations. Supplemented by computers, experts in comparative linguistics, translation, ancient cultures, and ancient languages should be able to determine whether the technical data, concepts, and achievements found in museums, existing at archaeological sites, and described in historical and religious documents could have originated with a pre-scientific people who spoke only non-technical and unsophisticated language. Surely such an effort would bring more probable results than will the expenditure of hundreds of millions of dollars from an impulse technology attempting to discover evidence of the existence of extra-terrestrial intelligences—an effort with which I nevertheless heartily agree. However, there is even less of a "smidgen," to use a favorite word of Carl Sagan's, of evidence in space. In fact, there is *no* evidence except for the "evidence" of extra-terrestrial interference (in the development of man) right here on Earth as it had been offered throughout our history by ancient astronaut theorists.

As it stands now, the ancient astronaut hypothesis is primarily a historical hypothesis and peripherally a scientific one. It is founded on documentary and circumstantial evidence and, in some cases, on hard evidence that may not be denied except by stretching the facts beyond reason and probability.

Passage 6. The Strategy of Social Futurism*

Can one live in a society that is out of control? That is the question posed for us by the concept of future shock. For that is the situation

---

*From *Future Shock,* by Alvin Toffler. Copyright © 1970 by Alvin Toffler. Reprinted by permission of Random House, Inc.

we find ourselves in. If it were technology alone that had broken loose, our problems would be serious enough. The deadly fact is, however, that many other social processes have also begun to run free, oscillating wildly, resisting our best efforts to guide them.

Urbanization, ethnic conflict, migration, population, crime—a thousand examples spring to mind of fields in which our efforts to shape change seem increasingly inept and futile. Some of these are strongly related to the breakaway of technology; others partially independent of it. The uneven, rocketing rates of change, the shifts and jerks in direction, compel us to ask whether the techno-societies, even comparatively small ones like Sweden and Belgium, have grown too complex, too fast to manage?

How can we prevent mass future shock, selectively adjusting the tempos of change, raising or lowering levels of stimulation, when governments—including those with the best intentions—seem unable even to point change in the right direction?

Thus a leading American urbanologist writes with unconcealed disgust: "At a cost of more than three billion dollars, the Urban Renewal Agency has succeeded in materially reducing the supply of low cost housing in American cities." Similar debacles could be cited in a dozen fields. Why do welfare programs today often cripple rather than help their clients? Why do college students, supposedly a pampered elite, riot and rebel? Why do expressways add to traffic congestion rather than reduce it? In short, why do so many well-intentioned liberal programs turn rancid so rapidly, producing side effects that cancel out their central effects? No wonder Raymond Fletcher, a frustrated Member of Parliament in Britain, recently complained: "Society's gone random!"

If random means a literal absence of pattern, he is, of course, overstating the case. But if random means that the outcomes of social policy have become erratic and hard to predict, he is right on target. Here, then, is the political meaning of future shock. For just as individual future shock results from an inability to keep pace with the rate of change, governments, too, suffer from a kind of collective future shock—a breakdown of their decisional processes.

With chilling clarity, Sir Geoffrey Vickers, the eminent British social scientist, has identified the issue: "The rate of change increases at an accelerating speed, without a corresponding acceleration in the rate at which further responses can be made; and this brings us nearer the threshold beyond which control is lost."

What we are witnessing is the beginning of the final breakup of industrialism and, with it, the collapse of technocratic planning. By technocratic planning, I do not mean only the centralized national planning that has, until recently, characterized the USSR, but also the less formal, more dispersed attempts at systematic change management that occur in all the high technology nations, regardless of their political persuasion. Michael Harrington, the socialist critic, arguing that we have rejected planning, has termed ours the "accidental century." Yet, as Galbraith demonstrates, even within the context of a capitalist economy, the great corporations go to enormous lengths to rationalize production and distribution, to plan their future as best they can. Governments, too, are deep into the planning business. The Keynesian manipulation of post-war economies may·be inadequate, but it is not a matter of accident. In France, *Le Plan* has become a regular feature of national life. In Sweden, Italy, Germany and Japan, governments actively intervene in the economic sector to protect certain industries, to capitalize others, and to accelerate growth. In the United States and Britain, even local governments come equipped with what are at least *called* planning departments.

Why, therefore, despite all these efforts, should the system be spinning out of control? The problem is not simply that we plan too little; we also plan too poorly. Part of the trouble can be traced to the very premises implicit in our planning.

First, technocratic planning, itself a product of industrialism, reflects the values of that fast-vanishing era. In both its capitalist and communist variants, industrialism was a system focused on the maximization of material welfare. Thus, for the technocrat, in Detroit as well as Kiev, economic advance is the primary aim; technology the primary tool. The fact that in one case the advance redounds to private advantage and in the other, theoretically, to the public good, does not alter the core assumptions common to both. Technocratic planning is *econocentric*.

Second, technocratic planning reflects the time-bias of industrialism. Struggling to free itself from the stifling past-orientation of previous societies, industrialism focused heavily on the present. This meant, in practice, that its planning dealt with futures near at hand. The idea of a five-year plan struck the world as insanely futuristic when it was first put forward by the Soviets in the 1920's. Even today, except in the most advanced organizations on both sides of the ideological curtain, one- or two-year forecasts are regarded as "long-range planning." A handful of corporations and government agencies, as we shall see, have begun to concern themselves with horizons ten, twenty, even fifty years in the future. The majority, however, remain blindly biased toward next Monday. Technocratic planning is *short-range*.

Third, reflecting the bureaucratic organization of industrialism, technocratic planning was premised on hierarchy. The world was divided into manager and worker, planner and plannee, with decisions made by one for the other. This system, adequate while change unfolds at an industrial tempo, breaks down as the pace reaches super-industrial speeds. The increasingly unstable environment demands more and more non-programmed decisions down below; the need for instant feedback blurs the distinction between line and staff; and hierarchy totters. Planners are too remote, too ignorant of local conditions, too slow in responding to change. As suspicion spreads that top-down controls are unworkable, plannees begin clamoring for the right to participate in the decision-making. Planners, however, resist. For like the bureaucratic system it mirrors, technocratic planning is essentially *undemocratic*.

The forces sweeping us toward super-industrialism can no longer be channeled by these bankrupt industrial-era methods. For a time they may continue to work in backward, slowly moving industries or communities. But their misapplication in advanced industries, in universities, in cities—wherever change is swift—cannot but intensify the instability, leading to wilder and wilder swings and lurches. Moreover, as the evidences of failure pile up, dangerous political, cultural and psychological currents are set loose.

One response to the loss of control, for example, is a revulsion against intelligence. Science first gave man a sense of mastery over his environment, and hence over the future. By making the future seem malleable, instead of immutable, it shattered the opiate religions that preached passivity and mysticism. Today, mounting evidence that society is out of control breeds disillusionment with science. In consequence, we witness a garish revival of mysticism. Suddenly astrology is the rage. Zen, yoga, seances, and witchcraft become popular pastimes. Cults form around the search for Dionysian experience, for non-verbal and supposedly non-linear communication. We are told it is more important to "feel" than to "think," as though there were a contradiction between the two. Existentialist oracles join Catholic mystics, Jungian psychoanalysts, and Hindu gurus in exalting the mystical and emotional against the scientific and rational.

This reversion to pre-scientific attitudes is accompanied, not surprisingly, by a tremendous wave of nostalgia in the society. Antique furniture, posters from a bygone era, games based on the remembrance of yesterday's trivia, the revival of Art Nouveau, the spread of Edwardian styles, the rediscovery of such faded pop-cult celebrities as Humphrey Bogart or W. C. Fields, all mirror a psychological lust for the simpler, less turbulent past. Powerful fad machines spring into action to capitalize on this hunger. The nostalgia business becomes a booming industry.

The failure of technocratic planning and the consequent sense of lost control also feeds the philosophy of "now-ness." Songs and advertisements hail the appearance of the "now generation," and learned psychiatrists, discoursing on the presumed dangers of repression, warn us not to defer our gratifications. Acting out and a search for immediate payoff are encouraged. "We're more oriented to the present," says a teen-age girl to a reporter after the mammoth Woodstock rock music festival. "It's like do what you want to do now. . . . If you stay anywhere very long you get into a planning thing. . . . So you just move on." Spontaneity, the personal equivalent of social planlessness, is elevated into a cardinal psychological virtue.

All this has its political analog in the emergence of a strange coalition of right wingers and New Leftists in support of what can only be termed a "hang loose" approach to the future. Thus we hear increasing calls for anti-planning or non-planning, sometimes euphemized as "organic growth." Among some radicals, this takes on an anarchist coloration. Not only is it regarded as unnecessary or unwise to make long-range plans for the future of the institution or society they wish to overturn, it is sometimes even regarded as poor taste to plan the next hour and a half of a meeting. Planlessness is glorified.

Arguing that planning imposes values on the future, the anti-planners overlook the fact that non-planning does so, too—often with far worse consequence. Angered by the narrow, econocentric character of technocratic planning, they condemn systems analysis, cost benefit accounting, and similar methods, ignoring the fact that, used differently, these very tools might be converted into powerful techniques for humanizing the future.

When critics charge that technocratic planning is anti-human, in the sense that it neglects social, cultural and psychological values in its headlong rush to maximize economic gain, they are usually right. When they charge that it is shortsighted and undemocratic, they are usually right. When they charge it is inept, they are usually right.

But when they plunge backward into irrationality, anti-scientific attitudes, a kind of sick nostalgia, and an exaltation of now-ness, they are not only wrong, but dangerous. Just as, in the main, their alternatives to industrialism call for a return to pre-industrial institutions, their alternative to technocracy is not post- but pre-technocracy.

Passage 7*

The central problem with the rationalist view of organizing people is that people are not very rational. To fit Taylor's old model, or today's organizational charts, man is simply designed wrong (or, of course, vice versa, according to our argument here). In fact, if our understanding of the current state of psychology is even close to correct, man is the ultimate study in conflict and paradox. It seems to us that to understand why the excellent companies are so effective in

---

engendering both commitment and regular innovation from tens of thousands or even hundreds of thousands of people, we have to take into account the way they deal with the following contradictions that are built into human nature:

1. All of us are self-centered, suckers for a bit of praise, and generally like to think of ourselves as winners. But the fact of the matter is that our talents are distributed normally—none of us is really as good as he or she would like to think, but rubbing our noses daily in that reality doesn't do us a bit of good.

2. Our imaginative, symbolic right brain is at least as important as our rational, deductive left. We reason by stories *at least* as often as with good data. "Does it feel right?" counts for more than "Does it add up?" or "Can I prove it?"

3. As information processors, we are simultaneously flawed and wonderful. On the one hand, we can hold little explicitly in mind, at most a half dozen or so facts at one time. Hence there should be an enormous pressure on managements—of complex organizations especially—to keep things very simple indeed. On the other hand, our unconscious mind is powerful, accumulating a vast storehouse of patterns, if we let it. Experience is an excellent teacher; yet most businessmen seem to undervalue it in the special sense we will describe.

4. We are creatures of our environment, very sensitive and responsive to external rewards and punishment. We are also strongly driven from within, self-motivated.

5. We act as if express beliefs are important, yet action speaks louder than words. One cannot, it turns out, fool any of the people any of the time. They watch for patterns in our most minute actions, and are wise enough to distrust words that in any way mismatch our deeds.

6. We desperately need meaning in our lives and will sacrifice a great deal to institutions that will provide meaning for us. We simultaneously need independence, to feel as though we are in charge of our destinies, and to have the ability to stick out.

Now, how do most companies deal with these conflicts? They take great pride in setting really high targets for people (productivity teams, product development teams, or division general managers), stretch targets. These are perfectly rational, but ultimately self-defeating. Why do TI and Tupperware, by contrast, insist that teams set their own objectives? Why does IBM set quotas so that almost all salespeople can make them? Surely TI has lazy workers. And no matter how intelligent IBM's hiring, screening, and training programs are for their salespeople, there is no way that this giant is going to get all superstars on its sales force. So what's going on?

The answer is surprisingly simple, albeit ignored by most managers. In a recent psychological study when a random sample of male adults were asked to rank themselves on "the ability to get along with others," *all* subjects, 100 percent, put themselves in the top half of the population. Sixty percent rated themselves in the top 10 percent of the population, and a full 25 percent ever so humbly thought they were in the top 1 percent of the population. In a parallel finding, 70 percent rated themselves in the top quartile in leadership; only 2 percent felt they were below average as leaders. Finally, in an area in which self-deception should be hard for most males, at least, 60 percent said they were in the top quartile of athletic ability; only 6 percent said they were below average.

We all think we're tops. We're exuberantly, wildly irrational about ourselves. And that has sweeping implications for organizing. Yet most organizations, we find, take a negative view of their people. They verbally berate participants for poor performance. (Most actually talk tougher than they act, but the tough talk nonetheless intimidates people.) They call for risk taking but punish even tiny failures. They want innovation but kill the spirit of the champion. With their rationalist hats on, they design systems that seem calculated to tear down their workers' self-image. They might not mean to be doing that, but they are.

The message that comes through so poignantly in the studies we reviewed is that we like to think of ourselves as winners. The lesson that the excellent companies have to teach is that there is no reason why we can't design systems that continually reinforce this notion; most of their people are made to feel that they are winners. Their populations are distributed around the normal curve, just like every other large population, but the difference is that their systems reinforce degrees of winning rather than degrees of losing. Their people by and large make their targets and quotas, because the targets and quotas are set (often by the people themselves) to allow that to happen.

In the not-so-excellent companies, the reverse is true. While IBM explicitly manages to ensure that 70 to 80 percent of its salespeople meet quotas, another company (an IBM competitor in part of its product line) works it so that only 40 percent of the sales force meets its quotas during a typical year. With this approach, at least 60 percent of the salespeople think of themselves as losers. They resent it and that leads to dysfunctional, unpredictable, frenetic behavior. Label a man a loser and he'll start acting like one. As one GM manager noted, "Our control systems are designed under the apparent assumption that 90 percent of the people are lazy ne'er-do-wells, just waiting to lie, cheat, steal, or otherwise screw us. We demoralize 95 percent of the work force who do act as adults by designing systems to cover our tails against the 5 percent who really are bad actors."

The systems in the excellent companies are not only designed to produce lots of winners; they are constructed to celebrate the winning once it occurs. Their systems make extraordinary use of non-monetary incentives. They are full of hoopla.

Passage 8.   Social Class, Minorities, and Conjugal Power*

The finding by Blood and Wolfe that white-collar husbands were able to make more important decisions than blue-collar husbands has not been seriously challenged, even though middle-class husbands espouse a more egalitarian ideology than do working-class husbands (Gillespie, 1971:134). The reason for this was mentioned in the discussion of different types of power bases early in this chapter. White-collar husbands can adhere to an egalitarian ideology but exert power as "experts" (L. Rubin, 1976:99). As William Goode summarizes, the white-collar husband "takes preference as a professional, not as a family head or as a male; nevertheless the precedence is his" (1963:21). By contrast, "lower-class men demand deference as *men*, as heads of families" (Goode, 1963:21). Blue-collar husbands rely more heavily on tradition to support their patriarchal authority.

Although blue-collar men may claim more relative power than their wives, studies show that their wives make more decisions than do middle-class wives. An explanation for this is that proportionally more blue-collar than white-collar wives work outside their homes, and those who do work make a proportionally greater contribution to the family income (Gillespie, 1971).

While white-collar husbands tend to exercise more marital power than blue-collar husbands, the relationship of income and status to conjugal power is not clear-cut. Research has supported Blood and Wolfe's early finding that lower-status blue-collar husbands have more marital power than do high-status blue-collar husbands. Mirra Komarovsky suggested a possible explanation: Because of their relatively high earnings, skilled workers may be able to marry women with as much or more education than they have. By marrying upward in this sense, skilled blue-collar husbands may lose a degree of power that the semiskilled worker exerts over his less well educated wife (Komarovsky, 1962).

Social-class patterns among blacks and Mexican-Americans are similar to those among whites. During the 1950s and 1960s social scientists believed that black marriages were characterized by a matriarchal power structure in which wives and mothers were dominant; howev-

---

*From *Marriages and Families: Making Choices and Facing Change,* Third Edition, by Mary Ann Lamanna and Agnes Reidman, © 1988, 1985, 1981 by Wadsworth, Inc. Reprinted with Permission.

er, recent research suggests otherwise. Black marriages tend to be more egalitarian than whites', but talk about "black matriarchy" was an exaggeration (McDonald, 1980; Gray-Little, 1982). One reason black marriages are more egalitarian than whites' is that proportionally more black than white wives are wage earners (Willie and Greenblatt, 1978).

Just as black matriarchy is a myth, so may be the belief that Mexican-Americans behave according to patriarchal standards. One study of seventy-six Mexican and Mexican-American migrant farm workers in California found that wives and husbands believed they made most decisions jointly. The one area decided more often by the husband alone was where the family would live. The authors concluded that "dominance-submission are much less universal than previously assumed. Either they never existed but were an ideal or they are undergoing radical change." (Hawkes and Taylor, 1975:807).

Recent research indicates that differences between minority groups, such as blacks and Mexican-Americans, and Anglo-Saxons are not more pronounced than social-class differences *within* these groups themselves (Cromwell and Cromwell, 1978).

Love, Need, and Power

Some have argued that a primarily economic analysis does not do justice to the complexities of marital power. Perhaps wives have considerable power through their husband's love for them.

The relative degree to which the one spouse loves and needs the other may be the most crucial variable in explaining total power structure. The spouse who has relatively less feeling for the other may be the one in the best position to control and manipulate all the "resources" that he [sic] has in his command in order to effectively influence the outcome of decisions, if not also to dominate the decision-making. Thus, a 'relative love and need theory may be . . . basic in explaining power structure [Safilios-Rothschild, 1970:548–49].

This theory is congruent with what sociologist Willard Waller termed the **principle of least interest.** The partner with the least interest in the relationship is the one who is more apt to exploit the other. The spouse who is more willing to break up the marriage or to shatter rapport and refuse to be the first to make up can maintain dominance (Waller 1951:190–92; Heer, 1963). Dependence on the relationship can be practical and economic as well as emotional. Women with small children are often financially dependent, for example. Aging women have less probability of remarriage after divorce or of significant employment (if they have not already established a career), so they may be reluctant to leave a marriage.

Like resource theory, the **relative love and need theory** is a variation of exchange theory. Each partner brings resources to the marriage and receives rewards from the other partner. These may not balance precisely, and one partner may be gaining more from the marriage than the other partner, emotionally or otherwise. This partner is most dependent on the marriage and thus is most likely to comply with the other's preferences.

The relative love and need theory does not predict whether husbands or wives will generally be more powerful. In other words, it assumes that women are as likely to have power as men are: "The man who desires or values the woman as a mate more than she desires or values him will be in the position of wanting to please her. Her enchantment in his eyes may be physical attractiveness, pleasing personality, his perception of her as a 'perfect' wife and mother" (Hallenbeck, 1966:201).

Generally, however, the wife holds the less powerful position. How does the relative love and need theory account for this? One explanation offered is that "love has been a feminine specialty" (Cancian, 1985:253). As we saw in Chapter 2, women are more socialized to love and need their husbands than the reverse (Firestone, 1970). They also tend to be more relationship-oriented than men are (Gilligan, 1982). According to the principle of least interest, this puts women at a power disadvantage (Cancian, 1985). Women "come to have a vested interest in the social unit that at the same time imposes inequalities on them" (Goode, 1982:138).

Moreover, Americans *believe* that women are more dependent on the marital relationship than men are. "If most people believe that women need heterosexual love more than men, then women will be at a power disadvantage" (Cancian, 1985:257). In our society women are encouraged to express their feelings, men to repress them. Men are less likely, therefore, to articulate their feelings for their wives and "men's dependence on close relationships remains covert and repressed, whereas women's dependence is overt and exaggerated" (258). Overt dependency affects power: "A woman gains power over her husband if he clearly places a high value on her company or if he expresses a high demand or need for what she supplies. . . . If his need for her and high evaluation of her remain covert and unexpressed, her power will be low" (258).

Passage 9.*   The Closing of the American Mind: How Higher Education Has Failed Democracy and Impoverished the Souls of Today's Students**

Introduction: Our Virtue

When I was a young teacher at Cornell, I once had a debate about education with a professor of psychology. He said that it was his function to get rid of prejudices in his students. He knocked them

---

*A more difficult passage for analysis.
**From *The Closing of the American Mind: How Higher Education Has Failed Democracy and Improverished the Souls of Today's Students* by Allan Bloom. Copyright © 1987 by Allan Bloom. Reprinted by permission of Simon & Schuster, Inc., pp. 42–43, 337–339.

down like tenpins. I began to wonder what he replaced those prejudices with. He did not seem to have much of an idea of what the opposite of a prejudice might be. He reminded me of the little boy who gravely informed me when I was four that there is no Santa Claus, who wanted me to bathe in the brilliant light of truth. Did this professor know what those prejudices meant for the students and what effect being deprived of them would have? Did he believe that there are truths that could guide their lives as did their prejudices? Had he considered how to give students the love of the truth necessary to seek unprejudiced beliefs, or would he render them passive, disconsolate, indifferent, and subject to authorities like himself, or the best of contemporary thought? My informant about Santa Claus was just showing off, proving his superiority to me. He had not created the Santa Claus that had to be there in order to be refuted. Think of all we learn about the world from men's belief in Santa Clauses, and all that we learn about the soul from those who believe in them. By contrast, merely methodological excision from the soul of the imagination that projects Gods and heroes onto the wall of the cave does not promote knowledge of the soul; it only lobotomizes it, cripples its powers.

I found myself responding to the professor of psychology that I personally tried to teach my students prejudices, since nowadays—with the general success of his method—they had learned to doubt beliefs even before they believed in anything. Without people like me, he would be out of business. Descartes had a whole wonderful world of old beliefs, of prescientific experience and articulations of the order of things, beliefs firmly and even fanatically held, before he even began his systematic and radical doubt. One has to have the experience of really believing before one can have the thrill of liberation. So I proposed a division of labor in which I would help to grow the flowers in the field and he could mow them down.

Prejudices, strong prejudices, are visions about the way things are. They are divinations of the order of the whole of things, and hence the road to a knowledge of that whole is by way of erroneous opinions about it. Error is indeed our enemy, but it alone points to the truth and therefore deserves our respectful treatment. The mind that has no prejudices at the outset is empty. It can only have been constituted by a method that is unaware of how difficult it is to recognize that a prejudice is a prejudice. Only Socrates knew, after a lifetime of unceasing labor, that he was ignorant. Now every high-school student knows that. How did it become so easy? What accounts for our amazing progress? Could it be that our experience has been so impoverished by our various methods, of which openness is only the latest, that there is nothing substantial enough left there to resist criticism, and we therefore have no world left of which to be really ignorant? Have we so simplified the soul that it is no longer difficult to explain? To an eye of dogmatic skepticism, nature herself, in all her lush profusion of expressions, might appear to be a prejudice. In her place we put a gray network of critical concepts, which were invented to interpret nature's phenomena but which strangled them and therewith destroyed their own *raison d'être*. Perhaps it is our first task to resuscitate those phenomena so that we may again have a world to which we can put our questions and be able to philosophize. This seems to me to be our educational challenge. . . .

The Student and the University: Liberal Education

What image does a first-rank college or university present today to a teen-ager leaving home for the first time, off to the adventure of a liberal education? He has four years of freedom to discover himself—a space between the intellectual wasteland he has left behind and the inevitable dreary professional training that awaits him after the baccalaureate. In this short time he must learn that there is a great world beyond the little one he knows, experience the exhilaration of it and digest enough of it to sustain himself in the intellectual deserts he is destined to traverse. He must do this, that is, if he is to have any hope of a higher life. These are the charmed years when he can, if he so chooses, become anything he wishes and when he has the opportunity to survey his alternatives, not merely those current in his time or provided by careers, but those available to him as a human being. The importance of these years for an American cannot be overestimated. They are civilization's only chance to get to him.

In looking at him we are forced to reflect on what he should learn if he is to be called educated; we must speculate on what the human potential to be fulfilled is. In the specialties we can avoid such speculation, and the avoidance of them is one of specialization's charms. But here it is a simple duty. What are we to teach this person? The answer may not be evident, but to attempt to answer the question is already to philosophize and to begin to educate. Such a concern in itself poses the question of the unity of man and the unity of the sciences. It is childishness to say, as some do, that everyone must be allowed to develop freely, that it is authoritarian to impose a point of view on the student. In that case, why have a university? If the response is "to provide an atmosphere for learning," we come back to our original questions at the second remove. Which atmosphere? Choices and reflection on the reasons for those choices are unavoidable. The university has to stand for something. The practical effects of unwillingness to think positively about the contents of a liberal education are, on the one hand, to ensure that all the vulgarities of the world outside the university will flourish within it, and, on the other, to impose a much harsher and more illiberal necessity on the student—the one given by the imperial and imperious demands of the specialized disciplines unfiltered by unifying thought.

The university now offers no distinctive visage to the young person. He finds a democracy of the disciplines—which are there either because they are autochthonous or because they wandered in recently to perform some job that was demanded of the university. This democracy is really an anarchy, because there are no recognized rules for citizenship and no legitimate titles to rule. In short there is no vision, nor is there a set of competing visions, of what an educated human being is. The question has disappeared, for to pose it would be a threat to the peace. There is no organization of the sciences, no tree of knowledge. Out of chaos emerges dispiritedness, because it is impossible to make a reasonable choice. Better to give up on liberal education and get on with a specialty in which there is at least a pre-scribed curriculum and a prospective career. On the way the student can pick up in elective courses a little of whatever is thought to make one cultured. The student gets no intimation that great mysteries might be revealed to him, that new and higher motives of action might be discovered within him, that a different and more human way of life can be harmoniously constructed by what he is going to learn.

Simply, the university is not distinctive. Equality for us seems to culminate in the unwillingness and incapacity to make claims of superiority, particularly in the domains in which such claims have al-ways been made—art, religion and philosophy. When Weber found that he could not choose between certain high opposites—reason vs. revelation, Buddha vs. Jesus—he did not conclude that all things are equally good, that the distinction between high and low disappears. As a matter of fact he intended to revitalize the consideration of these great alternatives in showing the gravity and danger involved in choosing among them; they were to be heightened in contrast to the trivial considerations of modern life that threatened to overgrow and render indistinguishable the profound problems the confrontation with which makes the bow of the soul taut. The serious intellectual life was for him the battleground of the great decisions, all of which are spiritual or "value" choices. One can no longer present this or that particular view of the educated or civilized man as authoritative; therefore one must say that education consists in knowing, really knowing, the small number of such views in their integrity. This dis-tinction between profound and superficial—which takes the place of good and bad, true and false—provided a focus for serious study, but it hardly held out against the naturally relaxed democratic tendency to say, "Oh, what's the use?" The first university disruptions at Berkeley were explicitly directed against the multiversity smorgasbord and, I must confess, momentarily and partially engaged my sympathies. It may have even been the case that there was some small element of longing for an education in the motivation of those students. But nothing was done to guide or inform their energy, and the result was merely to add multilife-styles to multidisciplines, the diversity of per-versity to the diversity of specialization. What we see so often happening in general happened here too; the insistent demand for greater community ended in greater isolation. Old agreements, old habits, old traditions were not so easily replaced.

Thus, when a student arrives at the university, he finds a bewildering variety of departments and a bewildering variety of courses. And there is no official guidance, no university-wide agreement, about what he *should* study. Nor does he usually find readily available examples, either among students or professors, of a unified use of the university's resources. It is easiest simply to make a career choice and go about getting prepared for that career. The programs designed for those having made such a choice render their students immune to charms that might lead them out of the conventionally respectable. The sirens sing *sotto voce* these days, and the young already have enough wax in their ears to pass them by without danger. These specialties can provide enough courses to take up most of their time for four years in preparation for the inevitable graduate study. With the few remaining courses they can do what they please, taking a bit of this and a bit of that. No public career these days—not doctor nor lawyer nor politician nor journalist nor businessman nor entertainer—has much to do with humane learning. An education, other than purely professional or technical, can even seem to be an impediment. That is why a countervailing atmosphere in the university would be necessary for the students to gain a taste for intellectual pleasures and learn that they are viable.

The real problem is those students who come hoping to find out what career they want to have, or are simply looking for an adventure with themselves. There are plenty of things for them to do—courses and disciplines enough to spend many a lifetime on. Each department or great division of the university makes a pitch for itself, and each offers a course of study that will make the student an initiate. But how to choose among them? How do they relate to one another? The fact is they do not address one another. They are competing and contradictory, without being aware of it. The problem of the whole is urgently indicated by the very existence of the specialties, but it is never systematically posed.

Empirical Theories and Explanation: A More Formal Approach

In previous sections of this chapter, we concentrated on the use of theories to explain *patterns* or *regularities* that are described by generalizations. But we can, as was mentioned, also explain the occurrence of particular events.

Suppose that someone tries to explain why the lamentable crack in Bruce's engine block occurred (Example 10.8). The person may point out that the temperature dropped substantially below 32°F and chide Bruce for failing to put antifreeze into his radiator. If Bruce presses for an explanation, the person might remind him of the "law of nature" (the generalization) that water expands when it freezes.

Philosophers of science have maintained that such an explanation of a particular event can be treated as an "argument" having the description of the event or condition to be explained as a conclusion and containing two sorts of premises: (1) generalizations that describe regularities or patterns (sometimes called "laws of nature") and (2) statements of particular relevant conditions. As we noted earlier in this chapter, although these explanations have the form of an argument, they *have a different purpose* than the standard arguments considered in much of the text. Those arguments aimed at establishing the *truth* of the conclusion. In an explanation, we assume that the conclusion is true (the event occurred). We want to understand *why* it occurred. Explanations of this type can be schematized as follows:

Example 10.11. An Explanatory Argument*

Regularities	$R_1 \ R_2 \ R_3 \ \ldots$
Conditions	$C_1 \ \& \ C_2 \ \& \ C_3 \ \ldots$
Description of event explained	E

There is considerable controversy about the extent to which *genuine scientific explanations* fall under this model. Nevertheless, some cases seem to fit comfortably. Bruce's unhappy experience with a cracked engine block, for instance, can be explained in all its painful detail by listing some of its relevant regularities and conditions.

---

*In this schema, the argument can be seen as resembling either a deductive argument, an inductive argument of the general-to-particular type (discussed in Chapter 9), or even some other kinds of inference. This model of an explanation is often called the "covering law model." If it is assumed that the argument is deductive, it is called the "deductive-nomological" or "hypothetico-deductive" model and is particularly associated with the philosopher of science Carl Hempel.

Example 10.12*

Generalizations expressing some observable regularities

(R₁) *(Pure) water turns to ice and expands when it is subject to temperatures substantially below 32° Fahrenheit for a substantial amount of time.*

(R₂) *The pressure exerted by expanding ice exceeds the ultimate tensile strength of cast iron.*

(R₃) *Whenever the ultimate tensile strength of a material is exceeded, it cracks (or breaks).*

Conditions

(C₁) *His water-cooled engine was filled with pure water.*

(C₂) *The temperature in his engine dropped substantially below 32°F for a substantial time.*

(C₃) *His engine block is made of cast iron.*

(E) *His engine block cracked.*

This model also provides a basis for understanding at least some cases of *prediction*. Essentially, a prediction can be seen as similar to an explanation except that we do not know that the event described in the conclusion has occurred. In the narrow sense of "predict," predictions are made about the future. We could predict that Bruce's engine block *will* crack in Example 10.12 if we have reason to believe that conditions C1, C2, and C3 *will* occur.

More broadly speaking, however, we can use the term *prediction* even when we are not talking about the future. In this sense we make a *prediction* about what we would find if we carried out a certain investigation, including past cases.** We could predict the existence of mineral deposits in eastern Washington given certain geological regularities (or laws) and statements about some specific geological formations in that area.†

---

*Adapted from *Political Research Methods* by Barbara Leigh Smith, Karl F. Johnson, David Warren Paulsen, and Francis Shocket. Copyright © 1976 by Houghton Mifflin Company. Reprinted by permission of the publisher.
**A prediction about the past or about unobserved cases is sometimes called a "retrodiction."
†This prediction was actually made by a computer program called PROSPECTOR. Field work indicated that there were, in fact, minerals of the type predicted at this unexpected location.

Not just any argument of the form given in Example 10.11 will provide an adequate explanation or prediction. What is crucial is that it contains some generalization that is at least a candidate for being labeled a "law of nature." The causal generalizations like those discussed in Chapter 9 are such candidates for "laws," and explanations containing them are called *causal explanations*. But laws come in other forms, such as the regularities about ice cited in Example 10.12. Such laws are principles that not only have held in the past but will hold for the future, not merely accidentally but as the result of fundamental interconnections in nature. One sign of such generalizations is that they are marks of what *would* happen even if it hasn't yet or won't. We know, by virtue of R_1, for example, that a glass of water left outside on that fateful night *would* have frozen. Similarly, Alvin might know that he *would* die if he ever succumbed to the temptation to drink a gallon of paint.

Compare this to a generalization that reflects an *accidental* feature of the world. It might be true that everyone who goes into the Oval Office of the White House is under 6'11" tall, but this gives us *no* grounds for supposing that some NBA basketball center over 7' tall *would* be (or would become) under 6'11" tall if he went into the Oval Office. Such an example is not even tempting.

Sometimes, as in the case of the fully controlled "true" experiment described in Chapter 9, we can have evidence that strongly favors a causal generalization. But even so, we need to depend on some background assumptions or theories, at least about the instrumentation that was used. Such a controlled "true" experiment cannot actually be carried out, for instance, to test the hypothesis that "All U.S. presidents are men" (that is, male gender is a causal prerequisite to being president) in the strong sense that has implications about the future rather than merely summarizes the past.* In practice we have to consider the broader context in which we can discuss the effect of gender on being elected to high public office in the United States. In short, we have to consider a theory.

A second type of explanation (or prediction) is the causal narrative or story.** Here we typically *explain* (or predict) *how* something came about, what *causal mechanism* was involved. We might explain how it happened that water was running out of the tailpipe on Diane's car by the following story:

---

*We call it a "hypothesis" in this context because it is a generalization open to *scrutiny* or *test*.
**Additional controversy exists about whether such causal narratives can be fitted into a complex version of the covering law model of explanation.

Example 10.13   *(1) When Diane brought her car in for routine servicing, the mechanic forgot to replace the radiator cap after checking the fluid level.*

(2) When Diane drove home the water boiled out of the radiator.

(3) The engine overheated.

(4) The head was warped enabling the water in the water jacket to flow into the cylinders and out the manifold.

(5) The water ran from the manifold out the tailpipe.

This sequence of events can be represented as a series of causes.

Example 10.14   *a caused b caused c caused d caused e*

Failure to replace the cap caused the water to boil out, which caused the head to warp, which caused the water to flow into the cylinder, which caused it to run out the tailpipe.

Note that even here our account presupposes some *theory* about the structure and operation of the automobile engine. It assumes, for instance, that water can move through the cylinder (of an operating engine) to the manifold if the head is warped.* These assumptions render the causal story plausible. Similarly, a detective in a mystery novel might explain *how* the crime was committed. But even here there are typically assumptions (theories) about how the murderer's mind worked, about how the murder weapon produced the wounds, and so on.

How can we represent the way theories enter into explanations and predictions? One tactic is to extend the model of an explanation presented in Example 10.11 to explain regularities in the same way these regularities explain particular occurrences, that is, by employing an argument that shows how the regularity follows from the theory and certain specific assumptions. Using this model, we have explained the regularity that water turns to ice and expands in temperatures below 32°F, when we show that it follows from a theory. But a theory typically does more than explain a single regularity; several known, predicted, and even unanticipated, potentially found regularities might fall within its scope.

---

*Note that such causal stories can be criticized by using the techniques we described in the previous section of this chapter. We can *subvert support* by pointing out that elements in the story did not occur, e.g., the radiator cap might still be on, the head might not be warped, etc.; or we can *note nonsupport*, e.g., that there is no reason for believing that water can flow through the engine; or we can *offer alternatives*, e.g., that the drain valve leaked or that there was a hole in the exhaust system that allowed rain to flow in.

In addition to statements of theory and regularities, we have identified a third level of particular pieces of evidence. Although it might be difficult to draw firm lines between these levels, they may be useful to you in picking out various kinds of statements in passages containing theories and explanations. Think of them as labels on an axis going from the more concrete and directly evidential to the more abstract and theoretical. There are two ways of looking at this relationship: from the top down, which distinguishes between what does the explaining and what gets explained, and from the bottom up, which distinguishes between what provides basic support and what ultimately gets supported. The process of explanation by theory is a "bootstraps" operation—like lifting yourself up by your bootstraps. A good explanation demands a well-supported theory, and the ability to explain items over a broad scope is a mark of a well-supported theory. These relationships are illustrated in Figure 10.2.

Marks of a Successful Empirical Theory   We have discussed techniques for criticizing empirical theories and have emphasized isolating fairly obvious faults that might be brought into the dialogue-process by those without extensive specialized or technical knowledge. But choice among theories, particularly by subject matter "experts," brings in some more refined criteria. Important among them is that a successful theory

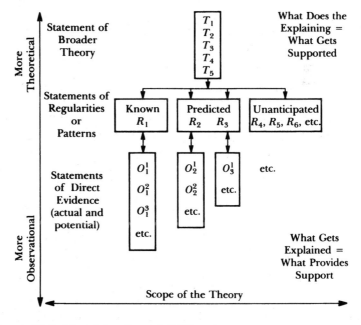

Figure 10.2. Model for Empirical Theories

typically provides a common explanation for a wide range of phenomena. The classical example is Newton's theory of gravitation explaining the orbits of planets around the sun and the moon around the earth; but the same theory that accounted for these regularities also had other applications. With a few additional assumptions it could be applied to explain the regular motion of pendulums as well as the parabolic path taken by cannonballs. The existence of these regularities supports the theory, and the theory in turn explains the regularities.

Several characteristics count as virtues in such successful theories:*

1. They have *explanatory power*. They actually explain patterns we know or suspect to exist with some accuracy and precision.

2. They have *broad scope*. They apply to a wide variety of diverse phenomena.

3. They are *systematic*. They consist of interconnected statements rather than an odd assemblage of loosely related items.

4. They are *fruitful*. They predict the existence of regularities that may not even have been suspected before the theory was propounded.

Nevertheless, at a given time there may be two different theories, both in some measure successful, covering some of the same phenomena. A number of studies indicate that police officers and prison guards measure high on various tests for authoritarian attitudes. Why? Two types of theories have been advanced. The first accounts for the pattern in terms of socialization. People coming into police and prison work are socialized (informally taught) authoritarian attitudes. According to the second theory, people who already have authoritarian attitudes are drawn to police and prison work. Both these theories explain the occurrence of authoritarian attitudes, can be applied to other occupational areas, can be systematically developed, and are suggestive of additional research, but at the moment, it is not easy to decide between them.

Furthermore, even if one theory can be considered better than another on the basis of evidence available at a particular time, this evidence might come to be seen in a different light at some later time. Not only is current evidence itself open to reexamination, the future may disclose new evidence or provide a revolutionary new theory that will bring about the rejection of certain currently accepted beliefs. But the more possibility that

---

*Various philosophers have included other criteria for a successful theory, such as simplicity and elegance.

we might have to give up a well-established theory is no reason, in itself, to reject the current theory—after all, it is equally possible that we now have it at least approximately right. Every time you shut the door it is barely possible (although hardly likely) that the floor outside has collapsed without your knowledge, but this is no reason for acting as if the floor has collapsed behind you.

Exercise 10.3   Putting Explanations Given by Empirical Theories into a "Standard Form"

Pick out statements of theory, regularity, and particular evidential data that occur in the following passages. Label the elements as in Figure 10.2.

1. A STAR NAMED GEORGE*

> In the 570 million years since the beginning of an abundant fossil record of the earth's biota almost every species has become extinct. Until recently the extinctions were thought to come at a roughly constant rate; the great biological crisis of 65 million years ago that resulted in the disappearance of the dinosaurs was thought to be one of a mere handful of exceptions to the hypothesis of continuity. Now a careful statistical analysis of the extinctions of more than 500 families of marine animals shows the dinosaur extinction to be less the exception than the rule. The analysis, conducted by David M. Raup and J. John Sepkoski, Jr., of the University of Chicago, shows that the rate of extinctions over the past 250 million years has increased systematically every 26 million years; the most recent ones were some 13 million years ago. The striking regularity of the extinctions suggests an extraterrestrial cause, and an astrophysical model that explains the regularity has now been proposed by Richard A. Muller and Marc Davis of the University of California at Berkeley and by Piet Hut of the Institute for Advanced Study. If the model is in accord with reality, it would bring about a fundamental revision in the understanding of the solar system.
>
> According to Muller and his colleagues, the sun is a member of a binary-star system. The sun's companion is most likely a faint dwarf star, perhaps a tenth the mass of the sun, that is now at a distance of about 2.4 light-years. It would be straightforward to suppose the periodic extinctions were somehow caused by the passage of the companion through the solar system every 26 million years; indeed, one of

---

Muller's initial hypotheses called for the companion to swing close enough to the sun to disturb the orbits of the asteroids between Mars and Jupiter and thereby subject the earth to an intensified planetoidal bombardment. That mechanism would not work, however, because an orbit with a 26-million-year period that passes so close to the sun would not be stable. Gravitational perturbations would probably cause the companion to miss the sun by 100 astronomical units on its second orbit. (An astronomical unit is the mean distance between the earth and the sun.)

In December of last year, meeting with Davis and Hut on the problem for the first time, Muller explained the apparent failure of the binary-star hypothesis to account for the periodic extinctions. Hut remarked that the hypothesis might be saved if the companion star, instead of passing through the asteroid belt, were to pass through the Oort cloud. That cloud is a huge shell of interstellar debris, weakly bound by the sun's gravity, in which comets are thought to form; it is named for J. H. Oort of the University of Leiden. Oort pointed out in 1950 that the comets observed in the inner solar system can be accounted for by perturbations in the orbits of some 10^{11} comets found between 10,000 and 100,000 astronomical units from the sun. The perturbations are caused by the random passage of stars in the neighborhood of the solar system. The comets that reach the inner solar system from this region of the Oort cloud are either trapped in relatively small solar orbits or swing so rapidly around the sun that they eventually leave the solar system.

Davis and Hut recalled that in 1981 a revised estimate of the population of comets had been published by Jack G. Hills, then of the Jet Propulsion Laboratory of the California Institute of Technology. According to Hills, comets must be far more numerous in the inner part of the Oort cloud—1,000 to 10,000 astronomical units from the sun—than they are in the region of the cloud considered by Oort. In the inner Oort cloud Hills estimated that there are roughly 10^{13} comets, although their total mass is less than the mass of Jupiter. The comets in the inner cloud are sufficiently well bound by the sun's gravity not to be much perturbed by a passing star, but Hills calculated that once every 500 million years the random path of a nearby star would come close enough to the sun to cause such perturbations. The perturbations would have dramatic consequences for the earth. Roughly a billion comets would arrive in the region of the solar system inside the earth's orbit over a period of from 100,000 to a million years. Of these comets, Hills estimated, perhaps 10 to 200 would hit the earth.

Most comets are believed to consist largely of ices such as solid ammonia, solid methane and ordinary ice, but some may also have a rocky core. The impact of a rocky comet on the earth could be the source of a thin layer of clay, highly enriched in the element iridium, that has been found in geologic formations at several locations. The enriched layer of iridium was first noted by Luis W. Alvarez and his son Walter Alvarez of Berkeley and their associates; it coincides with the biological crisis of 65 million years ago, when roughly 70 percent of the families or organisms on the earth, or more than 90 percent of the species, became extinct.

Many geologists and paleontologists now accept the Alvarez hypothesis that the origin of the iridium was extraterrestrial and that the impact of the extraterrestrial object with the earth threw up enough dust to darken the earth's atmosphere for at least six months. The dust cut off much of the sunlight that normally reaches the earth's surface, inhibiting photosynthesis and causing the disruptions in the food web that led to the mass extinctions. The mechanism is similar to the one that, according to many atmospheric scientists, would give rise to a "nuclear winter" after a large-scale nuclear war.

If the cometary impacts proposed by Hills can account for the kind of extinctions suggested by the Alvarez group, Muller, Davis and Hut reason that a consistent explanation can be given for periodic extinctions. The sun's binary companion must pass close enough to the inner Oort cloud every 26 million years to cause a shower of comets in the vicinity of the earth. Following Hills's analysis, they calculate that a dwarf star passing within 30,000 astronomical units of the sun should cause an average of three or four comets to hit the earth in every orbital period of the star. The statistical variability inherent in this number can account for the fluctuations in the extinction rate that are observed in the geologic record. Moreover, the mechanism leads to the prediction that several cometary impacts can be associated with a single rise in the extinction rate. That prediction is partially confirmed by the finding that associated with the iridium layer are at least three distinct layers of microtektites. Tektites are the glassy stones believed to originate when a large object strikes the earth and splashes out melted silicate.

A few days after Muller and his colleagues had reached these conclusions Walter Alvarez suggested to Muller that periodic comet showers should be reflected in the periodic excavation of large craters on the earth. Muller and Alvarez have analyzed 13 impact craters larger than 10 kilometers across that have been accurately dated, and they find another striking regularity: the impacts come on the average every 28.4 million years. The most recent increase in the frequency of the impacts was 13.5 million years ago, which nearly coincides with the most recent increase in extinctions. The probability that the increases are caused by random events is less than five chances out of 1,000. Muller points out that the discrepancy between the 26-million-year period and the 28.4-million-year one can be absorbed by uncertainties in the dating of the extinctions.

The most important prediction of the model is, of course, the existence of the companion star. The model makes no prediction, however, about the position of the companion in the sky. Several investigators are now searching among roughly a million stars brighter than the 12th magnitude for stars that show a small proper motion against the background of more distant stars. If the companion is found, Muller and his colleagues suggest in a footnote to their account several names: "Nemesis, after the Greek goddess who relentlessly persecutes the excessively rich, proud and powerful . . . Kali, 'the black,' after the Hindu goddess of death and destruction, who nonetheless is infinitely generous and kind to those she loves; Indra, after the vedic god of storms and war, who uses a thunderbolt (comet?) to slay a serpent (dinosaur?), thereby releasing life-giving waters from the mountains, and finally George, after the saint who slew the dragon."

2.* BUREAUCRATIC DOMINATION**

Usually the progress in death-dealing capacity achieved in the twentieth century has been described in terms of technological advances in weaponry. Too little attention has been given to the advances in social organization that allowed for the effective use of the new weapons. In order to understand how the moral barrier was crossed that made massacre in the millions possible, it is necessary to consider the importance of bureaucracy in modern political and social organization. The German sociologist Max Weber was especially cognizant of its significance. Writing in 1916, long before the Nazi party came to prominence in German politics, Weber observed:

When fully developed, bureaucracy stands . . . under the principle of *sine ira ac studio* (without scorn and bias). *Its specific nature which is welcomed by capitalism develops the more perfectly the more bureaucracy is 'dehumanized,'* the more completely it succeeds in eliminating from official business love, hatred, and all purely personal, irrational and emotional elements which escape calculation. *This is the specific nature of bureaucracy and it is appraised as its special virtue."* (Italics added.)

Weber also observed:

The decisive reason for the advance of bureaucratic organization has always been its purely technical superiority over any other kind of organization. *The fully developed bureaucratic mechanism compares with other organizations exactly as does the machine with the nonmechanical modes of organization.*

Precision, speed, unambiguity, knowledge of the files, continuity, discretion, unity, strict subordination, reduction of friction and of material and personal

---

*A more difficult passage for analysis.
**"Bureaucratic Domination" (pp. 21–31) in *The Cunning of History* by Richard L. Rubenstein. Copyright © 1975 by Richard L. Rubenstein. By permission of Harper & Row, Publishers, Inc.

costs—these are raised to the optimum point in the strictly bureaucratic organization." (Italics added.)

Weber stressed "the fully developed bureaucratic mechanism." He was aware of the fact that actual bureaucracies seldom achieve the level of efficiency of the "ideal type" he had constructed. Nevertheless, he saw clearly that bureaucracy was a machine capable of effective action and was as indifferent to "all purely personal . . . elements which escape calculation" as any other machine.

In his time Karl Marx looked forward to the eventual domination of the proletariat over the body politic because of its indispensability to the working process. Max Weber was convinced that political domination would rest with whoever controlled the bureaucratic apparatus because of its indisputable superiority as an instrument for the organization of human action. But, to the best of my knowledge, even Weber never entertained the possibility that the police and civil service bureaucracies could be used as a death machine to eliminate millions who had been rendered superfluous by definition. Even Weber seems to have stopped short of foreseeing state-sponsored massacres as one of the "dehumanized" capacities of bureaucracy.

Almost from the moment they came to power, the Nazis understood the bureaucratic mechanism they controlled. When they first came to power, there were a large number of widely publicized bullying attacks on Jews throughout Germany, especially by the SA, the brown-shirted storm troopers. However, it was soon recognized that improperly organized attacks by individuals or small groups actually hindered the process leading to administrative massacre. The turning from sporadic bullying to systematic anonymous terror paralleled the decline in influence of the SA and the rise of Heinrich Himmler and the SS. Himmler does not seem to have been a sadist. During the war, he did not like to watch killing operations and became upset when he did. But, *Himmler was the perfect bureaucrat.* He did what he believed was his duty *sine ira et studio,* without bias or scorn. He recognized that the task assigned to his men, mass extermination, was humanly speaking exceedingly distasteful. On several occasions, he praised the SS for exercising an obedience so total that they overcame the feelings men would normally have when engaged in mass murder. The honor of the SS, he held, involved the ability to overcome feelings of compassion and achieve what was in fact perfect bureaucratic objectivity.

Himmler objected to private acts of sadism, but his reasons were organizational rather than moral. He understood that individual and small group outbursts diminished the efficiency of the SS. One of his most important "contributions" to the Nazi regime was to encourage the systematization of SS dominance and terror in the concentration camps. At the beginning of Hitler's rule, Himmler, as head of the SS, was subordinate to Ernst Röhm, the head of the SA, the storm troopers. Himmler's position was transformed when Hitler ordered Röhm murdered on June 30, 1934. He ceased to be a subordinate. In the aftermath of the Röhm *Putsch,* there was a general downgrading of the SA. SA guards were removed from the concentration camps. Their places were taken by Himmler's SS. By 1936 Himmler was appointed *Reichsführer SS* and *Chef der Deutschen Polizei.* He then dominated the entire German police apparatus.

One of the examples of Himmler's organizing ability was his involvement in the concentration camp at Dachau which he founded in 1933. Originally, there was little to distinguish Dachau from any of the early "wild" Nazi camps. Under Himmler's guidance, Dachau became a model for the systematically managed camps of World War II. Under his direction, the sporadic terror of the "wild" camps was replaced by impersonal, systematized terror. Much of the systematization was carried out with Himmler's approval by Theodor Eicke who became commandant at Dachau in June 1933. Eicke had spent most of his career in police administration. His organization of the camp was modern and professional. His "discretionary camp regulations," issued on October 1, 1933, provided for a strictly graded series of punishments including solitary confinement and both corporal and capital punishment for offending prisoners. When corporal punishment was inflicted, Eicke's directives provided that the punishment be carried out by several SS guards in the presence of the other guards, the prisoners and the commandant. In a report dated May 8, 1935, Eicke's successor as Dachau commandant wrote to Himmler that individual guards were "forbidden to lay hands on a prisoner or to have private conversations with them." The intent of Eicke's regulations was to eliminate all arbitrary punishment by individual guards and to replace it with impersonal, anonymous punishment. The impersonal nature of the transaction was heightened by the fact that any guard could be called on to inflict punishment. Even if a guard was struck by a prisoner, he could not retaliate personally, at least insofar as the regulations were concerned. Like everything else at the camps, under Himmler punishment was bureaucratized and depersonalized. Bureaucratic mass murder reached its fullest development when gas chambers with a capacity for killing two thousand people at a time were installed at Auschwitz. As Hannah Arendt has observed, the very size of the chambers emphasized the complete depersonalization of the killing process.

Under Himmler, there was no objection to cruelty, provided it was disciplined and systematized. This preference was also shared by the German civil service bureaucracy. According to Hilberg, the measure that gave the civil service bureaucrats least difficulty in exterminating their victims was the imposition of a starvation diet. In a bureaucratically controlled society where every individual's ration can be strictly determined, starvation is the ideal instrument of "clean" violence. A few numbers are manipulated on paper in an office hundreds of miles away from the killing centers and millions can be condemned to a prolonged and painful death. In addition, both the death rate and the desired level of vitality of the inmates can easily be regulated by the same bureaucrats. As starvation proceeds, the victim's appearance is so drastically altered that by the time death finally releases him, he hardly seems like a human being worth saving. The very manner of death confirms the rationalization with which the killing was justified in the first place. The Nazis assigned the paranthropoid identity of a *Tiermensch,* a subhuman, to their victims. By the time of death that identity seemed like a self-fulfilling prophecy. Yet, the bureaucrat need lose no sleep over his victims. He never confronts the results of his distinctive kind of homicidal violence.

A crucial turning point in the transformation of outbursts of hatred into systematized violence occurred in the aftermath of the infamous *Kristallnacht,* the Nazi anti-Jewish riots of November 10, 1938. It is generally agreed that the riots were an unsuccessful attempt on the part of Propaganda Minister Joseph Goebbels and the SA to gain a role in the anti-Jewish process. On November 9, 1938, a young Jew, Herschel Grynzpan assassinated Legationsrat Ernst vom Rath in the German embassy in Paris. At Goebbels's instigation, SA formations set out to burn down every synagogue in Germany. Jewish stores were burned and looted and Jews were attacked throughout the country.

The SS was not informed that the operation was to take place. When Himmler heard that Goebbels had instigated a pogrom, he ordered the detention of twenty thousand Jews in concentration camps under his control and ordered the police and the SS to prevent widespread looting. According to Hilberg, Himmler dictated a file memorandum in which he expressed his distaste for the Goebbels pogrom.

In the wake of the *Kristallnacht,* there was widespread negative reaction against the pogrom from such leading Nazis as Goering, Economy Minister Walter Funk and the German Ambassador to the United States, Hans Dieckhoff. Goering was especially vehement in his opposition to *Einzelaktionen,* undisciplined individual actions. He expressed his opposition to pogroms and riots which led to unfavorable foreign repercussions and which permitted the mob to run loose. Goering's feelings were shared by the entire German state bureaucracy. This was simply not the way to "solve" the Jewish problem. According to Hilberg, the effect of the Nazi outrages of the thirties on the state bureaucracy was to convince the Nazi and the non-Nazi bureaucrats alike that measures against the Jews had to be taken in a rational organized way. Every step in the *methodical* elimination of the Jews had to be planned and carried out in a thoroughly *disciplined* manner. Henceforth, there would be neither emotional outbursts nor improvisations. The same meticulous care that goes into the manufacture of a Leica or a Mercedes was to be applied to the problem of eliminating the Jews. *Kristallnacht* was the last occasion when Jews had to fear street violence in Germany. Henceforth no brown-shirted bullies would assail them. Hilberg points out that when a decree was issued in September 1941 requiring Jews to wear the yellow star, Martin Bormann, the Chief of the Party Chancellery, issued strict orders against the molestation of the Jews as beneath the dignity of the Nazi movement. "Law and order" prevailed. There were no further state-sponsored incidents. The hoodlums were banished and the bureaucrats took over. Only then was it possible to contemplate the extermination of millions. A machinery was set up that was devoid of both love and hatred. *It was only possible to overcome the moral barrier that had in the past prevented the systematic riddance of surplus populations when the project was taken out of the hands of bullies and hoodlums and delegated to bureaucrats.*

When Max Weber wrote about bureaucratic domination, he did not have the Nazis in mind, nor was he proposing a prescription for slaughter. Yet, almost everything Weber wrote on the subject of bureaucracy can in retrospect be read as a description of the way the bureaucratic hierarchies of the Third Reich "solved" their Jewish problem. Furthermore, Weber's writings on bureaucracy are part of a larger attempt to understand the social and political structure and the values of modern Western civilization. Although there were bureaucracies in ancient China, Egypt, and Imperial Rome, the full development of bureaucracy in the Christian West came about as the result of the growth of a certain ethos that was in turn the outcome of fundamental tendencies in occidental religion. Bureaucracy can be understood as a structural and organizational expression of the related processes of *secularization, disenchantment of the world,* and *rationalization.* The secularization process involves the liberation of ever wider areas of human activity from religious domination. Disenchantment of the world occurs when "there are no mysterious forces that come into play, but rather that one can, in principle, master all things by calculation." Rationalization involves "the methodical attainment of a definitely given and practical end by means of an increasingly precise calculation of adequate means."

The earliest culture in which the world was "disenchanted" was the biblical world of the Israelites. When the author of Genesis wrote "In the beginning God created heaven and earth" (Gen. 1:1), he was expressing that disenchantment. Creation was seen as devoid of independent divine or magical forces which men had to appease. The world was seen as created by a supramundane Creator. As long as men came to terms with the Creator, the world was theirs to do with as they pleased. No interference need be feared from powers immanent in the natural order. On the contrary, Adam is enjoined to "subdue" the earth and to "have dominion" over it. (Gen. 1:28) As Peter Berger has pointed out, the biblical attitude that nature is devoid of magic or mysterious forces was extended to the political order. Thus, when David the king takes Bath Sheba in adultery and arranges to have her husband, Uriah the Hittite, slain in battle, he is denounced by Nathan the prophet. In the ancient Near East, the king was thought to be either a deity in his own right or to incarnate divinity by virtue of his office. By denouncing David, Nathan was insisting that the king was only a man, albeit one of preeminent importance, and that he was as subject to God's law as any other man. In ancient Israel, both the natural and the political orders were "disenchanted." The domain of divinity was relegated to the heavenly sphere. A beginning was made towards the secularization of the human order. The biblical world initiates the secularization process which finally culminates in the most extreme forms of secular disenchantment in modern political organization. There is, of course, a profound difference between the biblical conception of the political order and the modern conception. In the biblical world, all of human activity stands under the judgment of a righteous and omnipotent deity; in the modern world, the righteous and omnipotent deity has disappeared *for all practical purposes*. Man is alone in the world, free to pursue whatever ends he chooses "by means of an increasingly precise calculation of adequate means."

Berger maintains that the Christian doctrine of the incarnation, that Christ is simultaneously perfectly human and perfectly divine, was an attempt to find once again an intrinsic link between the supramundane realm of divinity and the desacralized human order which had become devoid of magic or mysterious forces. A partial attempt to *reenchant* the world took place in Roman Catholicism. Although the world is not the dwelling place of deities and spirits in Catholicism, it is at least a realm in which God's presence might indwell in his saints as well as in sacred space and sacred time.

Protestantism violently rejected the Catholic attempt at reenchantment. Its insistence on the radical transcendence of the one sovereign Creator and his utter withdrawal from the created order was far more thoroughgoing than the earlier Jewish attempt at disenchantment. Martin Luther proclaimed that the world was so hopelessly corrupted by sin and so totally devoid of the saving presence of God, that the Devil is in fact Lord of this world. The Protestant insistence that man is saved by faith alone *(sola fidei),* rather than works, separates man's activities in the empirical world from the realm of divinity with a remorseless logic to which biblical Judaism had pointed but did not reach.

It was the land of the Reformation that became the land in which bureaucracy was first perfected in its most completely objective form. The land of the Reformation was also the land where bureaucracy was able to create its most thoroughly secularized, rationalized, and dehumanized "achievement," the death camp. Before men could acquire the "dehumanized" attitude of bureaucracy in which "love, hatred, and all purely personal, irrational, and emotional elements" are eliminated in one's dealings with one's fellowmen, the disenchantment process had to become culturally predominant; God and the world had to be so radically disjoined that it became possible to treat both the political and the natural order with an uncompromisingly dispassionate objectivity. When one contrasts the attitude of the savage who cannot leave the battlefield until he performs some kind of appeasement ritual to his slain enemy with the assembly-line manufacture of corpses by the millions at Auschwitz, we get an idea of the enormous religious and cultural distance Western man has traversed in order to create so unique a social and political institution as the death camp.

When I suggest that the cultural ethos that permitted the perfection of bureaucratic mass murder was most likely to develop in the land of Luther, my intention is not to blame Protestantism for the death camps. Nor is it my intention to plead for a utopian end to bureaucracy. It must not be forgotten that the Protestant insistence upon the radical transcendence of a supramundane God, which was the indispensable theological precondition of both the secularization process and disenchantment of the world, was biblical in origin. Furthermore, Jewish emancipation in Europe following the French revolution was a direct result of the more or less successful overthrow of a feudal society of inherited, often mystified status by a secular society in which men were bound to each other primarily by contractual relations. The very same secularization process which led to Jewish emancipation led to the death camps one hundred and fifty years later. It is, however, crucial that we recognize that the process of secularization that led to the bureaucratic objectivity required for the death camps was an essential and perhaps inevitable outcome of the *religious* traditions of the Judeo-Christian west. One of the most paradoxical aspects of biblical religion is that the liberation of significant areas of human activity from religious domination, which we call secularization, was the cultural outcome of biblical religion itself rather than a negation of it.

This point is especially important in correcting the point of view that mistakenly regards the Nazi extermination of the Jews as an antireligious explosion of pagan values in the heart of the Judeo-Christian world. When Nazism is seen in such a light, its interpreters are quick to counsel a turning away from "modern paganism" and a return to the values of Judeo-Christian culture as the only way to avoid a barbaric repetition of the "pagan" explosion some time in the future. There may be good reasons for a "return" to Judeo-Christian values, but the prevention of future extermination projects is not likely to be one of them. Weber's studies on bureaucracy and his related studies on Protestantism, capitalism, and disenchantment of the world are important in demonstrating how utterly mistaken is any view that would isolate Nazism and its supreme expression, bureaucratic mass murder and the bureaucratically administered society of total domination, from the mainstream of Western culture.

One mistake often made by those who appeal to the humanistic ideals of the Judeo-Christian tradition is the failure to distinguish between the *manifest values* a tradition asserts to be binding and the *ethos* generated by that same tradition. The Judeo-Christian tradition is said to proclaim an ethic in which every man is possessed of an irreducible element of human dignity as a child of God. Nevertheless, beyond all conscious intent, it has produced a secularization of consciousness involving an abstract, dehumanized, calculating rationality that can eradicate every vestige of that same human dignity in all areas of human interchange. Furthermore, of the two elements that together form the basis of Western culture, the classical humanism of Greco-Roman paganism and the Judeo-Christian religious tradition, it is the biblical tradition that has led to the secularization of consciousness, disenchantment of the world, methodical conduct (as in both Protestantism and capitalism), and, finally, bureaucratic objectivity. Nor ought we to be surprised that the bureaucratic objectivity of the Germans was paralleled by the diplomatic objectivity of the British. They were both nourished by the same culture. *The culture that made the death camps possible was not only indigenous to the West but was an outcome, albeit unforeseen and unintended, of its fundamental religious traditions.*

(HINT: How does the passage explain "bureaucratic" mass murder such as occurred in the Nazi death camps?)

CHAPTER ELEVEN

Making Reasonable Decisions as an Amateur in a World of Specialists

This chapter examines your role as a creative individual in society. To what extent should you develop this role, as opposed to relying on others as sources of your opinions and decisions? Ours is an age of specialization. Technical or engineering backgrounds are rewarded by high salaries, public policy debate calls upon the testimony of experts, and colleges and universities encourage students to declare a major at an increasingly early point in their academic career. Given this trend, is it not reasonable to simply endorse the opinions of experts rather than relying on judgments, arguments, and theories of your own? But what then do we believe if experts disagree? How should we react when expert judgment turns out to be wrong? Should we become skeptics who use the critical reasoning procedures we have discussed to discredit the arguments and theories of others without advancing creative alternatives of our own? We will now consider some strategies for making reasonable decisions as amateurs in a world of specialists.

This book might seem to promote the passive role of sitting back and critically judging rather than actively creating new arguments and theories. You have been told that a *sound* deductive argument demands true premises and that the knowledge necessary to establish these premises often depends on specialized inquiry or technique, particularly when it depends on empirical theories. Given these suggestions, you might have lost confidence in your ability to make judgments yourself. You might be tempted to say: "In any area I might pick to create arguments and theories, there are people who have much more knowledge and expertise than I. Why not just find out what opinions they hold and adopt them for my own? If I try to figure things out for myself, it is very likely that I will be wrong."

The idea of "leaving things to the experts" is tempting enough that we shall spend some time exploring it. Unfortunately, we are faced with a very serious dilemma. We need to understand the world, but we can't understand what the experts say about it. If we try to figure things out for ourselves it is very likely that we will be wrong. But if we simply leave things to the experts without understanding their theories, we have difficulty in deciding who the experts are, in determining what to believe if the experts disagree, and in limiting the influence of experts to its proper domain.

This dilemma is extremely difficult to resolve—neither alternative is completely satisfactory. But we maintain that in the face of this difficulty it is important not to hide from the problem—not to take the view that it doesn't matter what you believe since all opinions are uncertain, or the view that in order to escape the uncertainty of rational processes it is necessary to rely on faith. It is crucial to continue to pursue reasonable belief, even if such belief is never certain, because belief is connected to *action*. Responsibility for our beliefs stems from responsibility for our actions.

When we say certain people are "experts," we are not assuming that society is divided into two groups—those who understand the world and the masses who do not. Even if you are an expert in one area, there are many other areas of which you are uninformed. We are not all equal in our general knowledge or in the breadth of our expertise, but for the purposes of this chapter we can consider each of us to be in the position of an amateur in a world of specialization.

Leaving It to the Experts

What do you really know about nuclear energy, the balance of trade, or the most effective ways of combating crime? Chances are you have expressed opinions on some of these issues in casual conversation, and you probably think that some views on these issues are *not* correct (such as, there are no dangers involved in nuclear energy; a trade deficit, i.e., buying from abroad more than we are selling, is good for the economy; crime will stop by itself). You are probably quick to acknowledge, however, that there are people who know more about these issues than you do. Why not, then, simply leave opinions on these matters to people who *do* know more—who have made it their business to learn all they can about areas such as these? You could say that for each issue on which you might need to express an opinion, you will just wait until the occasion arises and then try to find out what the experts think about it, and adopt their advice. Surely you would then have a greater chance of being right about each issue than if you spread out your time trying to learn a little about everything; and by leaving things to the experts you will have more time to do the things you really enjoy. What could be more sensible?

Let us imagine that we have adopted this policy of leaving things to the experts—what problems might we encounter?

Who Are the Experts?

Our first problem would be to determine who the experts are, so we could know whom to ask about the views we should adopt. Suppose the issue is how dangerous are nuclear power plants. As a starting point we might go to various professors of physics and of engineering and ask them who the best experts are on this issue. If there were some consensus as to who the experts are, and these experts all had about the same story concerning the major risks in nuclear power plants and the extent these risks could be minimized, then we would probably feel confident that our strategy of leaving it to the experts had been successful. But what might go wrong in this process?

We might pick the wrong fields of study in our search for experts. Perhaps the biggest risks involving nuclear power don't have to do with science and engineering, but with politics. Perhaps the technical problems of protecting against radiation leaks can be easily solved, but a revolutionary political group who wanted to gain power could get access to and control of nuclear power plants. How would we know this in advance when we began looking for experts? Perhaps the physicists and engineers we consulted would see the problem of political security and send us to the right experts on this part of the issue, but there is nothing to guarantee it. It is important to see that it would be helpful to know *something* about the dangers of nuclear power before we began looking for experts.

What If the Experts Disagree?

Second, we have a problem if the experts themselves disagree. Suppose the issue is what to do about the trade deficit—what causes it, how it might be reduced. Since this issue is an economic one, we would try to find out who the leading economists in the country are, and consult them. As a matter of fact, the answers we would get on this issue would be particularly varied, but this issue is hardly unique. Suppose we get three different answers from three widely renowned economists: How do we decide what to believe? We can ask for reasons to support the varying points of view, but the reasons will probably be imbedded in three different broad economic theories. We might need to learn the theories even to evaluate the particular views on the trade deficit.

Both of these problems—determining in which field an issue lies, and deciding among conflicting expert opinions—are related to a third, more difficult problem. If a supposed expert states a number of views on an issue, how can we tell which of these are based on his expertise, and which are based on his personal political or moral preferences? That is, how do we prevent technical expertise from spreading into political power?

How Can We Control the Influence of Experts?

Consider the issue of the most effective means of controlling crime. We might go to a famous criminologist who has studied carefully the variation of crime rates with different kinds of punishments, rehabilitation programs, police procedures, social conditions, and so on. But this criminologist also happens to believe that no one should ever be punished because all actions are socially caused and no one should be blamed for an act that is socially caused. Now this view about punishment is not one that is based on criminological investigation; it just reflects our "expert's" view about the way things should be. But on the basis of this political opinion, the criminologist might alter the answer he gives us about the most efficient way to control crime, because he wants to influence political opinion in a direction he would approve of. We might have the same problem with physicists and engineers generally *wanting* nuclear power production, and certain economic experts wanting inflation controlled in one way rather than another because of views they hold about the desirability of, say, a free market economy. And in each case, by relying on expert opinion, we as a society might be setting experts up so that they have things the way they want them—no longer will they just be giving us factual advice and letting us decide how we want things to be.

The *National Enquirer* Syndrome

The mentality of "leaving it to the experts" has further unhappy side effects. As the areas of expert knowledge become more specialized and more technical, the gap between the theories of experts and what the common person can understand becomes wider and wider. Many people lose contact entirely with the science of the day, and yet they want to understand why things happen. In this light, we can understand the immense popularity of newspapers like the *National Enquirer*. As you go through the checkstand at the supermarket, where these tabloids are usually placed, notice the headlines. You might find that all the political assassinations in the past two decades were a result of a single conspiracy; that a recent disaster was caused by visitors from outer space; that some common substance can cure cancer; that supernatural forces caused a plane crash; and so on. The upshot of all these theories is that you can understand what happens in the world without understanding all of the complicated and technical theories of the "experts."

Although the tabloid readers have, in a sense, "left things to the experts," they have not deferred to the judgment of experts out of respect. Rather, they have *abandoned* any attempt to comprehend specialized, technical theories. In most cases, the *National Enquirer* type of explanation is either one which is very simple—such as a single conspiracy accounting for many assassinations—or one which goes beyond science in a way that tells you: "You understand what is going on as well as anyone does, *because no one really understands.*" That is, the "explanation" is supernatural; it has to do with ESP, demonic forces, and so on.

We doubt that many theories of the *National Enquirer* type would withstand the critical tests we discussed in the previous chapters. The contrast between these theories, which are so popular, and the sophisticated theories of modern science, which have become so inaccessible, is striking evidence of the problem of the amateur in a world of specialization.

The Dilemma

The dilemma, then, is this: If we try to create our own arguments and theories without relying on experts, we will very likely be wrong. If we just leave things to the experts to figure out, thinking that we will adopt their opinions as our own, we have difficulty in knowing who the experts are, in deciding who is right when the experts disagree, and in controlling the influence of the experts on whom we rely. In addition, simply leaving things to the experts means neglecting the development of our own ideas so that we may find we fall back on explanations of the *National Enquirer* type in our understanding of the world.

If, by adopting the opinions of experts, we came to understand all that the experts understand, our dilemma would be resolved. However, when we spoke of "leaving things to the experts" we assumed that no one really has the time, energy, and intellectual ability to actually acquire more than a tiny fraction of the knowledge you would need to make expert opinions yourself. In this age of specialization it is a rare scholar who can keep up with the major developments in just one discipline such as psychology or physics. It is because of the rapid proliferation of knowledge that we run into the problems of determining who the experts are, resolving their disagreements, and so forth. We are forced to make these decisions in the absence of direct knowledge of the area in which we are seeking expert help.

How then are we to resolve this dilemma? Is some sort of compromise possible—a compromise between learning all that we can on our own and combining this with selective reliance on expert opinion? Are there particular strategies that might be used to control the influence of experts while still making use of their expertise? And how does all this relate to creating our own arguments and theories? Before addressing these questions, we should say a few words about certain attitudes that are easy to embrace in the face of the difficulties we have been discussing, but which we think are important to avoid.

Two Ways of Not Facing the Dilemma

Relativism A kind of disillusionment strikes many people as they come to realize how easily most opinions can be doubted. The fact that there is widespread disagreement, even among experts, on almost any issue of importance is unsettling. Perhaps this situation is grounds for a kind of skepticism—that is, we should be guarded in our claims to knowledge, and realize how many of our beliefs are uncertain. But it is tempting to go from skepticism to a more extreme point of view: that one opinion is as good as another and it doesn't really matter what you believe. It simply doesn't follow from the fact that people disagree that no one's opinion is more reasonable. And even if we granted that all our beliefs are uncertain, it doesn't follow that all our beliefs are *equally* uncertain.

Often, the kind of absolute relativism to which we are objecting comes out when someone is challenged about the truth of one of his opinions. A common reply is that some things are "true for me," and other things are "true for you," but no one can say what is *really* true. This may be an appealing point of view as long as the discussion remains abstract. But most if not all of the particular opinions we hold have implications for how we shall *act*. If you are riding in a car and you are of the opinion that it is heading for a cliff, but the driver doesn't share this opinion, it is doubtful that you will be satisfied to say that it is *true for you* that the car is headed for a cliff, but it isn't *true for the driver,* and that no one can tell what is really true in this case. Leaving aside questions of absolute certainty, one opinion is probably much more reasonable to hold than the other in this case, and it obviously makes a big difference which opinion you do hold. The consequences of many opinions are less direct and less drastic. But the fact that your beliefs determine your actions should be reason enough to reject the view that it doesn't really matter what you believe.

The "True Believer"
A second attitude is also commonly held in reaction to the uncertainty of most opinions. This is the attitude of the "true believer," who wants some firm doctrine to hang onto, does not find it through ordinary rational processes, and turns instead to faith. It is typical of the true believer that the doctrine she picks is one that explains anything and everything. And once she has accepted it, she is blind to any weaknesses. Whether the doctrine is Marxism, religious fundamentalism, laissez-faire capitalism, or astrology, she holds it so ardently that no conceivable argument will diminish her belief. We are not claiming that a person who holds any of the beliefs just listed is irrational and is a "true believer." We are concerned about the *way* in which the true believer maintains her doctrine. Perhaps she will undergo some personal change that will make her suddenly withdraw her faith in one doctrine and put it equally wholeheartedly into another, but this will not be the result of hearing a good argument.

Two tendencies, both partly the result of the difficult situation of the amateur in a world of specialization, contribute to the true believer syndrome. One is an insecurity resulting from the very tentative nature of belief based on science. With experts disagreeing, one theory succeeding another, and most theories only partly understandable by the common person, many people feel they lack a satisfying system of beliefs. It is comforting to put your faith in a single, understandable doctrine that will explain a great many things and will tell you where you stand in the scheme of things. But the fact that such a doctrine is comforting is not evidence that it is true.

The second tendency that contributes to the true believer syndrome is the tendency to see faith as parallel to and in competition with reason. This idea is especially attractive to the religious dogmatist who sees the uncertainty of belief, which we have been discussing, as a weakness of reason, a weakness that can be remedied by choosing faith instead. We do not maintain that faith has no justifiable role in our lives, but it is a mistake to see faith and reason as competing paths to knowledge. The true believer who sees faith as her path to knowledge is at a loss to answer one crucial question: Why have faith in one doctrine rather than another? The answer cannot be produced from within faith itself; it *must* be produced from within reason. Or if it isn't, it must be granted that the decision is arbitrary. It is not as though reason might choose one set of beliefs and faith another; faith does not choose.

Furthermore, the same point can be made against the true believer as was made against the relativist: Your beliefs form the basis for action, and as such you have a responsibility to choose them reasonably. Both relativism and the true believer syndrome may be *understandable* reactions to the dilemma of the amateur in a world of specialization, but this does not make them justifiable reactions.

Coping with the Dilemma

The first part of the dilemma we have presented is that if you try to figure things out for yourself you will probably be mistaken. Let's explore this half of the dilemma first, to see whether some of the problems associated with such a course can be remedied.

When we spoke loosely about "figuring things out for yourself," we had in mind developing your own arguments and theories. We did not suppose you would do this in a vacuum, with no help from other people and their writings. But even with this help, the arguments and theories you would develop would very likely be inadequate compared with those of experts in the different fields.

But even if your arguments and theories are inferior to those of experts, what is wrong with developing these inadequate opinions? The main drawback is that your opinions form the basis for *actions,* so you want to acquire opinions with the greatest chance of being correct. But is it *necessary* for us to use the opinions we develop on our own as a basis for action? Can't we develop our own arguments and theories, and maintain them tentatively, allowing them to be overridden by expert opinion when we decide that this is wise?

Developing Opinions without Acting on Them

Consider some examples. Suppose you were to read and think about physical health and how it should be maintained. You might adopt some theories of nutrition that you read about and came to understand; you might develop some opinions about exercise, based both on the theories of others and on your own experience and experimentation. You might form some ideas concerning your own ailments; what causes them, and how they should be treated. You could do all this and yet, when it came to diagnosing a certain ailment and providing treatment for it, you *could* decide to let one of your own beliefs be overridden by that of a doctor.

Suppose you read and thought about certain questions in the field of economics. You might read magazine articles on the nation's economy, discuss economic questions with other people, take a course or two in economics at a university, read some books in the area. You could come to understand and adopt certain theories you read or heard about, and you could develop certain variations of these theories yourself. You might acquire your own unique overview of economics, while hardly considering yourself an expert. And throughout this development of your own ideas you would probably remain ready to defer to someone whom you thought knew more about a certain issue than you did. If it came to giving investment advice, or even to voting for a political candidate who held an economic ideology quite different from yours, you might put your own opinions aside in favor of an expert's.

It seems clear, then, that it is possible to develop your own opinions in any area and still refrain from acting upon them. But what would be gained from doing so? Is there a way we can fit this possibility into a strategy for coping with the dilemma that confronts us?

A Proposed Strategy

There are two things to be gained from developing your own opinions, even though you probably won't act on them. First, self-realization is important to any person. And developing your own ideas, your own understanding of the world, is an important part of self-realization. There is a satisfaction—a feeling of autonomy—in taking the task of understanding the world into your own hands. This does not mean shutting out the opinions of others, but it means actively engaging in understanding rather than being a passive receptor of opinion. In the process, you will develop your mental abilities more fully.

Second, you reduce the problems involved in relying on experts. This point brings us, now, to what we see as the best strategy for coping with the dilemma of leaving things to the experts or figuring them out for ourselves. The strategy is to combine both practices. This is not a complete resolution of the dilemma because it leaves problems unsolved. But it does allow for self-realization while *reducing* the problems that arise from leaving things to the experts.

The more understanding you have, the better chance you have of minimizing the problems involved in relying on experts. The three major problems we anticipated were determining who the experts are, deciding what to do when the experts disagree, and controlling the influence of experts. Of these, the problem of disagreement among experts is probably the most difficult to overcome by gaining a limited understanding of the area in question.

Still a Problem: The Disagreement of Experts

When experts disagree, considerations beyond the credibility of the competing opinions may give us grounds for making a choice. If one physician advises that you have an operation but a second physician advises against it, there is an obvious reason for accepting the second opinion. It may also be possible to test competing opinions by putting each into practice for a trial period. A president, for example, might try one economic policy for a certain period and then shift to another. But the results of such trials are often difficult for the amateur to assess and there is not always time to experiment. Furthermore, a disagreement among experts may be such that you would need to understand both competing theories as well as the experts themselves do in order to make a reasoned choice between them. The other two problems, however, do not seem so intractable.

Creating Arguments and Theories and Determining Who Are the Experts

One fringe benefit of creating your own arguments and theories is that in the process of gaining background knowledge upon which to base them, you can become acquainted with a large number of areas. You can begin to understand how various academic disciplines, professions, and specialized occupations deal with the different sciences and their branches. This is precisely the kind of knowledge that is crucial in the age of specialization. Furthermore, by actually developing arguments and theories, you have a better chance of seeing the many different areas of expertise that apply to this issue.

There is a broad tendency to see generals as the experts on national defense issues, doctors as the experts on medical care issues, police chiefs as the experts on crime issues, and so on. In fact, all these issues have political, economic, and technological aspects that could be addressed by experts from dozens of fields. By attempting to develop your own ideas on these issues, you have a greater chance of seeing how diverse they are.

Creating Arguments and Theories and Controlling the Experts

The point that many different areas of expertise usually apply to a single issue is an important one when it comes to determining how to control the influence of experts. This is one of the few considerations that should give the amateur confidence when he considers his status in comparison to that of the experts. Very often, *no one* is an expert when it comes to seeing how the expert opinions from various fields should all be brought together to form a policy. And this is precisely the point at which the influence of experts can and should be controlled. At this point, the amateur who has tried to create arguments and theories concerning a broad issue need not defer to someone who is an expert on only one facet of the issue.

Furthermore, the relation between certain areas of expertise and their application to real world issues might be very indirect. Many academic disciplines develop abstract, technical theories and models whose relation to the real world may be poorly understood even by experts within the discipline. It is too often assumed that any behaviorist psychologist can give you advice on child rearing, that an economist can help you with your investments, or even that a mathematical logician can help you evaluate an argument from a piece of informal prose.

It is important that you see as best you can the limitations of each area of supposed expertise. The expert himself will not be anxious to limit his own influence—he might attempt to run a bluff, hoping that the amateur will be too meek to challenge him. The more you have adopted the habit of leaving things to the experts rather than developing your own arguments and theories, the greater the chance that such a bluff will succeed.

How Does One Create Arguments and Theories?

One central topic we have not addressed is how to go about creating arguments and theories. We won't discuss the *mechanics* of creativity—this topic is more suitable to a psychological study, or perhaps a biographical study of creative individuals. Nevertheless, the critical procedures described in the foregoing chapters can be used as a starting point in creating arguments and theories.

Criticizing and Creating

Criticizing and creating are not completely independent processes. One way of criticizing a theory is to see that an alternative theory is more plausible; this involves conjuring up, or creating, the alternative. When you reconstruct a fragmentary argument as a step toward criticizing it, devising missing premises requires creativity. When you ask whether a premise is doubtful or whether it is reasonable to believe, you *create* tentative arguments in an attempt to support it, and then critically assess these arguments.

Also, criticism is a part of a dialogue-process that is, on the whole, creative. You consider arguments or theories presented to you, reject them in part or entirely, and reconsider new or altered versions. This process is like an artist experimenting with a design. He might change it around haphazardly, and by using his critical eye to reject all bad configurations, arrive at (create) an artistically good one. This model of creativity is not completely accurate, however. An artist need not try different designs entirely at random. He has a sort of intuition that guides him—he can picture in advance the way the design *should* look. Similarly, in creating an argument or explanation you do not sort through random lists of statements to be used as premises or as parts of a theory. A kind of intuition guides you in seeing what would be plausible candidates for premises or for theoretical statements. Criticism plays a role, although a limited one, by rejecting poor candidates.

Criticism, then, if it is carried out well, involves you to some extent in creative activity. It is possible, furthermore, to pursue this aspect of criticism consciously. As a way of getting started at devising a theory to explain something, or an argument to support a belief, study theories that have been offered to explain the same phenomenon, or arguments that attempt to support the same opinion. Critically assess these arguments and theories and cultivate the creative aspects of this critical process—seeking more plausible alternative explanations; refining and altering the premises that support the conclusions; or, if they cannot be made adequate, either choosing other premises or considering arguments for rejecting the conclusion. Even going this far will do a great deal to bring about the benefits of "figuring things out for yourself," rather than "leaving it to the experts."

The Strategy and Its Prospects

The strategy we have recommended for the amateur in a world of specialization is one that combines creating your own arguments and theories, with selectively and cautiously relying on experts. As we have stated, we are not entirely optimistic about the outcome of this strategy. The number of problems and issues to study and the number of areas of expertise to monitor are overwhelming. Perhaps it is possible to gain back a significant degree of control over experts who affect you most directly and personally—your doctor, your mechanic. But the *social* effects that a single individual can have by carrying out this strategy are practically negligible. What must be hoped for, as specialization increases, is an increased intellectual activism on the part of a significant portion of the population.

But this point—that *one* person can't do much to guard against the dangers of relying on experts—brings into focus an aspect of our dilemma about which we have said very little so far. That is, the dilemma we have presented is *not* simply that of a *single individual* who wonders how to best attain knowledge. Neither, however, is it a matter of bringing together the knowledge of all the individuals of society. There is no repository for such an aggregation—society as a whole has no mind. If there were such a collective repository, it would be easy to combine the opinions of many experts to form a more complete and adequate body of knowledge than that which any single individual possesses. But in reality, *each* person must try to combine the opinions of experts from a position of relative ignorance. We each must to some extent *guess* which experts to trust. The problem becomes in part political, that is, power and influence become issues. How can each of us muster a picture of the world that has the best chance of accuracy, but also of not being biased in favor of the personal preferences of experts?

The Contemporary Problem of Knowledge

Through much of history, the problem of knowledge and the problem of the good society have been dealt with separately. A division of philosophy called *epistemology* attempts to answer the question of what knowledge is and how it can be attained. Political philosophy and social philosophy, on the other hand, deal with such problems as: How can a group of individuals combine to form a good or just society? In the modern world of specialization, the problem of how to attain knowledge becomes in part a social one.

In ancient philosophy, for example, Plato's *The Republic* stresses the connection between knowledge and the "good society." For him, true belief and knowledge could be ranked in levels depending in part on how specialized they were. A technician who assembled, for example, an electronic listening device (a "bug") would have more limited and specialized information than the electrical engineer who designed it and who could compare it with other devices having a similar function.* For Plato, knowledge about what might have counted as a "good" electronic listening device would not have been restricted to electrical engineering. An essential, more general question would have to be asked about whether, or in what form, such a device would exist in a good society.

Similarly, a "good computer" or a "good nuclear power plant" or a "good space station" would be ones that would exist in a good society. We are not accustomed to asking this general question about most of the objects, institutions, and policies that confront us. We don't typically move from a discussion about what is a good car (for us or for U.S. car manufacturers) to questions about whether a transportation system relying on the private auto is part of a good society. The problem, of course, with such a move is that it raises the difficult question of how to gain knowledge about the "good society."

Plato solved the dilemma by envisioning a class of super-specialists who sought knowledge about the good society. In the society Plato describes, knowledge was concentrated in a few individuals, and ruling was included among the specialized roles. In contemporary society, knowledge is at best spread among many specialists, and no one specializes in ruling— at least that is not seen as the ideal. Specialization, however, is compromised by an attempt at democracy. To put it pessimistically: for Plato, a few had knowledge and they would rule; for us, no one has very much knowledge, but everyone must try to rule.

It is doubtful that many of us would want to transform our society into the one Plato envisioned. It is difficult for us to part with the ideal of democracy, and we are justifiably suspicious of the "knowledge" of those who would rule. But to give our society the best chance of persisting, we must cope with its problems. Not the least of these is the problem of reasoning as well as we can from limited perspectives as amateurs in a world of specialization—reasoning both critically and creatively.

---

*Plato saw the "craftsman" as having only very limited skills; thus, technicians need retraining for each new project.

When Does the Conclusion Follow? A More Formal Approach to Validity

The informal discussion of validity found at the beginning of Chapter 4 provides several images for "picturing" the structural relationship among the premises and a conclusion in a valid argument. These images were selected to help you understand what it means for a conclusion to follow from the premises. We tried to capture the sense of logical necessity in which, if an argument is valid and its premises are true, then it is necessary for the conclusion to be true. Or to put it in another way: An argument is valid if and only if it is *impossible* for all the premises to be true and the conclusion, false.

The illustrations given in Chapter 4 appealed to your understanding of an idealized "physical impossibility." It is *impossible,* for instance, that the blocks are lined up in the appropriate way and pushed in the manner described, without a certain outcome occurring. Although these images can provide you with some insight into the idea of the impossibility involved when an argument is valid, they are quite limited in their application. For this reason, logicians (philosophers who are interested in the validity of arguments) have devised a variety of other techniques for illustrating the concept of *logical impossibility,* which in turn are ways of systematically illustrating the concept of validity. Further, these methods provide us with useful techniques for testing whether an argument is valid.

The method used by logicians is *formal* in the sense that it abstracts the form or pattern of an argument from its verbal content. This is seen as an appropriate move because *validity* is a feature of the structure of an argument independent of its particular content. More generally: An argument is valid if and only if all arguments of the *same form* are such that it is impossible for all the premises to be true and the conclusion, false. When validity is tied to *form* in this way, we can speak of the *logical impossibility* of having all the premises true and the conclusion false.

In an effort to characterize the *form* of arguments, logicians have introduced standard ways of presenting an argument. We have taken some steps in this direction in our table, "Some Common Successful Argument Patterns." For example, we gave the *form* of *modus ponens* as

Example A.1

> (1) If A, then B.
>
> (2) A.
> _____
>
> ∴   B.

In this example, the capital letters (A, B, and C) were used to stand for statements in an argument.* We have also numbered the premises, drawn a line, and used the symbol ∴ meaning "therefore" to indicate that we have an argument with premises and a conclusion.

Logicians commonly go even further in their use of symbolism. Whereas we have continued to use fragments of English such as "If . . . then . . ." and "Either . . . or . . ." to display more complex, logical features of statements, logicians typically illustrate form by use of special symbols that are roughly (but only *roughly*) the equivalent of the English language terms that we have employed. So for example, the following table gives these symbols for some common "logical words" that apply to whole statements. These logical words are often called *logical connectives* because most connect two or more statements.

Symbol	Name	Example	"Rough" English Equivalent
–	Negation	–A	It is not the case that A
&	Conjunction	A & B	A and B
v	Disjunction	A v B	Either A or B (or both)**
→	Conditional	A → B	If A, then B
↔	Biconditional	A ↔ B	A if and only if B

*We use the term *statement* rather than *sentence* because the same sentence (e.g., "He did it.") can be used to make different statements on different occasions depending on the reference of the pronoun, *he.* Further, different sentences can be used to make the same statement (e.g., "He did it," and "Jerry did it.")

**This use of *or* to include the case when both are true is called *inclusive* use of *or* as opposed to the *exclusive or*, which excludes this case.

Using these symbols we could illustrate some of the standard argument forms as follows:

| | | *Disjunctive* | |
Modus Ponens	*Modus Tolens*	*Argument*	*Chain Argument*
(1) A → B	*(1) A → B*	*(1) A ∨ B*	*(1) A → B*
(2) A	*(2) –B*	*(2) –A*	*(2) B → C*
∴ *B*	∴ *–A*	∴ *B*	∴ *A → C*

These symbols can be used to present a variety of more complicated arguments. For instance

(1) A → B	*(1) A → B*
(2) C → D	*(2) C → D*
(3) (B & D) → E	*(3) A ∨ C*
(4) A	*(4) –B*
(5) C	∴ *D*
∴ *E*	

Exercise A.1   Formalizing

1. Assign letters to each *simple* statement given below and use our connective symbols to "translate" the more complex statements built out of them into our formalism:
   a. The United States is now the world's greatest debtor nation.
   b. If the United States is a debtor nation, then future generations will be at a disadvantage.
   c. If the next session of Congress does not really limit the deficit, then the long-term economic outlook for the United States is bleak.
   d. Either Japan or the European Economic Community will be the economic power of the nineties.
   e. If the United States remains the world's greatest debtor nation, then either Japan or the European Economic Community will be the economic power of the nineties.
   f. Both the United States and the Soviet Union face significant economic challenges in the nineties.
   g. If either Japan or the European Economic Community are the economic power of the nineties, then both the United States and the Soviet Union will face significant economic challenges.

    h. The United States will again become the major economic power in the world if and only if it reduces its deficit and curbs its trade deficit.

    i. If not both Japan and the European Economic community are major economic powers during the nineties, then there will be room for renewed United States' economic prosperity.

(HINT: Use parentheses to group elements together. For instance, "Both A and B, or C" can be grouped ((A & B) ∨ C).

2. The following statements have less obvious translations into our formalism.

    a. It is not the case that the United States will not improve economically.

    b. The United States economic future looks bleak now, but we can overcome the obstacles if we again reward long-term economic investment.

(HINT: "But" can typically be translated like "and.")

    c. The United States will continue to decline economically unless it makes long-term investment more attractive.

(HINT: "Unless" can be translated like "or.")

    d. The United States will improve its economic position only if it makes long-term investment more attractive.

(HINT: "A only if B" can often be translated like "If A, then B.")

    e. Neither good intentions by the present administration nor reliance on an unfettered free market will improve the economic conditions in the United States.

(HINT: "Neither A nor B" can be translated like "It is not the case that either A or B" and also like "It is not the case that A, and it is not the case that B." As we shall see in the next section, these two statements in a sense say the same thing.)

3.   a. Translate the arguments in Exercise 3.1, 1a–e into our formalism. Be sure to indicate which letter stands for which statement.

    b. Translate the various reconstructions found in Exercise 3.1, 3a(i, ii, iii), 3b(i), and 3c(i) into our formalism. Be sure to indicate which letter stands for which statement.

4. Translate the following arguments into our formalism:

a. *(1) Either the United States will have to raise taxes or cut spending.*

(2) If the United States cuts spending, then crucial programs will be damaged.

(3) Crucial programs won't be damaged.

∴ *The United States will have to raise taxes.*

b. *(1) If the AIDS epidemic continues unabated, then there will be an increased burden on our already strained health care system.*

(2) If there will be an increased burden on our already strained health care system, then there will be increased pressure for the federal government to provide money to save the health care system.

(3) If there will be increased pressure for the federal government to provide money to save the health care system, then taxes will have to be raised.

∴ *If the AIDS epidemic continues unabated, taxes will have to be raised.*

c. *(1) The United States will succeed in overcoming its economic liabilities in the nineties only if it devotes more of its wealth to long-term economic development.*

(2) It will devote more of its wealth to long-term economic development only if the government changes its antitrust laws to allow much greater cooperation among competing countries.

(3) The United States will not change its antitrust laws unless American consumers become willing to pay much more for their consumer goods.

(4) Americans consumers will not become willing to pay much more for their consumer goods.

∴ *The United States will not succeed in overcoming its economic liabilities in the nineties.*

d. *(1) A widespread spiritual awakening will occur in the United States during the nineties if and only if personal success becomes measured by the quality of a person's character, not the size of his/her wallet.*

(2) *Personal success will continue to be measured by the size of a person's wallet unless American education concerns itself with issues of ethics and morality.*

(3) *America will continue to be able to accommodate an impressive variety of cultural groups only if American education does not concern itself with issues of ethics and morality.*

∴   *America will continue to be able to accommodate an impressive variety of cultural groups only if a widespread spiritual awakening will not occur in the United States during the nineties.*

Statements Containing Logical Connectives: When Are They True; When Are They False?

In order to evaluate whether an argument is valid, it is necessary to consider the situations in which the statements that make it up are true or false. If we are considering statements in our "idealized" form, the simplest situation is that in which we consider only a single letter. For instance, A. With respect to this statement, only two possible situations exist, either A is true or A is false. We can represent these alternatives as follows:

$$A$$
$$\overline{}$$
$$T$$
$$F$$

Given these two possible situations, we can determine the truth value of the slightly more complicated statement we obtain by negating A. In the situation in which A is true, the negation of A ("It is not the case that A. . .") is false, and when A is false, the negation of A is true. We can represent these alternatives as:

A	$-A$
T	F
F	T

We can extend this way of evaluating the truth statements to embrace compound statements created when we connect two simpler statements to form a conjunction, disjunction, conditional, or biconditional. In order to represent the possible situations when we have two statements linked by one of the logical connectives, we have first to display the joint possibilities. If we have two statements, when the first is true, the second can be either true or false, and when the first is false, the second can again be either true or false. This gives us four possibilities: (1) both are true, (2) the first is true and the second false, (3) the first false and the second true, or (4) both are false.

A	*B*
T	T
T	F
F	T
F	F

This allows us to define the various logical connectives. A conjunction (e.g., A & B) is true if both elements are true (e.g., both A and B). It is false otherwise.

This can be displayed graphically as

Possible Situations		Truth Value of Compound Statement
A	*B*	*A & B*
T	T	T
T	F	F
F	T	F
F	F	F

A disjunction (e.g., A ∨ B) is true if one element or the other or both are true (e.g., A is true or B is true or both are true). It is false otherwise. This captures the *inclusive* sense of "or" that includes the case in which both disjuncts are true.

Possible Situations		Truth Value of Compound Statement
A	*B*	*A ∨ B*
T	T	T
T	F	T
F	T	T
F	F	F

A conditional is true if either the first element is false or the second element is true. It is false only if the first element is true and the second, false.

Possible Situations		Truth Value of Compound Statement
A	*B*	$A \rightarrow B$
T	T	T
T	F	F
F	T	T
F	F	T

A biconditional is true if both elements are true together or false together. It is false if they have different truth values.

Possible Situations		Truth Value of Compound Statement
A	*B*	$A \leftrightarrow B$
T	T	T
T	F	F
F	T	F
F	F	T

The definition of the logical connective "&" is very closely related to our informal understanding of the connective "and." But you should not assume, even in this case, that the formal, logical connective is a perfect "translation" of the everyday term. Consider the two statements:

A: *He took the exam.*

B: *He looked at the answers.*

The statement A & B has the same truth value as the statement B & A although you might well distinguish the first from the second:

He took the exam and he looked at the answers.

He looked at the answers and he took the exam.

Sometimes "and" means "and then" in English. The connective "&" does not capture the meaning "and then."

Similarly, when a parent says, "You can have either cookies or cake," it is usually meant in the "exclusive" sense that the child can have one or the other but not both. If we translated this statement as A ∨ B, we are treating it as involving not this exclusive sense but the *"inclusive"* sense of "or" that allows for both to be true. To represent the strictly *ex*clusive sense we would need a more complicated expression:

$$((A \lor B) \mathrel{\&} {-}(A \mathrel{\&} B))*$$

The conditional "→" provides an even rougher translation of the English analogue *"If . . . then . . ."* Suppose we have the statement, *"If I lie, then I'll be sorry."* It seems reasonable enough to call this premise true if I do lie and I am sorry. And it is surely reasonable to call it false if I do lie and I am not sorry (rows 1 and 2 in the graphic display for the conditional). But why call it true if I don't lie but I'm still sorry, or if I don't lie and am not sorry (rows 3 and 4 on the display)?

There is no way on our display to distinguish a situation where the first element (the "if" part) is false but the whole sentence is true, from cases in which the first element is false but the whole sentence is false.** In order to preserve the simplicity of our method of relating the truth of the elements in a compound sentence to the truth of the whole so that the truth of the whole is a *function* of just the truth value of the parts, we accept some slack in our translation of the if-then statement. We take *"If I lie, then I'll be sorry,"* to assert nothing more than, *"It won't be the case that I'll lie and not be sorry."* That is, the only situation in which we say that *"If A, then B,"* is false is when A is true and B is false. Suppose I said, *"If you pay me ten dollars, then I'll juggle fourteen cigar boxes."* I might insist that my statement wasn't false if you don't pay me and I don't juggle. And if you don't pay but I juggle the fourteen boxes anyway, then you certainly can't complain that I lied. But if you do pay me and I don't juggle, then my statement clearly wasn't true.

---

*The truth table for exclusive "or," XOR, is

A	B	A XOR B
T	T	F
T	F	T
F	T	T
F	F	F

**For example, assume that I won't snap my fingers. The most natural interpretation in this contrary-to-fact condition treats as true the statement, "If I snap my fingers, then I will hear a sound," and as false, the statement, "If I snap my fingers, then I will turn into a bird," even though both are "true" in this counterfactual situation according to the definition of "→."

In the examples given above, we examined compound statements consisting of a logical symbol and one or two statement letters. But the definitions for the symbols apply even when they link more complicated expressions. For example, the following expressions are all also negations:

$$-(A \ \& \ B)$$
$$-(-A \rightarrow B)$$
$$-(\ (A \ \& \ B) \lor (C \leftrightarrow D) \ )$$

As in the instance of simple negations, the truth value of the whole compound depends on the truth of the statement it contains. So, $-(A \ \& \ B)$ is true if $(A \ \& \ B)$ is false, and $-(A \ \& \ B)$ is false if $(A \ \& \ B)$ is true. Since the symbols can link very complex elements, not just simple statements, we can display the various compound statements in a more general way. Let us suppose we represent one element of a compound (no matter how complex) with a square □ and another with a triangle △, then the following display "defines" generalized compounds involving the logical symbols:

Negation

Row	□	$-$□
1	T	F
2	F	T

Possible Situations			*Conjunction*	*Disjunction*	*Conditional*	*Biconditional*
Row	□	△	□ & △	□ ∨ △	□ → △	□ ↔ △
1	T	T	T	T	T	T
2	T	F	F	T	F	F
3	F	T	F	T	T	F
4	F	F	F	F	T	T

We can use these generalized definitions to evaluate complex statements. For example, consider $-(A \ \& \ B)$. It is a denial that contains a conjunction as a part. In order to evaluate the truth of the whole denial, we need to determine the truth of the contained conjunction. Suppose that the simple statement A is T(rue) and B is F(alse). In this situation (row 2 of the definition), the conjunction is F(alse). We have now evaluated the contained conjunction; we know that it is false. But the overall statement is a negation of this conjunction. If we look on row 2 of the definition for negation, we see that, if the contained element is F(alse), the whole negation is T(rue). So in the situation in which A is T(rue) and B is F(alse),

−(A & B) is T(rue). We can represent these steps diagrammatically as follows:

Example A.2

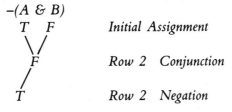

−(A & B)
   T   F   *Initial Assignment*

     F   *Row 2 Conjunction*

     T   *Row 2 Negation*

A similar technique will help us evaluate the compound −(−A → B), where A is T(rue) and B is F(alse).

Example A.3

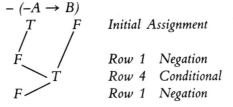

− (−A → B)
   T   F   *Initial Assignment*

   F   *Row 1 Negation*
        T   *Row 4 Conditional*
   F   *Row 1 Negation*

Finally, consider the following assignment and evaluation:

Example A.4

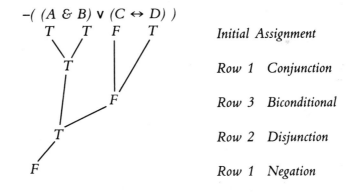

−((A & B) ∨ (C ↔ D))
   T   T   F   T   *Initial Assignment*

     T   *Row 1 Conjunction*

          F   *Row 3 Biconditional*

     T   *Row 2 Disjunction*

   F   *Row 1 Negation*

Exercise A.2   Evaluating Statements

1. Assume the following initial assignment of truth values to the statements: A is T(rue), B is F(alse). Use the technique of evaluation listed above to evaluate the truth value of the following compound statements. Be sure to list the appropriate row and connective to justify each step in the evaluation diagram.

a. A → –B
b. –B → A
c. –(A & –B)
d. –A ∨ –B
e. –(A ↔ B)

2. Evaluate the compound statements in step 1, but with the initial assignment A is F(alse), B is F(alse).

3. Assume the following initial assignment of truth values to the statements: A is F(alse), B is T(rue), C is T(rue), D is F(alse). Create evaluation diagrams for the following compound statements. (You don't need to list a justification for each step, but you should note to yourself how the definitions apply to each move you make.)

a. A → (B ∨ C)
b. (A & B) → C
c. (A ∨ B) → (C & D)
d. A → (B → C)
e. (–A → B) ∨ (–D → C)
f. (A ↔ B) ∨ (–C ↔ D)
g. –((A ∨ –B) & C)
h. – (–(–A → B) ∨ –(–C ↔ –D))

Truth Tables As a Test for Validity

The method of evaluation described in the previous section can be extended by constructing a *truth table* for an argument. Such a table lists the truth or falsity of *all* the statements in an argument for *all* possible situations. A truth table can be used to assess whether an argument is valid, that is, to determine whether there is a possible situation that makes all the premises and the conclusion false. If we find such a counterexample, then the argument is *in*valid. If there is no such counterexample, then the argument is valid. Consider the argument and formalization below.

Example A.5

(1) *Either I should jog or I should diet.*

(2) *I should not jog.*

∴ *I should diet.*

(1) *A ∨ B*

(2) *–A*

∴ *B*

This argument involves only two simple statements. We can construct a table that list the four possible situations, that is, initial assignments of truth or falsify to these two statements, much as we did in our definition of the connectives in the previous section. The truth table for the argument adds an evaluation for each of the statements in the argument (premises 1 and 2 and the conclusion) for each of these four possible initial situations.

Initial Assignments		Evaluation of Statements for These Assignments		
Possible Situations		Premises		Conclusion
A	B	A ∨ B	–A	B (Repeated)
1 T	T	T	F	T
2 T	F	T	F	F
3 F	T	T	T	T
4 F	F	F	T	F
		Disjunction	Negation	

Each row represents a possible situation. As in our previous discussion, the first line, for example, is a situation in which A is true and B is true; the second line is a situation in which A is true and B is false. The premise and conclusion columns evaluate the various statements in each of these possible situations. The column under "A ∨ B" merely gives the standard "definition" of disjunction. The column under "–A" gives the negation of A in each situation. Since A is T(rue) in the first two situations and F(alse) in the second two, its negation will be the opposite—F(alse) in the first two rows, T(rue) in the second two. Finally, in this simple example, the conclusion is itself a simple statement, so we merely repeat the initial assignment of B in each of the four situations.

Because a truth table displays all possible initial assignments of truth values to simple statements contained in an argument and allows comparison of all premises with the conclusion, we can use it as a test of *validity* for arguments. You will recall that an argument is *valid* if it is *impossible* for *all* the premises to be *true* and the conclusion, false. We can apply this account to arguments by asking whether there is a possible *initial assignment* of truth values to simple statements such that all the premises are T(rue) and the conclusion is F(alse). If there is no such counterexample, then the argument is *valid*.

In Example A.5, there are only four possible situations, and we can examine each possibility in turn. In the first situation, row 1 where both A and B are T(rue), the premise A ∨ B is T(rue) but premise –A is F(alse).

Since not all the premises are T(rue), this could not be a possible case in which all the premises are true and the conclusion is false.

Similarly, in row 2 where A is T(rue) and B is F(alse), again –A is F(alse), so not all the premises are true. In row 3 where A is F(alse) and B is T(rue), however, the premise A ∨ B and the premise –A are both T(rue), but in this possible case, the conclusion B is also T(rue). So here again, we satisfy the requirements for validity. Finally, in row 4 with the initial assignment of F(alse) to both A and B, we have the premise A ∨ B is F(alse), hence, not all premises are true, so again examination shows that we don't have a possible situation in which all the premises are true and the conclusion is false.

We have examined *all* possible situations (that is, all possible initial assignments of truth or falsity, T or F, to the simple statements that make up the argument). We have found *no* counterexample in which all the premises are true and the conclusion is false. (Alternatively, we could say that in every case in which the conclusion is false, at least one of the premises is false.) When this occurs, we declare the argument to be *valid.**

Notice, that, given this account of *validity,* the only cases that could show that the argument was not valid are those in which *all* premises are true. If one or more premises is false for a given possible situation, that is, for a row in the truth table, then it makes no difference whether the conclusion is true or false on that line, because it could not be a case in which *all* the premises are true and the conclusion is *false*. So, in order to use the truth table method as a test of validity, you need only to construct the table and examine the rows in which all the premises are true. The argument is valid if, for each such case, the conclusion is also true.** If we find even one line in which all the premises are *true* and the conclusion is *false,* we have found a counterexample (to the claim that the argument is valid).

Consider the following, *invalid* argument and its formalization:

---

*To be more precise, the argument is *deductively valid*. Note as well that an argument might fail this test and still be deductively valid. As we shall see below, some deductively valid arguments have a form that cannot be completely represented in terms of statement letters, negation, conjunction, disjunction, conditional, and the biconditional.

**In the strange case in which there are no rows where all the premises are true, we say that the premises are *inconsistent* (that is, there is no possible case in which they are jointly true). However, arguments with such an inconsistent set of premises are said to be *valid* because there will be no case in which all the premises are true and the conclusion is false simply as a consequence of there being no case in which all the premises are true.

Example 4.5   (1) *If I'm in Aspen, then I'm in Colorado.*   (1) $A \rightarrow B$

(2) *I'm not in Aspen.*   (2) $-A$

∴ *I'm not in Colorado.* $-B$

We can construct the following truth table:

	A	B	Premises		Conclusion
			$A \rightarrow B$	$-A$	$-B$
1	T	T	T	F	F
2	T	F	F	F	T
3	F	T	T	T	F	← (Counterexample: situation where all the premises are true but the conclusion is false)
4	F	F	T	T	T

Given this truth table, the only rows that we need to examine in order to apply the test for validity are rows 3 and 4. These are the only possible situations in which all the premises are true. In this example, row 3, where A is false and B is true, has all premises true, but the conclusion, −B, is false. So here we have an instance in which there is a possible initial assignment of truth values to the simple statements such that, given the definitions of the *logical connectives* involved, the premise statements are both true but the conclusion is false. Thus the structure of the argument (as given by the *logical connectives*) does not guarantee that if the premises are all true the conclusion is also. It makes no difference that row 4 has both premises true and the conclusion also true. Even in an *in*valid argument there can be situations in which all the premises and the conclusion are true, as in row 4 of this example. But this argument form does not guarantee that this happens as row 3 shows. In a valid argument, situations such as that in row 3 do not occur; truth of premises guarantees truth of the conclusion.

The truth table method can be extended to arguments that contain more than two simple statements. With each additional statement letter, we double the number of rows in our truth table.

one letter	2 rows
two letters	4 rows
three letters	16 rows
four letters	32 rows
and so on	

The test for validity can be quite straightforwardly extended to such arguments. Consider an argument of the following form:

Example A.6

(1) $A \rightarrow B$

(2) $B \rightarrow C$

(3) $-C$

———————————

$-A$

The argument generates this truth table*

| | A | B | C | Premises | | | Conclusion | |
				$A \rightarrow B$	$B \rightarrow C$	$-C$	$-A$	
1	T	T	T	T	T	F	F	
2	T	T	F	T	F	T	F	
3	T	F	T	F	T	F	F	
4	T	F	F	F	T	T	F	
5	F	T	T	T	T	F	T	
6	F	T	F	T	F	T	T	
7	F	F	T	T	T	F	T	
8	F	F	F	T	T	T	T	← (All premises true but conclusion also true)

This truth table shows that the argument is valid. Only in row 8 are all three premises true, but in this case the conclusion is also true. The form of the argument guarantees that, if all premises are true, the conclusion is true as well.

———————————

*Note that a simple way of getting the eight possible cases is to repeat the four possibilities for the two letters B and C. We have these four situations when A is true and again when A is false. If we had a four-letter argument, we could generate the sixteen possible situations by including the eight we have in this example, when this fourth statement is true and again when it is false, giving us the requisite sixteen lines for a table with four simple statements.

The truth table method illustrated here provides a useful way of testing an argument whose validity depends on the logical structure generated by negation, conjunction, disjunction, the conditional, and the biconditional as long as only a few simple statements are involved. It becomes quite ungainly if we have more than four or five different simple statements. For this reason, more general proof techniques are used in such cases. We will give you the flavor of these methods in another section of this appendix. Nevertheless, many commonly encountered arguments can be formalized and tested for validity using simple *truth table methods*. As we shall see in the next section, however, some arguments that fail the truth table test can still be considered *valid*. In order to show their validity we need to look at logical structure in a more fine-grained way. Logical form, as we have considered it so far, consists of rather coarse relations between statements. We have simple statements, represented by statement letters and compound statements built up of them. Consider the following argument:

Example A.7

(1) All pigs are beings having a four-chambered heart.

(2) Mike is a pig.

∴ *Mike is a being having a four-chambered heart.*

If we try to represent this argument using the methods discussed so far, we would have to assign a single, separate statement letter to each premise and the conclusion. It would have the form

(1) A

(2) B

∴ *C*

and the truth table

	A	B	C	A	B	C	
1	T	T	T	T	T	T	
2	T	T	F	T	T	F	← (Counterexample: both
3	T	F	T	T	F	T	premises are true but
4	T	F	F	T	F	F	conclusion is false)
5	F	T	T	F	T	T	
6	F	T	F	F	T	F	
7	F	F	T	F	F	T	
8	F	F	F	F	F	F	

As indicated by row 2, it is possible for an argument of this form to have both premises true and the conclusion false. This is just what we would expect. There need not be any logical relation between the three separate sentences. Nevertheless, there is another way of representing logical form that, so to speak, goes inside the simple statements to represent their internal structure. We have already seen this structure in our list of successful argument patterns. Example A.7 is an instance of pattern vi (p. 27).

(1) All P_1's are P_2's.

(2) m is a P_1.

∴   m is a P_2.

We will discuss techniques appropriate to arguments such as these in the next section.

Exercise A.3   **Truth Tables**

---

1. Complete the truth tables for the remaining two if-then argument patterns from our chart. Note that when three separate statements (A, B, C) are used to construct the premises and conclusion, there are eight possible situations represented by combinations of truth and falsity of these statements. Use the same interpretation of if-then as we used in the example above; that is, a statement of this form will be taken to be false only when the "if" part is true and the "then" part is false.

a.

		Premises		Conclusion
A	B	$A \rightarrow B$	$-B$	$-A$
T	T			
T	F			
F	T			
F	F			

b.

A	B	C	Premises $A \to B$	$B \to C$	A	Conclusion C
T	T	T				
T	T	F				
T	F	T				
T	F	F				
F	T	T				
F	T	F				
F	F	T				
F	F	F				

2. Complete the following truth tables for invalid argument patterns. Note which rows indicate a case in which the premises are all true but the conclusion is false.

a.

A	B	Premises $-A \to B$	A	Conclusion B
T	T			
T	F			
F	T			
F	F			

b.

A	B	C	$A \rightarrow B$	$B \rightarrow C$	$-A$	C
			Premises			Conclusion
T	T	T				
T	T	F				
T	F	T				
T	F	F				
F	T	T				
F	T	F				
F	F	T				
F	F	F				

3. Create truth tables for determining whether the following argument patterns are valid.

a. *(1) If A, then not B.*
   (2) B.
   ───────────
   ∴ *Not A.*

b. *(1) If A, then not B.*
   (2) Not B.
   ───────────
   ∴ *Not A.*

c. *(1) If A, then B.*
   ───────────
   ∴ *If B, then A.*

d. *(1) If A, then B.*
   ───────────
   ∴ *If not B, then not A.*

e. *(1) Either A or B.*
   ───────────
   ∴ *If not A, then B.*

f. *(1) Either A or B.*
   ───────────
   ∴ *If not B, then A.*

g. *(1) Either A or B.*
   (2) If B, then C.
   ───────────
   ∴ *If not A, then C.*

h. *(1) If not A, then B.*
   (2) If C, then B.
   ───────────
   ∴ *If not A, then C.*

i. *(1) If A, then not B.*
   (2) Either not B or C.
   (3) A.
   _____
   ∴ *C.*

j. *(1) If A, then not B.*
   (2) Either C or B.
   (3) A.
   _____
   ∴ *C.*

k. *(1) If A and B, then C.*
   (2) A and B.
   _____
   ∴ *C.*

l. *(1) If A, then either B or C.*
   (2) A and not B.
   _____
   ∴ *C.*

m. *(1) A if and only if B.*
   (2) If B, then C.
   (3) Not C.
   _____
   ∴ *A.*

n. *(1) (Not A) or B.*
   (2) (Not B) or C.
   (3) Not C.
   _____
   ∴ *Not A.*

Representing Structures Within Statements: Predicates and Quantifiers

In previous sections we explored the way in which the concept of *validity* could be made precise for arguments that could be formalized in terms of statement letters and logical connectives. Our aim in this section is to look more closely at logical form by examining arguments whose validity depends on structure within statements. We have represented statements such as "*Mike is a pig*" as having the structure "*m* is a *P*." We could represent it even more simply as "Pm" where the letter P stands for the predicate "is a pig," which is combined with name m, which stands for "Mike," to form a complete statement. Similarly, if I represent "Mike is a being having a four-chambered heart" by "Hm," H stands for the predicate and m, for the name that is the subject of the statement.

The aspect of logical form that generates validity depends on more than the simple relationship between a named individual and some characteristic represented by a letter standing for a predicate. In particular, these arguments depend on logical words such as *ALL, NO,* or *SOME,* that indicate the "quantity" of individuals having the characteristic. For this reason, the symbols used to represent them are often called *quantifiers*, in order to represent statements such as "*All* pigs are beings having a four-chambered heart," which we have represented as having the structure, "All P_1's are P_2's."

We can extend the formalism by noting that this sentence can be reformulated as "*For all things, if it is a pig, then it is a being having a four-chambered heart.*" Let us consider the symbol *x* as meaning "For all x," a term such as Px as meaning "It is pig," and Hx, as "It is a being having a four-chambered heart."*

We can then represent the sentence

Example A.7   *All pigs are beings with a four-chambered heart.*

as (x) (Px → Hx)

Given this formalism, we can represent the argument given above as

Example A.8

(1) All pigs are beings with a four-chambered heart.

(2) Mike is a pig.

∴ *Mike is a being with a four-chambered heart.*

(1) (x)(Px → Hx)

(2) Pm

∴ Hm

Similarly, we can represent the more complicated argument using this formalism:

Example A.9

(1) All pigs are mammals.

(2) Every mammal is a being with a four-chambered heart.

∴ *All pigs are beings with a four-chambered heart.*

(1) (x)(Px→ Mx)

(2) (x)(Mx → Hx)

∴ (x)(Px → Hx)

---

*In this and subsequent examples, lowercase letters near the end of the alphabet (e.g., *x*, *y*, and *z*) are used as *variables* that function much like the pronoun "it" in English. This is to be contrasted with lowercase letters from the beginning or middle of the alphabet, *a*, *b*, . . . *m* . . . that stand for names of particular individuals. Furthermore, we will assume that an uppercase letter stands for a predicate. We will allow any capital letter but it is useful to select one that reminds us of an interpretation (e.g., *P* for "is a pig"). But notice that the predicate symbol is always followed by either a name (e.g., *Pm*) or a variable (e.g., *Px*). This distinguishes it from a capital letter that stands for a statement (e.g., *A*).

Thus far, the formalism helps us capture the logical structure of statements containing the "logical words" such as *all* and *every*. We can also use it to represent statements such as "No clinically tested substance is a cure for AIDS." We can see the appropriate formalism if we realize that this statement can be rewritten as, "For all things, if it is a clinically tested substance, then it is *not* a cure for AIDS." So the sentence can be formalized as (x)(Tx → −Cx) where Tx stands for "It is a clinically tested substance," and −Cx stands for "It is not a cure for AIDS." This suggests the following formalization:

Example A.10

(1) *No clinically tested substance is a cure for AIDS.*

(2) *AZT is clinically tested substance.*

∴ *AZT is not a cure for AIDS.*

(1) *(x)(Tx → −Cx)*

(2) *Ta*

∴ *−Ca*

Finally, we can use another symbol to represent one more "logical word" important in representing argument structure. Consider the statements, "Some politicians are corrupt," and "Some politicians are not corrupt." There is no simple translation into statements involving *all* or *no*. We need a separate symbol (∃x) meaning "There exists at least one thing that . . .", so that "Some politicians are corrupt," that is, "There exists at least one thing that is a politician and corrupt," can be represented as (∃x)(Px & Cx) and "Some politicians are not corrupt," can be represented as (∃(Px & −Cx).* With this symbolism in hand, we can translate arguments as follows:

Example A.11

(1) *All people worthy of respect are honest.*

(2) *Some savings and loan presidents are not honest.*

∴ *Some savings and loan presidents are not people worthy of respect.*

(1) *(x)(Wx → Hx)*

(2) *(∃x)(Sx & −Hx)*

∴ *(∃x)(Sx & −Wx)*

---

*The quantifier x sometimes written (∀x) is called the *universal* quantifier—it applies to all or every item in our universe of interpretation. The quantifier (≡x) is called the *existential* quantifier—it asserts the existence of some, at least one, entity in the universe having a certain characteristic.

Testing Validity of Arguments Containing Quantifiers   As we noted above, the straightforward methods of the truth table do not extend to arguments containing quantifiers. Nevertheless, simple forms of these arguments can be checked using another tool: the Venn diagram. Consider the following formalized arguments:

Example A.12

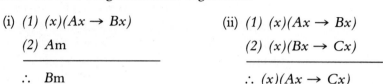

(i) *(1) (x)(Ax → Bx)*

    (2) Am

    ∴ *Bm*

(ii) *(1) (x)(Ax → Bx)*

    (2) (x)(Bx → Cx)

    ∴ *(x)(Ax → Cx)*

Arguments such as these can't be shown as valid with truth tables, because the internal structure of each statement plays a role in the relationship between premises and conclusion. However, we can illustrate a statement such as "All A's are B's"* using the following Venn diagram:

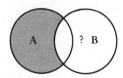

The left-hand circle represents the class of A's, and the right-hand circle represents the class of B's. By shading the part of the A's circle that doesn't overlap the B's circle, we are indicating that this part of the circle is empty—that all A's are B's. Now if we place an *m* in the unshaded part of the A's circle, indicating that *m* is an A, we see that *m* must lie within the B's circle, which is our conclusion—*m* is a B.

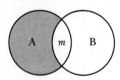

Again representing "All A's are B's" as before, we can add a third, overlapping circle to indicate the class of C's.

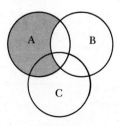

---

*We will use expressions such as "All A's are B's" in place of "all P_1's are P_2's" here and in following examples to indicate what predicate letters to use.

We shade a portion of the B's circle, representing "All B's are C's," and we see that our conclusion follows—"All A's are C's."

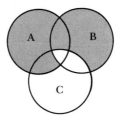

Contrast these cases to two invalid argument patterns:

Example A.13

(i)

(1) All A's are B's.	(1) $(x)(Ax \rightarrow Bx)$
(2) All A's are C's.	(2) $(x)(Ax \rightarrow Cx)$

∴ All B's are C's.   ∴ $(x)(Bx \rightarrow Cx)$

(ii)

(1) All A's are B's.	(1) $(x)(Ax \rightarrow Bx)$
(2) m is a B.	(2) Bm

∴ m is an A.   ∴ Am

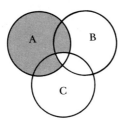

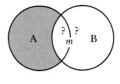

Again we can look for a counterexample. We construct the Venn diagrams to make the premises true. We can then ask whether the conclusion must be true. If it is possible for the conclusion to be false, then the argument is not valid. The possibility of objects that are B but not C as indicated by the upper unshaded portion of A.13(i) shows that its conclusion can be false of the Venn diagram even though the premises are all true of the Venn diagram. It serves as a counterexample. No valid argument can admit this possibility, so this one must be *invalid*. Similarly, the possibility that the named object *m* might be in the right-hand portion of the Venn diagram for Example A.13(ii) serves as a counterexample that demonstrates this argument is invalid as well.

The method can be extended to tested related arguments using the "logical" word *no* and related terms. For instance, "No clinically tested substance is a cure for AIDS," which has the form (x)(Tx → –Cx), is represented by the Venn diagram that darkens the overlap in the circles:

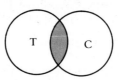

Notice that this is the same Venn diagram you would use for statements of the form "All T's are not C's." Indeed, we can easily combine Venn diagrams for many statements containing "no" and "not" with those containing "all."

Example A.14   *(i)*

No A's are B's.   *(x)(Ax → –Bx)*

All C's are B's.   *(x)(Cx → Bx)*

∴ No C's are A's.   ∴ *(x)(Cx → –Ax)*
        VALID

(ii)

No A's are B's.   *(x)(Ax → –Bx)*

m is an A.   *Am*

∴ m is not a B.   ∴ *–Bm*
        VALID

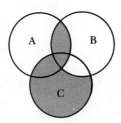

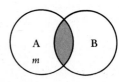

Finally, we can expand the method of representation we used for statements about some named individual to the more general case in which we are talking about some unnamed individual in statements such as "Some savings and loan presidents are not honest."

Example A.15   *(i)*

(1) (x)(Wx → Hx)

(2) (∃x)(Sx & –Hx)

∴ *(∃x)(Sx & –Wx)*
VALID

(ii)

(1) (∃x)(Ax & Bx)

(2) –Am

∴ *–Bm*
INVALID

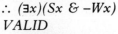

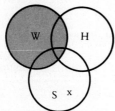

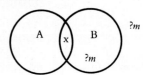

In Example A.15(i), the second premise assures us that there is at least one entity, call it x, that is in the S circle but not in the H circle. But as we can directly see, this means that there is at least one individual that is in the S circle that is not in the W circle. So we can see that it is impossible for both the premises to be true and the conclusion to be false. By contrast in Example A.15(ii), the two premises can be true as indicated by the x in the intersection and the name *m* in the left circle as well as outside either circle. (We don't know which from the information supplied in premise 2.) But we aren't assured that the named individual is *not* in the B circle. Hence, it is possible for the premises to be true of the Venn diagram without the conclusion being true. This provides a counterexample that indicates the argument is *in*valid.

Exercise A.4   **Venn Diagrams**

---

1. Give an example in English of an argument having each of the following patterns. Translate it into our formalism using quantifiers. Construct Venn diagrams to test for the validity of the patterns.

    a.   *All A's are B's.*
          All C's are B's.

       ∴ *All A's are C's.*

    b.   *All A's are B's.*
          m is not a B.

       ∴ m *is not an A.*

    c.   *All A's are B's.*
          All B's are C's.
          m *is A.*

       ∴ m *is C.*

    d.   *All A's are B's.*
          All B's are C's.
          m *is C.*

       ∴ m *is A.*

    e.   *All A's are B's.*
          All C's are B's.
          m *is not A.*

       ∴ m *is not C.*

    f.   *All A's are B's.*
          All C's are B's.
          m *is not B.*

       ∴ m *is not A and*
          m *is not C.*

2. Give an example in English of an argument having each of the following patterns. Translate it into our formalism using quantifiers. Construct Venn diagrams to test for the validity of the patterns.

a. No A's are B's.
    All B's are C's.
    _____
    ∴ No A's are C's.

b. No A's are B's.
    No C's are B's.
    _____
    ∴ No A's are C's.

c. No A's are B's.
    No B's are C's.
    _____
    ∴ No A's are C's.

d. No A's are B's.
    m is a B.
    _____
    ∴ m is not an A.

e. No A's are B's.
    All C's are B's.
    m is a C.
    _____
    ∴ m is not an A.

f. No A's are B's.
    All B's are C's.
    m is a C.
    _____
    ∴ m is not an A.

3. Give an example in English of an argument having each of the following patterns. Translate it into our formalism using quantifiers. Construct Venn diagrams to test for the validity of the patterns.

a. All A's are B's.
    Some C's are A's.
    _____
    ∴ Some C's are B's.

b. All A's are B's.
    Some C's are B's.
    _____
    ∴ Some C's are A's.

c. All A's are B's.
    Some C's are not A's.
    _____
    ∴ Some C's are not B's.

d. Some A's are B's.
    Some C's are B's.
    _____
    ∴ Some A's are C's.

e. No A's are B's.
    Some C's are A's.
    _____
    ∴ Some C's are not B's.

f. No A's are B's.
    All B's are C's.
    _____
    ∴ Some C's are not A's.

Glimpses Beyond:
Natural Deduction

Although truth tables and Venn diagrams serve to characterize *validity* for a variety of simple arguments encountered in everyday deductive reasoning, they are cumbersome techniques to use when arguments become complex. To handle these more complex cases, logicians have formulated a variety of systems of rules, which, if followed, allow us to say the conclusion follows from the premises. These systems of rules can themselves be shown to be justified.

The oldest of these systems of rules was given initial impetus by Aristotle in the fourth century B.C. His rules concerned the *syllogism,* a simple three-predicate argument of the type we examined in the previous section. The rules of the syllogism allow us to determine which of the combinations produce valid arguments. More recently, a variety of "natural deduction" systems have been developed that are roughly based on rules that human reasoners might *naturally* follow. One such rule might be a generalized form of *modus ponens.* Let us call a chain of reasoning in accordance with a set of rules for natural deduction a *proof.*

MODUS PONENS RULE

In a proof, if $\square$ is justified and $\square \rightarrow \triangle$ is justified, then $\triangle$ is justified.*

This rule would allow us to carry out the following *proof,* which consists of a series of lines that begins with a set of premises (above the line) followed by a series of "conclusions" that follow from the premises. Each line is justified either as a premise or as following from previous lines according to a rule of deduction.

		JUSTIFICATION
Example A.16	*(1) A & B*	*premise*
	(2) (A & B) → (C ∨ D)	*premise*
	(3) (C ∨ D) → E	*premise*
	(4) E → F	*premise*
∴	*(5) (C ∨ D)*	*(1)(2) modus ponens***
∴	*(6) E*	*(5)(3) modus ponens*
∴	*(7) F*	*(6)(4) modus ponens*

---

*The symbols $\square$ and $\triangle$ stand for any expression in our formal language.
**In this illustration, the numbers indicate the line numbers of statements previously given in the proof from which the current line follows in accordance with listed rule. We have only introduced one such rule, *modus ponens.*

We might add other rules. For example, we might have a conjunction rule that allowed us to join two separate lines and get a conjunction.

CONJUNCTION RULE

In a proof, if $\square$ is justified and $\triangle$ is justified, then $\square$ & $\triangle$ is justified.

This allows simple *proofs* such as:

JUSTIFICATION

Example A.17

(1) A   *premise*

(2) B   *premise*

$\therefore$ *(3) A & B*   *(1)(2) conjunction*

As well as more complicated *proofs:*

JUSTIFICATION

Example A.18

(1) A   *premise*

(2) B   *premise*

(3) (A & B) → C   *premise*

(4) D   *premise*

(5) (C & D) → E   *premise*

$\therefore$ *(6) A & B*   *(1)(2) conjunction*

$\therefore$ *(7) C*   *(6)(3) modus ponens*

$\therefore$ *(8) C & D*   *(7)(4) conjunction*

$\therefore$ *(9) E*   *(8)(5) modus ponens*

Natural deduction systems come in a number of varieties, differing in the particular rules they take as most basic. Furthermore, the two simple rules we have introduced deal only with statements. Additional rules might be used to handle quantifiers. For instance we could have a rule allowing us to go from the negation of universal quantified statement to an existentially quantified statement.

QUANTIFIER INTERCHANGE RULE

In a proof, if –(x) ☐ is justified, then (∃x)–☐ is justified. This could be used in the following proof:

			JUSTIFICATION
Example A.19		*(1) (x)Px*	*premise*
		(2) (x)(Px → –(x)Qx	*premise*
		(3) (∃x)–Qx → (∃x)–Rx	*premise*
	∴	*(4) –(x)Qx*	*(1)(2) modus ponens*
	∴	*(5) (∃x)–Qx*	*(4) quantifier interchange*
	∴	*(7) (∃x)–Rx*	*(5)(3) modus ponens*

A full set of rules for natural deduction is beyond the scope of this appendix. Many of the details are especially relevant only to those interested in logic or mathematics. But you should note that, even in everyday contexts, loose types of *proofs* are given to establish that a conclusion is actually supported by premises.

Example A.20   *Given political realities, taxes aren't going to be significantly raised soon. So the budget deficit will continue to remain high. Consequently the next generation of taxpayers will be saddled with an almost impossible debt.*

We can represent the three sentences in this passage as follows:

T: Taxes aren't going to be significantly raised soon.

B: The budget deficit will continue to remain high.

D: The next generation of taxpayers will be saddled with an almost impossible debt.

The *proof* is

			JUSTIFICATION
Example A.21		*(1) T*	*premise*
		(2) T → B	*premise (implicit)*
		(3) B → D	*premise (implicit)*
	∴	*(4) B*	*(1)(2) modus ponens*
	∴	*(5) D*	*(4)(3) modus ponens*

Notice that both of the conclusions, including the subordinate conclusion on line 4, are explicitly mentioned in the passage. What is left out are the obvious conditions 2 and 3. It is useful in interpreting arguments to keep in mind that some of intermediate steps employed in reaching a final conclusion are often included in order to guide the reader or listener from premises to ultimate conclusion.

The *modus ponens* (or chain) rule is used in *direct* proofs to spin out the implications of a set of premises. Another more *indirect* tactic is sometimes employed. Instead of trying to directly establish a conclusion, it is sometimes more effective to examine its denial. If this denial leads to an unacceptable (absurd) result, then the original statement can be embraced. This method of indirect proof is sometimes called *reductio ad absurdum* or just *reductio*.

RULE OF INDIRECT PROOF *(reductio ad absurdum)*

In a proof, if adding $\square$ to a set of justified beliefs leads to a contradiction $(\triangle \ \& \ -\triangle)$, then $-\square$ is justified.

Example A.22   *Complete tolerance is not acceptable as social policy. If it were, then Nazis and other tyrants would be allowed to enslave those who are tolerant. That's absurd.*

We can represent the statements in this passage as follows.

T: Complete tolerance is acceptable social policy.

N: Nazis and other tyrants should be allowed to enslave those who are tolerant.

The *proof* is

		JUSTIFICATION
Example A.23	(1) –N	*premise (implicit)*
	(2) T → N	*premise (implicit)*
	(3) T	*ASSUMPTION*
∴	(4) N	*(3)(2) modus ponens*
∴	(5) N & –N	*(4)(1) conjunction*
∴	(6) –T	*(5)(3) indirect proof (reductio)*

Here again, the comments in the passage present elements in the proof rather than a straightforward statement of premises. Recognizing this as a fairly common strategy might help you reconstruct the arguments of others and shape or edit your own arguments.

We have only touched on the issues that would be raised in a full-fledged presentation of a natural deduction system. Such a presentation would provide a systematic account of deductive validity that can handle all of the argument types we have considered in this appendix, as well as more that we have not explored.

Glossary

Ad Baculum ("To the stick") *See* Appeal to Force.

Ad Hominem ("To the person") *See* Attacking the Person.

Ad Misericordiam ("To misery") *See* Appeal to Pity.

Affirming the Consequent Any argument that exhibits the following *invalid* pattern:

> (1) If A, then B.
> (2) B.
> _____
> ∴ A.

Ambiguity A term in a context is ambiguous if it has more than one relatively distinct meaning in that context.

Analogical Reasoning Reasoning that justifies the claim that an item has a certain characteristic by appeal to a sufficiently similar (analogous) item, which is known to have the characteristic in question.

Appeal to Authority Appealing to someone whose expertise is not relevant to the issue at hand; or appealing to someone who is famous or admired, but not an expert on the issue at hand. (Note: We have just described *fallacious* appeals to authority. There are also *legitimate* appeals to authority—appeals to people who really are experts in the appropriate areas.

Appeal to Force The arguer tries to get you to agree by indicating that *you* will be harmed if you don't agree *(ad baculum)*.

Appeal to Pity The arguer tries to get you to agree by indicating that *he or she* will be harmed if you don't agree *(ad misericordiam)*.

Argument As opposed to mere dispute or disagreement, an argument is a structured discourse in which certain statements can be picked out as a conclusion and others can be picked out as premises that provide reasons for believing the conclusion.

Attacking the Person Arguing that a person's point of view should be doubted because the person has bad traits of character or because the person has something to gain by being believed. (Note: There are *legitimate* as well as *fallacious* cases of attacking the person.)

Begging the Question An argument that rests on a premise that is either a restatement of the conclusion or that would be doubted for the same reasons that the conclusion would be doubted *(petitio principii)*.

Causal Reasoning Reasoning that typically moves from observation that one thing is correlated with another to the claim that first causes the second. Such reasoning is not always justified and is best supported by controlled experiments.

Charitable Interpretation Principle A maxim for interpreting argumentative passages that enjoins you to give the arguer the "benefit of the doubt" if at all plausible. If you have a choice, interpret a passage so as to have the premises provide the best support possible for the conclusion. Sometimes an argument as presented is faulty, for example, invalid or unsound, in which case a charitable reconstruction would leave it faulty in this way. (See Chapter 2.)

Conceptual Theory A statement of the conditions under which a certain concept applies to an object. These theories are most plausible in domains in which clear boundaries can be drawn at least for some purposes. These theories are typically criticized by finding counterexamples and pointing to the need for a more extensive and illuminating statement of conditions.

Conditional A statement of the "if-then" form, represented by "A $\rightarrow$ B" in a formal language. The "if" part is called the *antecedent* or *condition;* the "then" part is called the *consequent*. (See the appendix.)

Conjunction A statement of the "and" form that links two other statements. It is represented by "&" in a formal language. (See the appendix.)

Consistency   A group of statements is consistent if it is possible for all of them to be true at the same time. If it is impossible for all of them to be true simultaneously, then the statements are *inconsistent*.

Contradiction   A statement that cannot (logically) be true. It is inconsistent in all contexts. Often used of statements having the form "A and not A," where "A" stands for a sentence, or the form "m is P_1 and m is not P_1," where "P_1" is a predicate.

Controlled Experiment   An experiment designed to determine whether one thing causes another. It involves comparing an experimental group or groups to which the suspected causal agent is applied to a control group to which it is not, all other conditions being the same. If assignment to the groups is unbiased (random), then any significant difference in the experimental groups can be attributed to the suspected causal agent. (See Chapter 9.)

Correlation   The association of two or more characteristics or events. That two events are correlated, that is, they typically occur together, does *not* in itself justify the conclusion that the first causes the second. (See Chapter 9.)

Counterexample   In a deductive argument, a counterexample is a clear case in which the premises are all true and the conclusion is false. It can be an argument that shares the same pattern as one in question, or, for an argument pattern itself, it can be a truth table assignment or Venn diagram configuration. (See Chapter 4 and the appendix.) For a conceptual theory, a counterexample either clearly fits the concept but not the conditions of the theory, or it fits the conditions of the theory but not the concept. (See Chapter 5.)

Critical Reasoning   In contrast to mere disagreement, a procedure for understanding and evaluating the support given for a point of view.

Deductive Argument   An argument in which the premises are put forward to guarantee the truth of the conclusion in the strong sense that it is "logically" impossible for the premises all to be true and the conclusion to be false.

Denying the Antecedent   Any argument that exhibits the following *invalid* pattern:

(1) If A, then B.

(2) Not A.

∴   *Not B.*

Disagreement   *Mere* disagreement takes place when people assert opposing points of view without being open to having their minds changed by reasons. Each seeks to maintain a prior set of beliefs. This contrasts with a dispute subject to critical reasoning. (See Chapter 1.)

Disjunction   A statement of the "or" form, which is represented by "v" in a formal language. (See the appendix.)

Elucidation   A criterion for evaluating conceptual theories. A conceptual theory can be criticized by showing that it uses terms that are no easier to understand than the concept supposedly being clarified (i.e., the theory *fails to elucidate*). (See Chapter 5.)

Emotion-in-Place-of-Reason Fallacies   The general category of fallacies that tend to persuade by making it desirable to believe an argument's conclusion rather than giving evidence to support it. (See Chapter 6.)

Empirical Theory   A set of statements of fairly broad scope that explains patterns or regularities more easily established by observation. The theory is only indirectly supported by observation. Empirical theories can be criticized by pointing out that expected regularities, predictions, or patterns do not occur or are questionable; that there is lack of evidence that required regularities do occur; that crucial concepts in the theory cannot be tested; or by offering a rival theory that is more plausible.

Equivocation   An argument in which an expression shifts its meaning from one premise to another, making the pattern invalid. Equivocation can exploit either ambiguity (more than one relatively distinct meaning) or vagueness (unclear boundary between objects to which the term applies and objects to which it does not).

Expertise   Specialized knowledge in a restricted domain. Expertise is difficult to locate and dangerous to blindly pursue. The amateur—the nonexpert—needs to be able to reason critically to be able to use expertise when and where it is appropriate. (See Chapter 11.)

Explanation   An attempt to indicate why or how something occurred rather than to justify our belief that it did.

Fallacy   A fallacy is an argument that tends to persuade us even though it is faulty and should not do so. Some fallacies involve a move akin to sleight-of-hand techniques used by magicians. Others tend to persuade because they put a motive for believing in place of support. (See Chapters 6 and 9.)

False Dilemma   The arguer claims that there are only two alternatives and one is unacceptable, so we should choose the other. But in fact, there are more alternatives than two.

Generalization   A statement that applies to some number of individuals rather than to a particular enumerated case. (See Chapter 9.)

Empirical Generalization   A generalization purporting to be based on empirical observation or induction.

Statistical Generalization   A generalization that applies to some, a few, or a certain percentage of cases.

Universal Generalization   A generalization that applies to *all* cases. A universal positive generalization contains words such as *all* or *every,* such as "All animals with hearts have kidneys," and "Everybody will be famous for at least 15 minutes." A universal *negative* generalization uses terms such as *no* or *none* to indicate that all cases do *not* have a characteristic. An example is "No one lives forever," which means "Everyone does not live forever."

General-to-Particular Reasoning   Nondeductive reasoning that moves from "statistical" premises, including those using words like *most,* to a conclusion about a particular item.

Hasty Generalization   Embracing a generalization on the basis of an unrepresentative sample, either too small or selected in a biased way.

Implicit Premise   An unstated premise. We determine that such a premise should be added to the reconstruction of an argument in accordance with the Principle of Charitable Interpretation. Typically, such a premise is needed to render the argument valid.

Inconsistency   A set of statements is inconsistent if it is impossible for all of them to be true simultaneously.

Inductive Argument   An argument in which the premises are put forward to make the conclusion likely or probable but not logically guaranteed.

Mere Disagreement   A difference of opinion in circumstances in which participants do not engage in reasoned criticism.

Misleading Definition   A case in which an unclear expression is given an "unusual" or technical meaning in the premises of an argument, but that peculiarity is not marked by qualifications or hedges in the conclusion.

Modus Ponens (mode of affirming)   A common, valid argument form in which we "affirm the antecedent" of a conditional (i.e., if-then) statement. It should be clearly distinguished from the similar but invalid argument called the "fallacy of denying the antecedent." *Modus ponens* is exhibited by this pattern:

(1) If A, then B.

(2) A.

∴ *B.*

Modus Tollens (mode of denying)   A common, valid argument form in which we "deny the consequent" of a condition (i.e., if-then) statement. It should be clearly distinguished from the similar but invalid argument form called "affirming the consequent." *Modus tollens* is exhibited by this pattern:

(1) If A, then B

(2) Not B.

∴ *Not A.*

Necessity   What must occur; the opposite of which is *impossible* or can't be. The conclusion of a valid deductive argument follows with necessity. It is impossible for all of the premises to be true and the conclusion to be false. A statement is *logically necessary* if its denial leads to a contradiction (a contradiction describes an impossible situation). Something is *physically necessary* in a situation if it is physically impossible for it not to happen.

Negation   A sentence of the "not" form, which is represented by "−" in a formal language.

Nondeductive Argument   An argument in which the premises are not put forward to logically guarantee the truth of the premises. Inductive arguments are one form of nondeductive arguments.

Non Sequitur   Conclusion does not follow from premises though it purports to do so.

Particular-to-General Reasoning   A type of nondeductive argument that typically moves from evidence about particulars (for example, evidence collected through sampling) to conclusions about a larger population. This type of reasoning is most commonly called *inductive*.

Persuasiveness   *Legitimate* persuasiveness is a criterion of success for an argument. A legitimately persuasive argument has premises that the audience can understand and will be inclined to believe. Fallacious arguments, by contrast, are persuasive due to tricks and gimmicks.

Petitio Principii ("Petitioning the Premises")   *See* Begging the Question.

Post Hoc, Ergo Propter Hoc ("After this, therefore because of this")   The fallacious or unjustified move from correlation to cause. (See Chapter 9.)

Prejudicial Language   The arguer uses language that biases you in favor of his or her position or against an opponent's position without giving evidence for his or her position or against the opponent's position.

Principle of Charitable Interpretation   *See* Charitable Interpretation Principle.

Quantifier   A symbol in a formal language used to represent the "quantity" to which a sentence applies. The *universal* quantifier (x) is used to formalize statements containing "all," "every," and related terms. It can be roughly translated "for all." The *existential* quantifier, ($\exists$x), means roughly "There exists at least one thing such that" and is used to translate statements containing the term "some." (See the appendix.)

Reconstruction   Reformulation of arguments, conceptual theories, or empirical theories that makes their structure more clear. This can include making explicit elements that are only implicit in the original presentation. Such a reconstruction puts argument or theory in *standard form*. (See Chapters 3, 5, 7, 9, 10.)

Reductio ad Absurdum ("Reducing to the absurd")   A technique of indirect proof that justifies a statement by showing that its negation leads to a contradiction (more broadly, to an absurdity). (See the appendix.)

Regularity   A less theoretical, more observational statement that describes a pattern to be explained by a broader empirical theory. (See Chapter 10.)

Relativism   The belief that one opinion is always as good as another, and that when two people disagree, it can never be determined whose position is more reasonable to hold.

Representativeness of a Sample   A sample is likely to be representative (similar to) a population from which it is drawn if it is sufficiently large and drawn in an unbiased manner. (See Chapter 9.)

Sample   A selection of cases from a population. In particular-to-general inductive reasoning, statements about a sample are used as reasons to justify similar statements about the whole population from which the sample is drawn. If the sample is likely to be unrepresentative, too small, or biased, then the reasoning can be criticized. A random sample of sufficient size improves such inductive reasoning. (See Chapter 9.)

Sleight-of-Hand Fallacy   The general category of fallacies that tend to persuade by distraction (taking the listener's attention away from weak points of the argument) or by counterfeit (presenting something that resembles a good argument but is not).

Slippery Slope   The arguer says we shouldn't do something, because it probably leads to something else, which leads to a third thing, and so forth down the "slippery slope" to a final consequence that is clearly undesirable. But in fact some of these steps are implausible.

Sound Argument   A valid deductive argument with only true premises. In such an argument the conclusion follows, all premises are true, and hence the conclusion is true as well.

Standard Form   For a deductive argument, standard form consists of a numbered listing of premises, separated by a line from a statement of the conclusion prefaced by the symbol meaning "therefore" ($\therefore$). For inductive arguments, the symbol for "therefore" is replaced by the term "likely". For conceptual theories, standard form has an underlined designation of the concept to be defined followed by "if and only if," followed by the condition(s) of the conceptual theory. For an empirical theory, standard form consists of a list of separate theoretical statements, regularities, or patterns, and any observational support.

Straw Man   The arguer makes his own position appear strong by making the opposing position appear weaker than it really is. He puts a weak argument in his opponent's mouth when stronger arguments are available.

Successfulness   A deductive argument is successful if it is valid (i.e., the conclusion follows), has true premises, and is legitimately persuasive. An inductive argument is successful if its premises make the conclusion likely, its premises are true, and it is legitimately persuasive.

Theory   *See* Conceptual Theory or Empirical Theory.

Truth Table   A way to systematically indicate possible assignments of truth values to initial statements and to display the truth value of more complex statements constructed out of them using logical connections. It provides a way to systematically search for counterexamples that might show an argument to be invalid. An argument that can be represented on a truth table is valid just in case there is no line in which the truth value, for all the premises, is true (T) and that for the conclusion is false (F). (See the appendix.)

Vagueness A term is vague in a context if it is unclear where to draw the boundary between things to which the term does apply and those to which it does not.

Validity A deductive argument is valid if and only if it is impossible for all the premises to be true and the conclusion to be false. (See the beginning of Chapter 4.) There is no counterexample showing that the premises are true and the conclusion is false. Truth tables or Venn diagrams can be used to determine validity for some arguments. (See the appendix.) In inductive reasoning, "internal validity" exists when threats to it have been eliminated using random assignment or other means. (See Chapter 9.)

Venn Diagram A way of representing simple predicate arguments using overlapping circles to represent the set of objects to which the predicate applies. The technique is useful in assessing validity and finding counterexamples to certain simple arguments that contain quantifiers. (See the appendix.)

Answers to Selected Exercises

Chapter 1

Exercise 1.1 (pp. 11–12)

(Wording of answers will vary.)

4a. MAIN POINT: America must cut its budget deficit.

SUPPORTING CLAIMS: America is the world's greatest debtor nation. We can change this only by reducing the deficit.

4c. MAIN POINT: Majoring in business but taking courses such as business ethics would be the best resolution of my problem about what major to select. [OR POSSIBLY: It's difficult to decide between a philosophy major and a major such as business.]

SUPPORTING CLAIMS: Philosophy is interesting but wouldn't get me a job. (IMPLICIT: Business courses would get me a job but aren't as interesting.)

Chapter 2

Exercise 2.1 (pp. 17–19)

1. *(1) You shouldn't lie to friends.*

   (2) Carla is your friend.

   ∴ *You shouldn't lie to Carla.*

3. *(1) Abortion involves the taking of a human life.*

   (2) Anything that involves the taking of a human life raises serious moral questions.

   ∴   *Abortion raises serious moral questions.*

5. *(1) All living things need some external source of energy.*

   (2) The sun is the only external source of energy for living things on earth.

   ∴   *All living things on earth need the sun.*

7. *(1) All pornography should be banned.*

   (2) Anything that contains pictures of naked people is pornographic.

   (3) National Geographic contains pictures of naked people.

   ∴   National Geographic *should be banned.*

9. *(1) Only adult citizens can vote.*

   (2) Peter is not a citizen.

   ∴   *Peter can't vote.*

11. *(1) The Pentagon is either in Washington, D.C., or in Baltimore, Maryland.*

    (2) My brother, who works at the Pentagon, says he has never been in Baltimore.

    ∴   *The Pentagon must be in Washington, D.C.*

13. *(1) We had a quiz on Friday.*

    (2) We never have quizzes on two class meetings in a row.

    ∴   *There will not be a quiz on Monday.*

15. CONCLUSION: *The United States has nothing to lose by cutting back on planned military expenditures.*

Exercise 2.2 (pp. 22–23)

1. *(1) If you take too much pride in your physical beauty, then you will come to dread growing older.*

   (2) You take too much pride in your physical beauty.

   ∴   *You will come to dread growing older.*

3. *(1) If you respected my opinion, then you would seek my advice.*

   (2) You don't seek my advice.

   ∴   *You don't respect my opinion.*

5. *(1) If Rob breaks up with Edna, then he will be free to date Karen.*

   (2) If he will be free to date Karen, then Arnold will be out of luck.

   ∴   *If Rob breaks up with Edna, then Arnold will be out of luck.*

7. *(1) Every person has the capacity to kill.*

   (2) Anyone who has the capacity to kill should avoid keeping loaded guns around the house.

   ∴   *Every person should avoid keeping loaded guns around the house.*

9. *(1) Either the United States will tackle the real social ills that beset its cities, or it will lose the "war on drugs."*

   (2) The United States will not tackle the real social ills that beset its cities.

   ∴   *The United States will lose the "war on drugs."*

Exercise 2.3 (pp. 28–30)

(Patterns for Exercise 2.2)

1. *(1) If A, then B.*

   (2) A.

   ∴   *B.*

3. *(1) If A, then B.*

   (2) Not B.

   ∴   *Not A.*

5. *(1) If A, then B.*

   (2) If B, then C.

   ∴   *If A, then C.*

7. *(1) All P₁'s are P₂'s.*

   (2) All P₂'s are P₃'s.

   ∴ *All P₁'s are P₃'s.*

9. *(1) Either A or B.*

   (2) Not A.

   ∴ *B.*

2a. *(1) All A's are B's.*

   (2) m is an A.

   ∴ *m is a B.*

   (1) Anyone who studies critical reasoning is bound to sharpen his argumentative skills.

   (2) John is studying critical reasoning.

   ∴ *John is bound to sharpen his argumentative skills.*

2c. *(1) A.*

   (2) If A, then B.

   (3) If B, then C.

   ∴ *C.*

   (1) Mary does find sensitive men appealing.

   (2) If Mary finds sensitive men appealing, then she will be attracted to Roger.

   (3) If she will be attracted to Roger, then she will end up being frustrated.

   ∴ *She will end up being frustrated.*

2e. *(1) If A, then B.*

   (2) A.

   ∴ *B.*

   (1) If Paul can find this strength, then he will be able to salvage some measure of self-respect.

   (2) Paul will find the strength to resist Sheila's advances.

   ∴ *He will salvage some self-respect.*

2g. *(1) Either A or B.*

   (2) Not A.

   ∴ *B.*

   (1) Either students will become more interested in learning for its own sake, or universities will become more vocationally oriented.

   (2) Students will not become more interested in learning for its own sake.

   ∴ *Universities will become more vocationally oriented.*

2i. (1) All P_1's are P_2's.

    (2) m is a P_1.

    ∴ m is a P_2.

(1) Everyone who goes to medical school will eventually become conservative.

(2) John will go to medical school.

∴ John will eventually become conservative.

3a. (1) All P_1's are P_2's.

    (2) m is not a P_2.

    ∴ m is not a P_1.

(1) All liberals support spending for social programs.

(2) Our senator doesn't support such spending.

∴ Our senator is not a liberal.

3c. (1) All P_1's are P_2's.

    (2) Some P_3's are P_1's.

    ∴ Some P_3's are P_2's.

(1) Anyone who has practiced law has been subjected to corrupting influences.

(2) Some judges have practiced law.

∴ Some judges have been subjected to corrupting influences.

Exercise 2.4 (pp. 32–34)

1a. If the first sentence is taken to be the point of the passage, then the third sentence could be kept as supporting this thesis, but the second and fourth sentences should be eliminated. Alternatively, a paragraph could be built around the point that God does exist, in which case the second sentence could be used as support, and the first and third sentences could be eliminated.

1c. The tone of the first sentence suggests that the writer favors equal rights for women but opposes sending women into war on the grounds that it is unfair to do so while not granting women equal rights. The last sentence, however, backs away from supporting equal rights, and the preceding sentence opposes having women receive military training alongside men on grounds other than fairness. If the thesis of the paragraph is that women shouldn't be trained for and sent into combat, then the last sentence should be eliminated, and the first sentence should be moved into the body of the paragraph and modified so that it is clear that it provides an *additional* reason against sending women into combat. A reconstruction might read as follows:

    Training women for combat exposes them to harassment and sexist abuse. Furthermore, it would be unfair to send women into combat as long as they have not been given equal rights. So training women for combat at the present time would be both cruel and unjust.

Chapter 3

Exercise 3.1 (pp. 46–56)

1a. *(1) If A, then B.*
     (2) [A].

    ∴   *B.*

[*The Nerdic computer runs Wordswift software.*]

1c. *(1) If A, then B.*
     (2) If [B], then [C].

    ∴   *If A, then C.*

If [I can't do word processing on it], then [it doesn't meet my needs].

Alternatively,

    (1) If not A, then not B.
    (2) If [not B], then [not C].

    ∴   *If not A, then not C.*

If it is not the case that [I can do word processing], then it is not the case that [it meets my needs].

1e. *(1) Either [A] or [B].*
     (2) Not B.

    ∴   *A.*

Either [I should buy a Nerdic computer] or [I should buy a Hacker 386 computer].

1g. *(1) All P_1's are P_2's.*
     (2) All [P_2's] are [P_3's].

    ∴   *All P_1's are P_3's.*

All [products guaranteed three years] are [products that give you a lot of protection against faulty workmanship].

1i. *(1) If A and B, then C.*
     (2) [A].
     (3) [B].

    ∴   *C.*

[*The Nerdic computer can run Wordswift.*] [*The Nerdic computer is cheaper than the Hacker 386.*]

1k. *(1) Either A or B.*

    (2) If C, then not B.

    (3) [C].

    ————————————

    ∴   *A.*

[*This money was given to me for my education.*]

2a. *(1) A.*

    (2) If A, then B.

    ————————————

    ∴   *B.*

(1) You promised to be here at eight.

(2) If you promised to be here at eight, then you should have arrived at eight. (IMPLICIT)

————————————

∴   *You should have arrived at eight.*

2c. *(1) If A, then B.*

    (2) If B, then C.

    ————————————

    ∴   *If A, then C.*

(1) If you tell lies frequently, then you must remember not only what you have done but also what you said you have done.

(2) If you must remember not only what you have done but also what you said you have done, then your memory becomes burdened. (IMPLICIT)

————————————

∴   *If you tell lies frequently, your memory becomes burdened.*

2g. *(1) A.*

    (2) If A, then B.

    ————————————

    ∴   *B.*

(1) There are not enough nuclear power stations under construction.

(2) If there are not enough nuclear power stations under construction, then we will face substantial energy shortages by the year 2000. (IMPLICIT)

————————————

∴   *We will face substantial energy shortages by the year 2000.*

2i. *(1) All P_1's are P_2's.*

    (2) All P_2's are P_3's.

    ————————————

    ∴   *All P_1's are P_3's.*

(1) Every successful politician has to compromise his principles occasionally.

(2) Everyone who has to compromise his principles occasionally loses integrity.

————————————

∴   *Every successful politician loses integrity.* (IMPLICIT)

2k. *(1) A.*

    (2) If A, then B.

    (3) If B, then C.

    ———————————————

   ∴ *C.*

(1) Taxpayers will take seriously the need for debt relief.

(2) If taxpayers take seriously the need for debt relief, then governments and banks will be willing to forgive some of the Third World debt.

(3) If governments and banks are willing to forgive some of the Third World debt, then the Third World countries have a chance to solve their mounting financial problems.

———————————————

∴ *The Third World countries have a chance to solve their mounting financial problems.* (IMPLICIT)

2m. *(1) The higher the interest rate, the better the bank.*

    (2) The interest rates at CASH National Bank are the highest in town.

    ———————————————————————

   ∴ *The CASH National Bank is the best bank in town.* (IMPLICIT)

2o. *(1) Either I should spend my tax refund on paying off my debts or I should buy books for this term [but not both].*

    (2) If I don't buy books, then I risk failing my courses.

    (3) I shouldn't risk failing my courses. (IMPLICIT)

    ———————————————————————

   ∴ *I shouldn't spend the refund on paying off my debts.*

2q. *(1) Every human action is determined by laws of nature.*

    (2) If a person deserves praise or blame, then she can act differently than she in fact did. [OR EQUIVALENTLY: If she cannot act differently than she did, then no person deserves praise or blame.]

    (3) If every human action is determined by laws of nature, then a person cannot act differently than she in fact did. (IMPLICIT)

    ———————————————————————

   ∴ *No person deserves praise or blame.*

2s. *(1) The existence of adult bookstores and the lawlessness they engender cannot be hidden from children.*

   (2) If the existence of adult bookstores and the lawlessness they engender cannot be hidden from children, the children are harmed by them. (IMPLICIT)

   (3) We must protect children.

   (4) If we must protect children, then we must prevent that which harms them. (IMPLICIT)

   ∴   *We must prevent the existence of adult bookstores and the lawlessness they engender.*

2u. *(1) If a bad environment caused people to become criminals, then everyone from a bad environment would be a criminal.*

   (2) Not everyone from a bad environment is a criminal.

   ∴   *It isn't a bad environment that causes people to become criminals.*

3a. Reconstruction (ii) is adequate. (i) needs an additional premise linking the two listed; in (iii) a linking premise that mentions the budget deficit is needed for the argument to be valid, premise 1 is unnecessary, and, even with these improvements, we would have reconstructed only part of the argument in the passage.

3c. Reconstruction (iii) is adequate, although quite "bold." Both ·(i) and (ii) take the "easy way out" using the if-then and are restricted to Mervin rather than to characteristics of people who are trying to make it to the top.

Chapter 4

Exercise 4.1 (pp. 76–78)

1. Valid. It is a variation of pattern (ii). A simple reversal of the game show example used for Example 4.9 provides a physical analogy.

3. Invalid. The argument has the form:

(1) All P_1's are P_2's.

(2) All P_3's are P_2's.

∴   *All P_4's are P_2's.*

which can be illustrated by the physical analogy of containers as

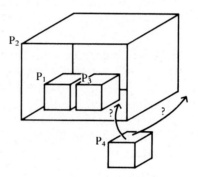

or shown to be invalid by the counterexample having the same form but with true premises and a false conclusion:

(1) All men are human beings.

(2) All women are human beings.

∴   *All computers are human beings.*

5. Invalid. The argument has the form:

(1) Either A or B.

(2) A.

∴   *Not B.*

In the game show physical analogy, a prize can be placed behind both curtains, since the only requirement is that it be behind at least one. In this sense, "or" is taken to mean "either one or the other or both." So, as a counterexample, we can imagine the case in which the drug crisis continues and we spend more money on social programs (perhaps we don't spend the money on social programs that will reduce drug use). In this case, the premises of the argument are both true but the conclusion is false.

Exercise 4.2 (pp. 80–81)

1. The practice of picking one's nose in public is harmful. It can transmit disease, cause wounds, lead to disfigurement, and cause others to think poorly of a person. Such a practice is harmful, but such details of conduct should not be cast in law. If such potentially harmful conduct should be outlawed, we should also outlaw a wide variety of practices that might cause minor injury or be viewed by others as in poor taste.

3. Not everything connected to the body is a part of it. A bullet fragment or piece of shrapnel might be connected to the body by being embedded in it, but is not a part of it. Similarly, a tumor, wart, or other growth might be considered connected to the body but not an integral part of it. Finally, two Siamese twins are connected but are not part of each other.

5. In spite of violence caused by drug-related activity in Colombia and Mexico, many citizens benefit from the illegal cocaine trade. For them, legalization would harm, not benefit. The legalization of other drugs would have uncertain effects. Mexico, for instance, has been a source of marijuana, but if marijuana were legalized, more of it would probably be grown in the United States.

7. States and countries without capital punishment have lower homicide rates than many of those with it. Indeed, the homicide rate in those states actively carrying out capital punishment are among the highest in the United States. This suggests that abolishing capital punishment is unlikely to cause an increase in the homicide rate. Indeed, if the "war on drugs" is successful, there might well be a decrease in the homicide rate, especially if there is a decrease in the male population aged sixteen to twenty-five—a more violence-prone age group.

9. Driving cars might make people aggressive, but it is certainly questionable whether this activity should be discouraged. Training for work in the military or security fields might well make people more aggressive, but such activity is (unfortunately) necessary and permissible.

Exercise 4.3 (pp. 86–87)

1a. Valid, unsound

2a. *(1) If L.A. is in Texas, then L.A. is in the Lone Star State.*

   (2) L.A. is in Texas.

   ∴   *L.A. is in the Lone Star State.*

2c. *(1) No bankers are overweight.*

   (2) All overweight people will have a heart attack.

   ∴   *No bankers will have a heart attack.*

3(i)a.   Misuse of terms; 3(i)c. Sensible use of terms; 3(i)e. Misuse of terms;
3(ii)a.   Inconsistent; 3(ii)c. Consistent

Exercise 4.5 (pp. 94–95)

1. The conclusion follows from the premises, but the premise "Any activity that makes people aggressive should be discouraged" has counterexamples. (See the answer for problem 9 in Exercise 4.2.)

3. The conclusion "The government's antidrug policies are effective" doesn't follow from the premises. It could be that drug use is beginning to decline for some other reason than the government's antidrug efforts. Perhaps it is because some well-publicized deaths from drugs are making users and potential users increasingly aware of the health dangers associated with drug use.

5. There is a subtle shift in wording that makes this argument invalid. The first premise says that if the *average* couple has more than two children, the population will rise drastically. The conclusion says that we should prevent *any* couple from having more than two children. All that would follow from these premises is that we should prevent the *average* couple from having more than two children. This would require much less drastic measures on the part of government than would the stated conclusion. The premises could also be called into question.

7. The conclusion "We shouldn't allow doctors to determine the gender of a fetus whenever parents request it" follows from these premises (at least if we allow "value arguments" resembling *modus tollens*):

   (1) *If we allow doctors to determine the gender of a fetus whenever parents request it, then (some) parents will abort a fetus simply because of its gender.*

   (2) *We shouldn't allow parents to abort a fetus simply because of its gender.*
   (IMPLICIT)

   Premise 1 assumes that when doctors determine the sex of a fetus, they will give this information to parents. It would be possible to have a policy that allows doctors to make this determination (for example, to detect sex-linked diseases) but that doesn't generally make this information available to parents. Premise 2 sounds persuasive, but keep in mind how strong an assertion this must be in order for the argument to be valid. The premise can't merely assert that allowing parents to abort a fetus because of its sex is a bad thing; rather, it must assert that we must prevent this state of affairs—using abortion for sex selection—from coming about. In reply, a critic could admit that sex selection by means of abortion is a bad consequence that we would hope to minimize but that the benefits of allowing doctors to determine the sex of a fetus (especially in detecting sex-linked disease) outweigh the risk that some parents will misuse information concerning the sex of the fetus.

9. The conclusion "Increasing user fees into national parks is justified" does not follow from the premises. Even if tax increases are unjustified, we needn't assume that an increase in other government fees (assuming they are not taxes) is thereby justified. Both tax increases and fee increases might be unjustified.

11. The conclusion "People without children shouldn't be required to pay for schools" follows from the stated premise, "People should pay taxes to support only parts of the government they use," plus the implicit premise that people without children don't use the schools. Both the explicit and implicit premises are doubtful. Arguably, government can function only if individuals are willing to pay for at least some benefits to others that they themselves will not directly use. Projects in some distant part of the country are "traded off" for projects close to home.

   Further, it is plausible to assume that if we interpret "use" in a slightly broader way than as direct personal use (by a person or at least by his or her family), then people without children do use the schools, contrary to the implicit premise. After all, the economic well-being of a community depends to a significant degree on the general educational level of its citizens, and a person benefits from ("uses") the economic resources of the community.

Chapter 5

Exercise 5.1 (pp. 106–108)

1a. The term "man" could refer to the human species or to individual human beings. "Free" could mean "having no constraints" or "having the power to do what one wants." It is probably true that the human species was, at some time in the distant past, free in the sense that it had no elaborate social constraints, but it was not free in the second sense. Individual human beings are or have been enslaved (so not all are free in the first sense); nor is anyone born free in the second sense.

1c. The expression "indirect suicide" is vague. If we interpret it in such a way that a person who plays "Russian roulette" with a loaded gun participates in indirectly suicidal behavior, the statement is true. If eating fatty red meat turns out to be as unhealthy as is sometimes suggested, then this too could be considered indirectly suicidal. But it is unclear, even with recent health warnings, that eating red meat should be "strongly condemned." If we specify the term in this broad way, the statement is false.

1e. The term "war" is ambiguous. It could mean either "an extensive armed conflict" or "a concerted public effort to eliminate or alter some unacceptable condition." Since the "war on poverty" was not a war in the first sense, interpreting it in this way would make the statement false. But it would be true if interpreted in the second sense.

1g. "Fine" is ambiguous. It could mean quite acceptable, or it could mean that a fine can be levied. The accused interpreted it in the second way; a conventional reading would have interpreted it in the first. From the legal point of view, the first statement is false given the first reading and true given the second.

1i. This passage trades on an ambiguity in the term "democracy." In one sense, a democracy is a form of government that has mechanisms to represent the views of the citizens. In a second sense, it must do more than merely permit these views to be represented. The citizens must actually participate in the process, at least to the extent that they vote for their representatives. The first sentence in the passage is false under the first interpretation and true under the second.

2a. RECONSTRUCTION:

(1) *The United States is ruled by the people.*

(2) *All countries ruled by the people are democracies.*

∴   *The United States is a democracy.*

ASSESSMENT: The argument is valid. The United States has a form of government that allows for "rule by the people" rather than by a king or an aristocracy. The actual power of the people has varied during American history. It is possible to have democratic institutions without having democracy in practice. If the conclusion is construed as meaning democracy in practice, then we must construe it as such in the premises as well. The degree of actual citizen participation and impact in the U.S. government is a matter of some debate, especially if we look at American political and social history.

2c. RECONSTRUCTION:

(1) *If space is expanding, it is finite.*
     [ALTERNATIVELY: *Either space is not expanding or it is finite; "A unless B" is interpreted as "A or B."*]

(2) *Space is not finite.*

∴   *Space is not expanding.*

ASSESSMENT: The argument is valid. The term "finite" can be interpreted in at least two ways. In the first sense, something is finite if it has a boundary. But there is another sense in which something could be bounded, like the surface of the earth, but still we could travel indefinitely without reaching a boundary—we could just circle the globe endlessly. Similarly, space could be expanding, but no path in space need end in a boundary. It could be infinite, but bounded. So the sense of "finite" that makes premise 2 true might not make premise 1 true.

2e. RECONSTRUCTION:

(1) We can't confidently predict the job market.

(2) If we can't confidently predict the job market, then we can't form a reasonable idea about what to do with our lives.

(3) If we can't form a reasonable idea about what to do with our lives, then we shouldn't go to college.
[ALTERNATIVELY: *If we go to college, then we must form a reasonable idea about what to do with our lives.*]

∴   *We shouldn't go to college.*

ASSESSMENT: The argument is valid, but the expression "confidently predict the job market" is vague. It is true that we can't precisely predict all the particulars about future employment opportunities. And all bets are off if a nuclear war occurs. But some general predictions can be made about broad trends, and this might be all a person needs in order to form a reasonable idea of what to do with his or her life. So the sense of the phrase "confidently predict the job market" that would make premise 1 true would probably make premise 2 false. Similarly, the phrase "reasonable idea" could be seen as shifting in meaning from premise 2 to premise 3.

2g. RECONSTRUCTION:

(1) If happiness involved freedom, then newborn children would be free (or would become free as they grow older).

(2) Newborn children are not free (nor do they become free as they grow older).

∴   *Happiness does not involve freedom.*

ASSESSMENT: The argument is valid. Two senses of "freedom" can be distinguished. Children are free, as Rousseau suggests, when they are subjected to few, if any, social expectations. As we grow up, society increasingly expects us to play socially defined roles. Skinner stresses a second sense of freedom, acting without constraint of physical environment or genetic endowment. According to Skinner, no one is free in this way. But if he asserted this conclusion without explaining his special meaning of "freedom," he would be guilty of misleading definition.

Exercise 5.2 (pp. 118–120)

1. A figure is a *square* if and only if:

(1) It has four sides.

(2) Its sides are equal in length.

3. A law is *just* if and only if it was passed democratically.

5. An event is a *traffic gridlock* if and only if:

   (1) It involves total standstill of traffic.

   (2) It lasts at least fifteen minutes.

   (3) It extends eight blocks or more in any direction.

7. Something is *human* if and only if:

   (1) It has an IQ of at least twenty.

   (2) It has self-awareness.

   (3) It has self-control.

   (4) It has a sense of time.

   (5) It has the capability of relating to others.

   (6) Other (unspecified) conditions.

9. A human activity is *art* if and only if:

   (1) A person creates external signs.

   (2) These signs are consciously selected to evoke feelings in another person that are similar to those the creator himself has previously experienced.

(Note—Tolstoy goes on to comment on what art can do rather than provide a further condition. The remainder of the passage asserts that art in Tolstoy's sense creates a union among people that is indispensable for progress of individuals and humanity.)

Exercise 5.3 (pp. 122–123)

1a. COUNTEREXAMPLE: A parallelogram can have four equal sides but not be square.

1c. COUNTEREXAMPLE: Prisoners in adjacent cells live close to each other but may not constitute a society.

1e. COUNTEREXAMPLE: Some people have several compulsions. A person might believe that time spent gambling or drinking fine wines is worthwhile and still be a compulsive programmer.

1g. COUNTEREXAMPLE: A person might be intelligent but have never taken the Stanford-Binet IQ tests or have been ill when taking the tests and got a score lower than 130.

1i. COUNTEREXAMPLE: At one point in history the belief that the sun goes around the earth was accepted by most people and was supported by some evidence—the sunrise—but was not true.

1k. COUNTEREXAMPLE: A person who recklessly exposes himself to certain death in order to try to do the impossible act of holding back floodwaters that threaten a town is not courageous, but foolhardy.

2a. "Follows from" is unclear. It could mean either that the conclusion is brought to mind by the premises or that its truth is guaranteed by the premises.

2c. Theory does elucidate. "Happiness" is surely better understood than "good," although it too requires some explanation.

2e. "Fair" is somewhat more clear than "just," but it is still an ethical concept over which there would be considerable disagreement.

2g. Theory does elucidate. Although it uses technical terms, their meanings are independent of the meaning of "arc."

2i. "Transmission of information" is somewhat clearer than "communicates," but not much.

2k. It is debatable whether "find worthy or valuable" is more clear than "appreciate."

Exercise 5.4 (pp 125–132)

1a. CONCEPTUAL THEORY: Something is *right* if and only if it is in the interest of the stronger.

CRITICISM: The expression "interest of the stronger" needs elucidation. If we interpret "stronger" to mean political rulers, as Plato points out in *The Republic,* then one important issue is whether we are talking about the real interest of the rulers or what they believe is in their interest. Even though justice may be in the *real* interest of rulers, counterexamples can be found in which what rulers believe is in their interest is not right. Hitler presumably believed that the concentration camps were in his (and Germany's) best interest, but that did not make them right.

1c. CONCEPTUAL THEORY: An action is *morally right* if and only if it produces more good than any available alternative. Something is *good* if and only if it produces pleasure in normal individuals.

CRITICISM: This version of utilitarianism faces counterexamples. An act might produce more good than any alternative but might distribute the goods so unfairly that some other act would be morally preferable (for example, telling a joke that thoroughly amuses most of those present but humiliates one person). Even giving the death penalty to a person known by a few insiders to be innocent (a scapegoat) might prevent an angry mob from rioting. In such a case, this alternative produces more pleasure than any alternative, but it is not just. Furthermore, proving a complex mathematical theory may be a good even if it does not produce (bodily) pleasure in a normal person or even in the mathematician who does so. The concept of pleasure and the methods of measuring it need elucidation. It is probably too narrow a concept to cover all things that are good.

1e. CONCEPTUAL THEORY:

Something is *human* if and only if:

(1) Its IQ is at least twenty.

(2) It has self-awareness.

(3) It has self-control.

(4) It has a sense of time.

(5) It is capable of relating to others.

The theory is not elucidating. The way in which humans have self-awareness and self-control, but other animals do not, is hardly more clear than is the distinction between humans and animals to begin with. Furthermore, there may well be extraterrestrials who satisfy the conditions but are not human.

2a. CONCEPTUAL THEORY: A work of art is *modern* if and only if it was created recently (in this century).

ARGUMENT:

(1) The Museum of Modern Art should show only modern art.

(2) A work of art is modern only if it was created recently (in this century). (FROM THEORY)

(3) French Impressionist works of art were not created in this century.

∴   *The Museum of Modern Art should not show French Impressionists.*

CRITICISM: The term "modern" reflects the style of the art, not the precise point in time at which it was created. In this sense of style, recent works can be done in traditional styles and not be modern in the stylistic sense. Native American totem art is not of the "modern" style even though it is still being created today.

2c. CONCEPTUAL THEORY: An argument is *good* if and only if it has a true conclusion.

ARGUMENT:

(1) All valid arguments are good arguments.

(2) All good arguments have a true conclusion. (IMPLICIT FROM THEORY)

∴   *All valid arguments have a true conclusion.*

CRITICISM: The conceptual theory about the goodness of an argument underlies the second, implicit premise. But this theory could be challenged by pointing out that certain deductive arguments—the valid ones—are *good* structurally even though they may have a false conclusion and that good inductive arguments need not have a true conclusion. If the theory is faulty, then premise 2 is questionable, and the soundness of the argument is in doubt. Furthermore, premise 1 is weak if "good" is taken as meaning "without defect." A valid argument could have the defect of false premises and conclusion. Incidentally, the argument itself is an example of a valid argument with a false conclusion.

3a. CONCEPTUAL THEORY: An object is *a work of art* if and only if it is put forward as a candidate for appreciation by people who constitute the art world. A person is a member of the *art world* if and only if her life and social relations are dedicated to creating, identifying, assessing, and evaluating objects as works of art.

SOME SAMPLE IMPLICATIONS:

(a) *Given the right circumstances, even an old, well-used urinal could be a work of art.*

(b) *If a work of art is consciously created, then the creator must have some idea about the standards of the art world.*

ARGUMENT FOR (a):

(1) *An old, well-used urinal can be put forward as a candidate for appreciation (as, for instance, when the French artist Duchamp did so in order to shock his contemporaries).*

(2) *If something is put forward as a candidate for appreciation by a member of the art world, then it is a work of art.* (FROM THEORY)

∴ *Given the right circumstances, even an old, well-used urinal could be a work of art.*

ARGUMENT FOR (b):

(1) *If a person consciously sets out to create a work of art, then she is consciously setting out to create something that can be put forward as a candidate for appreciation by the art world.* (FROM THEORY)

(2) *If somebody consciously sets out to do so, then she needs to have some idea about the standards of the art world.*

∴ *If a person consciously sets out to create a work of art, she needs to have some idea about the standards of the art world.*

Chapter 6

Exercise 6.1 (pp. 139–140)

1b. Straw man. This could be persuasive because your attention is caught by the weakness of the argument attributed to the opposition—anything that's fun is sinful. But there are much stronger arguments against legalized gambling.

1e. Slippery slope. A few people who begin with casual gambling are led through these steps to ruin. But for any individual who begins to gamble, this progression is not likely. You might tend to be persuaded because the first few steps sound plausible. Distracted by the thought of how horrible the bottom of the slope is, you don't think critically about the likelihood of all the steps following from the first few.

1g. False dilemma. This argument gives you the same kind of all-or-nothing choice as the argument in 1c. This simplicity might be appealing, but why not tackle a main part of the problem, even if it doesn't solve the entire problem?

Exercise 6.2 (pp. 146–148)

1a. Denying the antecedent. This resembles a valid argument.

1c. Affirming the consequent. (If we're nice guys, then we'll finish last. We'll finish last. Therefore, we're nice guys.) This resembles a valid argument.

1e. Begging the question. If this persuaded anyone, it would be because the premise is stated in slightly different words from the conclusion, making it less apparent that no additional reason is being given for the conclusion.

1g. Equivocation. Interest in art and religion might show that man is "spiritual," but not in a sense that would disprove the claim that mind can be reduced to matter. But someone who already wanted to reject materialism might overlook the shift in meaning.

1i. Equivocation. Even if each person's actions are selfish in the sense of being aimed at getting something the person wants, this is not incompatible.

3b. False dilemma. Not everyone who can beat you deserves to have you join him, but the two alternatives of beating or joining probably sound more comfortable than any third alternative.

3d. Equivocation. Just because someone loses graciously doesn't mean she loses constantly. But someone who is preoccupied with winning might lump these two categories together.

3e. Affirming the consequent. This resembles a good argument.

3h. "Reverse" of slippery slope. It is doubtful that *all* these things follow from this kind of peace of mind. But seeing some kinds of good follow from a practice leads one to expect all manner of good to follow.

Exercise 6.3 (pp. 154–155)

1. Appeal to pity
3. Prejudicial language
5. Appeal to pity
7. Appeal to force

Exercise 6.4 (pp. 162–164)

2a. Straw man, false dilemma, begging the question
2c. Equivocation ("duty"), prejudicial language
2e. Attacking the person, appeal to pity
2g. Equivocation ("welfare"), slippery slope, appeal to authority (depending on your view of Kennedy's expertise)
2i. Prejudicial language, attacking the person

Exercise 6.5 (pp. 164–166)

1. It might be claimed that this is the fallacy of appeal to pity. The question of whether this is a fallacy hinges on what the jury is deciding (or should decide). If the decision is simply one of guilt or innocence, then the appeal is fallacious. If the question is whether the accused should be imprisoned, then the appeal to pity is not fallacious.

3. If Joan is really offering an argument, then the last part of this passage is a fallacious attack on the person. But then the question becomes: Is Joan offering an argument or simply begging the question? If her premise is that it is not morally wrong not to give money to charities, this is very close to the same assertion as the conclusion—that giving money to charities is not an obligation. However, Joan might be making the more subtle point that not all acts that are good to perform are (strictly speaking) obligatory. Still, she needs to say more about why giving to charity should not be considered obligatory.

5. Is this a fallacious appeal to pity? This is debatable. All that is necessary to establish that Bert deserves compensation is to show that the company was responsible (the first sentence) and that Bert suffered damage. If a poor case had been made to establish responsibility, the arguer must be trying to compensate here by getting the audience to feel sorry for Bert because he can't feed himself. The degree of his suffering is irrelevant to whether he deserves compensation. But it would be relevant to the issue of how much compensation he deserves.

7. Is this a fallacious appeal to pity? Not according to our analysis of when it is appropriate for an argument to appeal to emotion.

Chapter 7

Exercise 7.1 (pp. 172–173)

1. *(1) If you're uncoordinated, then you can't be a good golfer.*

   (2) You are a good golfer.

   ∴ *You're coordinated.*

2. Description

4. Explanation

6. *(1) If three people who had a good education all went to Central High, then everyone (in town) who had a good education went to Central High.* [ALTERNATIVELY: *Only one school in town provides a good education.*] (IMPLICIT)

   (2) Dan, Homer, and Edna all have a good education, and they went to Central High.

   (3) Kathy had a good education.

   ∴ *Kathy went to Central High.*

8. Description

10. *(1) Anyone who is unwilling to help (do his share) with housework will make a poor spouse.*

    (2) Robert is unwilling to help (do his share) with housework.

    ∴ *Robert will make a poor spouse.*

Exercise 7.2 (pp. 173–177)

1. S1 explanation, S2 unsupported assertion, S3 description, S4 description, S5 editorial comment

3. All sentences are descriptions.

Exercise 7.3 (pp. 180–182)

1. Lazy people usually suffer; hardworking people benefit.

3. Only nature provides an escape from the harm of technological society.

5. A good teacher knows his or her subject, interacts well with students, and seeks objective feedback on his or her performance.

7. People don't really know what they want; their wants are created for them (by advertising, and so on).

9. GENERAL PARAPHRASE OF CENTRAL CLAIM: Schizophrenia can be healed through a natural process by which people who have recovered guide a patient through his or her madness.

Exercise 7.4 (pp. 188–191)

(Most arguments can be reconstructed in more than one way.)

Passage 1:

(1) If doctors are allowed to inform parents of the gender of their fetus, then they might abort the fetus simply because of its gender.

(2) We shouldn't allow the possibility that parents will abort a fetus simply because of its gender.

∴ *We shouldn't allow doctors to inform parents of the gender of their fetus.*

Passage 3:

(1) Whatever takes time from teaching basic skills and wastes money should not exist in the schools. (IMPLICIT)

(2) Sex education takes time from teaching basic skills and wastes money.

∴ *Sex education should not exist in the schools.*

Chapter 9

Exercise 9.1 (pp. 224–225)

1a. Particular; 1c. Generalization, statistical; 1e. Generalization, universal; 1g. Particular (unless the statement is construed as suggesting that Frankie and Johnny always act lovingly toward each other); 1i. Particular; 1k. Generalization, universal; 1m. Generalization, universal

2a. Inductive, general-to-particular; 2c. Deductive; 2e. Inductive, particular-to-general, then application with general-to-particular or deductive argument; 2g. Deductive; 2i. Inductive, particular-to-general (perhaps inductive, general-to-particular at end of passage); 2k. Deductive

Exercise 9.2 (pp. 232–235)

1a. *(1) Teachers in all three courses she has taken are men.*

(likely) Most university teachers are men.

Too small a sample. A better sample could be obtained by getting data from a random sample of universities; better yet, we could consult data collected and published by the Department of Education.

1c. *(1) An insufficient number of those sampled said that they would vote for Roosevelt.*

(likely) An insufficient number of voters would vote for Roosevelt to elect him.

The sample is not representative; the less well off would be less likely to read *Literary Digest* or to have a telephone or an automobile, especially during the Depression. A random sample of addresses for registered voters (those likely to vote) would have produced better results, but the data would have been difficult to obtain for the country as a whole.

1e. *(1) The records from recent years show that the National Football Conference has won more cross-conference and Super Bowl games than the American Football Conference.*

(likely) The NFC will (continue to) win more cross-conference and Super Bowl games than the AFC.

The sample may not be representative of future seasons, when the college draft might equalize the league or when restrictions on the number of players might make better players more generally available. A better sample might include records from a longer period of time.

1g. *(1) Most of those randomly selected people who were being treated for gout in the San Francisco area were not addicted to rich gourmet food and beverages.*

(likely) Most gout sufferers are not addicts of rich gourmet food and beverages.

The sample may not be representative of all gout suffers. A wider range of cities with various ethnic and cultural characteristics might be sampled.

1i. *(1) The [sample of?] guys down at the Beta fraternity house and Bernie's Disco [who are bachelors] are all unhappy.*

(likely) All bachelors are unhappy.

The sample is not representative of all unmarried men. A sample with a broader range of ages, social backgrounds, and cultural values would be better.

1k. (Among other arguments that generalize)

(1) A fifth of the 1,500 women surveyed at Harvard [said they] had been forced into sexual activity.

(likely) Sex is forced on 19 percent (about a fifth) of all college women [at Harvard? in the United States?].

It is unclear whether the sample was random or not. If it was taken from those using the health services, for example, they might be unrepresentative of the whole population. It is also unclear whether the article wishes to generalize to a larger college population outside Harvard. If so, the sample must be taken from other colleges and universities as well.

2a. Suppose it were argued that the percentage of minority group members in the United States is not increasing. The census report provides an estimate of the number of minority members for selected minority groups. Some urban minorities are apt to be undercounted because of a more mobile lifestyle—they might not be home much—or because they avoid government agents (for example, illegal aliens).

2c. An interview with individuals in randomly selected households in the neighborhood would be appropriate. Such an interview might be more easily done by telephone, given the emotional nature of the debate, though obtaining the telephone number of the household would be difficult. Care must be taken to avoid oversampling of one gender, perhaps by randomly asking for either a male or a female respondent from the household.

2e. Readings from monitors distributed in representative areas of the city could be used.

Exercise 9.3 (pp. 248–253)

1. Both heavy consumption of coffee and heart attacks might be joint effects of the same underlying cause—for example, a compulsive, hard-driving personality.

3. Going to the hospital and dying have an underlying cause—namely, some disease or injury that might account for both. There are, however, a variety of hospital-contracted infections that could in fact cause an elevated death rate for certain classes of patients.

5. Given the variety of types of studies underlying the correlation, the move of a cause is probably justified, though it is possible that both cancer and smoking spring from some underlying physical cause.

Exercise 9.4 (pp. 256–257)

1. COUNTERARGUMENT:

(1) Few drivers are drunk at 9:30 on Sunday morning.

(2) Armand was an auto fatality at 9:30 on Sunday morning.

(likely) Armand's death was not the result of the drinking driver.

3. COUNTERARGUMENT:

(1) Most clerical jobs have lower wages.

(2) American cities with a strong service economy have a great many clerical jobs.

(likely) American cities with a strong service economy have lower wages.

Exercise 9.5 (pp. 261–263)

1. A difference between the captain of a ship and the president of a country that makes the conclusion less likely is that the captain is supposedly an expert at handling his ship in all situations. An elected president may not be an expert at statecraft and may be unfamiliar with the kinds of crises that might confront him.

3. The implicit conclusion is that a government can't go on spending more than it takes in. One difference between a family and a government that makes the conclusion less likely is that a family has little or no control over the economic system in which it operates. For example, a government could affect the rate of interest on its debts through monetary policy, but a family could not. Furthermore, the premise that a family can't go on spending more than it takes in is somewhat doubtful. A family could do this for a long time, as long as it can pay the interest on its debt.

5. Rented tuxedos sometimes do fit. It is only if you abide by the myth of the perfect fit that you might think otherwise. Similarly, analogies might fit very well indeed.

Chapter 10

Exercise 10.1 (pp. 271–275)

1. WHAT IS EXPLAINED:	Why so many banks are failing.
THEORY:	Deregulation has resulted in bankers taking more risks.
3. WHAT IS EXPLAINED:	Why Bush won the 1988 election decisively.
THEORY:	Holding the conservative South and West for the Republicans while discrediting the Democratic candidate among his traditional supporters was enough to produce a decisive victory.
5. WHAT IS EXPLAINED:	Why the public interest group developed in America.
THEORY:	Change in the civil rights movement made white activists available to take up other causes. Formation of public interest groups took advantage of their social concerns and organizational talents.

Exercise 10.2 (pp. 284–302)

Passage 1:

STATEMENTS OF THEORY AND REGULARITIES:

T_1 Americans see themselves as members of primarily one group or another.

T_2 Americans tend to vote for parties that have historically represented the interests of groups of which they are members and that have an ideology similar to theirs.

R_1 Black Americans and members of labor unions tend to vote for Democrats.

R_2 Businesspeople and religious fundamentalists tend to vote for Republicans.

[Additionally]

R_3 Jewish people tend to vote Democratic.

R_4 Farmers tend to vote Republican.

SAMPLE CRITICISM:

(1) *(Subverting support)* Some of the supposed regularities cited are no longer so obviously the case. Labor unions such as the Teamsters supported Ronald Reagan, for example.

(2) *(Subverting support)* Statement T_1 would seem to predict that people would, if asked, identify themselves primarily as members of one particular group. But since many people are members of a variety of groups—a religion, an occupation, a hobby—and play a variety of roles—mother, money earner, citizen—it is likely that many of them would be unwilling to consider themselves as members of just one group. This pluralism undermines support for the theory.

(3) *(Subverting support)* Statement T_2 suggests that overall ideology is important in voting behavior, but recent elections have seen the emergence of the "single-issue voter," the person who votes for or against a candidate on the basis of the candidate's view about a single topic—for example, abortion or nuclear war—independent of the overall ideology of the party of the candidate. Again, this pattern undermines support for the theory.

(4) *(Alternative theory)* The regularity can be explained without appeal to membership in a group. Even if voting happens to follow group boundaries, it does not follow that people vote the way they do solely, or primarily, *because* of group identification. Such an alternative theory could explain these regularities by pointing out that in the past, Democratic political programs appealed to individual blacks and labor union members not because they were black or union supporters but because they provided direct economic benefit. Once this economic advantage disappeared, as when blacks became highly paid professionals or Teamster union members came to benefit from Republican policies, then voting allegiances altered.

Exercise 10.3 (pp. 309–319)

1. "A Star Named George":

T_1 The sun is a member of a binary-star system with a faint dwarf star about one tenth of the sun's mass at a distance of 2.4 light-years.

T_2 Passage of a star through the inner Oort cloud would cause comets to rain down on the earth.

T_3 Comets hitting the earth would spread enough extraterrestrial material and dust to darken the earth's atmosphere for at least six months (the Alvarez hypothesis).

T_4 Darkening of the earth's atmosphere for an appreciable period of time would cause mass extinctions.

T_4 The rate of extinctions increases systematically every 26 million years, the last some 13 million years ago.

O_1^1

O_2^2 } Data examined by Raup and Sepkoski.

O_3^3

R_2 [Unanticipated] Comet show impact craters occur about every 28.4 million years.

O_1^1 Alvarez' data on iridium.

O_2^2 Muller and Alvarez' data on thirteen impact craters.

Appendix

Exercise A.1 (pp. 337–340)

1a. A; 1c. −A → B; 1e. A → (B v C);
1g. (A v B) → (C & D); 1i. −(A & B) → C

2a. −A; 2c. A v B; 2e. −(A v B);
alternatively, −A & −B

3a. From problem 1a in Exercise 3.1:

(1) A → B.   A: *The Nerdic computer runs Word-swift software.*
(2) A.

∴ B.   B: *The Nerdic computer can meet my needs.*

From problem 1c in Exercise 3.1:

(1) –A → –B.
(2) –B → –C.
———————————————
∴   *–A → –C.*

A: The Hacker 386 does run Word-swift.

B: I can do word processing on it (the Hacker 386).

C: The Hacker 386 does meet my needs.

From problem 1e in Exercise 3.1:

(1) A ∨ B.
(2) –C.
———————————————
∴   *A.*

A: I should buy a Nerdic computer.

B: I should buy a Hacker 386.

3b. From problem 3a in Exercise 3.1:

(i) (1) A ∨ B.
    (2) –C.
———————————————
    ∴ *B.*

A: We should cut spending drastically to eliminate the budget deficit.

B: We should raise taxes to eliminate the budget deficit.

C: We should let our transportation, education, and health care systems deteriorate even further.

(iii) (1) D.
    (2) –C.
———————————————
    ∴ *–A.*

D: We should prevent the deterioration of social and economic systems in the United States.

4a. *(1) A ∨ B.*
   (2) B → C.
   (3) –C.
———————————————
∴   *A.*

4c. *(1) A → B.*
   (2) B → C.
   (3) –C ∨ D.
   (4) –D.
———————————————
∴   *–A.*

Exercise A.2 (pp. 345–346)

1a. A → –B

T F	Initial Assignment
T	Row 2 Negation
T	Row 1 Conditional

1c. –(A & –B)

T F	Initial Assignment
T	Row 2 Negation
T	Row 1 Conjunction
F	Row 1 Negation

1e. –(A ↔ B)

T F	Initial Assignment
F	Row 2 Biconditional
T	Row 1 Negation

2a. A → –B

F F	Initial Assignment
T	Row 2 Negation
T	Row 3 Conditional

3a. A → (B v C)

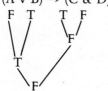

F T T	Initial Assignment
T	Row 1 Disjunction
T	Row 3 Conditional

3c. (A v B) → (C & D)

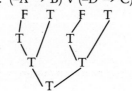

F T T F	Initial Assignment
F	Row 2 Conjunction
T	Row 3 Disjunction
F	Row 2 Conditional

3e. (–A → B) v (–D → C)

F T F T	Initial Assignment
T T	Row 2 Negation
T T	Row 1 Conditional
T	Row 1 Disjunction

3g. –((A v –B) & C)

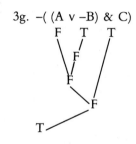

Initial Assignment

Row 1   Negation

Row 4   Disjunction

Row 3   Conjunction

Row 2   Negation

Exercise A.3 (pp. 352–355)

1b.

A	B	C	Premises			Conclusion
			A → B	B → C	A	C
T	T	T	T	T	T	T
T	T	F	T	F	T	F
T	F	T	F	T	T	T
T	F	F	F	T	T	F
F	T	T	T	T	F	T
F	T	F	T	F	F	F
F	F	T	T	T	F	T
F	F	F	T	T	F	F

Note that all premises are true in the first line only, and the conclusion is also true in this situation. So the argument is valid.

2a.

A	B	Premises		Conclusion
		–A → B	A	B
T	T	T	T	T
T	F	T	T	F
F	T	T	F	T
F	F	F	F	F

Invalid. Note second line.

3a.

A	B	Premises		Conclusion
		A → –B	B	–A
T	T	F	T	F
T	F	T	F	F
F	T	T	T	T
F	F	T	F	T

Valid. Note that only the third line has all premises true. The conclusion is also true in this situation.

3c.

A	B	Premise A → B	Conclusion B → A
T	T	T	T
T	F	F	T
F	T	T	F
F	F	T	T

Invalid. Note third line.

3i.

A	B	C	Premises A → –B	–B v C	A	Conclusion C
T	T	T	F	T	T	T
T	T	F	F	F	T	F
T	F	T	T	T	T	T
T	F	F	T	T	T	F
F	T	T	T	T	F	T
F	T	F	T	F	F	F
F	F	T	T	T	F	T
F	F	F	T	T	F	F

Invalid. Note fourth line.

3m.

A	B	C	Premises A ↔ B	B → C	–C	Conclusion A
T	T	T	T	T	F	T
T	T	F	T	F	T	T
T	F	T	F	T	F	T
T	F	F	F	T	T	T
F	T	T	F	T	F	F
F	T	F	F	F	T	F
F	F	T	T	T	F	F
F	F	F	T	T	T	F

Invalid. Note last line.

Exercise A.4 (pp. 361–362)

1a. *All men are human.* $(x) \cdot (Mx \rightarrow Hx)$

    All women are human. $(x) (Wx \rightarrow Hx)$

∴ *All men are women.* ∴ $(x) (Mx \rightarrow Wx)$

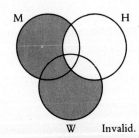

W   Invalid.

1c.   *All dogs are mammals.* $(x) (Dx \rightarrow Mx)$

 All mammals are animals. $(x) (Mx \rightarrow Ax)$

 Zeke is a dog. Dz

∴   *Zeke is an animal.*   ∴ Az

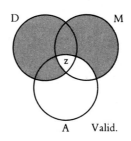

Valid.

1e.   *All men are human.* $(x) (Mx \rightarrow Hx)$

 All women are human. $(x) (Wx \rightarrow Hx)$

 Madonna is not a man. $-Mm$

∴   *Madonna is not a woman.*   ∴ $-Wm$

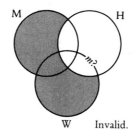

Invalid.

2a.   *No dogs are cats.* $(x) (Dx \rightarrow -Cx)$

 All cats are animals. $(x) (Cx \rightarrow Ax)$

∴   *No dogs are animals.*   ∴ $(x) (Dx \rightarrow -Ax)$

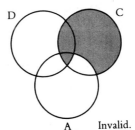

Invalid.

2c.   No women are men. $(x) (Wx \rightarrow -Mx)$

       No men are mothers. $(x) (Mx \rightarrow -Nx)$

∴   No women are mothers.   ∴ $(x) (Mx \rightarrow -Nx)$

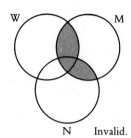

N   Invalid.

2e.   No men are women. $(x) (Mx \rightarrow -Wx)$

       Every female vocalist is a woman. $(x) (Fx \rightarrow Wx)$

       Madonna is a female vocalist.   Fm

∴   Madonna is not a man.   ∴   −Mm

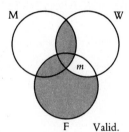

F   Valid.

3a.   All products high in fat are un- $(x) (Fx \rightarrow Ux)$
       healthy.
                                          $(\exists x) (Bx \ \& \ Fx)$
       Some cuts of beef are high in fat.

∴   Some cuts of beef are unhealthy.   ∴ $(\exists x) (Bx \ \& \ Ux)$

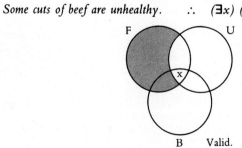

B   Valid.

3c.   *All bank presidents are human.*   (x) (Bx → Hx)

       Some men are not bank presidents.   (∃x) (Mx & −Bx)

∴   *Some bank presidents are not hu-*   ∴   (∃x) (Bx & −Hx)
       man.

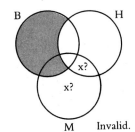

Invalid.

3e.   *No boring job is satisfying.*   (x) (Bx → −Sx)

       Some well-paying jobs are boring.   (∃x) (Wx & Bx)

∴   *Some well-paying jobs are not satis-*   ∴   (∃x) (Wx & −Sx)
       fying.

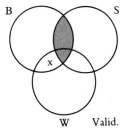

Valid.

Index